# CEPHIA
## AND THE
## DEVIL'S PANDEMIC

**ARPress**
ILLUMINATING IDEAS
EMPOWERING VOICES

SAMUEL KIRONDE NDAWULA

ARPress
45 Dan Road Suite 36
Canton MA 02021

Hotline:        1(888) 821-0229
Fax:            1(508) 545-7580

Ordering Information:
Quantity Sales. Special discounts are available on quantity purchases by corporations, associations, and others. For details, contact the publisher at the address above.

Printed in the United States of America.

ISBN-13     Softcover     979-8-89356-399-3
            eBook         979-8-89356-398-6
            Hardback      979-8-89356-397-9

Library of Congress Control Number: 2024903071

Disclaimer:

This is a work of fiction. Unless otherwise indicated, all the names, characters, businesses, places, events, organizations and incidents in this book are either the product of the author's imagination or used in a fictitious manner. Any resemblance to actual persons, living or dead, or actual events is purely coincidental.

This novel is dedicated to my mom, Joyce Nakibuka Nakawesi. She's the Pillar on which we have learned all our lives, the one who has seen us through our trials and tribulations. She's the reason this piece of work is possible today. Thank you very much, Mom.

And to my wife, Jose, for being so patient with me during the story's development and writing. It's always a solo, lonely, long journey, this writing. Thanks for your unwavering, total support, Jose. Your support made this work possible to the end. And thank you for believing in me.

# Table of Contents

# PROLOGUE

Hello there. My name is Robert Moolimer, and I am a pastor of a small, non – denominational Church, based in Dallas, Texas, United States of America. Now, it doesn't matter which faith you belong to, because what I am about to explain to you concerns us all, meaning it matters to every religious person or even non – religious people, who have faith and belief in the heavens above and the almighty God who governs them, who is also basically the creator of everything up there and down here in the world of the living and, maybe, the dead too. It means that he is the origin of all creatures and things known to man, meaning all things concerning life in general.

The story you are about to read is constructed out of a series of mysterious events evolving in different places and at different time periods, in different ways and for different reasons, but all culminating into one unifying effect. I and my colleagues put these pieces together after investigating these mysterious events that led to the conclusion of one major event of epic proportions.

This epic event revealed that beyond the world known to humans are invisible worlds of a spiritual entity as real as our own, where things unknown to us happen daily, where an unseen individual or individuals silently monitor the world of the physical human. We also concluded that if necessary, and if agitated or prompted to, these individuals can freely cross over into our human realm and create changes, altering our lives at their own discretion.

But just like in our world, the spiritual realm has both good and bad elements. Now it goes without saying that of the two entities, we the physical group are far more inferior, which makes the other side far more superior. For example, the spiritual individuals can easily cross over into our realm and back to theirs. On the other hand, once we cross into their realm, we can never come back to ours. That path is closed. Because of this one factor, the bad elements, unable to influence their equally stronger counterparts in their own realm, are said to cross over into our realm and take advantage of our inferior and weak physical individual beings, often leading us to intense and immense fatalities, very often to near total self-destruction, as seen in matters such as genocide, extremism, and tyrannical suppression of free living. As such, the only way we can survive the control and ultimate demise of our entity by these immensely powerful elements is when the good elements, who are constantly monitoring our side, intervene and stop the evolution of mayhem, especially of epic proportions. Both elements, invisible to our side, pursue and fight each other unknowingly to us, and face their fates without question. It's a game of cat and mouse, full of explosive reactions that sometimes spill over into our realm to a point where we ourselves can experience these reactions. Even then, we still never know how things came to happen the way they happened.

Yet there are some of us, in the human realm, some special people, perhaps gifted by God himself, that can experience the cross over, meaning, able to travel into the spiritual realm itself and visualize this world beyond ours. These chosen, special human beings are the ones who turn around and come back to the rest of us to warn us of the dangers of the other world beyond our own, that can, in turn, spill over into ours. Often unwilling to believe or listen to these individuals, we find ourselves totally helpless and unprepared for the onslaught from the results of the intentionally evil, bad elements that crossover from the other realm.

It's in such cases that we are forced to call, or pray to, the supreme maker of both realms, commonly known as God, or the holy spirit. And that's when the good elements respond, more often with force than compromise, to suppress the uprise.

Now I shall not delve deep into explaining what these actions and reactions are, because that, and I freely confess to it, will require interference with matters or issues that I myself have no understanding of or even jurisdiction over, simply because these issues are rather of a very complex nature. But I decided that by briefly exposing the concept of the two realms, I do hope it helps you to understand the story that we are revealing to you and why it is so dynamic. Our investigations, in form of phases, simply provide a framework to a story that reveals one such episode of deadly engagement that threatened to destabilize the delicate balance between the two worlds, forever. It will, hopefully, help you understand what's going on, and the reason why God's will, which is originally, yet basically, embedded in the soul of man, must prevail always.

I encourage you to read on.

# Chapter One

Bishop Peter Musolozza of the central Christian archdiocese in the city of Kampala, Uganda, was somewhat surprised when one evening, his close friend, the reverend Samson Ssekadde of the Namugongo township and parish church, invited him to come over and pray for his elderly mother, Edina, who he anticipated was about to end her journey of life on this earth. The bishop wasn't surprised because the last time he met with the mother Edina, as she was commonly called, she didn't look and sound good, looking very frail and weak. She also had lost her total appetite; the reverend had told him. Neither was the bishop surprised by this state of her life, for at ninety-seven years of age, Mother Edina was old by any standards and had indeed outlived a lot of her peers.

But the one thing that was of total surprise to bishop Peter Musolozza was that Mother Edina had not lost her mental faculties to old age. The old lady's mind was completely intact. She recognized everyone she had met in her life and knew them by name. She knew the names of all her twenty grandchildren and eleven great grandchildren correctly. She knew her calendar to date, able to correctly specify the current day, month, and year. She spent most of her day listening to her little radio and knew a lot about what was happening around the country and indeed around the world. She knew a lot about the bishop himself, having gone to the same school with the bishop's mother, who was already deceased, and had watched the two boys, meaning the bishop and the reverend, grow up together and forge a lasting friendship to the point that when the bishop's mother passed away several years ago, the bishop was quick to take on mother Edina as his adopted mother, confiding in her his deepest secrets and fears, and always seeking wise council from the beloved old lady.

So, on this day, when the reverend summoned him to come quickly and visit with Mother Edina because of what he thought was her end time being very close, the bishop cancelled all the day's activities and hastened to Namugongo to meet with and pray for the old lady. The reverend, his wife Rebecca, and three of their grandchildren lived in an old but well-maintained house not far away from the old church that he ministered to. Bishop Musolozza remembered that old church very well because, as a boy, he visited it every year because of the centennial celebrations concerning Christian martyrs that were killed a long time ago by an anti-Christian king, who had his henchmen burn these followers alive. Namugongo was the site of these executions and the site of a shrine for these fallen Christians. And to this day, he always asked his driver to slow the car down, so he can utter a silent quick prayer as they drove past the church, which was also part of the site. His driver, who had worked with him for a long time, now automatically knew what to do when they came here to visit.

The reverend was waiting for him at the front door when he arrived. "Peter, thank you for coming by at such a short notice," he said, smiling widely. "how's everybody at home and how's work?"

"You know I had to come straight away, Sam," the bishop said, shaking his friend's hand. "Because any issue concerning mother deeply concerns me too. Everyone is fine at home, and Sarah sends her greetings. I told her I was coming over because Mom wasn't doing well. She said she will pray for her. And work at the diocese ... you know how that goes."

After waving at the bishop's driver, who usually stayed inside the car, the reverend led the bishop to the back of the house, where a small independent housing unit had been built for Mother Edina and where she had stayed for years. It is where the old lady was now, in her bed, all neatly tucked up under clean white bed sheets and blanket. The aroma of Vicks ointment rub hung around the room, although a window was open to allow in the fresh breeze. Mother Edina always love fresh air, and rarely closed her door. She didn't look good at all, the bishop noted gravely.

"I forgot to tell you, Peter, but the old lady specifically asked for you to come see her," The reverend said.

"I understand," the bishop responded quietly.

"Petero, my dear, you are here," Mother Edina said, opening her eyes immediately and managing to smile broadly. She always stated his name in the same old fashioned, ethnic way. "I can barely see anymore, son, but I can sense your presence. Do come in and have a seat, here next to me. Both of you, my sons. Sit down here next to me."

There were two chairs and a wooden bench in the room. Both men picked up the chairs, moved them closer to the frail old lady, and sat down.

"Thank you, Mother Edina," the bishop said. "How are you feeling so far? Sam called me this morning and told me you're not doing well, so I came by to see you and perhaps share a healing word from the bible with you."

"Ooh, Sam, my loving son, always worrying and so concerned about your mother," she said, and reaching out, she parted the reverend gently on the back. "But now that both of my favorite sons are here with me, I am no longer sick. I feel good already. See, I can now laugh, smile, and speak clearly."

The two men looked at each other and grinned sheepishly but said nothing. They both knew that despite her hearty speech, mother Edina wasn't doing well at all. The frail look and altered breathing emphasized this, and so did her sunken eyes and drooping cheeks. Surprisingly, though, there were not that many wrinkles on her face. Her skin all over was almost as bright and smooth as a baby's.

"But there is something I wanted to talk to both of you about, a story I want to share with you," she said. "For now, I want you to just listen to what I am saying, and then give me your views when I am done."

"Ok mother. We are ready when you are," The bishop said. Mother Edina cleared her throat and the started talking.

3

"For the last three weeks to this date, I have been experiencing this one dream, where I am in this one place," she said. "Once I close my eyes, I fall asleep but then immediately find myself in another world, a place as bright and beautiful as the morning sunrise or the evening sunset. I can't tell the real difference in time, but I can feel that it's neither warm no cool, just sunny. The breeze is a constant flow, and I can hear the sounds from different birds. I am walking on a sand-less beach, following a trail, in the shadows of spaced-out tall trees of the same type. I can see the shiny, gleaming blue water of the lake on one side of the trail. I continue walking, feeling relaxed and good. As on the first day, a voice called me from nowhere, but all around me, bidding me welcome. I never see the person, but the voice tells me where to go. I end up in this one beautiful garden, as big as a public park, with green grass all over, neatly cut, and where all kinds of people are walking around. People of all kinds, laughing, smiling, talking to each other. No one says anything to me but smile at me as they walk by. I see beautiful animals everywhere, but mostly horses, camels, zebras and then all kinds of birds. But that was on the very first day."

"So, what happened the next day, mother?" The bishop asked, as the old lady briefly went quiet, catching her breath and clearing her throat. For some reason, he found himself immediately intrigued by her narration of the events in her dream.

"The next day I did the same." The older lady then continued with her narration. "I Lay down, closed my eyes and I immediately found myself linked to my new-found dream world. This time, a person simply appeared out of nowhere and started walking with me. I looked on my right side and there she was. I asked her who she is, and she said her name is Orayah … well that's how it sounded like, because she repeated the name several times as she spoke to me. She spoke in a strange way, like … Orayah welcomes you back, Orayah will show you around, Orayah wants you not to be afraid."

"What else did she say, mother?" the reverend asked.

"I am getting there, son," Mother Edina said. "Next, I asked her to tell me where I am, to which she replied that we are in the promised land, where everything begins but does not end. But before I could ask her what she exactly meant by that, she said "come, I will show you".

4

And then the world around me changed, and we were standing on top of a hill. Beyond I could see a very big bright light, like the sparkle of the sun against a shiny mirror or glass, bigger than a cathedral against a bright blue sky. She told me that it is where God lives. For some reason, I instantly asked her if she can take me there so I can see God, to which she answered yes, she will take me to the bright light so I can see God."

Both men now sat forward. There was no doubt both men had some questions in mind. "Did she take you, and did you see God? Is God a he or she?

"How did God look like, mother?" It was the bishop who finally voiced the big question, his eyes opening wider.

"She said she will take me to see the light, but later. She wanted to show me more of the place we were in first," Mother Edina replied. "And so, we walked on, but a lot of times I just found myself in different places, with different kinds of people, with different scenery, without warning of the changing. Everywhere I went, people stood up and greeted me with big smiles. There were all kinds of people … black, white, brown, people that looked Chinese but were black, some I recognized as from India while others wore turbans on their heads. I saw children, adult men and women, old folks with no walking sticks, healthy and strong, short people and very tall ones, and big people that seemed to be giants to me. And all of them greeted me warmly but no speech. One other thing I noted is that they were all dressed in bright, colorful clothes, and seemed to walk around without their feet touching the ground. The other strange thing is that there were all kinds of animals moving around with the humankind, and they all seemed to be directly communicating to me."

"And the third day?" Reverend Samson asked, sensing that the old lady had become somewhat shaky as she spoke of this episode or vision. He thought he could also help her get to the main point faster, that way she doesn't have to exhaust herself so much by talking too much about non – essential things. He too wanted to know of her vision of the almighty.

"There is a third day to this dream," she said, her voice trembling a little. "But this time, Orayah did not show up. Instead, this beautiful young woman, very light skinned, slender but not frail or thin, with the most beautiful, sky - blue eyes I have ever seen, appeared in her place. Her hair is wavy but short cropped, with bits of it being lifted by a drift of breeze that constantly surrounded her. Most amazingly, the lifted strands of her hair seemed to glow brightly every time they rose from her head. She was dressed in a flourishing sparkling light blue dress that went all the way down to her feet. Her hands were in bright yellow gloves, but not of cloth or other material. Her gloves were a thick form of mist, which also wrapped up both her feet. She smiled all the time at me, at times giggling nonstop, and tagged at my arm as we walked, or rather floated, around. When I asked her where Orayah was, she said that Orayah had gone to see God, that there was a meeting of all the angels. She said she was now going to be my guide until Orayah comes back. This time we went to different places below the hills, with areas of green grass and sun, numerous rivers and lakes, we walked on top of trees and ran around big hills, and when I woke up again, I felt so exhausted and then suddenly became very afraid."

At this point, the old lady closed her eyes and started breathing heavily. The trembling increased.

"Let's give her some water, maybe that will help," The bishop said quickly. He picked up a jug of water that was on top of a small table covered with a white tablecloth. Next to it was a pair of empty glasses. He picked up one of the glasses, poured some water in it, and while the reverend helped prop the old lady up, he placed the glass to her mouth. After taking several sips, she nodded her head and then mumbled that she had drunk enough. The reverend laid her back down gently, rearranged her pillow behind her, and covered her up again.

"Mother, what happened? What did you see that is making you tremble like that?" The reverend asked.

"It's because the dream is so vivid and real," she replied. "it's just like now. I still can feel the young woman's hand on my right hand as she held on to me and took me around and played with me. Her hand was so warm. I didn't want it to end, and I was not getting tired of the running around. I felt so alive and energetic. Yet it was when I woke up that I felt so exhausted. I am now afraid that I am living two lives, that this life in the dream is also real."

6

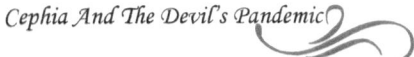
"Did the young lady in this part of the dream tell you, her name?" The bishop asked.

"No, but Orayah told me who she is when she came back from that meeting with angels," Mother Edina replied, her eyes still closed.

"Oh. So Orayah came back to you ..." the bishop said, sitting forward again. "So, who is the young woman?"

"Yes, Orayah returned in the fourth dream," Mother Edina confirmed. "She told me that the young woman's name is Cephia, and that she is the very youngest of all the archangels."

"Cephia, the very youngest of the archangels," the bishop echoed her words clearly, slowly and one by one. "Did she tell you what the meeting with God and all the angels was about?"

At that point, the bishop felt like he had to go micturate. Looking at his watch, he had already been sitting in mother's house for over ninety minutes. He didn't know how time had moved so fast, even if the old, frail lady was speaking very slowly, word by word, and he had to listen very closely. He had to leave fast, because his bladder was full, and the pressure was on. He excused himself and asked the reverend, who was holding his mother's hand, that perhaps he should refrain from asking anymore questions until he came back. The reverend agreed and whispered the bishop's request into the old lady's right ear. The bishop then left the room. The bathroom, an outside house unit, was not far away from Mother Edina's quarters and he quickly made his way back to the old lady's quarters.

"She just suddenly fell into a deep slumber, Peter," The reverend told him when he reentered Mother Edina's room. "I couldn't keep her from going, and neither can I now arouse her. But trust me, she is sleeping soundly, like a baby."

"Yes, I can hear her gentle snore," the bishop acknowledged. "Well, let's let her rest then. I will be back when she wakes up. I am cancelling today's activities to come sit with her. Sam, will you please give me a call when she wakes up?"

"Will do, Peter," The reverend affirmed. "Thank you. Let us now pray," the bishop said. The two men then bowed their heads in prayer.

# Chapter Two

Six hundred and sixty-six days later after the day mother Edina had debuted her dreams to her two sons, another event started taking place in Garache, a small, quiet town in the suburbs of Turikai City, the capital of the Turikai republic, a small island country and popular tourist destination in the Mediterranean Sea, strategically located North of Libya, East of Tunisia, and southeast of Italy. In number terms, the Turikai republic land territory covers about nine thousand square miles and has a population of about four hundred thousand citizens per world bank records. The officially known remaining indigenous folks, the Turikai, unfortunately only now account for about five percent of the total population. The rest were from elsewhere in the world, settlers from nearby countries, some from far and beyond. At a given time, these non - indigenous folks came in, systematically organized themselves, overpowered the indigenous population and its rulers, and took over governance of the island. These invaders then systematically organized themselves into a republic. In respect of the land's heritage and ancestral roots, the new rulers agreed not to change the Island's territorial name, thus calling themselves the Turikai republic. But the island's indigenous folks were generally under-represented in parliament and had little say in its politics and governance.

At eight o'clock, Turikai Mediterranean time on a breezy weekday evening, a time when most of its mostly rich, elderly residents have already retired for the day, a convoy of black cars rolled into town and headed for the town's council hall, a modern structure that also serves as the state's governing center and conference center. The building had been restored and rebuilt several times, and was now used for conferences, private parties, and other similar occasions on a rental basis. It was truly a monumental complex, with modern high-tech amenities. This was reflective of the country's current rulers, a group of middle-aged billionaire tycoons who were well vested in technology and its continuously evolving trends.

The island itself was a marvel of security and architectural wonders, boasting of an airport, a freight ship port and a wide tourist resort beach, a modern highway infrastructure or road network that made inner territorial commute easy and enjoyable, a special satellite control center that linked the world to the island via cyberspace and beyond, and facilitated high tech, twenty-four hours, seven days a week, all year around security surveillance over the territory. It even has a small army force, well-armed with sophisticated, up to date weaponry, but which also filled in as the island's police force. The capital, Turikai city, about one hundred and ninety square miles, has a few sky scraper buildings that mainly house hotels and shopping arcades, numerous small, ground level office type buildings that housed banks, private schools, post office, a money mint facility, small food stores and markets, gas stations, small entertainment arenas for its tourists, among others, and at least three communications towers which gave the city it's excellent mainland traffic control, the island's weather warning systems and cellphone operations. The Island has about two thousand square miles of elevated terrain, part of which is timber land. The country seemed to be out of the path of severe hurricane alleys or pathways, for it has no record of severe weather invasion in its known past, over three hundred-years history.

The island had a few mines of rare diamonds and natural gemstones, which commanded high prices on the world market and which the rulers protected fiercely.

Today's meeting in the conference center was a high level, secret business one, whose participants had been carefully selected and secretly flown into the island, and then secretly driven to the meeting location. The meeting was scheduled to last for not more than a couple

9

of hours, and then all participants were to be flown off the island and back to their hotels in the neighboring countries.

Before participating in this meeting, all participants had to leave their communication devices in their hotels in their cities, and intensive body searches were carefully conducted to make sure this rule was effectively adhered to. They had no travel baggage whatsoever, no watches, rings, jewelry of any kind on them. Not even sunglasses were allowed, and special, "scan - able" shoes had been issued to the participants to wear, to eliminate the possibility of secret shoe compartments.

They were asked to bring only their account numbers and or debit cards to initiate money deposits.

They were 12 participants all together, and all had one thing in common. They were all Filthy rich or represented someone filthy rich. But also, these people were part of the unpublished rich group, the type that you would never read about in Forbes magazine or see on the celebrity list. The group consisted of some prominent politicians or their representatives, some tech inventors, and some heirs and heiresses to big fortunes.

The meeting itself had been arranged in a mysterious fashion, centered around a fantastic business preposition with a promise of more than a hundred percent return on investment, a business so secret yet so big it would create guaranteed returns for years to come. There was no money back guarantee, because the masterminds behind the proposed business venture were so sure of themselves that they saw no need for future refund enactments. The business, they claimed, was designed to be a total, one hundred percent proof, success!

This was the fifth and last of such meetings. There were others going on elsewhere in the world, all recruiting capital, but this one was rather very special and exclusive, the members were told.

Once all the black premium cars had entered the perimeters of the ground of the meeting place, through a remotely controlled, electronically revolving metallic gate, twelve chauffeurs got out of the twelve cars and respectively opened the back doors for the limousines' backseat occupants. To meet the occupants at the marble tiled steps that led to the entrance of the building were twelve beautiful women all dressed in the same colored, same fashion design, matching silk attire, from top to bottom. Even the hair style was the same. These ladies spread out to match themselves to one of the twelves guests, to whom they handed an electronic iPad tablet and then gracefully led their individual to the inside of the magnificent building.

They were led straight to the conference room, through a quiet, well lit, carpeted hallway with glass doored entrances to other chambers. The conference room, a marvel of its own, boasted of tinted glass sliding electronically controlled doors on both sides of the room, three rows of polished oak tables and leather backed-chairs, bright, shiny chandelier lighting companioned with quiet, wide bladed ceiling fans that provided mild breezes of air all around the room. The walls were designed with soundproof material in place, and the ceiling was completely sealed. Laptop computers lined the tables, in front of the chairs. A podium with a microphone and a big screen, wall mounted television behind it was center stage at the front of the room, also left flanked by a single opaque glass door with no doorknob.

When all the occupants were carefully seated, and glasses of fresh water served from gold rimmed carafes together with fresh fig dates and biscuits, there was at-ease, loud talk as the twelve members of the group introduced themselves to each other. Soft Caribbean music was pouring out of carefully concealed loudspeakers in the ceiling.

Beyond the glass door, in another room above the conference room, a rather muscular man sat in an executive high - backed leather chair, gazing at a set of big monitors that provided him with live view of the entire interior of the conference room and its current occupants. Behind him was a long-legged woman wearing a mini dress over a well curved body and shiny, all leather, black knee – high women's boots, long black silky hair that fell all the way to the bottom of her back, ending on top of a well-balanced, sharply protruding buttocks, and a face that showed baby features with a touch of adult modesty. The woman's outlook truly befitted an effigy of a modern-day, top of the line, model. Her name was simply Pony, a bomb shell beauty of black and Korean human breeding who had earned the name back in her early twenties from those men who had the privilege to experience her level of naughtiness. Now in her mid-thirties, Pony was still a bombshell vixen, a beauty of unimagined magnitude, and a very well-

trained military combat professional. The worst part of all this was that she was also a killer that regular souls, minds, and eyes would never perceive to be as such.

Apart from being his personal assistant and or bodyguard, Pony was also the man's long-term mistress.

"They are all here, major," Pony said to the man. "I have gone through the list again, and every photo does match."

"Look at them … rich, snobbery bastards," the man said. "don't they look so pathetic, ah, Pony? They have no clue about what the real world is out there. All they care about is just their own kinky lifestyles and their money loaded accounts!"

"Yep, and they are all the same," Pony replied, laughing. "It's all clear when you look at them now. Similar behavior links them together and make them fit into each other's company well, yet they have never met before. Are you ready for the presentation, major?"

As she said that, she massaged his shoulders, using deep, slow strokes. He sighed heavily. Tall, with broad shoulders accompanied by lean muscles with strong arms, flat belly and legs meant to carry a man with a strong torso like his, the major typically looked the man who had with no doubt earned his rank and possibly more. He spotted a faint moustache that dipped into a sharp goatee on both sides of his grim mouth. The slightly slanted eyes and sharp nose could easily relate him to a Mongoose. These features gave him the look of a serious man who knows life for what it was worth and seldom takes it for granted; a man who has been to hell and back, and who is not used to pompousness. He had no time for soft spots and was always exact with his job. He had been code named "Rottweiler" after the final series of covert military operations he led, where he displayed a natural or rustic appeal, always strong, self-assured and steady, with a fearless behavior and attitude. During these tactical military operations, the major always led the way, and had done a lot of covert stuff out there that many considered impossible, quite dangerous and or deadly. Even his superiors respected him. This outstanding reputation led him to contracts of intense and private nature which needed a strong mind like his. He quit the military and started working with contracted missions only.

Dressed in plain green military officer's army fatigues, complete with boots and a beret tightly placed on his head, he got up with ease from his chair, poised straight up and then did a strong pivot to the left towards the elevator doors. Pony followed behind him, carrying a briefcase and a small electronic laptop computer. The elevator carried the two quietly to the ground or first floor of the building, enabling them to enter the conference hall through the glass door behind the podium. The major went straight to the podium and stood behind it. Pony stood to his left, just slightly behind him.

The conference room noise quickly died down. Everyone now focused on the new entries before them.

"Good evening, I am major Antoquake Haraabi. People who are close to me often call me Quake. So, you folks, too, are encouraged to call me major quake or simply call me major. No other exceptions, please," the man said. His British accent was quite self-sustaining. "The lady standing behind me is captain Pony, my personal assistant."

"Pony, like the small horse? Can I have a ride?" someone from his audience asked, prompting others to burst out laughing.

"Yes sir, just like the small horse, but no rides offered. Not today." Pony quickly replied from behind her boss, a faint smile on her face. If only these bastards knew what my capabilities are, they wouldn't be laughing at all, she thought. Apart from passing with A grades at small firearm use, captain Pony also possessed top credentials for a weaponless assassin. Her ability to kill a person with her bare hands and feet was remarkable. That, complemented by expert use of hand- held combat tools made her an extremely lethal entity! Even major Haraabi had on a few occasions bluntly confessed of being cautious with her.

But major Haraabi did not find that question amusing, and so did not react to it. He, instead, went on with his agenda. "Before I go ahead with the main topic and points this evening, I will first state that I prefer to let me speak first, meaning that I don't want to be interrupted while I am speaking. You will have plenty of time to question me after I am done with saying what I have to say. Do you understand?"

"Very well, let us now begin," he said immediately, not waiting for a response to his non – interference directive. A brief hand gesture at Pony, and she opened the briefcase, from which he slowly extracted a small, black rectangular box. Carefully opening it, he extracted two small, sealed glass vials. The vials resembled miniature wine bottles and had rubber stoppers on top. One vial was red, the other green. "Ladies and gentlemen, I present to you these two glass vials. They each contain a combination of different things, all very potent stuff . Let's talk about the red bottle first."

He then carefully placed the green vial back into the rectangular box and closed it. He then picked up the red vial and held it up in his hand. "This bottle, folks, contains an extremely deadly, scientifically enhanced airborne bacteria code named "La Puta". This specially enhanced bacteria, once freed, will seek out the closest human or animal temperature environment, and immediately enter it. Once it embeds itself inside its host, it then manifests itself into a multiple spore form, which releases exact replicas of itself in thousands of units, if not millions, into the host's blood stream. These infectious spores will then travel through the body of the host organism and soon embed themselves in the main body organs, but mainly the kidneys, the digestive tract, and the lungs, where they will release toxins that will cause the host organism to develop unique, multiple disease symptoms with deadly consequences if not treated immediately. The bacteria will also manifest itself into a rapidly infectious state, becoming mainly both an airborne and contact medium bound disease. Channels of transmission will be noted to be through urine, sweat glands and defecation outlets, and of course mouth and nasal discharges. This means, folks, that any sexual contact with the carrier host, or being in a room with multiple potential hosts, like bars, entertainment venues, mass transit units, crowded units like army barracks, mass worship centers, and even hospitals will trigger off an alarming rate of infection that will rapidly manifest itself in a period of about twenty-four hours. Symptoms will include a rapid fall in body temperature, causing acute stiffness and pain in most joints, appearance of itchy, ashy skin welts or patches from skin pores where some of those multiplying spores try to exit the body from whatever venue they can find including eyes, ears, and nose. Also, rapid diarrhea, as a major symptom of full compromise of the host organism's digestive tract, will start, together with flu - like symptom of repeated sneezing and coughing. Other spore results will cause extreme itching of the eyes which will suddenly evolve into a

14

heavy creamy discharge in the eyes as certain bacteria spores from outside invades the eyes due to natural eye defenses being knocked out by the invading organism. This, ladies and gentlemen, could lead to blindness if not quickly treated. The victim will also experience Uncontrollable bladder spasms and an uncontrollable urge to urinate will become part of the game. It will be possible to experience periodic, involuntary loss of chunks of mostly pubic hair from body, followed by extreme genital itching with warts. Some raptured blood veins on the inside and outside of host organism's body will cause painful welts or blood-filled blisters that could appear anywhere in and on the victim's body. These are just but a few of the major symptoms that I have mentioned, but there are a host of other deadly symptoms that could show depending on the host body's weaknesses and strength, like periodic headaches, nausea and vomiting, acute fatigue, loss of appetite, painful mouth sores, and others. This, ladies and gentlemen, is what we call our super bacterium."

At this moment, major Quake picked up a glass of water that had been set aside for him on a small table near the podium. He sipped from it as he let the information that he had just verbally delivered sink into his audience's minds. There was some silence now. Not for long, though.

"But... how did you get hold of this bacterium, and what do you intend to do with it?" one of the men, a middle-aged looking fella, asked, sounding frightened already. Others appeared to be quietly but intensively listening, eyes fixed on major Haraabi.

"Didn't I say absolutely no questions until I am done talking?" the major asked the man, sounding annoyed. "I repeat, do not ask any questions until I have concluded my speech. It's imperative that you listen to what I am saying first, make your own conclusions and deductions, and then ask me all the questions. Trust me, when I am done with delivering this speech summary, it will all come to you. It will make sense."

"But yes, when a mysterious bacterium reestablished itself in the middle of the amazon forest, the locals didn't know what to do," major Haraabi continued. "And neither did the national governments in the region. But it certainly attracted the attention of certain people elsewhere in the world. So, like any other curious scientific group, our organization sent our own scientists to the place and these guys collected samples from the sick people and brought them back to our laboratories. We isolated this bacterium that basically known to cause blood infections, giving the patient bloody diarrhea and general weakness for weeks. We then worked on it and modified it and made it stronger by infusing samples of it with samples of other deadly animal bacteria, not necessarily from humans. Not only did we succeed to create a super bacterium capable of bringing havoc to, and wrecking up, the human system, but we succeeded in modifying its infection rate and its resistance to common antibiotics. This modified strain, ladies and gentlemen, can cause death to its human host in approximately forty-eight hours if not treated, and the person will need active treatment for the next seven days to prevent reoccurrence. This super bacterium, folks, if released into a public venue, can single handedly cause an epidemic of spectacularly epic proportions, or in just hours in a relatively wide area. The havoc it unleashes will be so intense it will lead to a worldwide panic or intense pandemonium."

There was a total silence in the room as major Haraabi carefully put the vial back into the black rectangular box and then picked up the green vial. He raised it up in his hand for everybody in the audience to see. "But here is the good news. In this green bottle, folks, is the ultimate inoculation, and cure, for that bad news, super bacterium infection. Once we isolated the original strains, we took time to find out how it can be stopped or killed and developed the perfect serum. This means that for the capabilities we gave to the La Punta we have also created an opposite that can reverse the situation. We developed, in one cocktail capsule, a drug that can totally stop the La Puta's infectious pattern and annihilate it from the host body's system in just a matter of days. Ladies and gentlemen, in this green bottle is the ultimate cure to the super bacterium infection. We simply call it "el interceptor". Now, in the next few minutes, folks, I am going to show you a variety of our tests subjects, starting with the infected organism, and then the results of the interceptor drug after injecting it into this organism. The show is going to be presented via video recording. I now warn you that what you are about to see is real, but since it's not you or your loved ones, you should be able to handle it well. It means that

16

you're going to see actual people dying from the effects of the super bacterial infection, but we shall also show you those who were lucky to receive the interceptor drug and how they progressed to wellness. Our test subjects are captured animals from wild forests, while the human subjects are a bunch of notorious death row inmates and or a bunch of dirty, urban, homeless castaways or refuge, people who have nothing to lose or care for anymore in their lives. Please feel secure and don't freak out when you see the agony of these test subjects as the virus reaps through their bodies."

Major Haraabi then nodded at Pony, who went to work immediately with setting up the video show. Meanwhile, he carefully placed the "el interceptor" back into the black rectangular box. He then placed himself in a chair in one corner of the conference room, still in front of his audience, and made himself comfortable. In a few minutes, the room went dark, and the show began on a giant, one hundred forty-inch screen television screen.

# Chapter Three

Mother Edina slept through out that whole day. The reverend Samson did not leave her side, except if he had to go relieve himself or just to stretch his legs out briefly. He kept a cool piece of cloth on her forehead and held her hand all the time. He could feel the bounding pulse in her wrist, and the occasional light tremors that ran through her body accompanied by episodes of pauses in breathing. But these brief pauses only lasted for a few second and then normal, silent breathing resumed.

Mother Edina woke up briefly late in the night. The reverend then fed her a bowl of brown porridge mixed with milk, and then she went back to sleep. After that time, the reverend's wife came in and took over so he can go bath and himself take a nap. The reverend asked his wife to come get him up as soon as his mother wakes again.

However, Mother Edina did not wake up until the next day, in the morning, around ten o'clock.

Bishop Peter Musolozza did not return that day after he left, as he thought he could. The archbishop had an assignment for him that urgently needed to be taken care of. He returned the next day, early in the morning. As if on schedule, he arrived at ten o'clock to find Mother Edina awake. He was in perfect time to settle down and listen the next phase of Mother Edina's vision. Her fourth dream. This time he had a pen and notebook with him.

This time too, the reverend's wife Rebecca, who would usually leave her mother–in–law's bedside to go attend to household chores, stayed over to listen. The trio waited patiently while Mother Edina's personal care giver, a girl she had adopted from an orphanage, gave her a bed birth and changed her clothes and bed linen. She then also brought in a bowl of yellow, warm, mashed plantain covered with lightly salted vegetable in chicken soup. The reverend's wife then fed the food to her, and she ate most of it.

"So mother, in your third dream, or vision, you had just met with the youngest of the archangels, and you said her name is…" the bishop started to say after Mother Edina was done eating, but held back, trying to recall the name.

"Cephia, if I may recall. Is that right, mother?" the reverend intervened.

"Yes, Cephia, that's what it is," the bishop reiterated. "And you had also mentioned that Orayah, the very first angel you met, had returned from this place where all angels were having a big meeting with God. We were interested to know what that meeting was about. Did she tell you?"

"Yes, that gracious lady, Orayah, returned in my fourth dream vision," the older lady said. "When I inquired about the meeting, she graciously smiled at me and said all was not well, but that all will be well with God. As we continued walking, I asked her what would not be well, more especially where God is involved. Still smiling, she stated that all was not well with the seventh division of God's creation."

"The seventh division of God's creation," The bishop repeated, jotting down the phrase. "I wonder what that division is."

"Mother, did she tell you what this seventh division is?" The reverend asked, rubbing gently on one of her hands.

The old lady appeared to shudder, like she had seen something terrifying. The reverend's wife, Rebecca, moved her chair closer and held her other hand, gently rubbing on it too. She spoke to her in a soft voice, assuring her that all is ok, and that she is not alone.

"When I asked her what that was, she suddenly stopped smiling and her face became pale and empty, almost like a skeleton face!" Mother

19

Edina said, still looking terrified. "I had never seen anything like that. Her voice was not sweet anymore. I wanted to run away, but she held on tight to my hand. She told me that I was asking about things I wasn't supposed to know, that I am just a visitor, but that when I get where I am supposed to be, then I will know all about what goes on in her world. I became scared and was about to say am sorry when my face was redirected to look down. When I looked up again, she was gone. I found myself alone. I found myself on the very top of a mountain, where I could still see the shiny light that she had told me was God's home, and this time it was much brighter, like it was calling me to come closer. But I was so terrified to move. I repeatedly started asking myself where I was, and then I woke up. And that is when I summoned the two of you to come over."

"Yes, you looked very sick and for a moment I thought you were about to leave us," The reverend said. "But you eventually calmed down and then went back to sleep again. Did you have another vision?"

"Oh yes, I did. And it was all good this time," the old lady said. "I didn't get to see the lady Orayah again. This time it was that wonderful, beautiful girl who came back to me. And once again, we held hands and prayed. Oh, she is so innocent and so gentle, so fascinating. I love her so much and I just can't wait to fall asleep and see her again. She is so nice to me."

"Cephia..." the bishop mumbled.

The reverend's wife looked at both men and slowly shook her head. "That explains why Mother woke up in a fairly good state today. She was seeing good things," she said. "I think these visions are real. Mother is crossing over into heaven and back."

"Yes, Cephia. She told me about the seventh division of his creation," Mother Edina suddenly said.

All three people now quickly turned to her again, sitting forward in their chairs, once again making her the center of their focus. They wanted to know what seventh division of creation is. "Tell us about it, mother. Tell us what this seventh division of God's creation is," Rebecca encouraged her.

"She told me that where I come from, my world, is the seventh and last division of God's entire universe of creations," the old lady spoke out clearly and without hesitation. "And God's favorite too!"

"Hmmm… your world. Why your world?" the reverend asked.

"She means us, humanity, or to put it more correctly, our earth and all its occupants and stuff ," Rebecca quickly answered. "Maybe earth and its entire universe. We are God's seventh, his favorite and final, division of creation. But now, we are not doing so well like he wants it to be. Something is wrong. And so, if we are his favorite, God will then correct the situation. He will Save us."

"The young woman repeated to me that all was ok with God, the almighty father seated in heaven," the old lady said. A smile came on her face as she said this, and then continued. "What you are saying, Rebecca, is true. There is definitely something wrong, but God is going to correct the situation. She said that God is going to send another savior. A savior unlike any other, Cephia told me as we picked up some golden red roses that suddenly blossomed in front of us from nowhere. She told me that the task had fallen on the archangels to look amongst themselves for who would be most suitable to send to the seventh division to fulfil God's task of restoring order and to defend God's glory. But when I asked her what the problem was, she said she will let me know the next time we see each other, for now it was time to go see and do other things. Ohhh she is such a happy, sweet young woman. So, we walked on and then met more people. There are thousands and thousands of people in the heavens, the beauty of which never ends, the warm sun shines forever together with stars in the sky and streams and lakes keep changing. I wish you can join me in my dreams and see for yourself."

"Did she tell you which archangel was selected, and or when this archangel will be coming to the seventh division?" The bishop asked.

"No, she herself didn't know yet. All that she told me was that the archangels were holding going to hold another meeting today, to determine who to send," Mother Edina said. She started yawning. "She said that she will let me know next time we meet."

"Mother, are you getting tired?" Rebecca asked quickly. "You don't have to go on with this if you are exhausted. Rest now and we will be here when you wake up again to hear more."

"Thank you, daughter," Mother Edina said, smiling again at her daughter – in - law with her eyes closed. "I will see you when I wake up. Thank you so much for everything you do for me."

While the reverend's wife did a final checkup and fully tucked her mother in - law into bed, the two men stepped outside.

"What do you think of all this, Peter?" the reverend asked of the bishop. "Do you think Mother is simply hallucinating with all these things she is talking about?"

"You know, something tells me she is not, Sam," the bishop replied, his hands folded in front of him. "Mother is a very strong- minded person and I have never known her to be the one to make up stuff . Yet what she is revealing to us now seems to be real and well- coordinated, to the point that it influences her behavior when she wakes up. I think we are up to something here, Sam. I am thinking about inviting the archbishop himself to come in and listen what mom is saying. What do you think of that, Sam?"

"If you think if it's that important, I don't see why not," the reverend agreed. "But I still think that our savior is about to call her and take her, and we don't have much time before it happens."

"I have the same feeling, Sam," the bishop agreed. "But as men of God we both know that we cannot be afraid of her end in this life. We only must rejoice in her memory. That is why I think that we should pay more attention to what she is trying to tell us through her visions, as she appears to not to have much time left with us in this world. Maybe it is a revelation of what is to come, and God wants us, and wants this world, to know."

"Yes. But the questions on my mind, Peter, are why she was chosen for the task of conveying this the message, and why specifically to us. There's the pope, the archbishops, the Imams of Mecca or other religion figure heads," The reverend remarked.

"Only the lord has those answers," the bishop said. "All I can say is that I have a feeling that this is real, and we should not ignore it or assume its hallucinations from a sickened, aged mind. At the same time, we must continue to pray hard for hers and our sakes. We will ask the almighty God to give us the answers, and I am sure that he will, through her or other means. Tonight, I will contact the archbishop to seek wisdom on the issue and maybe ask him to come by and visit with mother. Meanwhile we must continue taking good notes on all the things that she tells us."

The two men agreed that whoever is there when she wakes up should write more notes on what she says and make them available for review when others concerned come by later. They left the pen and notepad in the room on top of one of the small bedside tables. Rebecca was notified of this, and she fully agreed. She also let the men know that Mother Edina was now soundly asleep and comfortable. The three people then prayed together, holding hands, and then the bishop left. Rebecca also commissioned one of her home helpers to stay by the bedside of the old lady with instructions that should she wake up, to be called immediately.

As soon as bishop Musolozza got back home, he made a telephone call to his archbishop and told him about the mother Edina's dreams and visions. But the archbishop was getting ready to travel the next day to a senior clergy's conference that was being held in England and cited that he won't be able to be present when the old lady wakes up to narrate her visions. The archbishop then appointed Bishop Musolozza to be his emissary, to represent and report back to him about every revelation. He asked that the bishop stay constantly in touch with him by phone, if possible, on a daily basis to tell him about the issues evolving around the old lady.

But Mother Edina did not sleep well that night either. In the middle of the night, she suddenly started crying in her sleep, shaking, twisting and turning in her bed. Rebecca's home helper immediately summoned the reverend's wife, who in turn woke up her husband and they both went to Mother Edina's room. They found the old lady all covered in perspiration, and the reverend's wife went to work immediately, placing cool wet wash - cloth on Mother Edina's head and exposing the frail lady to open air by removing all linen. Then the reverend stepped in and gently shook his mother by the shoulders until she woke up.

Upon doing so, she opened her eyes, looked at her two children's faces in front of, and very close, to hers, sighed in relief and then closed her eyes again. The vigorous body movements stopped, and so did the crying, but the breathing remained labored.

"Mother, I am sorry, but I had to wake you up. You were crying and raving in your sleep and your body was shaking terribly like you were experiencing epilepsy," the reverend whispered in her ear. "I am glad you woke up and that it has all stopped,"

"Yes mother, it was very scary to see you like that," his wife added, looking quite terrified.

"I am sorry, but I had another vision in my dreams and it was terrible," the old lady said, her eyes still closed. After a period of about five minutes of quietness elapsed, she opened her eyes wide. "The angel Orayah came back to see me as soon as I went back to sleep. She was back to her normal self, and told me that all was not well, that God's Seventh Division was indeed in great danger, that a catastrophe of great magnitude and suffering, an event not of divine planning and implementation, was about to happen. She was almost in tears while facing me and gesturing with her hands. She then started asking me as to why we are doing this to ourselves, why there is always trouble within or amongst ourselves, and why peace can't be forever in the seventh division. I told her that I don't know anything about that, or who is causing the trouble. It was then, at that moment, she suddenly told me to see for myself."

"See for yourself what, mother? did she show you what was going to happen?" the reverend asked, his eyes becoming questioningly wider, and all eager to know.

Mother Edina slowly opened her eyes wider and stared at her son again. Her face grimaced, and she slowly shook her head before talking again. "Yes, son. She reached out and touched my forehead, and I suddenly found myself back here, in our world. But not just here, I was everywhere. And everywhere I looked, people and all kinds of other creatures looked sick and dying. There were cries of agony, from mothers and their children as they witnessed their men dying. As I witnessed all this, I could hear Orayah's voice telling me that everything I see alive was simply waiting for its turn to perish! I saw a boiling river of blood as it fl owed by, I saw mountains crumbling. I saw a lot of blind people in a large gathering, looking stranded. I slowly turned around, and suddenly found myself standing on a wooden platform, and below me were so many people whose bodies looked deformed and dismembered, their arms in the air and faces looking upwards at the sky, full of agony. As I stood there, wondering what was going on, a huge, thick white cloud of mist came from nowhere and covered the entire place below me with all the people in it. But this mist quickly disappeared, and with it all the thousands of people I had seen at my feet. The place where these injured people had stood earlier had now turned into a barren land, like a desert, with miles and miles of space void of human life, for as far as my eyes can see. This area was now filled with multitudes of terrifying, big black birds with no eyes. My Son, this is the most terrifying dream I have ever had in my life!"

Mother Edina's eyes suddenly filled up with tears and she started sobbing. Laying her hands on each of their arms that were closest to her, she shook her head slowly again and again.

"Mama, what is it now? Are you seeing things now with your eyes open?" The reverend's wife asked gently, staring at the frail lady. Though she had a strange, faint smile on her face, she at this point didn't know what to do with her mother-in-law. The sudden mood change was dramatically profound.

"No, not right now. But what I saw was so terrifying and sad," Mother Edina answered slowly. "And that wasn't all. I was still standing there on that raised platform and asking myself what this was all about, when the platform suddenly crumbled, and I started falling into the barren, empty ground below. As I fell further down, the area suddenly erupted into big, smoke-filled flames. I literally felt the terrible heat on me and cried out for help. That was when Orayah reappeared and pulled me back up, away from the flames. And suddenly we were back in the place that I usually stay when visiting. She quickly told me that all my children were going to perish in this fire and that my children's children will forever be affected by this scourge of man's sinful nature. She said that all of you, my present children, will perish first, and then those who will survive this scourge, the very few remaining people and their people, will live forever to feel the pain. That is what is making

25

me cry, because I feel it inside me, and I am greatly worried about all of you, my children and my grandchildren."

"Mother, I thought you said that God is sending a savior, an archangel to take care of us, his beloved Seventh Division?" The Reverend asked, holding on to her arm. His wife was also doing the same thing with the other arm, because both of her frail arms were shaking uncontrollably."

"That's what I was told at first, but after showing me all that, I am no longer sure if that will ever happen," Mother Edina replied. "Orayah simply said again that the archangels were still debating on who to send and have created divisions amongst themselves. Orayah told me that earth appears to be so wretched that no Archangel wants to come down to us. Then she suddenly vanished and, in her place, instead, was the young woman with the shiny eyes.

When I again started crying, and shaking, she wanted to know why. But that's when you woke me up. I really wanted to tell her about those visions that Orayah had gotten me to see and what she had told me was going to happen. And so, when I opened my eyes and saw both of you, I closed them again, wanting to keep her there. To my surprise, she was still there, smiling and holding on to me, urging me to tell her why I was so sad. I thought I only could see them in my dreams, but now I could see her while awake and my eyes closed!"

"Did you tell her?" The reverend asked.

"Yes, I did," his mother replied slowly. "She simply frowned and then told me she will go check things out and let me know. She told me she didn't know about all those things, but that she will go ask Orayah or her brother Gabriel who, she said, seems to know everything divine. She promised to tell me what she has found out next time we meet, when I fall asleep again, and that I should stop crying, for everything will be ok. Then, to my surprise, she told me to open my eyes because you, my children, are waiting! Then she vanished, and I instantly opened my eyes again. Now, Can I have another drink of water?"

As mother Edina received the drink of water she had requested for, bishop Peter Musolozza was in his bed, very awake. He had been unable to sleep, thinking about what was going on with Mother Edina. For some reason, he was in total belief of everything that she was telling them. He believed that a voice, or voices, from heaven were talking to them through her. It was exciting, but at the same time terrifying, for this to be happening to the old lady, for the effects were visibly taking a profound toll on her. He was very concerned about what was going to happen after Mother Edina finally exited this world. Based on sheer belief, it is meant to be that God and his angels were never to reveal themselves directly to man, and that should that kind of contact ever come to be, that human individual or individuals would perish, erased to deter possible revelation of heaven's beings.

But that may be his own opinion or thinking. The lord of the heavens is mysterious in his ways, the bishop reminded himself. What we humans think may be totally different from his will, because he has his own reasons that can never, ever be predicted and or challenged. So, there is hope. Hope that Mother Edina's family might not perish at all because of this divine contact. He looked at his wife, sound asleep on the other side of the bed. As far as he was concerned, she had nothing to do with all this yet, and that's because he had not told her yet. It is probably the reason why, unlike himself, she was sleeping so soundly. Was the message meant for certain people only? If so, why?

An idea crossed his mind. He got out of the bed, very carefully so not to wake her up and made his way to the living room. On his way out of the bedroom, he picked up an old bible. He considered this bible the master bible of the house, as each room in the house, not excluding the kitchen, the toilet and the garage, all had a bible placed. He believed that the divine book is a protection from all evil, a lightless dispersion of evil will and spirits. After he checked on his two grandchildren in their bedroom, all sleeping soundly, he proceeded to the living room and immediately took to his knees in front of one of the big living room chairs, behind which hang a big silver cross with a fixture of the hanged Christ on it. He was going to appeal to God for answers, for a sense of direction, for what to do next. Maybe there would be a diversion, total or even partial, where he would separately experience all or share Mother Edina's visions. His sole purpose, he prayed, was to seek answers to know what this is all about, because he believed that it is all real, and perhaps too much for his frail old mother to handle.

But he also had another idea that he intended to pray to God for guidance. For some reason, and not even knowing even why he was thinking that way, he was beginning to believe that what was going on was a matter that could turn out to be a worldwide phenomenon, an issue that could affect the very fabric or nature of humanity. Therefore, his idea was to involve someone else, someone of a totally different path of faith or belief, someone to relay the heavenly message to another audience and make the undertaking of this event bigger. After a period of about forty-five minutes of silent prayer, the bishop returned to his bed, and got back into it just as quietly as he had left it. His wife still slept on.

Early in the next morning he called up the reverend. "How was mother last night?" he asked.

"Well, we had more revelations right a few hours after you left, and this went on into the middle of the night," The reverend explained. "The rest of the night was peaceful after that. The young female angel in her dreams promised to provide an explanation about the terrible nightmare, or vision, revealed to her earlier by the other angel, Orayah. We are now waiting for that promised explanation."

"I think I am going to come over this afternoon and spend the entire evening there with you for today, and maybe even tomorrow, to be closer to mother," the bishop said. "I intend to listen more to what is coming next. Samson, something big is going to happen, and I think heaven is communicating it us, basically through mother."

"I cannot disagree more to that," The reverend responded back. "I will make sure Rebecca prepares some tea for you and have a room ready in case you need to sleep over."

"Thank you very much, brother," the bishop replied, and then hang up.

His wife Sara was preparing his breakfast when he entered the dining room. "Good morning, Peter. You did not sleep at all last night. Is there something bothering you? If there is, then we should pray about it. Nothing is too big for the almighty God to fix, you know," she said.

"You won't believe what I am going to tell you," The bishop said, sitting down at the table. He proceeded to tell her about the old lady. "I think we are up to something big here, Sara. Something unimaginable, and I can feel it." He concluded.

Sara touched her husband's hand and smiled. "The almighty God has many ways of manifesting himself. I feel so blessed that my husband is part of a special group of people chosen by the heavens to be of the holy deliverance. I also suggest that you should go be with Sam and Rebecca. Stay by their side until this is resolved, my dear. This is because not only are they experiencing the sudden, and mysterious, holy deliverance but also the terrifying fact that mother is about to permanently leave them. They need our unwavering support, as you have always been to them. We need each other more than ever during this critical time."

"Yes, I think that's the right thing to do, but I will also be away from my wife, and this could take a few days. I will be missing you a lot," The bishop said, smiling and squeezing her hand gently.

"Yes, I very much understand that, and I will be missing you so much too, my husband," she replied. "But I think this is a direct call from heaven, Peter. In fact, I can almost feel it myself. You must heed to it. Such a calling is far more important than ourselves. It's even bigger than our love for each other. And, after all, it's God who created this love between people and other creatures and it is him, too, that can at his sole discretion also ultimately dissolve it. But now he wants us to put all aside and attend to his business. Maybe he wants to talk to you, all of you, personally. Who knows? So, go be present. I shall keep our home warm and safe until you return."

The bishop thanked his wife for her wisdom and for his breakfast, kissed her lightly on one side of her mouth and left the house, heading straight for the car parked in the yard and where his driver was waiting patiently. Now, had he turned around and looked at his wife one more time, he would have seen the very bright, sparkling yellow twinkles that became her eyes for about five full seconds.

At Namugongo, Rebecca, the reverend Samson's wife, received a phone call from her closest friend.

"Hello my dearest. I am letting you know now that I have dispatched my husband out of the house, urging him to come towards you now," Sarah the bishop's wife told her. "I want him to be in place when the revelations begin. How are you and your dear husband doing so far? It

must be so hard for him. He's always so concerned when it comes to his mother."

"Oooh, he's holding on. He will be ok for as long as I am on his side," Rebecca replied cheerfully. "After all, my dear, isn't that what we were sent here to do? To be their permanent shadows, to provide unwavering support for all their needs. For sure, Sara, I have come to enjoy and love the task so much I surely don't miss heaven anymore."

"Neither do I, my dear. They are such frail, pleasant, and innocent darlings to take care of, their nature being so vulnerable to their unknown foes that you find yourself totally committed to protecting them," Sarah affirmed with a giggle. "I intend to ask the light to reunite with mine when he is done here. I am so fond of him. By the way, how is mother doing? Will she be able to handle the possession process during the revelation? I am worried that her body is now so frail and weak."

"My dear, I am trying my level best to make sure she is strong enough for it," Rebecca replied. "I have tried to go through the angel medium to raise the same very concern, but I get no feedback. But I am also not void of self-reminding that we have become so much like them and that in doing so we tend to forget that nothing is impossible for the one who is the light and beyond. Remember, if he wills it, then it prevails. And clearly this is his will. She will prevail through it."

"Yes, my dear, you are right we have very much become like them," Sarah said. "We indeed forget, or sometimes fail, to have total faith in the light. We doubt his every word and vision. We indeed need to get to our knees and repent this sin of doubt."

"I am with you on that, my dear," Sarah reaffirmed.

"Can we meet in the medium and do the repentance as soon as possible?" Rebecca suggested. "I prefer doing it before her possession, and the revelation, take place. Can we meet this evening? Your husband will be here with mine. They will all be with their mother. And so, during this time we can find some quiet and privacy and get it done with."

"Amen, and Amen. Totally agree, all sounds good to me," Sarah replied. "See you later in the evening when we meet in the medium, my dear."

"Amen, and Amen," Came the reply from the other side. And then both simultaneously hung up.

# Chapter Four

$\mathcal{B}$ut now back to the business meeting in St Garache, the quiet suburb town of Turikai city, capital city of the island republic state of Turikai. Fast forward exactly Six hundred and sixty-six days from the events going on at the reverend's house in Namugongo.

Forty-five minutes into the meeting, Major Haraabi's audience finished watching the thirty minutes, pre - recorded show that visually demonstrated the devastating power of the "La Punta" super bacterium, first tested directed on mice, then livestock, then monkeys, and finally human beings, all in controlled environments. The video was so horrifically graphic and intense that the room went totally silent at the end. The Moments of shocked exclamations during its running time had also taken place, as audience members experienced the horrific reality of the power of this bacterium in its functioning reality. The way its victims ended up was very disturbing and sickening.

Captain Pony turned off the projecting device and turned on the room's lights. Major Haraabi, who had been carefully watching the reactions of each one of the members of his audience from his darkened corner to the left of the podium, got up and resumed position behind it. In the eyes of his audience, he appeared very calm and composed. His manner was reflective of indifference as he spoke again.

"That, gentlemen and ladies, was a demonstration of the power of our newest invention. A test, people, of its feasibility, its power," he said. "It will bring and strike terror into the hearts of men and women of this world and will unleash a whirlwind of confusion and mayhem into the inner cores of even the world's strongest governments. We will bring them to their knees, as they scramble to find the cure with useless tests and predictions. Religious institutions will call this the end of the world, which will bring more fear and chaos. Pandemonium, ladies and gentlemen, will be the new order of the day, because citizens will be looking at their governments for relief, and these governments won't know what to exactly do about the situation. And so, they will be willing to do anything to get rid of this deadly pandemic. They will be willing to spend all the money in this world to stop the scourge of this seemingly relentless, infectious bacterial infection. And that's where we come in, people. We will present our antidote, a patented cure to this disease menace! And yes, we shall name our price! A great return to your investment!"

"This is so ridiculous and evil," someone from the audience suddenly interjected. Standing up, he pointed a finger at Major Haraabi. It was the same middle-aged looking man who had questioned him in the beginning. "And you call this a great business preposition? The Mass destruction of people? This is mass murder, and so for God's sake we can't make money out of this kind of thing, huh… people! This is absolutely preposterous!"

"Sit down and let me finish!" Major Antoquake snarled, staring back at the man with visible menace. "And for future references, please leave God out of it, will you? Let me make it clear to you right now that we are not religious fanatics or terrorists. We are simply businessmen! I am still presenting this plan to you and once I am done it will all make sense to you. But until I am done, I will not entertain any panic-based interference whatsoever, in any form or way! Neither can you leave before I am done, ladies and gentlemen. You signed up for this private symposium and that's why you are here. I am not here to waste your time, and neither should you waste mine! So, sit your ass down and listen carefully. When I am done you will have all the time to ask questions and or express your wimpy concerns. Am I understood?"

The man seemed to be affected by the menace in major Haraabi's voice. He slowly sat down. The rest of the audience said nothing.

"Good. Let us now continue," the major said firmly. He made a hand signal to Pony, and she went to work again. Using her hand computer, she quickly did some typing and soon another bright screen came up behind the podium where they stood, replacing the video projection one. This one revealed the map of the world, with pointers to the world's most densely populated areas, which included all the world's major cities. The densely populated areas had a red indicator light that continuously flushed on and off. "As you can see, this is the map of the world showing all the world's hot spots. By hot spots I mean where a lot of people are at the same time in given country. These, gentlemen, are going to be our main target areas. Beijing, London, New York, Moscow and St Petersburg, Riyadh, Calcutta and new Delhi, Manila, Paris Dhaka, Dubai, Mumbai, Tokyo, Colombo, Cairo, Cologne, Cape town, San Paulo, Buenos Aires, Lagos, Barcelona, Mexico City, Melbourne, Rome, Toronto, East Africa's major cities, Java, united states of America states of Texas and California, Israel and Palestine, and a whole wide range of island states! We will dispatch the duplicated bacteria strains and release them simultaneously at the same time. For some of these complicated places we main need to use complicated delivery systems like long range stealth drones that will detonate once they reach destinations. But most of the strains will be delivered by human dispatch and then released into the general populations of these places. Once the pandemonium is on and raging, our already existing drug manufacturing companies and general pharmaceutical outlets will announce the antidote and money will start flowing in. That's the plan. Now, any questions so far on this?"

"Ok, we got that point," a guy with a typical south Texas cowboy accent, said. "So where does our money come in? Why do you need so much money from each of us? I mean, dude, personally I will be shelling out some millions of dollars when or once I press the button on your little computer in front of me. Tell us what our money is exactly going to do."

"Very good question, and expected," Major Haraabi responded. "First, understand that our group, the proposing side of this business, is also going to invest a lot of money in this. So, we will all be in the same boat, rowing together. Simply put, we need extra money to mass produce, and carefully package our super bacteria strain. We are hiring special lab scientists, chemists, infectious disease experts, and lab personnel to help us do this. We will need a secure location with a sophisticated security system, and for this we are hiring a top security team which will oversee highly trained security personnel all armed and ready to ward off any interference. We will need to set up out delivery systems for the duplicated La Punta strains which, like I said, will consist of both human and mechanical means. We are to replicate the antidote strain at a mass level and have it ready for delivery or mass distribution by opening pharmacy outlets and dispensaries and have trucks and planes to ship out the antidote. Before that we must set up the complex marketing teams and money accountants and banks who will make sure you receive back your money plus interest in such a way that you are not linked to all of this in anyway. We will set up a sophisticated, private online network with special passwords and fire walls for each of you so you can stay informed of our progress, and what to do when the plan is initiated. So, you see, ladies and gentlemen, all these things will require money to be done, and not just pennies, but lots of money, millions of dollars. But not so much as to when you start realizing the returns, gentlemen. Trust me, you will personally call us and thank us for being so genius."

Someone in the audience suddenly stood up and started clapping his hands in staccato fashion. "I think it's perfectly genius. Perfect!"

He was joined by another and another, until all of them were up and clapping to his rhythm. All of them except the middle-aged looking guy, who remained seated, hands folded in front of him.

Major Haraabi smiled and joined in the clapping. He was happy to have the majority and the meeting had turned out to be easier than he had expected. However, his eyes remained focused on the middle-aged guy, whose eyes were now focused on the floor. He had to deal with this one separately, he decided.

"Gentlemen and ladies, let me now assume that everyone is happy with our business proposal and is ready invest in it. I assure you, relax, because as we promised in our first approach which led to this meeting, you will get back your money at one thousand percent profit! With your money, we shall implement this operation to such perfection that not even God will be able to stop us! It is now time to use the iPad computer in front of you to wire us the money, your share of your investment. Simply type in the figures of your account number, type in the exact amount allotted to you for the investment exactly as indicated in the top right corner of the screen and hit the send button. Everything else has been set up for you. You will see a confirmation message of the wired funds and receive a confirmation number via the email you provided," Major Haraabi concluded.

His audience quickly sat down again and picked up the hand computers. As he watched them do it, he was surprised to see the middle-aged guy using the computer too. He felt a brief sense of relief. He didn't have to eliminate him after all. He wasn't going to let him leave and live after revealing the master plan of this operation. There was no doubt he would simply compromise everything, since he already signaled disagreement with the business proposal and or its functions. But neither was he trusting these rich people with his plans. They tend to carelessly talk too much and could easily spill the beans. And for that, he already had a plan in the works, one that could make sure that kind of thing doesn't happen.

In front of him was his own computer, and from it he could see the figure rising as the money transfers came in. It finally beeped and a green light flashed at the bottom of the computer, accompanied by a string of words that read "Total deposit complete".

He now had all the money he needed to run the operation. Everyone had met their obligation, including the nervous guy. It was now time for him to deliver on his own side of the bargain.

"Gentlemen, and ladies, you have all met your obligations, so thank you very much," he said. "It's now our turn to deliver on our bargain. The time frame is approximately six months from now for the results of your investment to materialize. Please rest assured, it will be done and each one of you will see a hefty return on your investment. After you leave here, we will contact you again in three months to update you on how far we have gone with your money, and from that point forward you will receive monthly updates until D day arrives. By that time, you will be seeing us in action on all news media in the world."

"How about us and our families' safety?" someone asked from the audience. "Aren't we going to be affected by the spread of this deadly bacteria?"

"Good question," The major replied. "In five months from now, which is one month before D day, you will each receive a small package in the mail delivered at your doorstep at the address you gave us. It will contain several bottles of the antidote and instructions on what to do with it. You shall also be advised to which areas to stay out of when and as we initiate the operation. Fair enough?"

"Fair enough, major," the question's origin responded back. "Good. Any more questions? Mr. Vonsberg, perhaps? Any questions for me before we end this session?" major Haraabi asked. He was making sure the audience was on the same page with him now, and in doing so directly addressed the middle-aged man, identified as Bernhardt Vonsberg.

"No. No more questions or concerns, Major," Bernhardt Vonsberg replied, staring straight back at the major, his face expressionless.

"Good then," major Antoquake acknowledged. "One more thing, people. I must let you know that at this juncture you are fully invested in this operation and there is no such thing as changing your mind or ranting about our business project. You would automatically be implicating yourself if you do. By sending us the money you have signed off on this and that makes you directly liable! Are we clear on that?"

There was no direct answer to his precautionary question, just loud mumbling and mild, random disgruntlement. The folks gathered in this room were either filthy rich or represented the rich and therefore were not used being cautioned. To them, any deal is a risk and if it fails, oh well, they move on the next one. Liability was no big deal to them because they could afford the best lawyers in the world. They were not used to being served ultimatums and that's what this guy was trying to do.

"Is there anything else you would like to tell us, aah, Major?" someone else asked from the audience. "Because if this meeting is over, I would like to move on to my next rendezvous!"

"Meeting is adjourned, gentlemen and ladies," Major Antoquake confirmed. He was already as tired of them as, perhaps, they were showing intolerance of him. "Use the center gliding door to the right. The ladies are waiting for you outside to lead you back to your respective cars and chauffeur, who then will take you back to the airport where the plane is waiting to fly you off the island and back to the mainland." His audience members quickly filed out. Still, the last person to step out of the room was the middle-aged guy, Bernhardt Vonsberg. Major Haraabi beckoned to him with his hand to hold on for minute. The man stood still and waited. Major Haraabi walked over to him and then looking straight into the man's eyes, he asked "Mr. Vonsberg, are you sure you have no more reservations about our business proposal and operations?"

Bernhardt Vonsberg stared right back at major Haraabi and replied. "Like I said, not anymore. But perhaps I would like to say one thing, Major …"

"And that is?" Major Haraabi asked quickly.

"If I heard right, you said that not even God will be able to stop you. I think that's an overstatement. Look, I am a man who strongly believes in God and the Almighty divine nature, which I fully believe is real. So, are you sure of that statement, Major? Especially when you're trying to mess with God's creations? I mean, you're going to be destroying lives here, lives that you didn't create or bring to this world. I think it's a bad thing, a bad way to go, and we shouldn't do it. But I can see that you're very determined to carry on with this evil deal, so…good luck with that man!" Bernhardt Vonsberg said. And then he left the room.

Major Haraabi turned to captain Pony. "For safety reasons, please run a complete data check on Vonsberg and email it to me a.s.a.p.," he instructed. Picking up his iPad tablet, he left the podium and headed for the elevator. Captain Pony grabbed her computer and quickly followed behind him.

Pulling out his cellphone, he quickly dialed a number, issued some rapid instructions to the recipient of the call, and then ended it.

"Yes sir," she replied to his order as she joined him in the elevator. The elevator took them back to where they had come from, his office. Once they were inside, he turned to her and embracing her fully, he started kissing her. After getting back a full response to his advances, he, in a matter of few minutes, started unbuttoning her blouse. But as this body-to-body engagement grew to a breathless level, she pushed back momentarily.

"Quake, did you mean what you said, that not even God can stop you?" She asked, looking straight into his eyes.

"Emm hmmm…," he mumbled, pulling her back to him.

She pushed him further away. "Are you sure of that? Because as far as I am concerned you just jinxed your entire plans and operations. You just jinxed the whole project! Quake, you just don't say things like that. How dare you …"

Major Haraabi's overall demeanor suddenly changed, and before she could say anything else, he grabbed her around the neck and squeezed hard. He lifted her much slender body off the floor and slammed it hard against the opposite wall.

"Let… me… go! I can't breathe!" she squealed.

"Don't you ever, ever question what I say again, woman!" he growled. "I mean what I say and say what I mean! I don't believe in luck, good or bad! I only believe in myself and my plans, and so your God, or for that matter anybody else's, has absolutely nothing to do with it! Divinity is a travesty of human thinking and ability! Do you understand? DO YOU UNDERSTAND?"

"I… get it, yes sir, Major… Haraabi," she said, amid gasping for air with her feet dangling in space. He suddenly let go of her neck and she flopped down to the floor like a small sack of potatoes. He started walking away from her.

"You are a fool to think the way you think, Haraabi," she managed to say as she gently rubbed at her now sore neck with her right hand, staring angrily at him. "You should, perhaps, know that no man or woman, and certainly nothing in this world, can openly defy or challenge the living God, the holy spirit!"

She managed to get herself back to her feet, but only to be slapped hard in the face by a glaring Major Haraabi, sending her flopping down to the floor again. So hard was that slap she immediately felt dizzy and nauseated.

"Oh, go to hell, you son of a bitch!" she hissed loudly glaring back at him. She was no stranger to major Haraabi's sudden temper tantrums and or hitting at her like that. She had realized that challenging this man got him overall frustrated and lashing out angrily was a way of expressing his frustration. And every time this kind of act happened, they would end up making passionate love afterwards, so passionate she considers it being raped, legitimately. And after each of those episodes, everyone ended up feeling much better, herself all worn out and sore, him much calmer. It's just that it had never been over something like this.

"Take your clothes off right now!" he commanded. She instantly obeyed, and the next thing she knew he was on top of her, naked and giving it to her hard with her legs wide open in the air, right there on the office floor. The grinding was hard, with him grunting at every thrust, and her whimpering loudly from her pain. It was an exhausting moment that lasted a full ten minutes before he released into her, and then quickly got up. She remained on the floor, curled up in a fetal position, trying to catch her breath.

"Come on, babe. Get yourself together, we still have lots of work to do, including a flight to catch," he said, looking down at her and shaking his head slowly. "We will have abundant time to chill when this is all over and done with."

Pony slowly started getting up from the floor.

Once they got outside of the building, the members of major Haraabi's meeting or audience were not allowed to congregate again. They were each ushered to their respective chauffeured vehicles and taken to the airport where their transport plane was waiting to take them off the Island. They all left at the same time, a line of black vehicles cruising the well illuminated freeway. Bernhardt Vonsberg's car was the last in line, keeping the rear of the entourage. His chauffeur, just like the other chauffeurs, did not say a word as he drove. They were forbidden to talk to the guests. However, this quiet momentum was briefly interrupted by a recurring buzzing sound when the chauffeur suddenly received a telephone call via a cell phone. He picked it up but didn't say a word while he listened to the voice on the other side of the line. Neither did he stop driving, still following the line of other cars ahead of him. He then put the phone back down and stared right ahead. About fifteen minutes later of non – stop driving they arrived at the airport, driving through a series of guarded gates and into the airfield. Suddenly, Bernhardt Vonsberg's chauffeur veered off the route and headed for the row of airport hangers to the far left, accelerating the speed.

"What are you doing?" Bernhardt Vonsberg asked immediately, sitting forward in his seat. "Hey man, where are you taking me? You are driving away from the plane."

But the chauffeur didn't answer his question. He continued driving into the darkness until he suddenly stopped the car, turned off the headlights, and shut the engine off. Only the dim lights from the dashboard illuminated the interior of the car. Before Bernhardt Vonsberg could ask him again about what was going on, the chauffeur opened the driver door and got out the car. He then opened his passenger's door and Bernhardt Vonsberg found himself staring at the long barrel of what appeared to be a silencer attached to a pistol held by the chauffeur, pointed at his chest.

"Get out of the car, now!" The chauffeur commanded, his voice deep and menacing.

Breathing heavily, Bernhardt Vonsberg did as he was told, and faced the chauffeur, who appeared to be a big, tall man with broad shoulders. It was clear that the man was going to shoot him, as he raised the barrel of the gun to his head.

But suddenly another man emerged from nowhere in the darkness and grabbed hold of the chauffeur's gun hand. In one reflex action, he knocked the gun out of the chauffeur's hand and in the next grabbed the chauffeur's jacket collar and yanked him around, forcing him to turn away from Bernhardt Vonsberg. This same man then hit the broad-shouldered, big, tall chauffeur in the middle of his body with a right hand, closed fist! The blow came with such brutal force that the chauffeur's body was flung backwards, smashing into the right side of the car a few feet away from Bernhardt Vonsberg, with a heavy thud. Bernhardt Vonsberg heard the chauffeur gasp heavily, like in a deep sigh, as he involuntarily expelled air out of his lungs. His body flopped to the ground with another thud, immediately going into convulsion.

41

But the attacking man wasn't done yet. Grabbing the convulsing chauffeur by the neck with his left hand, he yanked him off the ground like he was a light scarecrow doll and then lashed out with another vicious right-hand blow at the left side of his neck. When the man let go again, the remains of Bernhardt Vonsberg's chauffeur collapsed in a crumpled heap on the ground, next to the right front tire of the car.

All this happened so fast, perhaps in less ten seconds.

With no signs of shortness of breath that normally accompanies swift and sudden activity by a normal human being, the attacker looked down at the still form of what would have been Bernhardt Vonsberg's murderer. Grabbing the unresponsive man by his jacket collar again, he dragged his body a few yards away from the car. Standing upright again and clapping his hands together as if he was getting them free of filth, he kicked the chauffeur's gun away from the car in one swift leg movement. The man then turned to look at Bernhardt Vonsberg. Though much shorter than the broad- shouldered chauffeur, his built appeared stocky and or solid.

"Get back into the car, Mr. Vonsberg," he said. His voice was surprisingly calm and smooth.

Bernhardt Vonsberg did as he was told. The man closed the door behind him and then himself entered the car, sitting behind the wheel.

Starting the car, he veered it around with tires screeching and headed back in the direction from which they had come, driving towards the brightly illuminated area of the airport where a few planes were lined up.

Clearing his throat, Bernhardt Vonsberg finally found the guts to lean forward from the back seat, trying to look at the man. He still could not see his face clearly.

"Can you please tell me what is going on?" he managed to ask, his voice a husky whisper. "Who are you? Why was that driver going to kill me and why did you stop him from doing it? I am sorry to be asking all these questions and I thank you for saving my life, but I still want to have some answers for which, I am indulged to think, you do have."

"Yes, that man was ordered, and was indeed going to, end your life. I am glad we came in on time," the man said. "We stopped him from

42

doing it because of the courage you showed during that meeting of which you were part of just a few minutes ago. Not only were you concerned about the lives of the innocent, but you also questioned the validity of man's abilities above God's. Your courage caught our attention and we got permission to have this unnecessary end of your life, which was going to be today, revoked."

"I am not getting the meaning of all this stuff you are telling me about my courage and life, and you still haven't answered my questions. Who are you, and how do you even know about this meeting?" Bernhardt Vonsberg asked. "I don't remember seeing your likeness anywhere inside that meeting room, yet you seem to know so much about it."

They now entered the brightly illuminated area of the airport. Bernhardt could now see the rest of the convoy cars parked outside the single-story building, the airport's terminal. Beyond that, inside a fenced off area, were two planes. One, a big jet plane, had its full lights on and was slowly taxing on the runaway, while the other, a smaller plane, seemed to be warming up for departure but was still parked in one spot.

The man stopped the car after pulling up in line with the other convoy cars, which were all now empty of their human cargo. After he shut down the engine he turned around and faced Bernhardt Vonsberg. He had a dark complexion with strong facial features highlighted by pronounced cheek bones. He smiled faintly and then said "The heavens have opened today in your favor and protected you from those who sought to decease you. Know this from today, that the right hand of the one who is the holiest of the holiest, and who is seated in heaven, will always protect, and will never forsake, those who believe and trust in him. God's right hand has indeed reached out to you today, Mr. Vonsberg. You can now go in peace and continue living with, and or in your unwavering faith in God."

"Okay…" Bernhardt Vonsberg said hesitantly. "So, who are you?

An Angel, who is also a part of the "we" you referred to earlier?"

"If you want to know more, here is my number," the man said, offering him a small card. "Call me, at your time discretion, and then I shall not only explain about this phenomenon that has revealed itself to you, but also help you understand it, that way you will get to know who we

43

exactly are. Just remember that You must, at some point in time, call me, Mr. Vonsberg. Now get going. By the way, you are supposed to be on that plane that's taxing away on the runaway, but we delayed you, and you shall soon know why. You will now get on board the smaller plane. Everything has been cleared for you, just identify yourself and you will be taken on board."

"Wow!" Bernhardt exclaimed, shaking his head slowly. He stepped out of the car and shut the door. He still couldn't see the man's face clearly. "Thank you, thank you very much Mr....," he said as he walked away from the car.

When he reached the glass double doors at the entrance of the terminal, he turned around to look at the man in the car one more time, perhaps wave at him. But there was no one behind that steering wheel anymore. He blinked quickly and peered at the car again. Yep, there was nobody in that car. Shaking his head, he opened the terminal door and stepped into the brightly lit lobby. A female attendant in a neat light blue uniform immediately approached him. Smiling widely, she extended her hand to him. He shook the dainty hand.

"Your flight is ready for you, Mr. Vonsberg. Please follow me," she announced without asking for his identification. How does she even know who I am?

It was exactly two hours when major Haraabi and his mistress Pony left the main town hall of the main conference center of Turikai, the capital city of the island republic of the Turikai. Both still looked exhausted from bouts of rough love – making, for she had grabbed at him after her initial beat up, forcing him to disrobe again and get into it again, at least twice, and this time gentler. The driver of the four-wheel drive jeep wrangler had waited patiently outside until the pair emerged from the building and then promptly chauffeured them to the airport, where a private jet was waiting in a private hanger for use to fly back to a mainland. The major tipped the driver with one hundred euro note, which worked here very well as a domestic major currency, before boarding the rented forty–people passenger business jet. Both him and Pony were certified plane pilots and had flown themselves to the Island. For that matter, they were the only people on the plane.

As Pony prepped the jet for the flight, Major Haraabi got beeped on the plane's satellite communications apparatus and took the call from the back of the plane. It was one of his main employers.

"We realized you were going to let that rich son of a bitch Bernhardt Vonsberg walk off the island just like that," the voice on the other side stated immediately. "We didn't like his reactions to our plans, so we took care of that problem for you. We eliminated him before he left the island."

Major Haraabi did not care to hide his anguish at the news about Bernhardt Vonsberg. "But he gave us the money, hence he basically became part of this business. Obviously, he wasn't going to spill any data on the operation because then he would incriminate himself. We have all the info we need on him, enough to allow us to inflict havoc on him and his family using our worldwide network of hell raisers who work for us. We wanted his money, we got it, and that was that. Everyone in that meeting knew the consequences of betraying the cause. So why then kill the rich bastard while he's still on the island? All his phones are tapped. Even his personal friend, who's his finance manager, now works for us. I say we should have given him sometime, just to see how he reacts."

"From what we noted as we followed the meeting remotely, he seemed to be too much of a risk to be cut by loose into the public," the voice on the other side said. "We were monitoring the meeting, remember? Every one of us. And we all agreed to the same thing. To eliminate him immediately. We are going to set it up by putting a woman's dead body in the car together with his, so it looks like he was having an extra – marital affair while on the island. Our networks will broadcast it as an assassination of some sorts."

"That wasn't necessary at this time!" the major snarled back. He personally liked to be challenged more before getting to eliminate someone, and Bernhardt Vonsberg had not kindled that challenge level yet.

"Now you watch your temperament major, or I will have you kenneled for life too!" the caller snarled back. "For God's sake, have you lost your guts and nerves? Since when did you start giving a shit about any assassinations, huh? You have personally arranged and participated in

many of them so why should this one matter that much to you? Looks like you are going soft on us, Quake. Maybe it is time to replace you with some other crazy bastard."

The phone line went dead in his ears immediately after the caller made this final threat. Major Haraabi hang up the communication headset and returned to the pilot's cabin, where he took over from Pony in the pilot's seat.

"Bernhardt Vonsberg is dead!" he told her as she settled herself into the comfortable co-pilot chair.

"What?" she exclaimed in total surprise. "What the hell happened now?"

"Those bastards at corporate level had him killed," he said. "They activated his chauffeur into assassination mode, without even telling me. I usually arrange for those kinds of things to happen to people basing on what I deem is necessary. It's always been that way. They claim they didn't like his reactions during the meeting and didn't think he should be allowed to get off the island alive."

"Oh my god, they are so impatient," she said, sounding concerned. "They killed him right after taking his money too. That's not right!"

"Yea. And when I told the caller that it wasn't necessary at this time to kill him, the bastard threatened to get rid of me!" The major said. "But they have no godamned idea who they are messing with. After this assignment, you and I are calling it quits on them and going solo, on our own, Pony, and I need you to be ready for that change. I already have everything worked out."

"But they will come after us and try to kill us, right?" she said, as their jet finally went airborne. "It's always been like that, you know. For the mere fact that we already know too much."

"Not after you and I kill each and every one of them first," Major Haraabi replied. "I know where each and every one of them live and work, except for the one on top, the one everyone calls "the principal". I designed and now also have control their personal protection details. The men who protect them work for me."

"Hmmm… well then, they are as good as dead already," Pony mused.

Two hours ahead of them already, Bernhardt Vonsberg had landed at a private airport in Europe, where a car with a driver was waiting for him to take him to a major public airport. Even though he could afford a private jet of his own, he instead preferred flying on normal public planes. It suited his lifestyle, a quiet, non – stylish billionaire who had nothing much to do with lavish parties or public confrontations. It was normal for him to suddenly leave his office and call for a Taxi.

But now he was clearly rattled by his near execution. Although he loved taking business risks, for the first time in his life he felt threatened and realized that from now on he had to be very careful with whom he was dealing with. He had no clue who these people were and why they had suddenly decided to kill him even after he had given them a lot of his money. And then there is this other group, the group that had saved his life. He had no clue who they were either. He reached into his pocket and took out the small business card that his rescuer had given to him.

It was a plain white card with the word "Zeal" in the center, and a row of numbers below it. He assumed that was the name of the man and although he had never seen such an arrangement, that the row of numbers was his telephone digits. The name and number were all in gold script. A strange feeling came over him as he stared at the card. It was like the numbers leapt towards his eyes and were right in front of his nose, yet he was holding the card way down near his waist, something he has automatically been doing due to eyesight problems. The numbers also seemed to be radiating repeatedly. He shook his head repeatedly as if to clear his head, but that vision remained for as long as he was looking at the card. He put it back in his pocket, then brought it out again. Same thing still happened. He decided to put the card away and focus on his current trip. After his encounter with death, all he wanted to do now was to go home to his wife and children.

Two hours later he was airborne straight for Dallas-Fort Worth, a sprawling metroplex in the state of Texas, united states of America, where he lives in a gated mansion in a city called Southlake. He fell asleep on the plane, feeling tired and exhausted and for some reason, anxious. When he woke up, he turned on the personal television monitor in front of him. A plane had just crushed over the Sahara

Desert, killing all eighteen people on board as it flew into a mysterious heavy sandstorm and the pilot lost control. It was a business carrying executives from some big companies, some of them the company owners. Authorities in that area were on their way to further investigate and images of the wreck were to be released later. Bernhardt Vonsberg turned off the television immediately. He didn't want to listen to or see bad news today. He just wanted to go home. He unfastened his seatbelt for better comfort and then fell asleep again and was later awakened by a flight attendant reminding him to fasten his seatbelt again as they were about to encounter heavy turbulence.

Approximately ten hours later he landed at Love field airport, and since he had only one suitcase full of personals, it was easy and quicker for him to go through customs and then get hold of a taxi. About forty-five minutes later, time four thirty in the afternoon, he arrived outside his house in Southlake. He noticed that there were several cars outside his walled in mansion, among them a city of Southlake police cruiser. Also parked outside was a white van with what appeared to be a satellite dish on top. It was a News - eight anchor van. A man wearing a cap and a set of big headsets held a big video camera and was facing a woman with a wireless microphone in her hands. Other people were slowly moving in on them.

Bernhardt Vonsberg's heart started pounding hard inside his chest as he wondered what was going on. He knew very well that this was a live news crew convening outside his place. Why were they here? Something must have happened to his family, that inner voice inside his head immediately taunted his mind. That's perhaps why the police were here too. He told the driver to stop. He then pulled out a few crisp dollar bills from inside his jacket pocket to pay for his fare, but to his surprise the taxi driver declined it. Not understanding why, he asked the man why he was refusing to take the money.

"God has already taken care of it, sir," the man said, in what was clearly a middle eastern accent. "You're a good man, sir, so it's free. Go on, have a good day sir."

Bernhardt stared at the man for another five seconds, noticing the name Hassan Warried on the dashboard. Shaking his head, he repocketed the money, and stepped out of the car. The taxi immediately drove off. Slowly he made his way towards the now wide- open gates. He was beginning to feel a little nauseated, perhaps from the anxiety welling up inside him as he weighed in on what could have possibly happened. Suddenly, someone shouted something, and the woman with the microphone quickly turned around and looked at him, the camera man following closely. Her eyes widened when she apparently recognized who he was.

"Hold it," he said, raising his hands up. "Can you please tell me what's going on? What are you people doing outside my home? We certainly didn't call a news conference, did we? Is my family, okay?"

"Mr. Vonsberg, I am Megan Johnson of News eight," the woman with the microphone said, hastening to face him and standing in his way. "Mr. Vonsberg, you are one of the businessmen on the list of the people killed in that plane crash that occurred in the Sahara Desert this morning. The list was released this afternoon by the company that leased out the plane. Yet here you are now, suddenly showing up outside your home. How can that be? How did you manage not to be on the ill-fated plane unlike your other fellow businesspeople? It's even been confirmed by your own company spokesman that you were on that plane. Can you please tell us about what appears to be a bizarre twist in this event story?"

"I don't know, and I don't understand it either," Bernhardt Vonsberg replied, sounding frustrated already and looking quite stunned by the revelation. "Now, please get out of my way. I need to get to my family first."

Gently pushing past the news anchor, he proceeded through the main gates and hastily strode up the driveway that led to the front of the house. The news crew followed him all the way until he stepped on to the mansion's wide front porch. There they stopped but remained on the grounds. Inside the house, a small group of people were gathered, seated in the first living room. He recognized all of them, two of them being the city of Southlake police chief and the other one the city's mayor, both of whom he had met on several occasions during the city's charity programs. The others were Greg Green, his company's chief financial officer and his best friend, together with his company spokesperson Donald, his sister Adalicia Vonsberg, who was currently living at his house as a private duty nurse looking after his wife who was very sick, his twenty-two years old middle son Barret, and the pastor of his church, J. V. Curry. They all looked shocked to see him and the room went totally quiet.

"Barret where is your mother?" he asked immediately, breaking the silence without acknowledging anyone else's presence.

Suddenly everybody jumped up and all started talking at the same time. His son, Barret, hugged him tightly, and then took off running upstairs, shouting at the top of his lungs, notifying his mother that his dad was in the living room and not dead in a plane crush. The rest of the people in the living room now surrounded him. Everyone basically wanted to know how come he was here while, at the same time, he was said to have died on the ill-fated plane in the Sahara Desert. His chief financial officer restated that he had all confirmation records of his destination to the island and that all travel itinerary to and from the island was based on that plane.

"Listen, everyone, I myself don't know what happened," He replied. "All I know is that an incident on the way back to the Island's airport delayed me, and by the time I got to it the unfortunate plane had left without me. Nonetheless, I was already booked on another one."

"Heaven is still smiling down at us. Our heavenly father sent his angels to protect you and bring you back home safely," someone said from somewhere. It was his wife, Myra. Everybody now looked up at the slender, frail figure standing at the top of the stairs. She slowly started descending the stairs until she stood right before them, with her son Barret standing right behind her. Her eyes were bloodshot red, evidence that she had been crying.

Bernhardt Vonsberg stepped closer to, and then embraced, his wife. Myra Vonsberg was suffering from, and being treated for, a rare form of cancer in her throat, and had to undergo chemotherapy every other day for over three months now. As a result, she had lost her appetite and lost a lot of weight. The illness itself had taken a profound toll on her body. The cancer specialist looked like he was throwing in the towel and was going to give the Vonsbergs his final verdict on their next visit, which was also going to be their last. From the indications already noted, it wasn't going to be a favorable one.

"Yes, they are indeed protecting us, and yes, I think God told them to do so," Bernhardt reaffirmed, his face turned upwards, pulling his son Barret closer to him. His daughter, Benita, had also come downstairs and was holding on to her daddy firmly, tears rolling down her eyes. "I will never leave you guys alone again. I was very worried about you all until now."

But then he suddenly let go of the children and stared at his wife.

"Honey, you are up and walking by yourself?" He asked, a surprise look on his face. "The last time I left the house you couldn't stand on your own at all, couldn't maintain your gait, and could hardly look up without your nurse helping you. But here you are now, coming downstairs by yourself and standing upright, and staring right back into my eyes. How did that happen?"

"And she got out of bed by herself too, Bern," her other private home health nurse, who also happened to be her younger sister, Wendt, stated. She had just appeared at the top of the stairs. "Don't ask me how it happened, Bern, because I don't understand it either. I was in the bathroom when she did it."

"Dad, the moment you showed up through the front door, mommy suddenly opened her eyes, got out the bed, and started coming towards you, with no help at all!" Barret told his father.

For a moment, all attention turned to the frail woman standing next to her husband and children.

"I just can't explain it either," Myra Vonsberg said slowly, sounding puzzled, and sensing that everyone was staring at her in a strange way. "All I know is that this strange voice suddenly whispered into my right ear, telling me to get out of the bed and go meet my husband downstairs. And so, I did. But come now, Bern was telling us how he had an incident on the way to an airport that delayed him and hence kept him off that ill-fated flight. Why don't we let him finish with that?"

Bernhardt Vonsberg nodded his head in affirmation and cleared his throat to speak. But before he could start, a blaring noise suddenly took over the room. It was the sound of the original classic telephone ring tone and pastor J.V Curry quickly fidgeted with his pockets to

51

pull out his cell phone. As everyone turned their heads to look at him, he answered the call, listened to it, and then looked up at Bernhardt Vonsberg, a look of surprise on his face. "It's for you, Mr. Vonsberg," he said, stretching out his hand to with the cell phone towards Bernhardt Vonsberg.

Bernhardt Vonsberg took the cell phone from the pastor, equally looking totally surprised. "Hello?"

"Mr. Vonsberg, this is Zeal, the person who saved you from being killed today," the voice on the other side said. "Listen to me very carefully. I want you and your family to leave your house immediately. Move your family away from there to some other location and stay there until further notice. Do it now!"

"Hold on man, what do you mean I should move my family out of here immediately, and why are you calling me via the pastor's..." Bernhardt started, but the man cut him short.

"You have no time, Mr. Vonsberg. The people who tried to kill you earlier have found out that you are still alive and are coming after you again," the man said. "And so, start moving now. And for now, do not reveal to anyone where you are going. That's for their own safety."

"But can you please explain to me what's..." Bernhardt started to say, but the line went dead.

He stared at the pastor with a questioning look as he handed back the cell phone. "Who are these people?" he asked.

"I am sorry, Mr. Vonsberg but I have never seen that number before, don't know who the caller is, or why he used my phone to get to you," The pastor replied.

"What is it now, Bern?" Myra Vonsberg asked, getting instantly concerned about the look on her husband's face.

"The person who just called me via the pastor's phone says we are in danger and that we should leave this house now," he said, visibly frowning.

"Mr. Vonsberg, are you and your family in some sort of danger?" the Southlake city police chief asked. "Did you just get threatened over the phone? Because if that's the case then I can offer you full protection

52

from my police department until we get to the bottom of all this. You don't have to leave your home immediately without proper planning."

"Why are we suddenly being threatened, dad?" his son Barret voiced up. "Is there something crazy going on that we need to know about? Is anyone after you for now for something that you did earlier? Why don't you just tell us about it now dad?"

Bernhardt waved his arms in the air to calm the situation down. "Believe me, son, I myself have no clue of what's going on right now," he said, his voice calm and clear. "All I know is that I and this caller met several hours ago, under mysterious, extreme circumstances that I can't explain at this moment. But my instinct is urging me to just do what he says. I promise you that when the right time comes, I will tell you all about it. For now, I will go get the minivan out of the garage. The rest of you, go pack your personal stuff now, and please try to be quick about it. Someone, please go help park mom's stuff ."

He turned to the chief of police. "Paul, I need your help to clear all those people out of my front yard and to make sure nobody follows us when we leave here. Can you do that for me?"

"Sure can," the chief replied. He already had a cellphone in his right hand and in a moment, he was talking on it and issuing instructions.

Another phone went off, and this time it was Greg Green's, his best friend and chief finance officer. He excused himself and stepped out of the room.

"There is a sudden change in plans," he said to the caller once he was out of the room. "Vonsberg is leaving his residence for a destination currently unknown to me, and he is leaving immediately."

"We have already activated an active team in the States, and they are on their way to his house right now as we speak," the voice on the other side said. "So, he can't leave yet. Either find a way to stop him from leaving or try stalling him. If that's too hard for you, Mr. Green, then find out where he is going and let us know immediately." The phone went dead.

Greg green stared at his phone for a moment and then slowly put it back in his pocket. He didn't know what to do now, because there didn't seem a way to stop Bernhardt Vonsberg and his family from leaving. But he had to do something, because the people who had just called him wanted him to do so, because if not his own very life and his family would be in danger. These people appeared to be very dangerous, powerful people, and for the first time he regretted having got involved in this whole business, for it was him who had arranged for Bernhardt Vonsberg to go to this business trip. That was after a gentleman paid him a visit at corporate office and described a money- making plan that could earn the Vonsberg company millions of dollars, tax free. Greg already knew this gentleman and had already done enough business with him to trust him. But since it involved investing a large sum of money, Greg suggested to his friend Bernhardt Vonsberg to go check it out, that way if impressed he could instantly transfer the money. Bernhardt Vonsberg was savvier with business dealings than him and always spotted the right deals. And so, Bernhardt Vonsberg had agreed to go check it out.

But about forty-eight hours ago, before Bernhardt Vonsberg's mysterious reappearance after being considered dead in a plane crash, things started going into a different direction. First was the announcement of the plane crash carrying important business people and or, their representatives, right in the middle of a desert. It was feared that Bernhardt was on it. He had immediately contacted the Vonsberg family after reconfirming the flight data and numerous news outlets, and immediately convened an emergency company meeting with all department heads to figure out the next step. But while that meeting was going on, the gentleman who had brought him the business preposition called him and requested that he meet with him immediately. He was in the parking area of the Vonsberg business tower, a thirty-story glass structure. Greg Green had excused himself from the meeting and went out to meet with the man.

The man appeared very nervous. He told Greg Green that things were not going as planned per the business preposition and that the people who planned the whole thing were wanting to talk to Greg Green directly. He stated that he had given them Greg's business cellphone number and that they would be contacting him shortly. The man told him that he must answer the phone, and must do as they ask, because these people were very powerful and very dangerous and render great harm to Greg Green and his family and at their own discretion. The gentleman drove off before Greg could ask him any more questions.

And sure enough, the people called a few minutes after this man left. They wanted to immediately be notified if, and when, Bernhardt Vonsberg showed up or contacted him. They said they had close monitoring on him, Greg, and that if he did not comply, not only would he be in immediate danger, but his family will be too. He mentioned to them that Bernhardt Vonsberg had just been reported in a plane crush, but they said all that was incorrect. Greg Green had returned to the meeting with the department heads, telling them to disband themselves plus all company employees to their homes, and from there await further instructions. After that, he and the company's spokesperson immediately left for the city of Southlake to meet with the Vonsberg family to talk about the issue.

But by the time they got there, other people who had watched the news had already called the Vonsbergs about the tragedy of the plane crash on which Bernhardt Vonsberg was rumored to be. And then an hour or so later after the two men arrived at the Vonsberg home, Bernhardt Vonsberg himself mysteriously showed up.

Now while Bernhardt Vonsberg was hugging his family, Greg Green quickly stepped out of the room and contacted the bad business people, notifying them that they were right, the supposedly dead Vonsberg had showed up at his home. The people said they would be calling him back shortly. They stated they wanted to meet with Bernhardt Vonsberg again and in person, to discuss more business, and that it was up to Greg Green to see that this meeting happens, or he would face deadly consequences. But what really got Greg Green nervous and suspicious about the proposed meeting was that they also insisted that Greg Green should make sure Bernhardt Vonsberg does not leave the house before they arrived and that after meeting with the billionaire their business with Greg Green would be over. They also renewed their threat that if he let Bernhardt Vonsberg leave the premises, his own life plus that of his family would be in danger. That alarmed him, reminding him of what his gentleman friend, the man who had linked him to these bad business people, had told him, that these were very bad, dangerous and powerful people and he had to do exactly what they wanted him to do.

But Greg Green quickly reminded himself that Bernhardt was his best friend and that he would never do anything to harm him knowingly, even if his own life was in danger. This man has been so good to him all his life and he was worth dying for. Deep inside him he felt that these people were up to no good, that they wanted to do harm to Bernhardt Vonsberg, possibly kill him if they found him. And he wasn't about to let this happen to his best friend.

Greg Green decided that the only way to save his friend from danger is to not stop him from leaving. Let him go anywhere, away from here, before these people showed up. He walked back into the house.

"Everything ok, Greg?" Bernhardt Vonsberg asked him when he saw him walk back in.

"Everything is good, Bern," he replied. "it's just the wife wondering where I am at right now."

"Well, sorry Greg, but I must leave right away," Bernhardt said. "I don't really know what's happening to my life right now, or when it will stop being this way, but my whole conscious tells me that I must do what that caller asked me to do and that is to get out of this home right away. I will talk to you about my experiences with that business proposal thing and what happened thereafter after we settle down in the place we're going to."

"Got ya on that, boss," Greg Green responded back with the same answer he's always known to use when responding to the man who not only was his best friend, but also his boss. "I will patiently wait for that."

The police Chief also walked back into the living room. He too had stepped out of the house to make his phone calls. "You now can go get your vehicle ready and then get out of here, Mr. Vonsberg. My men are quickly clearing the press mob off your premises. I have also instructed them to make sure no one follows you to your destination. They will escort you to where they feel it's safe for you to be on your own and then will themselves pull back. Please don't forget to lock up the house before your leave. I don't want your place vandalized while you are away. Good luck in all your endeavors, Mr. Vonsberg."

56

"That I will do, chief, and thank you very much," Bernhardt Vonsberg said. "We have a central lock system on the house that will automatically close up the entire house via a remote control I have in my pocket, which is also linked to a code number in my cellphone." He winked at the police chief.

The rest of the other people in the living room also got up to leave, quietly exiting through the main door. And that was after he thanked each one of them for coming by when they realized his family was experiencing difficult times. He used a side door to enter the hallway that led him to another door that opened into the big garage. A brand-new Mercedes Benz minivan with tinted windows was packed in the middle, surrounded by a few other cars, with keys still in the ignition. He had just bought the vehicle for use by the nurse to transport his wife to and from hospital appointments. He decided to use the van for the drive out.

After the next several minutes, with his family finally all on board, Bernhardt Vonsberg drove the minivan out of the garage and into the yard, which, as the police chief had promised, was now empty of unwelcome people. Two police cruisers were parked at the outside of the gates, and as soon as he drove out of the compound, they started following him.

"Why, and where are we going, Dad?" Barret Vonsberg asked. "I hate going on sudden, unplanned trips. And late in the evening on top of that."

"Barret, it's ok, son," Myra Vonsberg said from the front passenger seat, next to her husband, before he replied. "I trust your father knows what he is doing and why. Let us not ask him too many questions at this time, lest we frustrate his efforts. And I am very sure he will explain this to all of us once we are settled down at our next stop, won't you my dear?"

"Hmmm, ok mommy," Barret replied, slowly shaking his head at the same time. He slumped down further in his seat and remained quiet.

"Yes, I will," Bernhardt Vonsberg replied, sighing in relief. He was always weary of his son's nagging inquisitiveness.

She smiled as she placed her frail hand gently on top of her husband's right hand, which was on top of the armrest.

They did not notice a black ford sedan parked a few yards away from the main gates, most likely because its lights were turned off and it was parked in the shadows. There was one man in this car and for the past one hour after Bernhardt Vonsberg's return he had been monitoring the Vonsberg house through a pair of military-type binoculars equipped with night – vision capability. He now particularly zoomed in on the minivan as it left the compound, immediately followed by two police cars. He could see only two heads in the front part of the van, a man and a woman, because everything else was tinted. Reaching over to the front passenger seat, he picked up a cellular phone and engaged a speed dial number. It buzzed for two minutes before it was answered from the other side.

"What have you got for me?" the call's recipient asked.

"I think our subject just left his place in a minivan with tinted windows and some people," the man said. "He's got two police cars following him. What do you want me to do?"

"Follow them, find out where they are going and give me a call back immediately," the recipient replied. "Do not lose sight of them. Understand?"

"Got it boss," The man replied, and then hung up. He could see the minivan and its police escort ahead and down the street, where they had been stopped by a red traffic light signal. Starting his car, he drove out of the shadows and into the route towards the small convoy. As he drove past the Vonsberg house, he could see that the lights in the house were still on. He eased on his gas pedal a little bit as doubt clouded his mind. Maybe the subject was still in the house, he thought. Would he be wasting time following the wrong people? It wasn't very clear who was in that minivan because of its tinted windows. It would be disastrous for him if he did, because he had just told his employer that the subject left the house. His employer did not tolerate mistakes and could follow up with quick punishment for those who failed him. Nonetheless, the man decided to go with his instincts, and that is to follow the van and its escorts.

He finally caught up with the small convoy, and just as the red light turned to green. The convoy started moving again. He also noticed another car, a big white Sport-Utility-Vehicle, in the opposite lane also begin moving in the opposite direction. His keen attention to his immediate surroundings helped him note that the S.U.V was filled with men who looked like they were headed for a mission. He knew those type of people, all sitting up straight, staring forward with grim faces and this automatically registered in his brain before he returned his focus to the vehicles ahead of him.

Meanwhile, back at the Vonsberg house, Greg Green and the Southlake City chief of police were shaking hands and getting ready to part ways when they noticed that the main gates, which are electronically controlled, were still wide open and a car drove through and came up the driveway. It stopped in a parking spot a few yards away yards away from the front of the balcony. The driver's door slowly opened, and a bald-headed man slowly came out of the car, a shiny silver colored Jaguar sedan to be exact. He was dressed in a black suit but no tie, matched with shiny black shoes as part of his perfectly fit looking attire ensemble.

"Nice Jag you've got there, man," Greg Green said, unable to resist the external appeal of the sleek looking Sedan. "You must be a friend of Bern Vonsberg's. For some reason, he prides in these jaguar cars and has a collection of earlier models stacked up somewhere in a private garage."

"Thank you. For the type of work, I do around here I decided to ask for a nice-looking vehicle. But also, just to fit in with the general crowd around here," the man said, smiling. "Hello there, Mr. Green. Howdy there, chief Roberts."

"Hey! How do you know me, huh?" the chief of police asked, staring blankly at the man. "You appear to know who I am. Now, you may be a familiar acquaintance of this guy here, but I am certainly sure I don't know you."

The smile did not leave the man's face, despite the suspicious look from the chief of police. "Almost everyone in this city knows who you are, Chief Roberts," the man said.

"Aaah, I don't think I know you either, man," Greg Green said quickly.

"My friends call me Zeal," the man said, nodding his head in affirmation to both men's inquiry, and as he walked up the steps to where the two men were standing at the edge of the balcony. "And yes, Mr. Vonsberg is indeed a friend of mine." The man's hands were now in his pockets. He did not attempt to shake hands with the two.

"Okay. But Mr. Vonsberg is not available at this moment. So, what can we do for you, Zeal?" The chief of police asked.

"Well, I also happen to work on behalf of Mr. Vonsberg and I am here to make sure that everything is ok," Zeal said. "In fact, as you are about to see for yourselves, I am also going to make sure that you guys stay out of harm's way."

"Well, Zeal, I am not sure I understand," the chief of police reiterated. "As you can see, we are perfectly fine, but I am now getting more concerned about you suddenly showing up on private property, unannounced, and that's because Mr. Vonsberg did not mention anything about you coming by. It's called trespassing, and since what you are saying is not making any profound sense to me and Mr. Green here, I am about to ask you to leave immediately, or I will have to arrest you."

Chief Roberts slowly placed his right hand on the gun in a holster on his right hip.

At that very moment a big white sport – utility vehicle glided through the open gateway, and it too slowly made its way up the driveway. The first thing to note was that all its headlights were off and it had no plate numbers. But then they suddenly came on, brightly illuminating the three men standing on the balcony, and whoever turned them on deliberately used the full beam, perhaps the fog light option, making it intense. As the big car came to a stop just a few yards from the balcony steps and a few yards in front of the sedan, Greg Green and the police chief covered their faces with their hands to block the intense glare of its lights from their eyes. Zeal, however, appeared not be affected by that as he simply turned around and fully faced the new arrival on the scene. He's hands now quickly came out his pockets.

"Oh, come on guys, that's not right," Zeal said, and then quickly clapped his hands. The big car's headlights suddenly dimmed, and then went out altogether.

"That's better, "the police chief said, uncovering his face. "don't do well with them bright lights in my eyes. I am literally blinded." "And that's rude of them to do that," Greg Green lamented.

All the big car's doors opened at the same time, and five men came out of it. They all wore long black trench coats, unbuttoned, and wore their hair long, rock star style.

"What can we do for you, gentlemen?" The police chief said. He didn't seem to like these guys. They looked like they were up to no good.

"We are here to see Bernhardt Vonsberg," the man in the lead of the group, who also was driver of the S.U.V, said. "He is expecting us."

"He's not here. Not on the premises," the police chief answered.

"But he told us he will be here, at this time," the man insisted. "And like I said, he's expecting us. So, you see, there is no way he can't be here, at least inside his house. This is his residence, right?"

"Yes, this is the Vonsberg residence, but he is not available at the moment, not even in the immediate future as far as I am concerned." the police chief replied.

"Well then can we go in and look?" the man said. "Just to look, make sure he's not on the premises, like you claim. We just want to make sure, man."

"That's absolutely a no!" Greg Green said.

"Tell you what, you boys can be good, law – abiding citizens by getting back into your vehicle and driving off these private premises, before I arrest you for trespassing," chief Roberts said, sounding clearly annoyed. His right hand was still resting on the butt of the holstered gun on his right hip.

"I wouldn't do that, friend," the lead man said, a smile coming on his face. Turning around and nodding at his four colleagues, he added. "Guys, show these fellas we mean business. Get them out of my way."

The four men flipped aside the front of their trench coats and suddenly each of them was armed with a gleaming submachine gun rifle. At the same time, Zeal turned to the two men standing next to him and spoke. "Let me take over from here,"

As Zeal spun around smoothly on the toes of his black shoes, like a seasoned ballet dancer, he spread his arms out wide, at the same time raising them up, palms facing the five men. A light blue vapor randomly sparkled by tiny, colorful specks floating in it came out of his hands and spread out in front of him, quickly creating a vapor wall that remained in one place like a non – moving low mist or clear fog. And in the next ten or fifteen seconds, four of the five men aimed their submachine guns at him and the other two men behind him and suddenly opened fire. A flush of lightning sparked the area in front of Zeal, causing the two men behind him to step back immediately. The gunshots were quite deafening, but to everyone's amazement, the bullets could not go past Zeal. All bullets kept falling at his feet, hot shells rolling on the ground before him. It was like the mist or foggy wall was a bullet proof screen or barrier shielding him and the two men standing behind him.

"What the hell…" the lead man exclaimed.

"Your bullets can't touch us!" Zeal shouted out. "So why don't you just do what he asked you to do. Leave!"

"I will be damned!" the lead man shouted back, at the same time pulling out a big pistol from his waist belt. Pointing it at Zeal, he started firing the weapon, at the same time moving forward until he got almost face to face with Zeal. Still, his bullets, just like the other shots, could not penetrate through the mist to hit the target. And then Zeal suddenly lashed out with his left hand through the misty barrier and grabbed the lead man's neck, holding on tight, eventually lifting him off the ground until his feet were dangling in the air. He was squeezing hard. The man let go of his gun, which fell on the ground below him, and started grasping at his neck with both hands, trying to free himself from Zeal's powerful one hand grasp, and gasping for air.

"Let go of him, put him down, now!" chief Roberts ordered from behind zeal. "I will take over from there. Do it now or I will be forced to take further action."

Without letting go of the man or putting him down, Zeal turned his head around in a one hundred- and eighty-degrees swivel to the right, and stared at the chief of police, who had pulled out his gun and was pointing it at him, with unblinking blank eyes. At the same time, Greg

62

Green shifted his evidently horrified look from Zeal to the police chief, the look on his face instantly transforming to that of surprise. Greg Green slowly placed his hand on top of the police chief's gun wielding hands and slowly forced him to lower his aim down and away from Zeal.

"What are you doing, man? Can't you see he's protecting us from these peoples' gunfire? And can't you see that what's happening is very unusual?" Greg Green quickly said to the police chief. "It's evidently out of this world and definitely beyond our comprehension! In any case, if those bullets fired off by those guys couldn't touch us or him, then neither will yours!"

Both men now looked at Zeal, whose blank eyed stare was still fixed on the police chief. They found themselves staring into a face with raised eyebrows, eyes round and wide open, and a closed mouth that had transformed Zeal's face into a mean, daring look. Greg Green felt within him that this individual, at this moment, would not hesitate to turn his magic, or whatever his powers are called, on them if deemed necessary. Zeal's wide-open eyes had turned a complete bright yellow with no visible pupils. The chief of police's face turned grim as he heeded to Greg Green's advice, and both men stepped back and away from the now scary individual staring blankly at him.

Shaking his head, Zeal slowly turned his head back to focus on what now appeared to be his upheld, still dangling and squirming, victim. In a quick lash out with his right hand, he smashed his clenched fist into the man's midsection, let go of his neck, sending his body flying backwards in the air until it slammed into the windshield of the big car with such shear force that the big glass shattered to pieces. The man's body remained motionless on top of the big car's bonnet.

"Human beings, you're all so pathetic!" Zeal said, shaking his head slowly again and folding his hands in front of his chest. "Ok guys, you heard what the chief said. Leave now, or I will come after the rest of you next."

His arms unfolded and with one simultaneous gesture of his right hand all the big car's door flew open.

The other four men seemed to hear him loud and clear. Quickly putting their guns back in their original place, they turned around, grabbed hold of their downed friend, who was still unconscious, and shoved him into the backseat of their big car. While two men got into the car on each side of the unconscious man, the other two quickly got into the front. The two in the front stared at Zeal one more time, looking rather terrified, before reversing the car off the Vonsberg compound and quickly driving away. They could not even turn their headlights back on, for the car's light system had completely malfunctioned!

Zeal suddenly started to clap his hands repeatedly, in a hearty fashion that usually depicts victory, and then turned around to face the two men behind him. His eyes were now back to normal, and he was smiling again. The transparent fog with its tiny multi - colored specks instantly faded away.

But it was quite the opposite for Greg Green and the police chief. Just like their now gone adversaries, they too looked very terrified. What they had just witnessed was indeed out of this world.

"Please, please... don't... don't... harm us," Greg Green suddenly and quickly said, his voice low as he mumbled the words out. He suddenly went down to his knees. "We will do whatever you want us to do. Just don't do any harm to us."

The police chief looked down at the shaken man next to him, on his knees. He slowly did the same, and then looked up again at Zeal.

"Listen, what or who exactly are you and why are you here?" he asked. His voice, though shaky, was loud and clear. "We have no problem with you, and we thank you for protecting us from those villains. But please tell us what you want from us, and we shall try to comply. Just don't take us down like you did with that guy."

"Oh, come on, guys," Zeal said, still smiling. He reached out and assisted Greg Green up to his feet again. He did the same with the chief after that. "I am not here to do harm to you, but rather to protect you from those men, who were here on a murder mission. They had orders to kill Mr. Vonsberg and his family and then burn down his entire house with the bodies in it. They are professional killers who are hired by other people to kill other people. And they were going to stop at nothing to accomplish their given task. Since you were in their way, they were simply going to kill you and get into the house, thinking the Vonsberg family is in there."

"That wasn't going to happen. Not on my watch!" the chief of police said.

"What, if I may ask you, chief Roberts, was your one gun going to do against their five fully automated guns, huh?" Zeal asked. "Especially if they opened fire at you without warning, right? Absolutely nothing! But I am here to tell you that when it comes to God, the holy spirit from above, even the protector will need to be protected! Those men had more terrible weapons in their car's trunk than you can ever imagine, enough force to kill a substantial amount of their fellow human beings in a very short time and do a lot of damage too. They were going to start with you two. And this was just the beginning of it all. That is why I was dispatched to come out here and dissuade them from doing so, by showing them there is a greater power than their guns, that there is another force to reckon with if they did not stop."

Greg Green still looked shaken, but he was trying to quickly restore his composure. He was still fearful of Zeal, who now stood close to him. As a result, he let the chief of police do the talking.

"Ok, great. Now excuse me for asking again, sir. Who are you and who do you work for?" The chief of police asked. "And how did you stop those bullets from reaching us? You must be using some very expensive technology to do that, one that only the government can afford to buy. Which means you work for the government, right?"

"Yes, I work for the government, but not your government," Zeal replied. "Let's say I work for a government that is so powerful it governs all the governments of this world. And yes, my government owns the technology that stopped those bullets from reaching you. No other government around here has it or will ever even have it."

"So, what is your position in this government?" the police chief asked.

"Don't you get it, man?" Greg Green suddenly intervened, making both men immediately turn their attention to him. "He's not from anywhere around here or anywhere in this world. He's definitely not of our world. I think he is very supernatural!"

Zeal smiled at Greg Green, and then turned around again and faced chief Roberts. "He's right on that one, chief. I am indeed not from your world. Simply said, I am one of God's Secret Agents and we have been sent down here straight from heaven to put a stop to a very deadly event that is bound to cause so much misery to you humans and threatens to destroy the very core of God's perfect creations out here on earth. We are also here to persuade you human beings to abstain from self-destruction, which is a seed of sin planted into human minds by the devil. This seed of sin has grown so massive and has branches everywhere. If humanity doesn't abstain from self - destruction which, by the way, has already begun, then God's seventh dimension, which is your world, will diminish and his original intentions of a glorious paradise of creatures that he mirrored himself into will be forever lost. God's intentions are being thwarted by elements of evil, and from those who fell short of his glory in heaven."

"But why can't God come down here himself?" chief Roberts asked. "Fix his own flaws instead of sending his agents. Besides, we want to see him with our own very own eyes. I am sorry, but his appearance is long overdue!"

Zeal suddenly clapped his hands again in rapid or quick successions and then slowly shook his head. As he did so, the sound of the clapping vibrated through the ground they were standing on and bright red sparks of fire came out of his hands, causing the two men to flinch.

"Sorry, didn't mean to do that," Zeal said, putting his hands down again. "That's just my way of signaling impatience with that very question which has been thrown at us so many times by your kind. Mankind must first, and most of all, understand that God doesn't do things the human way. It's not that simple, my friend. Why? because you human beings don't really want to see him down here in all his glory! You really don't want to see how he looks like; you wouldn't even dare to face him. I myself have never looked up to see what the almighty looks like, for fear of seeing what I will see but not meant to see. Just his appearance alone will completely dissolve the very soul of the onlooker. He is the holiest of the holiest, the soul of all souls, the spirit of all spirit. And so, my friend, if he showed face out here, you really don't want to be there to see, because you will perish! God only manifests himself through his actions, which are completely beyond human control and understanding."

"So, why did you come here to save us from those hoodlums?" Greg Green asked. "We are not directly affiliated with the evil that is about to befall the world, are we?"

"No, you are indeed not directly affiliated, but you almost got caught up in it,' Zeal replied. "There was a deal done with the devil at a meeting place forty-eight hours ago and Bernhardt Vonsberg was involved in it. The only difference is that he, unlike the rest of his fellow participants, invoked God on it when he objected with insight to the loss of innocent human lives and lives of other creatures, upon execution of the devil's plan. He thus unknowingly triggered off the heavenly mandate to restore the original conduct of peace in God's backyard, also known as the seventh dimension, setting off heaven's retaliation against all vile elements prevailing within this realm. My part is to immediately ward off possible loss of innocent human souls pertaining to this evil. I want you to note that Satan and his agents are everywhere in the seventh dimension, but now so are we. There are other angels like me dealing with other issues right now, as we speak. But there is one major difference with this case, and that is it's signifi cant, unprecedented deadly massive impact on this world. It will therefore also be handled by an individual way higher than myself in the hierarchy of heavenly beings. There is an archangel, one of much superior holy nature and one who will yield the most powerful heavenly mandate ever unleashed. The archangel will be here to completely erase the devil's menace that's currently looming over humanity and will wage a full-scale war against the devil's manifesto! My friends, I can tell you right now that my actions here today are nothing compared to what's coming with this archangel! The magnitude of the mandate this war archangel is coming with is so big, so diverse it's effect will be terrifying and felt everywhere the archangel goes!"

"When is this... archangel coming?" The chief of police asked. "We sure could use some of those services here in America and the rest of the world."

"You're very right, chief. This whole world needs God and his angels, or agents, to intervene, and the sooner the better," Greg Green stated, and then turning back around to face Zeal, he added "Mr. Zeal, I set up this deal for Bernhardt, but I didn't know it involved such evil.

What's going to happen to me then? Is the archangel coming after me too?"

"No, but listen to me carefully," Zeal said. "Leave this place now and go back to your homes, gather your families and pray for protection from the devil. We will hear your prayers and respond accordingly. Tell your neighbors to do the same and ask them to tell their neighbors too. Henceforth the word will spread out, and soon the devil will be flashed out into the open. The rest will be up to us to deal with."

With those words, Zeal suddenly reached out with both hands and lightly touched both men on their foreheads. Suddenly both men were surrounded by a very bright light, in the middle of nowhere, and all around them was vast darkness. And before them stood Zeal, no longer dressed in a black suit. His now bare chest body was muscular, almost bronze tanned. He was clad in white harem pants, bare feet. His right wrist was clad with a shiny metal bracelet and in his right hand was a sparkling long double-edged, golden sword. In his left hand was a huge, shiny metal shield. The angel was staring at them, a grim look on his face.

But the most significant object of this transformation was the pair of huge black and white feathered wings attached to the back of his shoulders, like those of an eagle in structure. The gigantic wings were flapping up and down in slow motion and the two men could feel the breeze generated by the movement of the wings on their bodies.

Zeal's right hand moved, pointing the sword at them.

"Now go do as I told you. Go back to your families, and neighbors, and ask the holy spirit to protect you from the devil's aggressions," he commanded.

Suddenly the bright light vanished, and the two men found themselves back in the same spot, standing on the Vonsberg balcony. They looked around them.

Zeal had vanished, together with his gleaming, silver jaguar sedan.

Major Haraabi is a man who works with precision and this character trait always compelled him to insist on job updates at specified times or within a time range. These imposed, timed responses on his subordinates and or employees allowed him to have the much-needed time to plan

68

changes and reactions, to get the job done the way he wants it. And perhaps, also, to keep his own bosses happy. Just because in his line of work, where unpredictable changes are part of the inevitable, and could easily ignite into an uncontrollable spin of events, it is rather hard to keep your bosses all the way happy. His bosses always want to hear the good news only, not the bad stuff. In other words, fix the bad stuff first, then talk to us. That's what we hired you to do!

This time, though, now back in his East London, U.K, apartment with his assistant / mistress Pony, he got the update before the time he had expected it. The call was from his hired mercenary group in the United States of America. He had commissioned them to do a job in Texas. News had come up that the Texas billionaire who was said to be dead earlier was still alive and had actually showed up on live TV news outside his home. His bosses, despite the fact that they tried to do the job without first consulting him and messed up, now wanted him to fix their failure. They still wanted Bernhardt Vonsberg dead! So, he got in touch with an elite killer group in the United States and instantly commissioned them to do the job, half down stat and half when job done.

But what he didn't expect to hear was what he was being told later on, given the fact that this mercenary killer group is very well organized, has the resources, and is known to be very efficient. In other words, quite reliable and to date, had never failed him.

"Mission accomplished?" he asked when he answered the phone call bearing their contact number.

"On the contrary, this time around, nope!" the caller replied. "To begin with, Cory is in the hospital, unconscious, all messed up. Doctors at the hospital think he had been involved in a motor vehicle accident of some sorts. His internal organs are all disorganized and as we speak, he is undergoing surgery to have those organs put back in place. But they say he will live."

"What the hell happened?" Major Haraabi asked.

"Resistance, boss. We met heavy, bad ass resistance," the caller said. "We went to the site to do the job and this one guy… he fought us back and prevented us from getting to the target and eliminating it."

"One guy?"

"Yes, one freakin', deadly son of a bitch!" the caller replied quickly, sounding frantic. "There were three men on the job site, but only one of them prevented us from carrying out the task. He had strange… what should I call it… powers with him! Our bullets could not get past him! He placed some strange foggy vapor shield or barrier that came out of his hands, between him and us which apparently turned out to be bullet proof. I mean, impenetrable! And that's when Cory went up close and personal, with his pistol blazing. But that didn't work out well either, boss, because this son of a bitch reached out through his fog and grabbed Cory by the neck, dangling him in the air like he's some two-pound, Wei – Wei doll, and then struck out at his body with his fist, tossing him back to us! We tried to react back, but boss, this… this guy, he proved to be too much for us. Just with a wave of his hands, the doors on our truck flew open, and then he shouted at us, commanding us to leave immediately. We had no choice but to abort the mission. I have never seen anything like this before. This shit isn't normal, boss. He even knocked out the car's headlights with a wave of his right hand! It was out of this world stuff! We are just lucky that Cory is still with us," the caller said in a quick succession of words. From the way he sounded, the man was still in shock of whatever he had experienced earlier.

"Bull crap!" Major Haraabi shouted back instead into the phone and immediately hang up. He already had his answer, that the job was still not done. Bernhardt Vonsberg was still out there, alive and now the loose. His bosses were going to be furious, more especially that he had told them that this was a "piece of cake" job, and he would take care of the issue quickly.

But he was also getting concerned about the failure to eliminate the billionaire, who seemed to be getting help from somewhere. And if so, who are these people and why were they protecting him? And they seemed to be unique, because he had been informed earlier that the same thing had happened to the man sent to eliminate Vonsberg the first time. The chauffeur turned assassin, too, had suffered grave fatalities, confirmed to be very terrible injuries to his internal body structures before his death. And now there is this talk of invisible bullet proof barriers? Hard to believe! But if true, what kind of adversary was he facing now and how much does he know about his plans? A red alarm went off in his brain, something telling him that he must refocus intensively on the task at hand, to make it happen, before someone with strange "powers" tried to stop him.

He picked up the satellite phone in front of him and tapped the keypad. After beeping for a minute or two, his call was answered.

"Yes, boss…"

"Are you still following that minivan?" he asked.

"Yes boss," the receiver replied. "Actually, I have some good news. Vonsberg is in it, boss. He's driving it, and I think he's with his family. They stopped at a gas station, and I pulled up next to them. It was then that I was able to place the tracker on their vehicle, just as one of the kids stepped out and pumped some gas into it, I pulled up behind their van and quickly attached the tiny gadget. So now I can see their movement on my phone, which will provide a location address every time the car stops. Now they are on the road again, and I am following them at a distance. What do you want me to do, boss?"

"Good job. Keep following them. Also, share the tracker operation with me via my cell so I can also see what's going on," the major instructed, and then once again hung up the phone immediately. In about five minutes, he heard a ding sound on his phone and when he looked at it, it was a notification that he was now part of the tracking device's operation and could now see every movement the Vonsberg minivan was making.

Pony was in the shower room, bathing. Major Haraabi made his way to the shower door and opened it abruptly, without knocking. He instantly found himself staring into the extended fore end of a CZ Scorpion EVO semi-automatic pistol held by a naked Pony, dripping with steamy water from the steady flow of hot water coming out from the shower head. The hot steam escaping from the shower room briefly revealed only her silhouette.

"My, my, my, you're one hell of a nervous wreck, Pony!" he said, shaking his head slowly. "What are you so worried about that makes you partner with a gun even when bathing?"

71

"Dammit, Quake, how many times do I have to ask you to knock before you enter, huh?" she reacted back, sounding annoyed and lowering the gun. "I hate your surprise barge - ins, because they startle me. With my kind of life, versus the world we live in today, I have the right to be nervous, and therefore ready, to tackle adversaries at anytime, anywhere, with whatever means possible. You of all people should know that it's no longer safe anywhere, for anyone on this planet! Least of all of us."

With that she slammed the shower room door shut in his face. "It's safe here, Pony. And you, of all people, should know that" Major Haraabi said, still standing outside the shower room. "This apartment is very secure, one of the safest spots in the world that I am proud to claim. And since I own it, I go wherever I want without announcing myself. Unless, of course, you are trying to hide something from me."

"Whatever, Haraabi. But I am telling you that one of these days you will get shot, and it will be your fault. Don't say I didn't warn you. I repeat, no place is safe enough anymore on this planet. Only God can save or protect us every day!" she shouted back.

"Here we go again with that God bullshit. Seems like I am hearing that a lot lately. Well, get ready to travel, Pony. You are going to the United States now," he said loudly as he walked away from the room.

The shower door opened, and Pony stepped out of the shower room, now wrapped up in a towel bathrobe.

"To the United States? Now?" She asked, looking surprised and sounding bewildered.

"Yes, to the United States yes now, my dear," the major repeated. "Looks like our nemesis, Mr. Vonsberg, is becoming rather difficult to eliminate. He seems to be getting help from someone, or some people. I sent in our team in Texas to do the job, and they couldn't even get to him. Instead, their leader, Cory, ended up getting messed up by a guy who appears to be protecting Vonsberg and his people."

"Colonel Cory McCrary? He got messed up? Now that's crazy! He's one of the best-known assassination mercenaries in the world, and has never been known to fail," Pony said, raising her eyebrows. "He's one of the very best in the business, so confident in himself and in his team that he doesn't demand payment until the job is done. He's never known to fail, and that's why he commands a high price. So how come he got messed up? Who messed him up?"

"I don't know, Pony," Major Haraabi replied. "But I just got a phone call from one of his guys, telling me that he is somewhere in a Texas hospital undergoing surgery after being tackled by Vonsberg's protector."

"Now that's crazy," Pony said, shaking her slowly. "Cory McCrary is one crazy son of a bitch, definitely not one to mess with, armed or unarmed. I find it difficult to believe that this kind of thing happened to him."

"Me too," Major Haraabi reiterated. "That is why it is time to send in someone with similar special skills, but more so someone I trust to do whatever it takes to get the job done. And that's you, captain. You have my mandate on this one, and I will notify our benefactors that you are going in to clear the problem once and for all. You will then have their full support, everything you need to get it done. I don't care if you blow up an entire stadium full of people or gun down an entire village or mess up a car or bus full of kids. Just get it done. Just erase this guy and his family, friends, neighbors, bodyguards, his dogs, cats, whatever stands in your way, off this planet! We have no time for games anymore, we have a mission to accomplish, and it's now timed. That is why you must leave now, immediately. So, get dressed. While you are at it, I will call up a connection in Texas to go ahead and prep up for your arrival."

"Yes, sir," Pony replied without any more reservations. She was firmly attached to this man, had been with him at least half of her professional life, had been through so much with him, learned so much from him, and he had gone, in her thinking, beyond the proven measures to prove that he cared for her beyond anything and anybody else. So much was she into him that she was ready to do anything for him, to protect and or die for him, as long as it made sense to both of them. She always had that strange reservation of sensibility on issues.

So, she wasn't going to make this the exception. Killing the billionaire was only a side effect, she told herself, and so she was going to travel the United States and do whatever it takes to erase this rich guy, Bernhardt

Vonsberg, off this planet, once and for all. And yes, anyone who stands in her way would face the full brunt of her attack, even if it meant eliminating an entire town! She was going to unleash hell. Such was her determination. . .

But she still had some emotional reservations.

Wait a minute, what the hell is going on? What's happening to me, huh? She had never felt like this in her entire professional life! For the first time she had second reservations about her mission for him. Her heart kept skipping as an irregular, sickening feeling of fear and doubt settled down deep inside her. That second voice she never knew she had before, never thought she will ever get to hear, suddenly began gnawing at her conscious. Major Haraabi had warned her about it, had told her that should she ever hear it, then her career would all be over. He had emphasized repeatedly that they were now soldiers, but of a different kind, because unlike regular soldiers, they are not fighting for cause or country, creed or flag. They are soldiers of fortune, soldiers on private quests and mission. They had digressed from that typical soldiers' creed of for God and country, and now their skills were up for sale to the highest bidder. For that matter, theirs is a never – ending warfare. And in this kind of warfare, there was no going or looking back. They fight private wars, global or civil, personal or general, for other people, and as such there is no space for thinking about the aftermath. We simply go in, do whatever we are paid to do, and get out, he said. No room for failure, for failure would defame the brand.

And they could also become the enemy, he proclaimed. The target of other similar groups, if they compromise a mission because of second thoughts, and could then end up fighting a never ending, possibly deadly war, but without pay. Such was the side effect of this kind of warfare. We don't want that to happen to us. We must stay always focused and determined, he concluded.

So, to avoid the compromise, to avoid having a war against their brand, they had to act in one faith and without looking back, without hesitation. The client comes first, Major Haraabi had affirmed, before anything else. "And that includes family, friends, personal interests, religious beliefs or convictions. There was no room for that, it's all gone down the drain, Pony. It all becomes trash! Therefore, I am warning you about that second voice. It must never be listened to, must never be allowed to overcome your conscious. Because the moment it does, you are compromised, and so no longer a part of the brand!" People like that we can't trust anymore, Major Haraabi had said, and so we find a way to get rid of them quickly before they contaminate the rest of the syndicate.

But now she was listening to this second voice. She was questioning the purpose of this mission. It wasn't humanitarian, it wasn't Godly, for it is going to mess up a lot of people. Major Haraabi had mentioned the effect of this project was going to be worldwide, and that includes south Korea, where her mother and baby sister live in Seoul, one of the major cities targeted by the Haraabi project. These two were the only family she had, and although she rarely saw them physically, she didn't want them to die.

She had to go help them, make sure they were secure and as far away from capital city as she can take them. She had enough money to do that. She was going to go to Seoul first before going to the United States to carry out the elimination. Once she was sure they are safe, then she would embark on the American assignment.

The rapidly repeated, loud knock on the bedroom door woke her up from her deep thoughts.

"Hey, Pony, you are all set and ready. I have also pulled out your passport for you from the safe," Major Haraabi shouted on the other side of the door. "What's taking you so long, huh?"

"Almost done, boss," she shouted back. The only time he ever talked to her without shouting was when she was within direct eyesight, especially during sex. And she found this very annoying, because it didn't matter if she is around the corner, in the same house, and within hearing range. He doesn't have his eyes on her, he shouts!

She had already pulled out her own emergency passport from one of her "quick - pack" emergency packages she carefully kept concealed in his apartment, together with an international credit-debit card. First, she quickly put on a pair of loose – bodied boxer shorts on top of her leather thongs, slapped on a pair of loose, black military style cargo trousers or pants with multiple pockets, some on the inside, where she put the passport. Instead of a typical belt, the pants were complimented by an almost wire thin titanium rope belt with small metallic pointer clips. Her leather comfort bra was concealed under a Calmi – De - Sontee brand polar neck jersey. Opening a jewelry box, she selected a few items from it, laying them down on the dresser. One of these items was a necklace with several thick black beads on it, which she carefully placed around her neck. Then she proceeded to place the other selected items on other parts of her body, all visible. Black Takipani, all leather, ankle high, flat soled, slip-on boots completed the outfit, concealing the thin foot-liners which are not exactly socks because of their stretch capabilities. She finally covered up with a silver- buttoned jacket with no buttonholes. Shades? Hmmm, a pair of gold rimmed Cat eyeglasses and she felt ready to roll. Alright mother, and little sis, here I come, she reflected in her mind.

She stepped out of the bedroom and walked into the living room, her hip swaying gayly, like a lazy big cat. Major Haraabi was doing something on the laptop when she walked in. He looked up at her and smiled wryly.

"Going for a night out cat party, babe?" he asked, getting up slowly and coming over to where she stood. He kissed her lightly on the lips, squeezed one side of her bottom, and then went back and sat down again.

"Yeah, solo girl's night out," she acknowledged. "Just that lone bitch wolf style, the "put your Paws on me and you instantly die" kind of stuff ."

"Hmmm, I sense that," he acknowledged back.

"Quake, do we really have to do this? A lot of people are going to die. I feel bad about that. Baby, maybe we can just abandon everything and simply vanish. We have enough money now stashed away to keep us going safely for life," she said.

Major Antoquake Haraabi slowly turned around in his chair and looked up at her. He did not get up this time, but his face registered a deep frown.

"Excuse me? Since when did you look at the things we do in that way, huh, Pony?" he asked. "I have never heard you talk like that before. You are suggesting we backout now, after all the planning and hard work we have put in this project? How about our clients? These people are very dangerous, and they can't be double crossed or let down. So, backing out now is not going to happen. We get this thing done and over with as planned, tie up all loose ends and then, perhaps, or maybe, we can call it quits. But not before we give them what they want. We can only be free after it's done."

"I am just concerned about all those innocent people, baby…"

"Stop! Stop right there and stop baby - shitting me!" He shouted. "And from now on, you need to address me with full respect. In case you need to be reminded, I am major Antoquake Haraabi, clandestine military operations specialist by merit, due to military camp training and years of proven field experiences. That means I have paid my dues, captain. Now to hear an officer of a lower rank question my motive and intentions is unimaginable and, in fact, given the right settings, warrants instant court martial proceedings! In this setting, captain, I AM THE COURT MARTIAL! Not God, not the clients, not a government or military establishment, not my mother or deceased father either. I am the judge, jury, and executioner! So, just go do what you have been ordered to do, soldier, before I change my mind and initiate judgement on you. And Captain, make sure you do it right, for failure is not an option! Or I will be forced to kill you myself! Then after that I will go after your mother and sister, and then possibly eliminate anyone else who is close to you! Now, the bag is over there on the couch with everything you will need for travel. I have already called our armory group in the U.S and they are on their way to Dallas Texas right now where u will meet with them. They will arm you with everything you need for the assignment. Now get the hell out of my face!"

"Yes sir, Major Haraabi," Pony acknowledged slowly, shocked and overall terrified by the sudden, indifferent outburst of animosity directed at her, and then including her family. And all that just came out of the man she had come to consider as her lover. The look on his face, complimented by his tone of voice, left no doubt that he meant what he said. She now felt that she had just witnessed the verbal outcome of a devious, crazed mind. Yet she all along had come to believe that she had mastered his soft side, that when it came to her, he would put her first. She suddenly realized now that she barely knew who this man really was, and that even though she had this deep love for him, she suddenly felt the need to be as far away from him as possible.

None of that love mattered anymore now, because he had just threatened her family, her only family. An instant deep hatred for him now welled – up inside her. Therefore, without looking back, she walked past him and out of the apartment via the front door, slamming it shut behind her.

The moment she exited, Major Haraabi looked at the bag on the couch, shook his head slowly, and then picked up his cell phone and pressed a speed – dial digit. The call was answered in ten seconds.

"I think I have a run - away," he said immediately. "It's my assistant, Pony. I hereby request that we invoke the EWTI code on her. Attach the T penalty on it too. She just left my place in East London, and she is now at large."

"Are you sure about this, major?" the person on the other end asked. "I don't know what she has done to invoke such a decision, but we also know that Pony is not only just your assistant in this organization, but also your personally groomed flower, one that you have grown to be so fond of. You and her, come long ways together, major, and have both done so much work together for our organization. I would think that you would give her the benefit of the doubt, perhaps a second chance to reinvent herself before calling for such an invocation."

"Yes, that's my final decision and please spare me your verbal condiments, meant to perhaps detract the request," Major reasserted. "Your job is to initiate it, not to question it. Do I make myself clear?"

"Very well, major Haraabi, sir," the person said. "I will activate the order to Eliminate Without Trial Immediately, Total penalty attached. It's going on record now as we speak that you, major Antoquake Haraabi, as one of the senior commanders of this organization, is declaring your assistant miss Pony as no longer a viable asset to the organization and therefore request use all necessary means to immediately and completely eliminate her entire existence plus all known relatives or next of kin. Is that correct?"

"Correct, and thank you very much," the major confirmed.

78

"Alright then, it's all done," the person said with a sigh, and the line went dead.

Major Haraabi slowly put the phone down and picked up another phone set. He tapped some digits and waited. "Pedro, have you figured out the address where the subject is currently relocated?"

"Yes, boss, I have it," Pedro replied. He was packed right outside the fenced perimeter of the house where Bernhard Vonsberg had just moved in with his family. He gave the address to the major. "This guy has a sort of forest around his house, boss. The big house is tucked away in trees and bushes. Why do rich people live in seclusion like this? You should see it, boss. It's crazy!"

"That's Ok, let me worry about that. Thanks for your services, Pedro. You can go home now. I am sending a new team to take care of that vermin." the major said. "Your payment will be on your account by tomorrow morning."

After he hang up with Pedro, he used the same phone to dial another number. When the call was answered, he said, "Change in plans. My assistant will not be taking care of business as previously planned. So, activate the other field sector using the same orders, to go to this address I am going to give you now. I will notify the principal about what's going on. You ready?"

He repeated the address given to him by Pedro and then hung up. Major Antoquake then sunk down deeper in his chair and lit a cigarette.

A few miles away, driving a rented sedan and headed for the airport, Pony's cell phone pinged a message. Using her free hand, Pony picked it up and quickly glanced at it. What she saw made her pull over immediately, to fully comprehend the message. She could hardly believe it:

"This is an all systems alert, worldwide. EWTI, attached with the full TP, ordered STAT on miss Pony profile. Subject still at large."

"Son of a bitch!" Pony hissed loudly. "Very well, he wants a war, he's going to get one!"

With tires screeching, she got back on the route to the airport, but now at a much faster speed. The route was busy, even at this time of the evening, and suddenly came to a standstill as a long line of cars patiently stopped at a busy railroad crossing with a train passing through. Reaching inside her small duffle bag on the passenger seat beside her, she retrieved her mobile phone and pressed a speed dial number. A human voice answered after a few sound blips.

"Express travel systems, Asian East connections, how may I help you?" the person asked in a Korean dialect.

"Min - Seo, this is miss Po. Please arrange for me an all through clearway non - stop chatter to Seoul. No waiting, I need it immediately. Private pay please," Pony replied in fast Korean, her mother tongue. "Use my red account if necessary. Boarding is at Heathrow. I Should be getting there in about twenty-five minutes."

She needed to get to Seoul fast, without any delays.

"Yes, miss Po, got it," Min – Seo confirmed, and the line went dead.

She had just booked a special private charter jet plane to that effect through one of her special quick travel connections.

Pony thrust the phone back into the duffle bag. Then she suddenly started sobbing, her eyes suddenly welling up with tears.

"I am so sorry, Ma, so sorry Sue - Ann," she muttered to herself, tears running down her face. "I didn't mean to do this to you, didn't want these troubles coming to you at all. I hope I get there in time to protect you from harm. I swear I won't let anyone do harm to you."

Pony found herself suddenly pleading with God. "Please God, help us, keep them safe for me until I get there. They have nothing to do with all this, they are innocent and don't know a thing about what's going on. Please have your angels watch over them for me until I get there."

She now felt betrayed. How could Haraabi, a man who she had truly considered her lover, do this to her? He had even met, and sat down to dinner, with her family once, when she wanted her mother and sister to meet her man friend. Now he's after them, intending to harm them because of her? It is first class betrayal, equivalent to treason, she declared!

She now felt scared. These people were everywhere, meaning the organization that her and major Haraabi worked for, or with. The organization, a global criminal business undertaking of underground international assassins like her, also were money launders, mercenaries, weapons of war traders, coup d tat specialists, to name a few operations, that worked with governments, counter – government agents or guerilla movements, drug cartels, and other illegal territorial entities to make big money. They made big, bad, impossible things possible and were even feared by drug cartels and world police systems. Because of these mostly secret dealings, if anyone of their own senior operatives was to be noted as defective, a back lash would be unleashed on them immediately to ensure that the organization's secrets remain intact. Pony was one of those senior operatives, highly regarded and trained in the organization hierarchy. And so now that Major Haraabi, a senior figure in the hierarchy of the organization and her handler, has declared her a liability, that backlash was on, and one way they would get to her was to grab her family, hence force her to capitulate, to come to them. She knew this because she had carried out a few of these orders herself. The one thing she did, though, was to always free the kidnapped family member or members when the defective company agent has surrendered. The organization left this part solely to the discretion of the apprehending operative or operatives.

But other operatives weren't necessarily like her. Once the defective operative was apprehended, and consequently killed, the family would never be freed either. They would also be killed. And if the defective operative did not show up as ordered, these innocent folks would ruthlessly and mercilessly be tortured, and pictures loaded on the organization's dark website for the operative to see. Every member of the organization, once certified, had access to this website twenty – four seven, worldwide. It didn't matter if it's the operative's infant children or elderly parents, the treatment was harsh and horrible. So now she had to get to her mother and sister as quickly as possible to protect them before this happens to them.

She finally made it to the airport. Pony recomposed herself, making sure her eyes were dry and not puffy, and then got out of the car and dashed to one of the entrances. She knew where to go, because she had used this service several times before on the organization's business, most times with Haraabi. Once she realized how handy this express

81

travel service was, she had set up an account with them, not knowing if or when she would need it.

There was someone at the private charter desk. This person run her passport names through the computer in front of her, confirmed that the jet was already booked and ready to go, gave her a one-piece document to sign, of which she received a copy, and then re - directed her to another area. When she got to this other area of the airport, a man viewed the document and then after scanning her backpack, he drove her in a go-cart to an area with a string of private hangers. There was a pilot already waiting for her outside one of the hangers. She was to fly solo and immediately, on a ten-passenger gulf stream jet all the way from the UK to south Korea.

Fifteen minutes later, she was airborne. A moderate sense of relief settled down on her, reducing some of the anxiety. She was going to her family, to make sure they are ok, and had managed to get going without the usual public hassle, thanks to one of those private money accounts she had set up for personal emergencies. She was going to get to them as quickly as possible. Once they were safely out of harm's way, she was going to find a way to get back to that son of a bitch, Antoquake Haraabi, for retribution. She was going to expose all his illegal dealings, including the current one. It was going to be payback time for betraying her love for him, and for betraying her fam.

# Chapter Five

Mufti Musa Mugabi begun his morning as usual, leading a congregation in an early morning prayer at the town mosque, discussing neighborhood issues with the town's youth Islamic believers, and restocking his small shop with merchandise for his wife to sell. Now he was back home and preparing for his mid-afternoon journey to Kampala city when his youngest son, Musa Mugabi junior, came running out of the living room to tell him he had a phone call. He frowned, not used to getting phone calls at midday.

"A' Salam - 'Alaikum, Mufti Musa here," he said when he picked up the phone.

"A 'Salam, Musa. It's me, Peter," the caller mentioned.

"Peter, well, well, buddy, how are you, old friend?" the Mufti greeted again, his tone becoming more jovial immediately upon recognition of one of his childhood best friends. "We haven't talked for over three months now and I was beginning to worry about you. How is wife, family, and work?"

"All is good, Musa, thanks be to God, and I hope you and yours are all ok too," The bishop replied heartily. Talking to Musa was like talking to a blood brother. Both men had grown up in the same diverse neighborhood and had gone to the same primary and high schools. They had played soccer together, attended numerous social functions and even dated each other's sisters at one time. The only thing that separated them was the religious faith, one Christian the other Muslim. Their families knew each very well too, their fathers not only meeting at village or town functions but visiting each other's homes occasionally. Their mothers, too, were best friends and Musa was well acquainted with mother Edina, and well known to Reverend Samuel Ssekadde.

Both men's families had deep, mutual respect and the two men had kept it that way ever since, despite following different, but similar professional paths. Given family responsibilities now, they at least spoke once a month, but lately, and for some unknown reason, it had taken longer than one month. Maybe all the sudden changes in the world were keeping both men busy and away from one another. And that was why each side was now very glad to know the other is ok.

"Musa, I need your help today, brother," Bishop Musolozza said.

"Anything you need, I will gladly help, brother," Mufti Musa replied immediately. "Just ask and I will do my best, as usual, to have it done."

"It's Mother Edina. I think she is actively dying," the bishop replied. "But that's not the main issue here, because her health has not been good for at least the past two years and has gotten worse lately. We figured at her age it was probably that time. The old lady is tired. We had committed her to the almighty. Our problem right now is the way she is dying."

"I am very sorry to hear that about Mother Edina, God bless her soul," the Mufti replied. "But I don't understand. Did you say that the problem is the way she is dying?"

"That's Correct, Musa," the bishop confirmed. "Her situation has taken a strange turn, one that is clearly very puzzling to us. I think something divine, but also exciting, is going on with her. She seems to be commuting to heaven and back in her sleep. She's telling us about it every time she wakes up. From what she's saying, it sounds very real."

The bishop then proceeded to tell his friend the Mufti all about the mysterious circumstances happening with Mother Edina, and how her family was interpreting it one episode at a time.

"I think we are going to have some concrete answers tonight," the bishop concluded. "And that, Musa, is why I need you to be with us tonight, around Mother Edina, to witness this possible phenomenon and perhaps help us to understand it more. I believe this is an issue for all of us, an issue for all human faith. Perhaps it will be you who will transfer the message, if any, to the followers of your faith."

"Indeed, I hear you, brother, and thank you asking me to come to be part of it," the Mufti. "If it is today, then I am putting everything on hold and will be coming your way as soon as possible."

"Thank you very much, and see you around this evening, Mufti," the bishop replied to his best friend.

"See you around, Bishop" the Mufti replied.

And so, on that same day, late in the evening, Mufti Musa bid farewell to his wife, Halima, and headed out for Namugongo, and that being after he explained to her why he must travel so abruptly that evening. Of course, Halima knew of one of her husband's best friends, the bishop, and his family, very well and as soon as he drove away, she picked up the phone and dialed a number.

"Yes, my dear," the call was answered within a few seconds, with a lot of enthusiasm.

"Sarah, I just saw him off now, and he's coming to you," Halima said. "It's all going as per the orders from above. Yours called on him this morning to come over to Namugongo and attend the revelation. Is Rebecca ready for all this?"

"As ready as she can be," Sarah replied. "We are very excited about this evening, but for the moment we doubted if Mother Edina will be able to handle it. Her body is so weak."

"Aaah, you doubted the heavens? Why?" Halima asked, though not sounding shocked. "These revelations and their timings were indicated in all heavenly schedules before we were sent here. That means that the revelation phase will, and must, manifest itself. His words are the very words and can never ever be doubted. Only the inhabitants of the seventh dimension are yet to understand, and receive, the words of the holy decision. They are the last ones to receive it, and that is to be so tonight."

"I know, I know, and Rebecca and I will enter redemption to seek forgiveness for the sinful doubt," Sarah said. "We plan to do so while the revelation phase itself is going on. Perhaps when you are done with

your earthly chores you can enter the redemption phase with us and help appeal our case, that our judgment of the human spirit corrupted our understanding of heavenly assertion."

"Indeed, I will, my sister," Halima replied without hesitation." We are part of them now, so the prayer is to ask that the heavens side with us on the error. I think its excusable. After all, heaven sent us here."

"I think it will be excused and thank you for accepting to be part of our redemption," Sarah replied happily. "We will receive your presence when the time comes."

There was a deep sigh from both sides of the phone line, a sign that the discussion was over, and the line shut itself off without both sides hanging up. From their respective dwellings, they simply put the phones away.

Mufti Musa was graciously received and welcomed into the reverend Samson's house, at Namugongo, that evening. The reverend's wife, Rebecca, served hot milk tea with lightly salted, roasted peanuts and grilled soft sweet potato slices and then left the men in the dining room to resume bedside care for Mother Edina in her room.

Mufti Musa was quickly briefed again about the situation and its mysterious circumstances and told that Mother Edina had requested for him, specifically by name, to come see her. To the old lady, these three men where all her boys. She had seen them growing up together, and the Mufti was an occasional visitor who always came by to pay his respects to the old lady. She had always done the same when she travelled to the Mufti's hometown in the suburbs of the capital city, stopping by to chat with him.

Just like the other two men, Mufti Musa was intrigued by the whole story, and asked for a basin of fresh water to cleanse himself and be ready for what was presumed to happen. He was shown to the guest bathroom where he washed up and changed into a clean, sparkling white garment and clean, white Taqiyah, or rounded skullcap. The other two men also changed into fresh pastoral garments.

It was around 9pm that night Rebecca sent the maid into the house to inform the men that Mother Edina was now awake, and she was getting ready to feed her. She wanted the three men to come in and be present while the old lady was awake.

The three men left their shoes at the entrance of Mother Edina's room, and the door was then closed. Rebecca then notified Mother Edina about the presence of the three men at her bedside. The men then offered their individual respects to the old lady and then sat down in the three chairs that were placed around, and close to her bed.

"I already knew that all three of you are going to be here. my three favorite boys," the old lady acknowledged feebly. "I always think about all of you, and I want you to know that. Tell me, you all out there, what would life be without my three boys?"

Right after saying that, the old lady abruptly closed her eyes.

As the three men looked at each other, not understanding what the frail old lady meant by that statement and not knowing exactly how to respond to it, Rebecca turned her face away from Mother Edina and looked up at the three men, a big wide smile on her face, perhaps a feature that denoted her understanding as to why the three men appeared perplexed.

"You don't have to respond to what she says, or asks," the reverend's wife said. "At least not now. Mother has been saying strange things lately, but mostly in her sleep. Just listen, and maybe acknowledge now and then. While it may be difficult to make sense of what she is saying, I hope you agree with me that it's fascinating to hear her talk." The three men nodded their heads with understanding.

Rebecca continued dabbing mother Edina's forehead with a soft, white piece of cotton cloth, absorbing small beads of sweat as the frail old lady appeared to have perspiration despite the fact that there was no excessive heat in the room and the outside was relatively cool after the sun went down. A light breeze was blowing through the two small windows plus a small, rectangular vent at the top of, but centered, the left side wall of the room. These three airways no doubt provided enough ventilation.

Suddenly, Mother Edina's body quivered, and her lips started trembling. All three men sat forward, fearing that the old lady was about to experience a seizure. Rebecca quickly leaned forward and

cradled the frail old lady's head and shoulders in her arms. She slowly started rocking her like an infant that needs attention.

"Water … water … please," the old lady mumbled, her eyes still closed. Another tremor went through her body, a much stronger one.

Mufti Musa, who was closer to a carafe filled with fresh cool water and four clean empty drinking glasses, all on top of a small table, reached over and quickly poured some water into one of the glasses, passing it on to Rebecca. Rebecca connected the lip of the glass to Mother Edina's mouth.

"There you go, mother, there you go," She calmly said to the old lady, not unlike talking to a baby that was trying to fall asleep. "All is ok, Mother, all is fine. Just stay with us please, stay with us."

Rebecca's whispering plea to the old, frail lady then turned into low - toned sobbing as fear and anticipation of what could happen next took over. Mother Edina, in her later years, was no stranger to seizure activity, and some of those attacks had been quite severe, almost taking her life. The reverend moved closer to his wife and put his hand around her shoulder, trying to comfort her without saying anything.

"I am alright," Mother Edina suddenly said. But this time there was no mumbling, even though her voice was low pitched. "From now on, there should be no more crying or worrying so much. I want you to rejoice, and understand, that God has not forsaken you. He will protect us, protect you, his children."

After that statement, the old lady slowly raised her frail, skinny arms up in front of her and clapped her hands loudly … One, Two, Three times …

The light in the room went out. At the same time, the windows suddenly slammed themselves shut, while something loudly scraped the outside of the closed door at the entrance of Mother Edina's room. It was like someone from the outside was reinforcing the door with an extra bolt or barricade. The entire room was cast into pitch blackness. No one in the room moved, or even made a sound, for no one knew what was happening or going on.

And then tiny bright balls of glowing lights started streaming through that little vent on top of the left wall, floating into the room like tiny soap bubbles, shiny and glowing in all sorts of colors you can ever margin, their flow very graceful as they piled up in the center of the room right above Mother Edina's bed. As more flowed in, the glowing entities engulfed the tiny bed and its now quietly still occupant, like they were embracing her. They were so many that the room became filled up with them. It was like a city's Christmas exhibition lights, made of many colors. Then they started rearranging themselves into a shape, until a complete human form was formed. Behind this form, other balls of light attached themselves to it, maintaining constant movement like the wings of a slow floating butterfly.

The spectacular array of tiny, colorful glowing lights had just arranged themselves into the form of an upright human being with big, gently flapping wings. It now stood right next to Mother Edina's bed, to the left of her head, facing them. Complimented by a warm aroma of wild bush roses, the site was obviously magnificent, a dazzling vision to behold and feel, perhaps one to last forever in the minds of those present in the room. There was no doubt then, to the onlookers, that this magnificent, floating apparition before them is indeed the glorious appearance of an angel of God, of and from heaven.

Then the angel started talking.

The voice was male, void of dragging, void of faintness, void of squeakness. It was a bold, clear and calm, yet authoritarian voice full of booming resonance that seemed to heighten at points of emphasis, and each word said was stated in its singularity, not linked.

"You three men are not here by coincidence. It is by divine choice. You are here to receive a message from heaven, to receive and be witness to the divine decree from the almighty father of all, who sits in heaven. Your will hear it with your human ears but receive it with your soul. I bid you to listen to the word from God, as it's being uttered in its very absoluteness."

There was a brief pause here, the angel seemed to sigh, like he really didn't want to say what he was about to say. When he did this, a rolling vibration briefly shook the entire room.

"I am not happy with what I see in the seventh dimension, in my own back yard. You have all turned against me and sought comfort elsewhere. My love and creations have been corrupted by unjustified means and ways, of division and destruction, of selfless greed and deceit. My seventh dimension now reeks of impurity and death, and now represents the very ways of one who fell from glory, Satan. He has totally confused and sought to divide, by settling humanity into so–called races and religious sects, by introducing the so-called god which you humans call money. This second so-called God has no doubt corrupted civilizations, nations and its leaders, communities of people, families and friends. Even great minds sanctioned by me have been corrupted. Yet haven't I made myself clear enough, that there is only to be me, your creator? That you are all made of the flesh and bone and blood? That the populace of humanity will be of male and female, as clearly defined at creation, and the reasons why so clear? Haven't I revealed myself through obvious and absolute ways, with pure clarity, by making evident the sheer power of my will through miracles of nature, through the obvious disparities in human and other creatures' traits? Haven't I shown humanity that I, alone, hold the key to the difference between life and death? I have forced entire communities and nations to listen, to bow down to me. My angels, at my command, have altered the lives of individuals, man and woman and child alike, this to remind humanity of my presence, my greatness!"

Another brief break of quietness here, and then another rolling vibration through the room was felt.

"But now I see that a lot of you have failed me, and for that reason I am sending one with my mandate to restore my order, a fire that will reinstate my sanctity. Henceforth, mark my words, the innocent, the weak, and the faithful shall be protected, but the devious and the wicked are going to be crushed and destroyed. So go now, tell your people, your congregations throughout the masses that listen to you, to turn back to the righteous way, my way. I am going to help them stand up against the evil and the devious. I will spare them the peril that is now imminent."

Another brief, quiet break moment again, but this time the reverend Samson Ssekadde spoke, remaining very calm as he spoke to the divine being before him. "What about our mother Edina? She has been having these dreams in which she purportedly has been travelling to and from heaven. Are these dreams real? Are they linked to your message?"

90

"Your mother has been quietly praying for your world ever since she reached the human age where she can do so herself," the angel answered. "Through her humble soul we have been able to take note of what is going on inside the seventh dimension. We have watched, reviewed and deliberated, but every night and morning she has prayed and begged the heavens to spare your world from divine wrath, to have mercy on all defaulters, and not to call the world to judgement too soon. She has asked the heavens for a second chance for human beings to redeem themselves and correct their ways and be saved from destruction. She is the main part of the whole."

"I know she is frail and sick due to aging, but we still want her around, still love her so much," The reverend said. "I am humbly requesting that heaven delay her departure from this world and grant us more time with her."

"Your request is fully granted, but on the condition that none of you human beings in this room will ever reveal, at any given moment, the reasons of, how and why, she is having this second wind of life" the angel replied. "Your mother has also made a special request. She wants to see her divine creator. While that request has been looked into, and possibly granted by the council of heavenly angels, the time phase for this to happen has yet to be deliberated upon. So, until then, we release her back to you per your request. Now I see that every one of you has one prominent question on their mind. You all want to know when the one with the heavenly mandate will arrive. This heaven-sent holy fire will arrive unannounced, yet it's divine presence will be felt, the mightiness of the mandate being delivered witnessed. But most of all, the ways and means of her final act of judgement shall be swiftly and precisely delivered. Thereafter, God's message will again be announced to those worthy of receiving it."

The array of shiny, numerous lights suddenly became brighter to the point whereby the entire room was brightly illuminated by a spectacular, colorful glow of brightness such as they have never seen before. The form became more revealing, showing a barefooted, tall human being clad in a flowing gold robe, the skin on the face, arms and feet glowing with a fiery brownness in skin texture. A shiny halo surrounded the bold head of the angel, whose face was expressionless upon self-revealing.

"Now go in peace, and continue to serve the almighty God faithfully," the angel said. And with those final words, the vivid apparition transformed itself back into the tiny lights, graciously moved upwards and above their heads to the ceiling level, and then slowly, completely disintegrated, extinguished themselves at the same time.

Another loud banging noise on the outside of the door happened again, just like the one at the beginning of the meeting. It was like a heavy barrier was being removed, and the lights from the electric bulbs in the bedside and ceiling light fixtures suddenly turned themselves back on.

Total silence now ensured. Everyone was, at this moment, totally speechless! After a few minutes another voice, devoid of fear or distress, shock or surprise, suddenly broke through the silence and took over the room again.

"Can I please have a sip of water? I feel so hot and thirsty," Mother Edina said in a normal, regular voice. Her voice, unlike before, had none of that previous frailty in it.

Rebecca quickly picked up the almost full glass of water at bedside and offered it to Mother Edina, again as before, connecting it to her mouth. But the old lady took the glass from her with both her hands and drank all the water, to the last drop.

It was a sudden strange, and complete, transformation.

"Thank you very much, Rebecca," Mother Edina said, smiling. "Now please help me sit up straight in this bed. I want to be able to see the three boys sitting in front of me without straining and stretching my neck."

Rebecca complied with the request, propping her up with pillows. After she set Mother Edina up comfortably, Rebecca turned around to look at the three men, who still sat still, not talking. It was quite evident that this evening's event, which they had just been part of and witnessed firsthand, had mesmerized them and taken its toll to the core. The message had indeed gone to their souls, as the lord's angel had commanded.

"Let us pray," Rebecca said, smiling graciously, and instantly bowing her head.

The battle for the Seventh dimension had just been declared.

# Chapter Six

Six years from that evening in Mother Edina's room also saw another similar conclusion, in another corner of the world, in an apartment living room. In the living room a solo soul sat, a man that had meticulously set up, following the guidelines from his employers, the ambitious and deadly project that could impact every human being on earth and change the world forever.

But to major Haraabi, the project promised to be the biggest payday of his life, one from which he expected to completely retire from living the life and job of creating death for other people, which was his specialty, usually involving and impacting hundreds, sometimes thousands, of people. Not that his mind itself was impacted, not in the least, because he rarely involved himself directly in the nitty gritty onset and final effect. He simply takes up his client's plan and envisions it, create a "how to do" plan, and then sets it into action. Once set into motion, he would see it through by monitoring the situation, drawing the conclusion, fixing up loose ends and then the proof would be out there for his clients to see. He then gets paid the rest of his money and walks away. He moves on to the next project.

But this was big and even though he had never met the actual individual behind the entire idea and project, he was willing to see it through. From what he had noted so far, these people were far from small. He was dealing with a behemoth, an organization that seemingly had all the funds and means, the resources and power, and had no boundaries. For a period of over ten years now he successfully handled projects for them and in turn got paid very well. But the organization kept coming back with more projects, small and big, with this one being the most ambitious and deadliest ever. And the payoff was beyond his wildest imagination.

But with all the past time success, he had never met the organization's top boss. The leader seemed to work through individual, personalized connections, branches, subsidiaries and digital outlets. But it mattered less to major Haraabi, sort of, for as long as he got paid, and these people paid well, he really wasn't in a hurry to meet the big boss face to face.

It was hours later after Pony's departure that he finally concluded the final planning of the project, and everything seemed to be in place.

He had made so many scripted phone calls and digital communications that his head now hurt. He still had to eliminate that billionaire, Bernhard Vonsberg, from the equation, but that wasn't his main concern. He had his eyes on the main deal, the project itself. He was determined to see it through. He would always deal with the billionaire and or his family later.

Major Haraabi usually treated his stress headaches with a glass of scotch whisky, and he was about to pour himself one when his private phone started vibrating. It was the same phone he used to communicate with his mysterious employers.

"Hello?" he carefully said, always avoiding revealing his identity instantly.

"What happened when the man delivered our stuff?" the caller asked.

"We took it," major Haraabi replied.

"How was it delivered? By car, plane, or boat?" the caller persisted.

"It was in his stomach,"

"What did he bring back to us?"

"Nothing. We already got paid and he was already..."

There was a pause in the communication for at least thirty seconds. In this coded introduction, to make sure that the recipient was the right one, the caller always finished that last sentence. If the receiver answered it fully, the call would be disconnected immediately.

"Dead!" the caller finished the sentence. "You are scheduled to meet with the school Principal to address issues concerning your child tomorrow. Please do not miss this appointment as there will be severe and or direct consequences for both you and the child if you do. A car will pick you up at zero six hundred this morning from where you are right now to take you to the meeting place. Between now and then, do not leave your place or go anywhere. Do not carry any tools on you. At zero fifty-nine, step out of your door and wave at us. We will acknowledge back, and then you will walk to us and get into the back seat of the car. You should be seated in the car at exactly zero six hundred." The caller hung up.

Major Haraabi put the phone back down on the table. A meeting with the principal? Hmmm, he mused. After ten years plus of service to the organization he fi nally gets to meet the top guy, code named the principal. The code word for individualized projects like his were always referred to as a Child. They must be very pleased with the way things were going, he mused. During meetings with fellow top operatives like himself, which always took place anywhere on the globe, this top boss was always never present. Nobody seemed to know who this person really was.

But one of those operatives, a high-ranking lieutenant feared by most of the others, was gracious enough to seat down and talk to him. This was at one of those grand introductory meetings, where he was being inducted with honors into the organization. This lieutenant told him that the big boss only met with a selected few, and that to meet with the principal you must have done your job well, exceeded expectations beyond normal standards. This guy claimed he was one of the few ever privileged to meet with the principal, and that the experience was one of a kind and indeed very rewarding.

Major Haraabi looked at the analog clock on the wall. It was three o'clock in the morning, so he had three hours to prepare himself for the meeting. He picked up the alarm clock at his desk and primed it to ring at five o'clock. After over seventy-two hours without sleeping, he badly needed a nap. Two hours were good enough to power him up. In his world, one gets used to these kinds of naps, which are taken anytime, and anywhere it's deemed safe enough. He also wanted to be awake and alert during this meeting with the principal.

The alarm promptly woke him up at five o'clock. He still felt exhausted, but after taking the ten – minute cold water shower he felt much better. Inside the shower room, he had found the gun that Pony had pointed at him after he abruptly opened the shower door on her while she was bathing. It was on top of the counter, by the sink. That made him think about her. He now felt that he missed her presence. He was already missing her looming female warmth that always overpowered him and reminded him of his humanity and the meaning of intimacy with another human. He remembered that with her, he didn't need the whisky to tame his stress. She always found a way to sooth him. Now he wished he had not sent her away. She could have come with him to meet the principal. He was willing to show off his favorite toy, Pony.

He also now felt bad about issuing that death warrant on her and her family. But that was the job and its rules, he told himself. The job rules required him to do that in order to protect his client's interests.

And he was sure the principal would approve that step taken, even on his own mistress, a longtime confidant now presumably gone bad.

With a brief sigh, picked up the gun and placed in the cabinet below the sink. He then quickly brushed his teeth, combed his hair, then left the bathroom for the bedroom. He selected a clean white polo - neck shirt and black dress slacks with a sheath belt, then chose flat – soled, crocodile skin boots that resembled the Cavender style in America. He then closed with a midsize trench style overcoat and a red scarf around his neck. It was nippy cold out there, but this scarf was also a special present from Pony, and he liked moving around with it during private functions.

He looked at the clock. Man, time flies by fast, he told himself. It was already ten minutes to six o'clock! He left the bedroom and went back to his study, where he made sure everything was in its proper place and or tacked away neatly. At two minutes to six o'clock he turned off all the lights and stepped out of his flat's front door. Right across the street was parked a long, white limousine sedan, with all lights off. He looked at it briefly, and then raised his hand and waved. The lights on the outside of the limousine, including the headlights, all came on instantly. The driver's door opened, and a rather short man stepped out. He beckoned at Major Haraabi. After making sure the apartment security system was on and front door locked, major Haraabi quickly ran down the steps and made his way to the limousine. When he got to it, the short man, who turned out to be the stocky, solidly built type in his black overcoat and fedora hat ensemble, opened the passenger door for him to get in without saying a word. Once the major was inside, he slammed the door shut and got back in the driver's seat. There was another man sat in the front passenger seat. He too had broad shoulders and even from the back Major Haraabi could tell the military type, complete with a square jaw. A notable contrast between the two, one short and dark skinned, the other tall and light skinned, but both shared one outlook. They had that cold, hawkish look of professional killers.

The man in the passenger seat turned around and faced him. He had a glass full of liquid in his left hand, and a pistol with a long silencer, pointed at the major, in his right one.

"Drink this, now!" the man said, in a whiny voice which, surprisingly for his size, was small like a little girl's.

"Don't think so, bud. I don't do breakfast this early," Major Haraabi said.

"Then I will shoot you dead!" the man said.

"Tell me why I must drink your stuff , and not smash it back into your face instead, and then perhaps I will think about drinking it," major Haraabi said, showing a lot of indiff erence to the man pointing a gun at him.

Now the man in the driver's seat turned around to look at him. "it's a means and ways to make sure that no one finds their way back to the principal unannounced, after the visit, if you know what I mean," the short, black man behind the wheel said. His voice was deep and heavy and booming, with a growl in it. He said this with a smile on his bulldog, hairless face.

"Ok. But please tell your buddy here that it's important to be polite when communicating to people, especially those that you meet for the

98

first time," Major Haraabi said. "Because that rudeness could cost you your life, bud."

"Are you threatening me?" the little girl – voice man responded instantly, his gun still pointed at the major.

"Call it what you want, but consider it a warning, or an advisory tip off," the major said, staring right back at the man. He was the least intimidated. As much as he hated guns being pointed at his head, he had faced too many guns in his career so one pointed at him made no difference. And from his evaluation of the current situation, he could easily turn this one into a simple close call, turn it around very quickly to where it would be this gun pointer's turn to face the crazy aftermath of his actions.

"Gentlemen, please let's cut out all the unpleasantry," the deep voice man behind the wheel intervened. "Let's instead strive to work together and make it a wonderful day. G, put the gun away, man. From what I see, he means exactly what he said. His threat is real and deadly, G. And you, sir, please do comply. We are under strict orders to do this with everyone we pick up for this kind of appointment with the big boss. No offense to you, sir."

The man with the little girl voice, or G, as his buddy called him, mumbled something, but mostly to himself, and then put the gun away. But he still extended the liquid - filled glass to major Haraabi.

"Now that's a much better approach," major Haraabi said, and then taking the glass out of the man's hand, he downed its contents into his mouth. The liquid tasted very blunt and had a mucoid or gooey texture to it, like some bad, raw egg concoction. It instantly made him gag.

"Damn, this stuff is so yucky!" major Haraabi said.

"There is water in a fridge behind you, if you want to wash it down or out of your mouth," the driver said, starting the car immediately.

"Any alcohol?" major Haraabi asked.

The man with the little girl voice stared at him, this time with a big grin on his face. "In the small cabinet to your left, and the glasses at in the cabinet in front of you. You already look pathetic, dude," he said to major Haraabi.

Major Haraabi reached over to the cabinet on his left. His first thought was for scotch whisky, for a heavy feeling of nausea was intensifying, and he was trying to fight it. He felt that the car was moving in circles, like spinning around and around, yet he remained in one position. He stuck his fingers into his throat, but nothing came out.

His breath now smelled like ammonia. His entire body felt drenched in sweat and his forehead was hot. Where is that scotch whisky again? That punk had told him in the cabinet on his left... but suddenly his hand was too heavy for him to reach into the cabinet. He suddenly felt very exhausted, wasted, lethargic.

He decided not to fight it anymore. He slumped back into the spinning car seat and closed his eyes. He couldn't hear a thing except his own thoughts. If this is what death is like then I am ready, he told himself, but it was all in that black abyss that was now his mind. The abyss grew deeper and deeper, until it turned into total floating blackness.

But wait a minute! Oh no, he wasn't dead yet. He was seeing some light, and the abyss was disappearing fast. Then it suddenly all turned into a very bright light. He was in a big room that had several chairs and a glass coffee table in it. There was a clock on the wall, a closed window to his right. A ceiling fan running on high speed maintained a cool air flow that reminded him of an early morning autumn breeze. His head was pounding heavily and persistently, like every blood vessel in his head was about to burst.

"Give this guy a glass of cold water, now!" he heard someone say. Someone brought some water in a glass and placed the glass to his mouth. He took a few sips of it, and then turned his head away.

"Whisky. Give me some scotch whisky," he said in a sluggish voice.

"You heard what the man said. He wants whisky! So, what are you waiting for, huh? Go get him the godamned whisky! Are you deaf?" someone else yelled. It was a female's voice this time.

The glass of cold water was withdrawn. A few minutes later, another glass was rather shoved onto his lips. It was the whisky, his beloved scotch whisky. He opened his mouth and gulped the entire glass - full up.

100

"Damn, man, he just zapped the entire glassful, like it is simple water!" a male voice said.

Major Haraabi now started coughing nonstop, which then turned into gagging.

"Water, where… is… that water?" he mumbled quickly, his lips trembling.

The water quickly reappeared, and he drank on it slowly, until he drained the entire glass.

"Thank you," major Haraabi said, and then remained quiet, his head hanging down, chin on chest. About ten minutes later, his foggy vision had somewhat cleared up and the pounding in his head receded, slowly fading away. He realized that he was tightly tied up in a chair.

Across the coffee table and at least ten meters away from where he sat was a big ornate circle on the floor with strange symbols and artwork such as he had never seen before. It looked like it was right in the center of the room. Beyond this circle, again about ten meters away from it, was a single, big, upright chair with long armrests, like a throne, and in it sat an individual dressed in a floral, multi – color summer dress with long sleeves. Underneath that dress was a pair of pants, or trousers, that completely obscured the wearer's legs and only revealed the high heeled leather boots on the feet. With arms stretched out on top of the long armrests, the hands were out of the long sleeves of the dress and revealed multiple ornaments on all the fingers, and that the throne occupant had these most ridiculously long nails that major Haraabi had ever seen, all painted red. The fingers on the left armrest kept tapping on it, not so unlike a deliberate twitch.

But perhaps the most chilling thing about the individual on the throne was the red, jagged skinned, Japanese Oni devil's mask, complete with the horns and short tasks, covering the throne occupant's face. Major Haraabi felt goosebumps and chills on his whole body by just looking at it.

On both sides of this figure were two similar, but smaller, upright chairs, but not as regal looking as the big one that they flanked. In both chairs sat a woman, one black, the other one white. Unlike the throne person, they were dressed in a black business suit attire with mini- skirts

101

that barely touched the top of the knees and had no masks. Their hair was a neat, short cropped, military type crew cuts and none of them spotted any make up except for the red lipstick, that made them look rather cute. They each had a gleaming metal ornament around their slender necks that very much looked like a dog collar, and numerous bracelets on their right wrist. These two women, Major Haraabi noted, with their prominent cheek bones and dazzling eyes, among other fine body attributes, were very beautiful and elegant, seating upright and poised with confi dence, knees clamped together, hands resting on their laps.

"I am the principal, and these are my assistants, Kimbi and Kimba," the figure behind the mask suddenly said, without moving any part of her except the lips and the twitching fingers still tapping on the armrest. The voice was laid back, almost sluggish, yet deep and icy with a no – nonsense tone in it, a relay of a commanding, authoritarian overtone. "Please don't let our general appearance rattle you. We like looking this way during our leisure. We finally meet, Major Haraabi. You have done such great work for us in the past decade or more, which is very much appreciated. And so, I must say it's a pleasure to finally to meet the man himself."

"Pleasure is mine, principal, and I have been looking forward to the day I get to meet you," Major Haraabi responded back. "Not like this, though. I didn't expect to meet my boss tightly bound to a chair. I detest being in any form of captivity, which I perceive this is. Given the commendable service record that you yourself just stated, may I ask why I am bound up like this?"

"Just precautions, major," the principal replied. "My people go to great length to protect me. But you are right, this is no way to welcome an esteemed guest, especially for the first time. Someone, please free up the major immediately."

Someone from approached him behind and quickly cut the ropes that bound him to the chair. Major Haraabi gently massaged his sore wrists. Whoever had tied him up had relentlessly tightened those notes so hard his wrists were bruised.

"Precautions?" major Haraabi asked. "I thought I was a major asset to you and your business, not a major threat to you and your body."

"Presumably, until yesterday, when we reviewed your file again," The Principal said. "The review was triggered off by your decision to activate the EWTI on your lover. By doing that, you indicated sudden deep mistrust for her, and we really wanted to know why you did that. Even though your plan to carry out our business is well set and in place, it has now come to our attention that a few loopholes that are rather very dangerous to our very commitments, elements that we cannot allow to thrive because of their ability to cause major disruptions, are now prevailing. We note that you have failed to effectively diffuse these elements. In our business, major, failure is not an option. We prefer decisiveness concluded with active precision. That is where you have failed us."

"May I ask how, or where, this has happened?" Major Haraabi asked, sounding very surprised. On the contrary, he had expected a very warm welcome, not a rebuke, of his efforts. "Perhaps these mistakes can be corrected."

"It's now too late for your corrections, Major," the principal replied. "We are already taking these matters into our own hands. But first, let me explain it to you. There is your total failure to eliminate this billionaire man threat, Bernhardt Vonsberg. He already knows too much of our intentions and our plans and could easily expose us. Given the vast resources availed to you, this threat should have been eliminated by now. Yet Vonsberg is still at large as we speak. Major Haraabi, your record to deal with foes bigger than this is very commendable, which is why we brought you on board. Yet you have failed to erase this one."

"Excuse me, but didn't you originally send someone to eliminate Vonsberg right after the meeting and instead your killer was himself eliminated with deadly force?" major Haraabi retorted. "You too failed. Vonsberg has someone, or something, that is protecting him beyond imagination and perhaps once you and I figure this out we shall act with precision. And I am already working on that."

"There is no more time for you to act on anything, major Haraabi," the principal said. "And for future reference, don't you ever voice your disagreements with me again until I ask you to, and only when I am done talking. That alone can easily make matters worse for you and cost you the ultimate, meaning your life. Are we clear on that?"

"Alright. Very clear, boss," Major Haraabi answered carefully. His sense of awareness of danger was beginning to kick in. He didn't like the sound of this at all.

"Good. Secondly, and most of all, you allowed your lover, also known as your assistant and confidant, to leave and be at large, instead of eliminating her there and then," the principal continued. "She too already knows too much and should not have been let free into the public just like that. And now that she knows you have issued a death warrant against her and her family, she is bound to expose our plans as pay back. An angered confidant turned femme fatale is the last thing you want in yours, and ours, kind of life! We are now working on taking care of that too, hopefully in time. As of you, major Haraabi, you must now pay for your mistakes."

"And what, exactly does that mean?" Major Haraabi asked, sitting forward quickly.

"It means that we are terminating your services with immediate effect," the masked principal replied. "These kinds of errors are unacceptable and only tell us that you have lost the competitive edge, the talent of the ruthless maneuverer who uses the tactical, quick-thinking approach that we hired you for and expect from you. You are no longer part of this organization, no longer one of us."

Major Haraabi couldn't believe his ears. On the eve of meeting the top boss of the organization, a day he had so much looked forward to, he gets fired instead? That's the craziest, most surprising, and least expected thing that ever happened in his life. At this moment, he didn't know what to say or how to react or respond. He now wished Pony was here to comfort him. Together they would have handled this situation. She was always there to support him during complex, difficult times, and it always worked. But now she was gone, probably dead already. He now regretted what he had done to her, and in his mind, he uttered a weary sorry to her for doing her that way.

"Major Haraabi, do you have anything to say about all this? I am now done talking, and so now is the time for you to speak your mind,"

He heard the principal say. The haunting, icy voice now brought him back to the present.

"Like I said, Bernhard Vonsberg has a force protecting him that I am yet to understand. It's a force that seems to be, in some way, taunting and defiant to our cause and mission. They have shown this by their determination to use overwhelming force to protect him," Major Haraabi said. "It's like they are sending us a message, telling us to back off. I have sent one of the best killer teams in the world to eliminate him, and these men tell me that whatever that force was that they ran into wasn't normal and vowed not to go back. Another team is on their way to Vonsberg's hiding place now and I hope they succeed where the other group failed."

"Hmmm!" the principal responded. "Please carry on."

Major Haraabi cleared his throat, and then continued. "And as for the girl, Pony, I couldn't bring myself to do it. You want to know why? Because I loved her, and now I think I still do. For the first time in my life, I saw value in something, in someone. Until I met her and got to know her, my life was full of excerpts of ruthless anger and punishments endured from my father, an evil entity that finally destroyed my mother, killing her right in front of me. I realized later on in my teenage life that my father acted that way because his inferiority complex, his failure to provide what he wished for his family, which ultimately turned to ruthless anger. So, I ran away, determined to make something out of myself regardless of the cost. The military was the only entity that would take me in without questioning my life. So, I joined and trained hard, developing skills that I myself didn't think I was capable of. I was involved in numerous covert operations, most of them successful, building a reputation for myself as a hardcore, relentless, operative. With it came the disregard for human life, the remorseless killings done because someone deemed it necessary, someone in an office somewhere. I was so good at it I decided to retire from the military and work for myself. I still did the same thing, but this time my own way, and my money. But when Pony came into my life all that changed. She showed me that there is another side of life, which is the ability to be part of the love evolving around humanity again."

Major Haraabi said all this while looking down. Now he slowly raised his face up and stared right back at the masked figure and her posse. He was no longer afraid of the ugly, dreadful mask. "And that is why I let

105

her go. Because I love her, I could not bring myself to kill her. I didn't want that blood on my hands. I sent someone else to do it, someone unrelated to her and who didn't have a deep connection to her. I still did what was best for the organization. But if truly loving someone is a crime to this organization, it's something I wasn't aware of, and so be it."

"I find it difficult to understand, after this confession of love, why you still went ahead and put her in this most difficult situation," the principal said vehemently. "And because of your self-proclaimed, foolish emotional stunt you have now put the organization and its agendas at risk! Do I need to remind you that the organization always comes first? You have shown weakness, failed at your job because of petty emotions. And for that reason, you will pay the ultimate price."

Major Haraabi sighed in resignation. It was clear that this wasn't going anywhere. There was not going to be any understanding or common ground.

"Ok. I understand I am fired, no longer for and with your organization. Can I now go home?" he asked. "It's been rather a long day. I have given you all the final plans per my work via the computer, so you are good to go. We can now call it even. I don't owe the organization anything, do I?"

"Oh no, we are not even at all!" the principal said, suddenly getting up from the throne and pointing a finger. The two women assistants also stood up. "You think we are just going to let you go? We are not going to make the same mistake that you did with your little lover. We are not going to let you leave here alive! You know too much about our business secrets! Prepare to meet your maker, and that is if you even have one, major Haraabi!"

The big ornate circle on the floor in front of him suddenly started moving, splitting into two and revealing a blazing fire underneath. The heat was so great Haraabi could feel its burning radiation from where he sat. It was some form of incinerator, he figured. These people were about to kill him by incinerating him. He quickly looked around him, searching for an exit of some kind, a way out. There was a closed double - sided door to his left. He must have been brought in through that door, therefore it must be the one to lead him out of this bedeviled

106

room and house. He quickly got up and started moving towards it, moving quickly.

"There is only one way to move, major Haraabi, and that is forward, right into the incinerator," the masked Principal shouted out at him. "There is no escape this time around. Your demise has already been set, so why don't you save us the trouble and just walk right into the fire, huh? Just get over with it, just like everybody else before you who suddenly found themselves in the same predicament, has done. Why torment yourself? It doesn't make sense anymore! Dying never makes sense to anyone, to anything. Everyone, every live creature, wants to live for eternity, yet that can never happen. Every creature has its day, and today is yours!"

The door suddenly burst open, and two women walked in, dressed in white kimono style attires and wielding long knives. They stood there and blocked the doorway, their weapons poised. Major Haraabi stood back and surveyed the situation.

"Hmmm, what do we have here, huh? A group of maiden kittens with big knives ordered to stop me from leaving," he responded back loudly and gravely, turning around to look at the masked figure beyond the blazing incinerator. With a smile on his face, he turned back to face his deterrers. "Alright, come to Papa, girls, because I am about to make my way through, and you are indeed not in position to stop me!"

One of the women pointed the sharp, double-edged blade at him, and shouted out at him. "You! Go back there. You belong to that fire! You are not getting out of here! It's not going to happen!"

Major Haraabi started making his way towards the guarded door, but suddenly the two women also advanced on him, weapons still poised. In quick motion, major Haraabi pulled loose the scarph around his neck and stretched out. A finger on his right hand easily found a small button at one end of the scarph and pressed it. The long piece of neck cloth stiffened out, activating a thin long piece of titanium wire. He lashed it out at the woman on his left, the one closest to him. The metallic strip lassoed around one of the woman's hands and then he yanked it back, hard. The thin metal noose around the woman's hand tightened before suddenly unwrapping off her wrist, slitting it, and forcing her to drop the blade as her other hand clutched at the injured blood vessel at the bottom of her wrist. And at that moment he got to her, kicking her hard in the right knee. She screamed in pain as her knees buckled simultaneously and she fell to the floor. It took the other woman a few seconds to realize that her partner had gone down so fast, and that was enough time for him to force his hands around the downed woman's neck, stringing her tightly with the titanium rope and cutting deep inside her neck tissue. Yanking her up, he spun her around and off the floor and swiftly tossed her body in the direction of the incinerator. The woman landed a few yards away from the fire, attempted to get up to avoid the blaze, but lost balance and fell right into it.

Major Haraabi didn't wait to see what had happened, attacking the other woman. She wielded the blade with experience, bringing it down on him with all the skill and strength she could master into it, aiming at slicing him up. But he jumped out of the way, left and right and then right again, the deadly blade smashing into the floor inches away from him. In a matter of seconds following that move, he lashed out again with his scarf weapon, hitting her in the waist area, then made for the door. It was like she didn't feel the pain of the lethal slash, which tore through her clothing and tore at her slender abdominal wall with an immediate bloody outcome. She flipped backwards, vaulting three times in the space above him and then landing in front of the door before he got there. He found himself facing her blade again. Wielding it expertly, she slashed at his face, left and right, then thrust forward, hard. But major Haraabi counteracted every move, ducking right and left then skipping out of range of the blade's lethal tip. His feet touched something hard, and he was quick to note that it was the other woman's big knife. With one flip of his foot, he tossed the big knife into the air and then reached out and grabbed with his free left hand. He started engaging his adversary with both the sword and the scarf weapon skillfully and vigorously.

As they taunted each other, lashing out viciously, blocking defensively, major Haraabi lashed out at the woman with the sword knife in his left hand. As she went in to block the blow with her weapon, he lashed out with his right hand with scarf metal, hitting her in the back of her knee. The string latched onto her leg and then he yanked. She screamed in pain as the lassoed end cut into her flesh. Then the woman's free hand dashed into her dress's cleavage area, and came out again in a flash, throwing two metallic pieces at him, left and right, simultaneously. These objects, if thrown skillfully, are meant to embed themselves into the flesh and cause damaging wounds to the body. Major Haraabi ducked away from the deadly objects, twisting his body while bending backwards. The pieces narrowly missed him by inches on both sides, embedding themselves into the wall behind him. Seeing that his body balance was temporarily destabilized, she took advantage and flipped her body sideways, vaulting into the space above them and landed a right flying kick into his chest. The blow came with measured strength, and sent him reeling backwards, falling on his back. This action let him loose grasp on both of his weapons, causing him to cough and spit blood out of his mouth. As for his adversary, she landed back upright on both her feet in no time. She now poised herself majestically a few yards away, her sword knife weapon raised to strike position, glaring down at him. There was blood running down the back of her left leg and the abdominal wall, onto the floor, coming from the wounds caused by the scarf string weapon.

Major Haraabi quickly looked around him. The blazing incinerator inferno was a few yards behind him, and he could feel the scotching heat from its blazing inferno again. There was not much room for him to roll or push himself back if she attacked him from the front, which he already anticipated she was going to do. Beyond and behind the incinerator, he noted that the principal and her two lieutenants were still up on their feet, eyes focused on him, a sign that they were monitoring the fight closely. The only way was going forward again, but with no weapons in his hands, engaging his fierce weapon - wielding adversary was going to be almost impossible. He had a plan B, and with the right timing, he could ultimately incapacitate her.

She attacked as anticipated, leaping forward and off the floor, screaming with murderous rage and wielding the weapon upwards and bringing it viciously downwards at him. Major Haraabi quickly flipped his legs upwards, then brought them down again, the heels of his boots tapping hard into the floor. As she came down again on top of him, his legs came up quickly again. She landed squarely into a pair of sharp steel blades that had ejected from the front of his boots when the heels had tapped the floor. The blades pieced through the area below her diaphragm and below her left breast area. A huge gasp of air escaped through her mouth as she dropped her arms, still holding the big sword knife, and froze in midair, the tip of the double-edged blade inches away from his chest. Major Haraabi turned his body sideways in one hard vigorous twist to the left, flexing his thigh muscles backwards into his midsection. As he did this, his adversary's body lowered down closer to him, and he was able to look into her blood- shot eyes. They had that last total look of surprise, and absolute shock, that mirrored back at him. Then he flexed his thigh muscles outwards again, feeling the light weight of her body as it leaned forward against his legs. Blood was already dripping from her nose as he pulled back his right leg, withdrawing one blade, then kicked hard into her midsection with the freed foot, mostly using the heel of his shoe, avoiding blade reinsertion, ultimately tossing her body off him. Her body fell on the floor to his left with a thud, and her hands let go of her weapon, which fell to the floor next to her still body.

Breathing hard, Major Haraabi slowly got up from the floor and then tapped the heels of his boots left, then right, into the floor. The blades retracted back into their respective chambers inside the toes of his shoes. He looked down at his opponent and shook his head.

"You should have stayed out of my way, bitch," he mumbled, and stepping over her body, he started making his way towards the door again.

"Not so fast, major!"

Those words came to him in form of a terrifying, shrill voice, the sound of a feat of forceful rage from within a deranged human with such an intense magnitude only seen with the likes of those who have crossed the usually hard to define line between intolerance and intractable, intense, volatile anger! The voice of the principal was clearly recognizable even in what sounded like a deranged state.

Major Haraabi looked back behind him, instantly drawn to the shrilled, aggravating sound. He was just in time to see the principal airborne, a leap that took the masked figure from the front of her throne and over the wide open, blazing incinerator, hands spread out like the wings of a mighty bird of prey, and before he took sense of what was really going on, the principal was vaulting over him. As the

110

principal's upside-down body went past him, the hands reached down to his shoulders and sank the long nails into his flesh, between both pit areas of his clavicle. For about a total of about five seconds they remained buried in him, and then the principal pulled out, flipped over and landed smack down on both feet on the floor in a normal upright position, in the doorway behind him.

He grimaced in searing pain from the forced, piercing entry into his flesh, and the jagged withdrawal of the principal's long ugly fingernails! He felt like the flesh in his shoulders was disintegrating in fire, his shoulder blades feeling like they are melting from his body. He had never felt anything like this before, and so fast. As he turned to face the principal, and saw the figure standing in the doorway, he was hit by a flying left kick into his face which threw his body completely off balance, thrusting him backwards. His feet temporarily left the floor and then his body landed hard on the floor with a thud.

As he tried to hoist himself off the floor with his weakened arms, his face all bloody and torn from the vicious flying kick made more lethal by the kind of shoe the principal was wearing, the enraged masked Principal now slowly and gracefully walked towards him. squatting down a few yards away from him, head corked sideways, the principal looked down on him as if assessing his fatalities.

"I told you that you are not getting out of here alive, Major Haraabi," the principal growled. "When I sank my nails into you, I also injected lethal doses of the Cicuta Maculata poison that's infused into my finger extensions. You will not be able to survive it. But in gratitude of your service to our organization, I will save you from the agony that comes while you are dying from it. Goodbye, Major Haraabi. I hope your soul rests in internal pieces! Throw him in, girls."

Girls? The principal's assistants, he figured. In his weak state of shock, as the poison took over, Major Haraabi managed to look around him. He may as well look at something so beautiful, for at least one more time. It would be a wonderful way to die, staring insanely beautiful women.

He, however, did not see any beautiful women.

He was, instead, confronted by two fiercely growling, abnormally big and long dogs with big mandibles each bearing a set of massive white teeth. They were probably a likely result of Doberman pinscher and Great Dane crossbreeds, he mused. The dog collars around their necks looked familiar, but the excruciating headache could not allow him to jog his memory to determine why those collars stood out.

Then the dogs attacked. Their massive teeth tore at his arms and yanked them off his body. As blood splattered everywhere from the exposed, torn, major arteries, Major Haraabi cried out in pain. As the ceiling above him started reeling in slow, dizzy motion, the dogs attacked again, sinking their teeth into his thighs from both sides, and started dragging him towards incinerator.

He then knew that he was finished. Closing his eyes, he mumbled these words out loudly. "Here I come, God. I hope you forgive my sins so done by me to mankind. Amen!"

Still growling menacingly, the dogs withdrew, and then sunk their big jaws into his flesh again lifting what was left of his body off the floor like a rag doll and thrust him the blazing inferno. A thick cloud of black smoke came out of the incinerator and engulfed the room, while his body exploded to pieces as the intense fire diminished his bones and tissue. The dogs stopped growling, stepped back, and stared into the fire. The principal now walked over and stood between them, the tips of those long nails gently touching their big heads, then looked at the clock. It was six O'clock in the evening. The principal then looked down at major Haraabi's sword wielding female adversary, her still body spread out on the floor, blood still oozing from her wounds. She was barely alive, but the masked principal decided there was no need for her anymore. After all, she had failed miserably at her job. The principal spit down on her body.

"What a waste!" The principal said. "Throw this one into the fire pit too, girls!"

The big dogs obeyed immediately, sinking their teeth into the sword woman's body and dragging her close to the edge of the incinerator. Then together, using their front paws, they pushed her still body forward until she finally rolled over the edge and fell into the blazing inferno. The animals quickly retreated from blazing heat and once again sat back and stared at the fire and the grey-black smoke mix that resulted from another body's decimation.

The principal revealed a small gadget in the hand that resembled a small television remote control. It had a few colored buttons on it. The principal then touched one of those buttons and the blazing incinerator fire died down to smoke. The cover panels that were the floor above it moved back into place to become the big ornate circle with its strange symbols again, completely obscuring the empty furnace place below it.

"We are now done here, girls. Get yourselves prepped up because we've still got places to go and things to do," the principal added, and then left the room.

The two big dogs growled, and then slowly and simultaneously rose to stand on their hind legs. Then a most amazing transformation began taking place, from their feet upwards. The hind legs' hairy outlook yielded to a smoother human skin, folding inwards, with dog paws transforming into human feet. Their bodies continued with the rapid transformation, to the arms where the front dog paws transformed into strong and beautiful human hands, to the bare chest that opened in robust transformation to pop up a pair of well-formed human female breasts, the boobs expanding like balloons being filled with neon gas. The animals finally howled loudly, appearing like they were yawning from a deep sleep, as their heads finally transformed back into female human heads. The transformation became complete when all facial features reformed into well edged human profiles, oral fangs reshaping into well segmented, shiny white human teeth. The only glitch in their appearance was the obvious smear of dried blood around their mouth.

And so right there in this corner of the room stood two perfectly shaped, manikin – style, human females, skin glowing with purity, and all very naked. The women hugged each other and started leaking the blood off each other's lips and parts of their bodies.

Someone suddenly appeared in the doorway, which the principal had left open. Both women's heads automatically turned in that direction, doing a three hundred and sixty degrees turn around on their neck bases.

"Hey, bitches, you need to make it quick. Come on now, your boss isn't going to wait for you all day! Boss is already getting tired of waiting for you lazy asses, so step on it, or I will have to come closer and pull some hair ... wow!" the new entry started to say and then froze when his eyes befell their naked beauty. "Ok now, can you do something about your nudity? You bitches been doing a last-minute make out or what? Quite disgusting! I will wait outside!"

It was the tall, big guy with the little girl voice, otherwise known as G. The one who had given that nasty drink to major Haraabi while in the car several hours ago.

The two young women looked at each other and nodded their heads slowly. Then the white girl walked over to the doorway to where he was standing. The man was indeed looking away, staring down the well illuminated hallway.

"You don't have to step out, Mr. G," she said in a soft voice. "What is it now, aah ah? You can't handle two naked girls standing right before you, in the same room? You can come in here and watch us dress up while you wait. We have no problem with you looking at us, unless and of course, if you do."

G turned around to look at her, and his eyes once again widened as they settled on the naked super modelish specimen before him. He exhaled heavily, and then grinned widely.

"No, of course I don't," he said in his small girl voice. The woman was already standing aside and out of the way, more in the inside of the room where her copper color skinned, black partner stood waiting, to let him through. Big Mr. G strolled into the room. The woman slammed the door shut behind him the moment he walked through that doorway. When he heard the door slam shut behind him, he turned around in response to the sound.

"You may not have a problem with that, but we damn right do, sucker!" the white beauty suddenly said, and then suddenly lashed out with a clenched fist blow at his face that twisted his head in the opposite direction, sending him reeling further into the room. Being a heavy, tall guy, he stumbled but didn't fall off his feet.

But the now vicious white beauty wasn't done with him. She slammed the back of his left knee with a hard kick, spinning around instantly and administering another hard foot blow to the back of the right knee. This time the big man went down, his knees slamming into the hard floor. And that put him in direct focus with the black beauty, who

114

pounced on him and viciously swiped at his face, lashing out at him with sharp wolf - type claws that had suddenly protruded out of her fingers on both of her hands. His two eyeballs fell out of their sockets to the floor before him, viciously clawed out of his face!

"Today you die, you godamned, arrogant bastard!" the black beauty shouted. "You have treated us like we are nothing, always rude and threatening us, shouting at us like we are your little kids or servant girls, even in the presence of boss lady. Just because she favors you doesn't give you that right to be arrogant and abusive! Now let's see how you do without your eyes, you blind piece of shit!"

As the frightened man screamed in pain, frantically trying to strike out aimlessly with his fists, his face now a horrifying bloody mess, the white beauty struck again, this time at his neck, and like her partner, she used her now exposed claws to slash at the right side of his neck, literally tearing apart his jugular vein. The now blinded big man, still on his knees, froze! His aimless, frantic arm swinging ceased, and his arms flopped down to his side as blood gushed out of his torn neck wound.

"I hope this teaches you to be polite and nice to other people in your next life, big buffoon!" she hissed at him.

"Ye, in your next life you go! Rest in pieces!" the black one said and spinning around, she landed a head twister kick at the left side of his neck that brought his body down to the floor with a thud. The two women stared down at G's still body, and then they both simultaneously spit down on it. They linked their hands together as they turned away from his now dead body and left the room through a side door behind the principal's throne.

A few minutes later, they reemerged, all fully dressed and looking clean and cool in jean slacks, white long-sleeved T-shirts covered by black leather jackets, feet in brown military boots. They walked across the ornate circle, past his dead body and left the room through the same doorway through which Principal had exited the room, closing the door behind them.

The principal was seated in the back seat of a black range rover with no license plates, the short, solid black guy at the wheel. The black

woman got in the back seat with the principal, while the white one got into the front seat next to the driver.

"Where is G?" the driver asked in his heavy drawling voice.

"He went to the bathroom first," the white beauty said to him, smiling broadly. "He said he's got an upset stomach."

"Man, now that's going to be some long wait," the driver said. "I think G has the longest defecation duration time in human history. I don't know why he takes so long on the damn toilet!"

"Let's get going. G will catch up with us later. He knows what to do," the principal said, looking straight ahead. The principal already knew what the girls had done but kept quiet on it. The man was known for his arrogance and bad attitude, so he got it coming for him.

"Yes boss," the driver said, starting the car. The range rover slowly left the compound through a pair of open iron gates and entered the main road, leaving behind a cloud of dust.

Behind them, on top of the mansion, a bunch of black crows that had been hovering in the air above it gently settled down on its rooftop and remained still.

# Chapter Seven

The principal was right on one issue. Never take for granted a disgruntled, belligerent and vindictive, woman! Especially one who happens to know you in and out, like your former lover!

Such was in the case of captain Pony, feeling so betrayed by the man she had come to love so much. She was so distraught, she planned to break him in every way she could. And so, when her privately leased plane took off from England's Heathrow airport, and finally levelled off in the sky, she began the ditching of his secrets. She wrote a single, well detailed email from her mini laptop's electronically advanced, satellite - linked communication module and sent it to several established governments' intelligence and military establishments. She made sure that it included certain global coordinates that indicated the heart of major Haraabi's deadly project, which she had opposed right from the beginning. She was totally shaken up by its projected deadly outcome and always prayed that someone could intervene and stop the madness! But because the love of her life was involved, and dedicated to this very inhuman project, she felt that if she went out of her way to fight it, it would be betraying him. For that very reason she had held back.

Pony felt that she had come from far, her body a temple to many men on her journey of life, mostly for reasons of survival. But in major Haraabi she had found something different. Unlike other men, he had treated her differently. He was kind and gentle with her, like she was something so delicate to handle, someone very special to him. She had finally found a soulmate. And so, for her this was it, she always told herself. She was prepared to follow him anywhere, like what he liked, and grow with him for the rest of her life. And because of her love for him, she deliberately dedicated herself to now and then try to talk him out of the evil project, which by itself wasn't an easy thing to do.

He was such a dedicated professional to whatever he did, and always delivered to the end point. It didn't matter to him whether the deal is right or wrong. As long as the money is right, it's simply a job he is hired do and so he did it well and did it right. He left it to the client to worry about the moral part. His job always meant almost everything to him. But now it was even more than apparent that it meant everything to him, since he valued it more than that one person, he had confessed to repeatedly that she meant everything to him, the one person he said he couldn't do without, the person who supported him all the way, one hundred percent. He had crossed the line by unleashing the elimination kill code on her and her family. She would never, ever forgive him for that. Not in her lifetime!

And so now that she felt bedeviled by him, betrayed to the core, she had a reason to do the same, betray him the same way, all the way. It was an intense, uneasy feeling prevailing inside her mind as she wrote the email, because she knew that it wound lead to his ultimate destruction. She hated herself for the failure to instantly shake off the love she had for him, the endearment that had finally culminated inside of her as a result of several years of carefully cultivated feelings of love for this one man, which had crossed over into attachment and dedication. This moment of intense, turbulent and enraged bouts of emotions finally overwhelmed her, led her into quiet sobbing, and she fell asleep.

Only to suddenly wake up and find herself dripping with sweat and her heart was throbbing heavily. She felt like her chest was about to burst open and spill its inner contents. At the same time, she felt an overwhelming feeling of nausea. She had never felt like this before in her life. She felt like something had evidently gone wrong somewhere, like something bad just happened, she just didn't know what. Then she realized that she was still on the plane, still on her way to Seoul to protect her family. The digital clock on the dashboard above her head showed that it was four o'clock in the morning. She immediately became frantic again about her mom and little sister.

"Where are we?" she shouted out at the pilot. "We should be in Korea by now, we should be! That's why I paid a lot of money for this plane and a good pilot to get me home as quickly as possible! So why are we still flying? Do we even have air in this thing? It's too hot in here!"

"We are flying over Incheon international airport right now, Madam," the pilot replied, maintaining a calm demeanor, despite being yelled at. "I have just received permission to land. We will be landing in about five minutes. Cabin temp is a comfortable seventy degrees madam, but at your request I can always make it cooler, or you can actually change it to your comfort using the personal thermostat control panel in front of you."

"Well make it snappy, pilot! I have no time to waste!" she said. Unbuckling herself, she stood up and stumbled her way to the toilet. She kicked the door open and barely made it to the commode where she wretched as she vomited out all her stomach contents.

"You ok, madam?" the pilot asked from his cockpit area.

"Yeah, I think I am ok!" she shouted back. "don't worry about me or what I am doing. Just focus on getting me to my destination. I really need to be there, and the earlier the better!"

"Yes madam," the pilot acknowledged. "Since we are preparing to land in a few minutes. I recommend that you now get back into your seat and fasten your seatbelt."

After gagging and spitting for another couple of minutes, Pony flashed the toilet, then rinsed her mouth out and washed her hands in the restroom sink. She cleaned a few tiny vomit residue splatter spots off her jacket with paper towels, checked herself in the mirror, noticing she looked pale, which didn't really matter to her, and then made her way back to the seat. As she sat down in it and buckled up, she realized that she felt much better. The air in the cabin now felt much cooler and fresh, and there were no more strange abdominal pains. She pondered about what that body reaction was all about, wondering if she was falling sick. Falling sick was the last thing she wanted to experience right now, for until she was sure that her family was safe, she needed

119

every ounce of energy in her body to stay focused and remain ready for any possible hostile encounters that may come her way.

What she didn't realize was that at the very time her body reactions were happening was the exact time major Haraabi, her now ex–lover, was thrown into the raging incinerator inside the principal's mansion and killed, rendering any possible reconnections between him and her completely null and void, forever. Such had been the spiritual connection between the two, another part of God's amazing wonders!

The pilot landed the jet in about ten minutes and then was guided by a ground crew member to a private hanger where he parked it. After thanking the pilot and quickly, in as few words as possible, apologizing for her angry outburst, Pony picked up her stuff and disembarked quickly from the plane. She jumped onto a motorized, internal airport passenger transporter which took her to the checkout area. She only had one backpack which contained her small laptop and a few personals, so she was able to quickly leave this area and to a car that was waiting for her outside. The car's standby delivery driver gave her the keys to a barely used black Rav4 without a word and walked away immediately. She planned to drive herself solo to her mom's apartment house, which was on the outskirts of the capital city, an approximately forty – five minutes' drive. But first, she had to bypass a self-storage place right outside the airport to pick up some stuff she needed. In her line of work, these places are used as retooling stations, since airport security would become problematic if she tried to walk in with stuff like that.

She had several "ready" bags in place. She picked up the biggest one, threw it into the front passenger seat of the car, then locked up the storage unit and got back into the car. Unzipping and reaching into her backpack, which she had placed at the floor of the passenger seat, she retrieved her mini laptop device and switched it on. After typing in some figures and letters a new screen showed. This gave her access to a special site, part of the dark web that specialists in her line of work use to almost retrieve data on anything, from purchases that are illegal to general public data, to very classified computer information or data. She had found it very handy and now had a one – year paid subscription to it. She also pulled out a pair of cables and quickly hooked them up to two small outlet ports below the car's dashboard. She placed the

120

device on a device- holder attached to the dashboard on one side of the steering wheel and where she could easily reach its digital keypad. She also turned on the device's voice recognition software application, in case she couldn't use the keypad. Then, out of experience and instinct, she unzipped the big bag's main zipper, exposing its contents, and then drove off.

It appeared to be a fogy morning, but the road was smooth and clear of traffic, as the early morning commuters had not hit the road yet. It was also a Saturday, a day when, generally, nobody jumped out of their bed so early.

Pony's mind was also clear now, the intense thoughts or feelings gone. I think it was the feeling of being home, breathing in that air that reunited her with her birthplace environment. And that was until she saw this car trailing behind her. This went on for the next ten minutes or so. She made it to the next exit and pulled off the highway. But the car followed her. Her instincts instantly heightened, Pony stepped hard on her brake pedal and lingered on it just to see if the car would drive past, but that never happened. She also noticed that it was a police cruiser, and sure enough, it's emergency blue and red lights started flashing.

"Man, I have no time for this bullshit now," Pony told herself as she pulled over to the side of the road. The police cruiser pulled up right behind and she could see the number plate. A figure in police uniform stepped out of the police cruiser's front passenger side and approached her. She noted that the police driver remained behind the wheel. That prompted her to think that these people were on high alert, like she was likely to take off without notice. She quickly wondered why, as the car she was driving had clear number plates, and she had not exhibited any erratic behavior on the road. That told her that they already had issues with her. She rolled her window down halfway as the officer arrived at her door side.

"What seems to be the problem, officer?" she asked, using a popular Korean local dialect.

"License and insurance, please," the officer said in the same language, and ignoring her question.

Reaching into her backpack, she pulled out a small booklet with a few papers in it and handed them out to him.

"International business driver," she told the officer.

"Hmmm," the officer noted, and then without another word, he walked back to the cruiser with her paperwork.

Pony turned around and looked at the police cruiser's number plate, then touched some letters on the keypad. The screen lit up and some open prompts came up. "Need Data on south Korean number plate 00XX5050", she quickly said. There was a repeating beeping sound as the dark web went to work. The message came back in ten seconds, basing on the self - timer on the device screen, and was flashing back in red. "Unregistered vehicle. Recheck?"

That was all she needed, and there was no time for a recheck, she told herself as she quickly reached into the unzipped big bag and retrieved a black tactical machine pistol complete with fresh ammunition magazine and long silencer. These people are not police at all, she told herself. They are assassins that had waited for her at the airport and had followed her. Through her rare view mirror, she saw both figures now step out of the police cruiser and approach her car from both sides. They both had guns, and not just pistols. They had full assault, tactical rifles. There were here to make sure she is dead.

"You suckers have no idea who you are dealing with or what you have just gotten yourself into!" Pony mumbled under her breath. A mischievous smile came on her face as she quickly assessed her adversaries one more time via the rare view and side mirrors, like a cat timing its prey. Snapping the safety catch off her own gun, she slightly and quietly opened her car door, waited for about five seconds, then thrust it wide open and moved, fast! Pony literally thrust herself out of the vehicle, sideways, smoothly landing on her side upon the paved sidewalk of the road. Instantly coming up and adopting to a crouched posture, the silenced gun barrel aimed at her closest adversary, she fired her weapon. Pop, pop, pop! He flopped to the ground without a sound as the armor - piercing bullets hit home into his forehead, below his chin and in his chest. The aim shifted in a flash second to the second adversary and Pop! The shot hit this one in the middle of the chest. The impact of the heavy caliber bullet thrust his body backwards. He hit the ground with a thud! Pony frantically scanned the area for another party but saw none.

Regaining an upright posture, she strode over to the second hit. She didn't even bother looking at the first one as she stepped over his still body with his assault rifle across his abdomen. Judging from the way she had shot him at him, she already knew he was a done deal. Dead!

But the second fake police officer was still alive, his body now spasming as he lay there on the ground, blood coming out of his mouth and nose. Pony shook her head slowly. He looked young, probably in his early twenties. His eyes were fixed on the sky above him as she squatted down next to his right side and pulled up the right arm sleeve of his police uniform to reveal a tattoo with the same marks as seen on that ornate circle in the principal's mansion that sealed up the incinerator. Pony already knew what it was as she had worked with some of the organization's killers, and they all bore it. It was the organization's logo, a devious symbol of membership recognition. All operatives were required to have it. The only reason why major Haraabi and herself didn't have it was because he had been privately contracted to set the organization's plans and ideas into active mode and she worked for him. Even though he had the option to be become one and was ranked as a senior operative because of the nature of his role, Major Haraabi was not yet a bonified member of the organization. He worked for himself.

Pony grabbed the man's mandibles and squeezed hard. The spasms suddenly increased, and his body jerked. His eyes rolled in her direction. "Listen to me, buster. I am not going to finish you off, and I sincerely hope you do make it out of this situation. And if you do, I want you to tell whoever sent you after me to stop messing with me. I am a force to reckon with, so they should totally back off!" she said, once again in the popular Korean dialect. She released his face, glared at him, and stood up. Walking over to the fake police cruiser, on the driver's side with the door still open, she reached inside and grabbed back her paperwork. Her face was still on the cruiser's computer, which was still turned on. They practically didn't have to check anything out anymore, because they had already found their quarry. The paperwork had simply been thrown on the floorboard on the driver's side. Pony fired off a round

123

into the computer set up, completely disabling it, and then walked away, headed back to her car.

"They are... on... the... way... already," the injured man mumbled, coughing up blood, as she walked past him.

Pony stopped walking and slowly turned around to look at the wounded, bleeding man. "On the way to where... to what?" She asked.

"To... get... to... your family. You... still lose!" he replied, somehow mastering a painful bout of fading energy to deliver the reply, his voice a shrill attempt at feeling triumphant.

Pony glared down at the man again, shook her head slowly as what he had just said sank into her conscience, pointed the gun at his head, but hesitated to pull the trigger. She noticed a cell phone sticking out of one of the man's pockets. Grabbing it, she quickly retreated to her car, got in and drove away from the scene. The cellphone was one of those cheap flip ones. She flipped it open and tapped 911.

"Police emergency dispatch, how can I help you?" the answer came back.

"There has been a deadly shooting on a service road off airport freeway, approximately twenty miles from Incheon airport. Need an ambulance, fast!" she told the police dispatcher, and then closed the phone up. She tossed it out of the window.

Pony suddenly found herself sobbing again, her eyes watering heavily. She started talking loudly to herself, as if there was someone else in the car with her. It was a passionate plea with God, an appeal to at least take her and instead spare her mother and baby sister from the hands of those horrible, ruthless people whose company she once flocked. They were merciless, demonic people who would use extreme measures to force their intended victim to capitulate. As mentioned earlier, she had participated in a few of these routines, as directed by major Haraabi, and had witnessed firsthand how ruthless they can be. She did not want this to happen to her mom and sister, and she was going to do all it takes to make sure that it doesn't come to that. Yet, basing on the dying man's words, she feared that it could possibly bd too late.

"Please, God, please hear me out," She found herself sobbing the words out loud. "I know I have done things you don't approve of, but please give me one more chance, one more blessing, towards solving this problem. Save my people, my family, because they are innocent, and I am the one to blame for all this. Punish me instead, not them. Just help me out this once, almighty God, please. Because I believe, God! I have always believed in you and your holy angels, and I know you can deliver on urgent requests. I promise you I will be a better human after this."

She suddenly stopped sobbing. Her tears started fading away. An overwhelming feeling of strange relief suddenly took over, and she didn't know why. At that moment, she suddenly saw things for what they are, and she was going do whatever it takes to correct these things.

Her mother and sister lived in an apartment in the Gangnam – gu district, south of the Han River, and she was determined, more than anything else, to get there as fast or as quickly she possible.

She arrived in Gangnam - gu and quickly drove through the streets that led to her family's apartment section. When she arrived on their street, she slowed down. She noticed that there were several of police cars on the street, and that black smoke was coming from one of the apartment blocks. She parked the car a few blocks away from the one with the smoke and looked closely. The smoke was coming from her mom's apartment block. Pony's heart sunk and she quickly jumped out of the car and started running towards that block. The entrance was already surrounded by police and a fire track with a full crew had just pulled up. She pushed through the police cordon, trying to get through. A strong hand grabbed her wrist and pulled her back.

"Madam, we cannot let anyone go up there yet, "the grabber, a policeman, said to her. "It's too dangerous. We are evacuating all tenants from the building as quickly as we can so that the fire team can take over and do their complete investigations."

"Well… what's going on? What happened?" She asked the policeman, shrugging herself free. "I need to know because my mother and little sister live here."

"There was an explosion inside one of the apartments that rocked the entire building," the policeman said. "From what we've heard, it sounds like it was a small bomb explosion."

"I need to go up there, right away!" Pony said.

"I said we can't let you go up there, because it's too dangerous," the policeman said. "We are going to seal off the entire place even after the fire team is done with doing their stuff."

"But you don't understand! My mom and sister live here. I need to know if they are ok. Please don't try to stop me!" she snapped back and started making her way to the stairs.

"Lady, stop right there! You can't go up there!" the policeman shouted, attracting attention from others around him. His right hand went to the holstered gun on his hip as he poised himself, ready to use it.

Even with the fact that she was already moving in what appeared to others as the opposite direction, Pony still visually took note of the policeman's moves from the corner of her eyes. It was part of those danger instincts, a brain so good at anticipating an adversary's intended reactions as a result of combined years of repeated hard, rigorous commando, combatant, survivor training from some of the world's best in these categories. She was taught to be instinctively aware of her environment and or surroundings, and never to take things for granted. To be precise, that move alone could have cost this policeman his life. But to Pony, this wasn't the time to kill a policeman who was trying to stop her, because that would cause more chaos which would hinder her primary intention, which was about finding her family, alive or not. But she had to make sure the police stayed out of her way. Plus, she didn't know what he was going to do with that gun once he pulled it out of that holster. After all, he could be one of those people trying to kill her, disguised as a policeman.

And so, in a blink of a moment she rapidly turned around and instantly became airborne, leaping straight towards him. She landed on her feet right behind the policeman, though more to his right side. She then gave his body a rough shove forward with the palm of her stretched out left hand, while at the same time tapping into his holster with her right. He definitely staggered, almost losing his balance. The policeman quickly regained balance, and of course turned around angrily to face his aggressor, only to find himself staring into the barrel of his own pistol, which Pony had smoothly yanked out of its holster on her way to upright position again while shoving him. His hands slowly went up as that barrel touched his forehead.

Taken by surprise at how so fast things had happened, everyone in that lobby room went quiet, all activity ceased momentarily, as the anticipation of what could possibly happen next took over.

"Wow, wow, wow, lady, put that gun down, now!" Another policeman present in the room nervously and loudly blurted out the order. He quickly drew his own gun and pointed it at Pony. Now several other police and security personnel in the room did the same, and in just a matter of time, Pony had over ten guns pointed at her.

"I shouldn't have tried that if I were you!" Pony hissed at the policeman who had attempted to stop her. Lowering the gun down, she flipped the safety catch back on and then offered the gun back to him. After the now vividly frightened policeman took it back, she turned around to face the rest, appearing oblivious of the guns pointed at her, and calmly addressed her nervous audience. "Now listen to me, people, I appreciate your concerns and I know you are trying to do your job, but I am going to go upstairs to look for my mom and my little sister. I am willing to shoulder the risk. I happen to be visiting them, I just came in from overseas and this has really shocked me. So, let me warn you that from the way I am feeling right now, it's for your own sake that I ask that you don't try to stop me again."

"Let her go upstairs," a policeman with a sergeant's rank marks on his uniform, the one who first drew his weapon on her, said. He lowered his gun. The others did the same.

But the policeman who had first tried to apprehend Pony now turned around and confronted his sergeant. "So, we are just going to let her do whatever she wants up there? That violates all police investigations rules, Serge," he proclaimed.

"What rules are better than your life, aah?" the sergeant responded back impatiently. "Didn't you see for yourself how fast she moved when she disarmed you? That's no regular Jane doe, man. That's a very well trained, well-seasoned, lethal force combat professional, the one-man army type that governments spend so much money on in combat training, the ones that they send solo on deadly covert missions. She didn't kill you because she knows it's bad to kill a policeman. In my line of duty, we are trained to quickly recognize those types and hence be able to use good judgment and precaution to protect our personnel from harm. So, my friend, be happy that I just saved your life, and probably the lives of others here too, by letting her go in. After all, it's her own decision to risk her own life going up there. Let it be man. Stand down!"

The man stared at the sergeant like he couldn't believe what he was hearing, shook his head, put his gun back in its holster and left the room.

"The bomb squad people have arrived, serge," someone announced. "Good! Let me go talk to them," the sergeant said. "The rest of you stay here and be alert, make sure people get out of this block safely. Let me know when that woman comes back down. I need to talk to her." After saying that, he left the area.

Meanwhile, Pony took to the stairs that led to different apartment levels on the block, taking on three steps up at a time, until she reached the level where she knew her mother lived. And sure enough, as she had expected, the smoke was coming from this level, indicating that this was the site of the explosion. She made it to her mom's unit and looked inside.

Her hand went to her mouth.

Everything was completely messed up, tattered, broken, burned and charred. Her guess was that they had probably tossed a small hand grenade in there. Pony started crying as the feeling of finding her mom and sister dead in the charred remains of the apartment sunk in. She frantically started calling them out by name, kicking through the shattered front door, her eyes focused on the floor, everywhere, trying to spot a body or bodies.

A bunch of firemen, all suited up and equipped with special handheld fire extinguishers and heat detecting devices, had already entered the place. The heavy smoke had cleared, and she could see them clearly sorting through the rubble.

"Excuse me, sir, have you found any people, dead or alive, in this apartment?" She asked one of the firemen as he approached her.

"No madam, there is nobody here," another fireman, instead of the one she asked, responded said clearly. "But we found this phone somewhere around here. Maybe it belongs to your folks."

Puzzled, Pony took the phone from the fireman and stared at the gadget in her hand. It was a cheap flip phone, like the one that she took off the fake policeman she shot. She immediately realized what the phone was about, and quickly looked up to confront the person giving it to her. But he was already gone, mixing up with the rest of the fire team. Pony now realized that it wasn't a coincidence that they had found the phone. It was simply delivered to her. They were here, her seekers, her designated killers, and they were probably monitoring her every move. They had staged the apartment explosion so that she would be forced to come right into their arena where they would confirm her whereabouts from now on, by making sure that she got the phone. They were also exercising precautions, making sure that despite her lethal capabilities, she wasn't going to cause a public commotion which would attract attention and complicate things.

The phone was from now going to be their way of direct communication to her. And she had no choice but to fully cooperate, otherwise they would torture her mom and little sister and eventually kill them.

There was nothing here at all. Just a waste of time, and it was best for her to get out of the doomed apartment before she aroused suspicion and end up being apprehended as a person of interest, she told herself. Meanwhile the clock would be ticking in disfavor of her folks. All she had to do now is to wait for their phone call and see what they had to say. She knew the drill very well. It was, on a brighter side, also a way to know that her mom and sister are still intact. A positive assumption. And that was likely to lead her to where they are being held captive, and from there, she would then deal with the problem hands on. But until then, she was powerless and at their mercy.

So, she left the apartment and slowly made her way back down the stairs. All sorts of uniformed people rushed past her, headed up, unaware of the real dilemma, the reason behind all this. When she finally made it into the lobby area, more security personnel were milling around in the area. To her surprise, they all stopped what they were doing and stared at her, at the same time stepping aside to let her pass. She simply walked on, not looking back, and definitely not acknowledging anybody. It was like the world around her did not exist. When she got to the outside into the sun streamed street, she carefully observed her environment. Nothing looked out of place out here except for people standing on the sidewalks, looking up at the block, talking about the explosion. There were also people expressing dismay at being evacuated, some crying, while security and fire teams did their jobs, which included controlling the curious crowd. There was even a news crew setting up shop in the middle of the street. Yet she knew that someone within this multitude of people was watching her every step.

The cellphone in her hand started ringing. She quickly flipped it open and put it on her ear. "Listen, you bastard, if anything happens to my mom or my sister you will leave to regret it!" she said quickly.

"You are in no position to make any threats, Pony, and you know it too. So, stop acting like you don't know what's going on!" The voice on the other side, a female one, responded back.

"Where is my mom and my sister? I need to know that they are still alive before I do whatever you want," Pony said, snapping off into the phone.

"If you adhere to our instructions, they will stay safe, you have my word," the woman replied.

"I need to know first that they are alive and well," she insisted.

"We both know that if I don't turn up in the next twenty-four hours the principal will lose patience, get mad as hell and turn her other dogs on you, citing failure due to incompetence. So, if I don't hear from my mom and or my sister then I will delay the process and you yourself will also become a victim of the circumstances."

"Alright!" the other person said. Pony now heard her yelling at someone, then other distant voices responded back. Then she thought she had someone whimpering in the background.

"There, woman, talk to your bitch daughter!" She heard the female operative say.

"Hellooo….," her mother's unmistakable voice came on the line.

"Mommy, it's me, Anna - Maria," Pony said, her maiden name that only her mother and sister knew and called her. "Are you all ok? Are they handling you well?"

"Anna, please tell me what's going on," Her mom said in reply.

"Mommy, it will all be ok. I swear to God it will be and I will explain it all to you when it's all over," Pony said. "But I need to know if you are being handled well. How's Sue – Ann doing?"

"They are rough and very impolite, especially this witch of a woman who gave me this phone," her mother replied. "But we are both ok. Are you coming to get us out of here, Anna?"

But before Pony could answer her mom back, the female operative returned on the phone. "There, you now have the answer to your demand. There won't be another chance, Pony, so listen up carefully. I am going to give you an address and you must be at this address in exactly twenty minutes after I hang up. If you don't show up at that time, I swear to you Pony, that will be the last time you see and or hear from your folks. I will kill them both! You must come alone, totally unarmed, unwired, no phone. Before you walk into our building, you make sure you remove your shoes. You will walk in here barefoot, hands up and behind your head, front of your shirt unbuttoned, and no bra on. No jackets, no sunglasses, not even bracelets. You must have nothing in your pockets at all. You will park your car at least ten yards away and then walk to the location. Failure to follow those directives will mean a death sentence for your folks, understood? Now, stand by for the address!"

The woman stated the address and immediately hang up. Pony looked at her watch. 9:15am. Knowing these people, she knew that they meant what they said, and if she did not show up in the time frame given something was going to happen to her mother and sister.

As she instantly took off running towards her car, she almost got run over by another car, a gleaming black jaguar sedan. The driver stepped on her breaks right on time.

"Hey, watch where you are going, woman!" the driver yelled at Pony after instantly rolling down her window. Pony glared at her briefly, just for a few seconds. The driver, a female, wore fancy big, dark sunglasses that completely covered her eyes, a hat on head, long black silky hair tied up in a long-split ponytail, a smiley face even as she yelled out, and was chewing on something. And that jaguar emblem on the car's engine hood seemed to be turning its head and snarling at her.

But then Pony took off running again, without saying a word back. The jaguar sedan also immediately sped off in the opposite direction, tires screeching. Pony got to her car and jumped in. Looking at the front passenger seat, she realized that the big bag, with all her equipment, was gone. So was the small duffle bag with all her documents. But the tablet computer that she had attached to the dashboard was still there. It was as if whoever had taken her stuff had intentionally left the device for her to use. Pony quickly turned the device on and plugged in the address she was told to go to. The GPS was ready.

Damn, man! Now she remembered that in her rush to get to her mother's smoke-filled apartment block she had left the car with door open. Oh well, she might not need that stuff anymore anyways, she told herself. Her main concern now was the safety of her family, nothing else.

Pony closed her eyes briefly, forcing her mind go blank for a moment except for one thing. Inside her mind, she asked God to please not forsake her at this dire moment. Then she opened her eyes, started the car, and drove off . She now had fifteen minutes left to get to her destination.

Ahead of her, about fifteen miles away, the gleaming black jaguar sedan pulled up into the front parking lot of an elegant, first class ten-stored hotel/restaurant building. The driver gracefully stepped out and went to the back of the car. One touch on the small car remote in her hand and the trunk popped open. She reached inside the trunk and pulled out a big, pink shoulder bag that resembled a guitar case, closed the trunk, and then lazily made her way to the hotel entrance.

The hotel lobby, which was also the entrance to the restaurant, was crowded with all kinds of people, talking or laughing loudly, and eating. Some appeared to be impatiently waiting for something, most likely their food. You could see the anxiety on their faces. But for whatever reason, the moment the lady driver of that gleaming jaguar sedan made her debut into the busy noisy lobby, averagely tall and well poised, her curvy body a showcase of elegance and beauty, all heads male and female turned and looked. The noisy diner went quiet. Her entire body dress up, including make – up and ornaments that jingled strangely only on her left ear, left wrist and left ankle, didn't spell extravagance or exorbitant pricing, but was perfectly marched without defying the young or the old. Even the strong perfume around her cocoa - brown skin colored body blossomed the place with an overwhelming freshness that modified the Asian food aroma to regular day in and out living room breeze. But perhaps the most appealing sensuality of this new entry was the enchanting, joy -wielding smile, complete with bilateral facial dimples, that seemed to be a permanent fixture on her face even as she gaily chewed on what seemed to be gum and looked straight ahead at the reception desk. The sensuality of her appeal was so distinct it created an aura of total and complete enchantment on everyone who beheld her.

"Welcome to The Candlelight Hotel and Restaurant International, madam," the receptionist said pleasantly, herself mesmerized. "How can I help you?"

"I do have a hotel suite reservation with you," the lady cooed. "Your Names please?"

"Pabitra Zeal, Ms."

The receptionist found her name in the computer and promptly offered her two guests keys. "There you go, Ms Zeal."

"One key will do, thank you very much," the lady told the receptionist. She placed one of the keys on the counter in front of her.

"On a note, though, once I am inside my room, I wish not to be disturbed by anyone, whatsoever, as I will be practicing my special music and any unsolicited interference could lead to me being distracted from my focus. That means no housekeeping, no deliveries or courtesy calls at my door. It must be a matter of acute emergency for anyone to knock on my room door. I hope this does not make me an abnormally for the hotel staff and or its management."

"Absolutely not, Ms Zeal," the receptionist replied instantly with a smile. "One more thing, though. Would you like me to ask one of

our bellhops to escort you to your suite, perhaps help you carry your musical instrument?"

"That won't be necessary, but thank you very much for the offer," the lady replied. "This is because it's a very special kind of instrument, delicate and all, and I prefer carrying it myself to avoid speculations over liabilities should anyone of your people damage it, unintentionally, of course."

"Yes madam, no problem," the receptionist acknowledged without question. "Elevator number three will take you straight to your floor, make a left upon exit into the hallway and that will lead you to your suite. We do hope that you thoroughly enjoy your stay at the Candlelight, Ms. Zeal."

Ms. Zeal, after acknowledging back with a simple bow of her head to the receptions, now graciously made her way to elevator number three, stood aside when its doors glided open to let the current occupants get out, still graciously smiling at everyone, and then entered the elevator herself. There was no one else in it and it took just a few seconds to reach the fifth floor. Neither did it take long for her to find her room.

Once inside, she placed the guitar bag on top of the neatly made queen size bed and then she closed the door, making sure it is double locked. She looked around the room, carefully scanning the ceiling and room corners through her sunglasses for cameras. There was None. Good!

Next, she went to the big windows and pulled the thick curtains back to reveal the sun outside. Across the street was another competing hotel, a bed and breakfast only, a fifteen – story high rise that was considered a high-end temporary dwelling for all sorts of wealthy, very discrete people.

Ms. Pabitra Zeal now opened part of the window and felt the warm morning air breeze through. Then she went back to the bed and opened the guitar case. She carefully removed all its contents, placing everything on top of the bed, and then placed the empty case on the floor next to the bed. She briefly stared at the different metallic pieces for a few seconds, and then went to work, skillfully and incredibly fast, attaching the parts together one by one. She was effectively done with it in exactly one minute.

The result was a fully assembled long range sniper rifle system complete with silencer, with an automatically reloading cartridge magazine, an advanced telescopic sight or scope, a foldable tripod stand, shoulder shock guard and other parts that make up the formidable weapon. But this gun was different from the usual military stuff out there, for it was designed for use by "an out of this world" military entity.

"The Angel Blow torch!" Ms. Pabitra Zeal mused, mumbling out the words with enthusiasm, her hands fingering the big gun. "I finally get to use you, huh? Come on now baby. Let's get to work!"

Ms. Pabitra Zeal took the big gun off the bed and strategically placed it near the window, its long, silencer rigged muzzle sticking out beyond the window edge. A ray of sunshine came through the window and settled down on top of the machine at exactly where three tiny, glass – sealed panels joined together. In a moment, the gun system became alive, activated by slightest touch of solar energy, and then she could hear the internal mechanism setting itself up automatically, just like a computer's initial auto startup. A single beeping sound alerted her that the bootup process was complete, and the tiny glass – sealed panels all went red. She grabbed a room chair and put it behind the gun. Sitting down on the chair, she took grasp of the gun, getting the feel of it. She adjusted the chair a few times until she felt that she was in a good position, and then got up again and went back to the bed, where she picked up a small leather wallet. Unfolding it, she removed a ward of chewing gum, spit out the one in her mouth into a trash can in the bathroom, and plugged a new strip into her mouth. She then adjusted the cap on her head so that the front face shield went to the back. She then she went back to the gun and sat down behind it.

"Ok then, let's check out our neighborhood a little bit," she said, and taking hold of the gun, she placed her eyes behind the scope. The gun seemed to respond to her touch, as all kinds of strange lights lit up on it. For this gun, too, the big telescopic sight allowed the user to focus through it like a binocular, the end view narrowing into one stream. The user had a control adjuster on the side of gun that helped set the sights on the target with a guided precision of 99.9 percent to the whiff of a gliding shadow, meaning that the gun automatically calculates the target proximity and angle, using its shadow bearings. The user didn't have to necessarily focus on the target itself. With its direct target-seeker, explosive impact projectiles, the victim's chances of not being compromised were very narrow or limited.

"Well, well, well, look what we have here," she said, grinning even more. There were many cars parked on the street, outside in her hotel's parking lot and in the hotel space across the street. She mused when she realized that several of the cars in her hotel parking lot were parked directly facing the opposite street and it's dominating hotel structure, and each car had at least two people inside it. The people in these cars were smoking so bad she picked up the swirls of gray smoke coming from their cigarettes. She checked out the hotel building, directly across from her, and noticed that each individual suite had a balcony. At least six of these had an individual on them. Now, there was one very interesting common factor with the people in the cars and the people on the balconies. They were all armed with guns, assault rifles at most. These armed people seemed to be posted in place to be on guard for something, or an event, about to take place. Something coming up via the same route, she acknowledged to herself.

"My oh my, Anna – Maria!" She mused again. "You must be one hell of a "bad news" human female to warrant a reception like this, for just your appearance only."

All combined, she counted seventeen well-armed people in total on guard at the front of both hotels. She couldn't wait to find out how many more were inside. This special weapon's telescopic sights also zoomed out ultra-supersonic X-ray type rays that could penetrate through walls to allow the user to view objects on the other side of the wall in pure 3D shadow mode form.

Ten minutes after her initial scan, a black Toyota Rav-4 slowly emerged on the scene and parked in one of the parking slots on the street parking of the other hotel, a few yards away from the hotel's main entrance. The gun men in all the cars sat up, levelling their weapons. She watched as Pony stepped out of the Toyota car and quickly look around her. She appeared to be nervous. A man approached her, coming from within the building across the street facing Ms Zeal. Pony closed the door and faced the man. She was barefoot. The man thoroughly patted her down from neck to ankles, taking his time to doing it. He appeared to be enjoying himself having his hands on her exposed breasts and then all over her body.

"Get over with the groping, you sleezy low life!" Ms. Zeal mumbled under her breath from her window spot. "I can see your mind is full of all kinds of nasty fantasies! Human beings, ughh!"

The man finally made a thumbs up, a gesture that all was clear. Two more men approached the pair. After the first man secured her hands tightly behind her back with what looked like sisal rope, the three men walked her to the entrance of the building and then the entire party disappeared inside. The rest of the guards stayed put in their positions on the hotel balconies and in the cars, settling back down.

Once pony entered the hotel lobby, which had a few customers with luggage seated around and drinking coffee, a woman approached her, entering the lobby through a side door that was an exit to the other side of the building, the hotel's backyard with a big swimming pool and other amenities. Pony had been here before and knew very well that the hotel was just a front for the organization's torture and killing rooms for this continental zone of the principal's deadly global crime network. The principal fully owned the property, and the entire third floor was set up for just that, remaining completely off bounds to other customers and axillary hotel staff, with armed guards posted to deter interference. The third-floor chambers were also completely soundproof.

Pony immediately recognized the woman.

"Katarina Kuznetsova?" Pony exclaimed, faking the surprise. In reality, her line of work had taught her never to be surprised by anything, but rather be ready for any surprises. But then she also wondered why the principal's main manager of east European operations was particularly sent out of her zone to handle her issue. Katarina was at a higher rank than her, the positional equivalent of Major Haraabi, but with the same assassin and or killer training. Within the organization, and unlike Pony, Katrina was known to be an extremely ruthless, mindless or insensitive, cruel and deadly individual, and one to never to be trusted by anybody. It was even rumored that even though she was close to the principal, the latter was weary of her unpredictable, cold-blooded ruthlessness and always kept her at bay.

Pony and Katrina had a shared history. They had met in several training zones and then in later years ended up working for the same organization, with Katarina and her man friend full time lieutenants in the principal's crime organization, while Pony remained on contract and under major Haraabi. The two women had liked each other one bit. Katarina's man friend Boris, another field operations assassin, was hunted down by, and eventually put down, on orders from the principal, who had deemed him rather incompetent. Pony was, on orders via major Haraabi, one of the operatives who helped capture him, but she did not participate in his killing. Her orders were simply to track him down and reign him in. But Katarina had vowed to make Pony, amongst others, pay for her man's death, just because Pony had been part of the process.

"Why are you all the way out here?" Pony asked. "Don't tell me there aren't enough killings in Russia for you to quench your coldblooded killing thirst, or that you needed an extra one to be able to thrive. Or is it that the principal didn't trust our Korean counterparts to handle my demise?"

"Hello there, Pony. Yeah, it's me!" Katrina said, a grin on her face. "And yes, I was asked, and gladly accepted, to handle this one. The principal wanted it well handled, to make sure it was efficiently done and concluded. But I also get to appease my Boris's killing, to make it even. Call it payback time, revenge! But just because of your deadly nature, I had to apply a lot of precaution by bringing in extra manpower. You are a celebrity in our ranks, Pony, and I really felt that apprehending you wasn't going to be a piece of cake. But surprisingly, it wasn't that difficult at all."

"For the record, I didn't kill your Boris, Katrina," Pony replied. "I may have helped bring him in, but after that it was out of my hands. I simply followed orders from above. If I didn't, the organization would hunt me down too for failure to comply. You know how it works."

"It's the same thing to me, Pony. You helped get him killed!" Katrina shouted back, her facial outlook suddenly becoming extremely grim. "So now I too get to follow orders from above by not only bringing you in but also making sure that you're dead. But there's only one difference, that is that I am going to enjoy doing it. I am going to enjoy seeing that last look on your face, when your life exits your body. And then Boris will get to deal with you on the other side. I promised him that I will one day deliver you to him, promptly. And that day has come!"

"Oooh, I am so ready for that, Katrina. I have always remained ready for this day, since you already told everyone who can listen to you about your intent for revenge on me, and in turn these people told me," Pony said. "Just remember, though, that we are both party to the same thing. We're all being used, bedeviled to do someone else's dirty work. And when they feel like they no longer have any use for us, they turn us against each other, make us kill each other. And so, remember that on someday to come, perhaps sooner than what you think, it will be your turn to face up to the same. I may just not be there to see that last look on your face when your life exits your body."

"Thank you for reminding me about it, but that won't necessarily change anything for you today, bitch!" Katrina retorted. "And damn right you won't be there to see it happen to me either, because for sure you will be dead by then. You get to die today. And that's final!"

"Ok. But now I am going to ask you one more time. Let my mother and sister go. They have nothing to do with all this. I won't ask you again, Katrina." Pony said.

The grim look on Katrina's face now disappeared and the grin came back. She now came closer to Pony until she was almost face to face with her. "You know what, Pony, this is not only for Boris. I also hate your guts, your smooth illusiveness, and your skillful abilities. And I may as well add this, that I also envy you for the way you look. In other words, you're beautiful and sultry, and I hear very talented in bed. Even Boris used to fantasize about you. That son of a bitch used to mention it even when he was in bed with me. Sorry, girl to girl jealousy! Now, let me let you in on a little secret. The way I see it, as long as you are alive, I will always be second place in the eyes of others, a shadow against your existence! I am so weary of your presence that I am going to make sure I wipe the rest of your genes off this planet, lest they reproduce another one of your kind! And I am going to force you to watch them die. After that, I will then kill you!"

"So, the rumors about you are really true, Katrina. You are really insane. You're a dangerous psychopath on the loose. You really need help, Katrina. I just didn't know it was this bad," Pony said, nodding her head slowly.

Katrina took several steps back, confronting the men guarding Pony. They were all Korean natives. "Take this bitch to the chamber, now! Watch her closely, she can be very dangerous, given the circumstances. If she tries anything, shoot her mother and sister immediately. Make sure she's well strapped to that metallic chair and then give her the full works. Do whatever you want with her first, and fast. I want to hear her scream for mercy, over and over again until she can't scream anymore. When you're done messing her up, call me in and I will finalize it. Do you understand?"

"Yes madam, we got it!" one of them answered back. The other two simply nodded.

"Good. Now go! Let's get this over with. I want to get back to my hotel as soon as possible so I can relax myself," Katrina said, and then walked away.

The three men ushered Pony into a small elevator, and then someone hit the number three button.

"You guys really don't want to do this," Pony said in that popular Korean dialect again, immediately after the elevator doors closed.

"You know this is not right at all. My mother and sister have nothing to do with this. They are all I am concerned about. Free me up now so I can go save them. Don't listen to that crazy, foreign bitch. And don't forget that what's happening to me, or my folks right today can happen to you too someday in the future. All I can promise you right now is that if you let me and my folks go, God will remember your kindness done today and will free you the same way on your day of reckoning."

The three men each looked at her, then at each other, then looked away without saying a word. Their faces remained expressionless.

"Alright. But don't say I didn't tell you," Pony said, her brain already seeking other possible alternatives to her blunt, psychological attempts convince them to cut her loose. There must be another way to get out of this, she told herself. Her life wasn't going to end just like that. She was going to try to fight back the best way she could. Right now, she had no choice but to do nothing, because they still had her mom and sister.

Ding! The elevator arrived at floor three and the door glided open. The three guards and their captive entered a hallway full of multiple doors on each side. These rooms had people in them, men and women, and they all came out quickly to their doors, stood there with hands folded on their chests, and stared at her as she and the three guards walked past.

"Why are they staring at us like that?" She asked.

"They are staring at you, not us!" One of the men replied without facing her. "You are a legend in this organization, Pony. A lot of these newer recruits have heard about your fighting skills and some of the stuff that you have done, at the same time how beautiful you are. These home-grown murderers now crave to get their hands on you, Pony. There is a price on your head of course, but some just want to simply prove themselves. They fantasize about you."

"Do you think I am beautiful?" She asked the man.

"I think that what we have heard about you is all true," the man replied. "Behind that prettiness is a deadly, lethal tiger waiting to come out. That's why we're not taking any chances on you, Pony. Sorry!"

They arrived at the end of the hallway, where there was a closed door. One of the men opened the door and Pony was ushered into a large room with metal chairs and tables, and all kinds of surgical and cutting tools. The room had a weird, stale smell to it. The smell of death. So many people had been tortured and killed here. Men with guns stuck in their belts sat in some of the chairs, doing something or nothing. Pony looked around the room until she saw two lone chairs on one side, and in them sat two people, tied up, blindfolded, and their mouth gagged up with thick tape. She instantly recognized her mom and sister.

"Mommy! Sue-Ann! Oh my God, what have they done to you?" she instantly reacted, shouting out in her native Korean dialect, and sounding very dismayed and or alarmed by the way they looked. They were barefoot and the front of their bloused had been ripped open, exposing their chests.

But before she could react, a man quickly stepped in between her and them and roughly shoved her back.

"Not yet, Ponei, not yet!" he growled in English. His voice had a heavy accent to it that definitely changed the sound of her name.

"You let my people go right now or I will be forced to kill you!" Pony shouted back.

"Oh really?" the man counteracted, and then in a move unannounced, he slapped Pony so hard in the face she reeled backward. But just in time, two of her three guard escorts grabbed her and prevented her from falling down to the floor. One of those men grabbed her hands, grasping the ropes that bound her hands behind her back, at the same time blurting out a word in Korean that sounded like he was cursing at her, and then they both roughly pushed her back into upright position. Pony felt a gush of hot air rush into her head from below and out through her nostrils. She looked down at her bare feet as drops of blood from her nose dripped down on them. She shook her head quickly so as clear the fog created by the blow, and then slowly looked up at the man.

She glared at him. He definitely wasn't Korean, but he looked like somebody from south Asia. A heavy-set man, with a thick moustache, wearing a white overcoat with no shirt inside, exposing his bushy hairy chest and the top of his distended stomach, with wrinkled trousers held in place by a brown buckle belt. His breath reeked of liquor. He was one of the organization's torture specialists, usually brought in to do exactly that. They were also known to be ruthless and merciless at their job, usually ripping out their victim's organs while they are still awake and alive, making a bloody mess out of the victim's body before killing them.

She looked around her. There were four other men in the big room apart from this man, all of them armed with guns, now ready to shoot. Which now made a total of eight men surrounding her and her family. "Do I have your full attention now, huh, Ponei?" he growled again. "You will have to answer some questions, like what information about the organization's operations did you disseminate and to whom exactly, before I let you go to your mama and sister."

142

"No, not yet. My attention is still focused on my family. But now, you listen to me carefully, my friend," Pony replied, breathing heavily. "It's me you want, so please let them go. That's all I am asking for. They are innocent folks, and don't deserve this, never have. Like I did with Katrina, I am pleading with you not to harm them."

The man laughed gruffly, and slowly shook his head. "I really admire your demeanor here, Ponei. Your self-denials of the truth about the facts, about why you and your family are here! But I will remind you that it is you who betrayed the organization, not me or anyone else here, and there is a heavy price to pay for that. You have no say, whatsoever, about anything here anymore, Ponei. It's now my sole jurisdiction, and I will do whatever I want at my sole discretion. You will tell me what I want to know, and then you and your wretched family will die. It's just that simple!"

"Anna-Maria, don't you worry about this man, or anyone else like him for that matter," someone else said. "In God's name you are going to be alright. You are going to win this war!"

"Who said that?" the man reacted, shouting out and angrily looking around. "And who the hell is Anna – Maria?"

Everybody was now looking around, including Pony herself. Then it downed to her. In this room, only two people knew her by that name. Pony looked beyond the man, at her mother and eleven years old sister. Her mother was still tied to the chair and her mouth still gagged with tape, but her sister was now, and she had no clue how it had happened, totally free of all her restraints.

"I did, over here," her sister said, slowly standing up from her captive chair. She slowly waved at Pony with her left hand. "Hey mister, that's Anna – Maria, my big sister. Hi, Anna."

The man now looked bewildered. "I told you guys to tie these people up. Both! Why is the girl free?"

"We did, boss! They were both properly tied up to the chairs and their mouths gagged!" one of the men replied, sounding surprised. "She must have somehow freed herself. And I don't know how she did it."

"Can someone please tell me what's going on here, aah?" the heavyset man bellowed. "You over there, tie her up again, and make sure that this does not happen again, or I will kill you with this axe! Now!"

The man picked up a big, rusted metal axe from the assortment of tools on the table "Nobody is touching my sister again!" Pony said, her hands coming out from behind, free of the rope. Unknown to the heavy-set man, the third man who had grabbed at Pony by the rope that secured her hands behind her when she got heavily slapped had cut it, and had alerted her with a single word, in Korean, that sounded like a curse, but meant "careful!". They had set her free. Perhaps the psychology talk had worked after all. And that was all she needed. It was now up to her to get them out of here.

But it wasn't totally up to her to do so, at least not yet.

Across the street on the outside of the torture building, in her hotel room, Ms. Pabitra Zeal had already started her work. First, she closed her eyes and put her hands on her ears. In a couple of minutes, all kinds of images came floating into her mind, of people talking and eating, people entering and leaving the hotel, of the busy street outside, the building across the street, and then inside its lobby. It was quieter here, with a few people coming and leaving, way less busy than her hotel. Her mind floated more, through the walls and well-lit hallways.

She suddenly got bombarded with all sorts of high-pitched noises, of people screaming and crying in pain, people begging for mercy, and to be freed. Her vision now showed blood everywhere in this part of the building, with all sorts of human body parts on the floor plus human waste as she had never seen before. This scenario was so gruesome, so horrid and frightful that she almost pulled herself out of it. These were the spirits of the people murdered in this place, crying out to her and showing her what had happened, the horrible things that had been done to them. They were crying out for her to free them from this place, their maimed hands reaching out to her, their tormented faces vivid and real.

But within all this horrendous, ghastly and ghostly frightful outlook, there suddenly appeared a strangely bright ball of light, so bright it seemed to blur out the horrible stuff with all the ghostly wailing. The light became brighter and brighter as she got close to it, and then suddenly she was the light. She looked at herself now. She was in the body of a small girl and was facing a group of people. One of them was Pony. A strange looking man was standing between her and pony. She wanted to reach out to Anna Maria, but when she tried to move the body, only her spirit form came out. She tried to talk, but the words could not come out of her mouth. She realized that the little body was tied to a chair and the mouth was gagged.

Ms. Zeal moved out of the little girl and worked on the knots tying her to the chair, setting her free. Then she gently removed the gag tape off her mouth and the blindfolding cloth off her eyes. After all that was done, she quickly got back into the little girl's body.

"You will tell me what I want to know and then you and your wretched family will die! It is that simple!" She heard the strange looking man say.

"Anna–Maria, don't you worry about this man, or anyone else like him for that matter," she said through the little girl. "In God's name you are going to be alright. You're going to win this war!"

She saw the man turn quickly around and heard him shout out. "Who, said that? And who the hell is Anna-Maria?"

"I did, over here," Ms. Zeal replied. She could see the other people, except the older lady next to her. They were all facing her. The strange man was talking, but now the wailing was coming back, overwhelming and strong. She saw one of the men moving towards her. She realized that it was the spirit medium warning her that something was about to happen, something bad. That fresh blood was about to be spilled.

"I must leave now, but part of me remains with you. Will be back in a few seconds," she told the little girl's spirit, which was the bright light.

She partially detached her spirit from the little girl and felt the heavy spark of instant transition engulf her body like a tremor. It was like holding her breath for about ten seconds and then suddenly exhaling deeply. She was now breathing deeply, because some of herself was still with the little girl. Eyes wide open again, Ms. Zeal grabbed at the gun, focused the scope on the building across the street and positioning it on the middle of the building's third level. There was a balcony there which, through a door behind it, linked to a room that had a joint wall with the torture room.

"Point the finger, baby. Point it at any of those men," she said, the words coming out quickly but in a hushed tone. Through their connected spirit mediums, she could hear the little girl's heartbeat as she slowly raised her right hand and pointed it at a man who was closest to her and who was now ferociously approaching her with an object in his hand. Ms Zeal then instantly pulled the trigger.

Back inside the torture room, things were beginning to change, and fast. The man closest to the little girl had picked up a long, gleaming, surgical scalpel and was moving in on her. "Sit down, you little maggot!" he yelled at her.

But Pony's little sister stood her ground and, instead, raised her right hand and simply pointed a finger at the man. The room shook, like something very heavy had suddenly crashed into it. The wall panel to her right cracked open and then blew up, developing a big round hole in it. Then everybody heard the sonic boom of a cracking sound similar to that of a whiplash! Then something shot out of that hole in the wall right after that whiplash sound.

What came out of that hole in the wall hit the man with the scalpel and instantly and completely disintegrated his body, the body pieces plummeting to the floor into a smoldering pile of shredded flesh and bone coated with dried-up blood. Even his entire body - fluid system had instantly been vaporized, together with the metallic scalpel!

Everyone in the room remained mesmerized, their eyes transfixed on the smoldering remains of the man who, until a few seconds ago, had been angrily wielding a sharp scalpel towards the little girl, not knowing what had exactly happened to their colleague.

"Good! Now point your finger again to the next bad guy," Ms. Zeal said from her room. There was a buzzing sound as the next bullet projectile moved into position inside the gun.

The little girl slowly turned around and randomly pointed a finger at one of the men with guns who was still seated on a chair to her left. The room shook again, another hole exploded through the wall, and the cracking sound made a rebound. This man, too, suddenly exploded to pieces, completely minced up, his gun and chair inclusive. The small finger, with yet another urging from Ms Zeal, turned to another man with a gun, pointing at him. But this man, now instantly so scared, dropped his gun and tried to run away, towards the door, terrified and screaming like hell. The little, pointed finger followed him as he took off. The next special, dynamically intense bullet exploded through the wall, reverberating strongly and leaving behind another hole with smoldering edges, followed the terrified man, and before he could reach the door, it hit home and completely obliterated him!

The rest of the men in the room, obviously terrified, now also tried to leave the room at once, crushing through the door like a mad dog was chasing after them. All of them, including Pony's three guards, somehow managed to make it through the doorway and into the corridor beyond, screaming loudly as they fumbled to get into the elevator. All of them except the heavy-set guy with the alcohol breath who had been threatening to kill Pony and her family.

Pony was standing right behind him, and now as the small finger slowly turned towards him, the man started shaking like a leaf, and fell to his knees. His quivering mouth started mumbling unintelligible words, his arms up and his hands forwardly clasped together, like a fervent beggar asking for support. He was suddenly sweating profusely.

"Anna-Maria, step away from him. Get out of the way!" the little girl said, her voice sounding strong and calm. But it was Ms. Zeal talking through her as her finger curled up on the gun's trigger, her view focused on the target, ready to send him to hell in pieces.

"No, sis, or whatever you have become. This won't be your fight alone!" Pony said, not trying to understand, at this time, why people and things were totally getting shattered up and obliterated when the little girl pointed a finger in their direction. Instead, she suddenly pounced on the man, and in one quick move she grasped the man's neck and part of his head and viciously implemented a jerky, twisting move, ultimately snapping his neck. The man fell on the floor, dead.

Pony looked down at the still body and slowly shook her head. A few minutes ago, this very man was threatening to kill her and her innocent folks, seemingly enjoying his power. But now here he was, dead on the

floor! Pony couldn't help but wonder, for a few seconds, how things in someone's life can instantly turn around so fast!

"For your information, buster, it's not Ponei, it's Pony!" she said, and stepping over his still form, her attention reverted to her sister and mother. They were the only people left in this room alive, apart from herself.

"Damn you, Anna-Maria!" Ms. Zeal exclaimed from where she was, after witnessing Pony kill the mean guy. She immediately shifted her aim of the gun. "Full recall, now!" She said inside her mind. She was recalling that part of herself attached to the little girl back to base.

Back inside the torture room, Ms. Zeal's remote, partial spirit presence broke its attachment from the little girl, instantly reattaching itself to its full base in the hotel room. Ms. Zeal once again felt her body receive a jolt of extra energy that completely diminished the persistent headache that she was experiencing as a side effect of splitting her spiritual form. At the same time, Pony's little sister suddenly collapsed to the floor, the intensity of Ms. Zeal's spirit detachment from hers instantly overwhelming and weakening her physically.

In an instant Pony was by her side, picking up the little girl's weak and now unresponsive body. Pony started shaking the girl's body vigorously, trying to wake her up. She felt the side of her neck with her fingers. The girl's neck was warm and yes, there was strong pulse. Ok, she's still alive, but needed medical attention immediately. She had to get her out of this place immediately to go seek medical attention for her.

"Anna-Maria? Is that you?" her mother suddenly spoke. For all this time, with all the loud explosions from the wall, the screaming of terrified men and the now the horrible smell of charred flesh and bone from the remains of the human beings after being obliterated, her mother had remained still and quiet, like she was not affected at all.

Pony now suddenly realized that something unusual and abnormal was going on, something that she herself did not yet understand or have answers for at this time.

"Yes mama, it's me, and I have come to take you home," Pony said. Gently Laying her sister on her shoulder, Pony managed to stand up and look over at the table with all the torture tools on it, some still coated with dry blood. She picked up one that looked like a Garab knife and had no dried blood on it. She then went over to her mother and cut the ropes that were binding her to the chair, removed the blindfold and gently pulled the tape off her mouth. "We must get out of here right away, Mom. Are you able to walk right now?"

Upon asking that, Pony quickly shifted her attention back to her little sister who was still unconscious.

"Yes, I think I can," Mom replied. She was a prominent, well- seasoned Tai chi woman herself and so held on very well through physically draining circumstances. "Where is Sue–Ann?"

"Over here, mom. I have her on my shoulder," Pony replied. "She's weak and needs immediate medical attention."

Her mother walked over to the middle of the room, finally able to hold her nose over the smell of burned flesh. "My goodness, what happened here? Did you do all this, Anna-Maria? And what happened to your sister?"

"She fainted, a few minutes ago," Pony answered. "But I don't have time to explain all that right now, for we must get moving immediately. I am also going to ask you to take this knife or pick something of your choice from that table, in case you need to defend yourself. I will carry Sue-Ann with me."

Mother nodded in agreement, sensing the urgency in her daughter voice. She picked up an item from the table, sticking it into her one of her pockets on her pajama pants. She also picked up what was clearly a tomahawk axe. "You should find one like this for yourself. You will probably need it. I am not good with knives except in the kitchen."

"An axe, mom?" Pony said as she checked up on her frail sister, who suddenly shifted from her shoulder to her arms. Sue – Ann's arms now slowly curled around her big sister's neck. The little girl was now breathing regularly.

"I want a piggyback, Anna-Maria," the little girl suddenly said, her voice sluggish. Pony looked at her, smiled, and then went down on one knee, waiting for the girl to switch positions, from front to back. She climbed on to her back and wrapped her arms around her neck again.

"Just a decoy, my dear," Mom replied. "It's an unusually formidable weapon to wield around and people are easily scared of it. It will make me look tough."

"Ok, let's go," Pony said. "Hang on tight now, Sue-Ann."

And so, the little convoy slowly made its way back out of an area reminiscent of sudden death, one of them a witness of the occurrences, past and present, the other two not fully aware of what had just happened, unable to clarify why the room was littered with debris of all kinds, including what looked like burned up pieces of meat and bones, and unable to identify the horrible stench that prevailed in the air. None of them even gave second thought to the dead body of the man who, as Pony had realized, had hung a death sentence on them less than an hour ago.

The hallway to the elevator was deserted, and so were the adjoining rooms. Maybe the survivors of the torture room situation had spread the word about a little girl with the finger of death, and so nobody wanted to stick around and wait for their turn.

"Can I, do it?" the little girl said from Pony's back. She wanted to press the button that opened the elevator.

"Ok," Pony said, and slightly turned around to let her have access. Little Sue-Ann pressed the button and following the "ding" sound, the elevator doors opened, revealing a lone figure holding a semi auto, tactical shotgun.

Katarina Kuznetsova opened fire immediately. Out of quick reaction instinct, Pony jumped out of the way the moment she laid eyes on Katarina with the gun, ramming her back, with Sue – Ann on it, into a side wall. The little girl cried out in pain caused by the impact, letting go off her sister's body. Both girls slid down on the wall and below the firing line, and then Pony rolled into a side door, dragging her sister into the room with her by her ankle. But her mother took the blast, the impact thrusting her off her feet to several meters away from the elevator and through the doorway of, and back into, the deserted torture room. Pony looked at her sister. She was breathing heavily, but her body looked limp, her eyes slightly open. Pony sighed with relief after she noted that the little girl was breathing, and now hoped that

150

she had not broken any bones due to the impact of the rapid, instant fall back.

She looked around for her mother, but she wasn't anywhere within sight or range. Pony's heart sunk as realized that her mother could be dead from Katarina's gunshots. But instead of believing it, she told herself that this can't happen to her mother now. She wasn't going to die today, and certainly not this way.

"Mother, are you okay? Mom ..." Pony called out loudly. But there was no reply from mother.

"There is no mom for you anymore, Pony," Katarina responded immediately. "She took the full shot! You failed to protect her, Pony. You killed your mother. And now I am going to find and kill both of you bitches too!"

"Mommy ... mother ... are you there?" Pony called again, even louder, ignoring Katarina's rant. "If you answer me back, I will come get you, Mommy. Please respond back to me, please mother."

"Mommy, mommy, mommy ... you sound so pathetic, Pony!" Katarina said and then fired off several shots through the doorway. Bullets ricocheted off the wall opposite from the corner where Pony was crouched, and Sue-Ann lay motionless on the floor. "Are you afraid of dying, huh, Pony? If you come out into the hallway now, I will spare you the agony of seeing your little brat sister die by shooting you down first and fast, right in the middle of your head. You won't even feel a damn thing, I promise you that, Pony."

Pony looked at Sue – Ann. Her eyes were now fully closed, and she was breathing normally. For now, at least, she didn't seem to be in acute distress. But now she had to go find out about her mom's fate, and to do so she had to find her way past Katarina without being shot at or shot down.

"Katrina, I need to see my mom, to determine if she's dead or not," Pony said. "My little sister is severely injured from bashing her against the wall as I tried to dodge your bullets. They are now both done. But I need to know my mom's real fate, and then you can kill me too."

"Ok. Just come out now, slowly with your hands up on the back of your head," Katarina shouted back, her voice sounding harsh and determined. "And I am warning you in advance, Pony, don't even think about playing any fancy tricks with me, for I am not in the mood for that. I want to be done with all of this once and for all. I am going to kill you, Pony. You and your wretched little family! I need to avenge my sweet Boris, and I am going to do whatever it takes to make sure it's done, even if it means blasting my way through that doorway using this gun or any other means possible!"

Pony sighed, and then slowly and carefully took off the necklace with the big beads from around her neck. Her hands quickly found it's connecting end areas and quickly twisted them. There was a clicking sound followed by a tiny spark of yellow fire as an inside connection in the thin holding wire was made that sent off a chain reaction to all the beads, which were small, nucleated explosives. Each one of these beads, when activated was capable of entirely blowing off, or dismembering, an adult person's hand, completely off its arm if placed within close range of that limb. A single activated bead, if stepped on or within range, could completely maim an adult person's foot or lower leg. In addition to that, the beads also had tiny, sharp, metallic shrapnel, the size of a small pin, that once released after the explosion, embed themselves into the target, causing tiny, painful, pea - size wounds. That entire explosive reaction would be followed by colored smoke, designed to make it difficult for the victim to see the rest of the scattered beads, hence stepping on them or blindly falling on or remaining within range of their deadly explosive range. There would be no telling what other parts of the body could be maimed or blown off . Just total disaster!

Quickly plucking them off the chain one by one, Pony peered through the door joint and saw Katarina approaching her door from one side, her body slightly crouched with her gun at shoulder level and aimed at the doorway, ready to shoot. At the same time, Pony counted in the equivalence of eight seconds, just shy of ten seconds, the actual time it takes for the reactive elements inside the beads to explode once activated. When she saw Katarina's light shadow nearby, Pony quickly popped her hand out of the doorway and threw the entire handful of beads in her direction, quickly withdrew her hand and fell back into position.

Katarina reacted at the movement in the doorway by letting off a volley of bullets, at the same time quickly advancing forward to get a better view of her target. Peeew pop, pop, pop… Pop! Pop! Pop! Poom! Poom! Boom! The bead bombs exploded in succession.

"What the fuck …" Pony heard Katarina exclaim, and that was followed by a loud shriek from her, before she lost hold of the gun, which fell on the floor in the center of the doorway and a couple of yards away from where Pony was holding up, making a clattering sound. This was ultimately followed by thuds from Katarina's body bouncing off the side wall and then falling onto the floor.

Pony instantly jumped out of her hiding place and scooped up Katarina's gun off the floor. Holding the gun at waist level, finger on trigger, she fully stepped into the hallway. Katarina was seated on her bottom, on the floor. Both of her legs looked severely damaged, her military trouser legs completely tattered all the way to her knees. Her military boots were all now split into pieces, her socks looking like they had gone through a shredder. Both of her feet were bleeding profusely, and her upper body cloth had visible, randomly placed, pea-size holes in them. Both of her hands, which were shaking non - stop as she tried to reach out to her feet, were now spotting multiple skin hematomas. Only her face looked intact, and she was able to quickly look up and glare at Pony. Her lips were quivering, clearly demonstrating a lot of fear mixed with anger and anxiety. She clearly hadn't seen this coming.

"Look who is looking so pathetic now, huh, Katarina!" Pony said, glaring back at her. "Any last words for me before I blast you off to hell? Don't you worry, I will spare you the agony of painful defeat. I am going to shoot you down fast, right in the middle of the head. You won't feel a damn thing, I promise you that."

"Go ahead and do it, Pony. You are still a bitch anyway. That's what you always will be to me!" Katarina mumbled back. "Like I said, I want to be done with all of this anyway. My damn life! That's all I need!"

"As you wish!" Pony said, levelling the gun at her Katarina's head. For a moment, Katarina's eyes widened with fear as she stared at the gun's silencer rigged barrel, and her breathing became faster and labored. Her body tensed and then shuddered. She looked very scared.

"Anna–Maria, please don't hurt her anymore. She now needs help. She needs to go to a hospital," a small, shaky voice said from behind Pony. "Where is Mommy?"

Pony quickly turned around and standing right behind her was little Sue – Ann, looking beat up, her gait very unsteady, like she was still half asleep. She was staring right at Katarina, looking concerned. After several seconds, Pony slowly lowered the gun down, conceding to the little girl's request. She didn't want her to have that bad experience of seeing someone being shot at close range, of seeing someone's head explode like a mashed watermelon, and the resulting bloody result after that. It would traumatize Sue – Ann's mind forever.

"So, this must be the little bitch I was told that blows up people with her little pointed finger," Katarina said, straining to talk. "Must be nice, having that power. I wish I had the same. Imagine what I could with it."

Pony now turned around and looked down at the incapacitated woman. Slowly shaking her head, she said "I myself don't understand at all the reality of what went on in that room, how my little sister did that. But I am sure of one thing, Katarina, which is that if we are to believe in what happened in that room, you should never have, and probably never will, have that power! Why? Because for the longest I've known you, you've always harbored evil intentions inside your head and or mind. You are full of evil, Katarina. You are the epitome of evil itself! You're always hurting people, killing people and for no genuine reason. You intended to kill us, despite my plea to at least let my mother and Sister go. They are innocent, and you know very well that they totally have nothing to do with all this. That's why I unleashed the "hell beads" on you. You remember those beads, right? One of our instructors talked about them, said they were rather an expensive investment, but one that could come in handy in a tight situation. I went ahead and bought the hell necklace as a last resort defense, even if they were expensive as hell. Looks like it was a good investment after all, it has paid off. But now my little sister, the one you refer to as little bitch, just saved your life. So, consider this as a life lesson, that not every so-called enemy of yours must die. You always have the power to give them a second chance, even at their most vulnerable moment.

That even weakens even weakens your enemy more. Come on, Sue-Ann let's go look for Mom. Thanks to you, I am done here!"

Taking little Sue's right hand with her left, her right hand still holding Katarina's gun, Pony made her way back into the torture room. Her bare feet now hurt, having stepped on all kinds of things on the floor in this room. Her heart was racing too, for fear that her mom was dead.

"I think you talk too much, Anna – Maria," someone said from one corner of the room, when they reached the entrance. "You should stop talking and instead focus on getting us out of here."

It was her mom, but she sounded distant and weak. They both instantly turned their heads towards the direction of the voice, spotted her crumpled up in the corner, and immediately went to her. Her eyes were closed, and she had a big, red stain on the front of her right shoulder, above breast, and all the way to shoulder – arm joint. Sue – Ann looked at her mother and started crying.

"Is she going to be ok, Anna-Maria?" she asked, as both knelt around their mother.

Pony put the put the gun down on the floor nearby and then squatting down next to her mother, she carefully pulled back the charred parts of her mom's bloody blouse. It looked like the bullet had shattered most of left shoulder blade, and part of the upper side of her right arm. She could see the clearly see the wound. There was blood on the floor all around her, an indication that she had already lost a lot of blood. From what it looked like, her mom had dragged herself into that corner and away from the doorway with her good hand, just to get out of Katrina's view.

"Mom, don't worry, I am still going to get you out of here. She will be ok, Sue – Ann, she will be fine. She just spoke to us, so she's alive," Pony answered. "We just need to get her out of here and to a hospital so that her injury can be treated."

"I can't feel anything on my right arm," her mom mumbled. "But I think I can walk, slowly. Help me up, Anna-Maria."

Pony pulled her up, first to a sitting position, then pulled her up against the wall so that she could lean on it. Pony carefully positioned herself, lowering her body below her mother's left side, and then put her arm around mom's waist. With one heave she pulled her upwards, at the same time hoisting herself up. Her mom wasn't big or heavy, just short and skinny. Straightening up, she held her mom in place with her right arm, while she had the gun in her left her finger resting light on the trigger. She could quickly raise the weapon up and fire it, if need be, thanks to meticulous firearm training. She then looked at Sue-Ann and nodded at her. "Let's go, Sue-Ann. Please grab hold of the back of my blouse so you can tag along."

And so once again the small, three - people convoy left the torture room, with Pony praying that this is the last time they do so. They entered the same corridor that had not too long ago turned into sudden terror, with terrifying results. Pony now prayed that it doesn't happen again, because she needed to get her mom to a hospital quickly to save her life, and surprise attacks would delay the effort to do so.

Katarina had now dragged herself towards the elevator and was on one side of its entrance. She was trying to pull herself up to where she could touch the button to open it when they walked up to her. A trail of smeared blood on the floor marked her efforts clearly. She immediately stopped her attempts when she saw them.

"Sorry about your mom," she said, her voice surprisingly sounding stronger now. "That wasn't intended for her. It was meant for you!"

"Get out of my way, Katarina," Pony said. "And I won't ask again. Sue – Ann, please press the button."

"You are not leaving me here, are you, Pony?" Katarina asked, sounding uneasy. "This place stinks! It reeks of death. And I need to go to a hospital right away for treatment. Help me get into the elevator, and I will take it from there. Get me into the elevator, Pony. That's all you need to do."

"No Katarina, the elevator is full now, so you can't be on it with us," Pony replied. "I will send the elevator back up to you after we get off."

"You need me, Pony, to clear your passage through," Katarina said quickly as Sue – Ann stepped forward and pressed the elevator button. The doors swung open. "I instructed the guards to shoot you on sight if you stepped out of this building. I also have people posted all over the place and outside this building covering the front, ready to do the

156

same. But if you help me get on the elevator, I can order them to back off. You have my word on that."

"We will see about that when we get down, and out, there," Pony replied. "I can't, and I will never ever trust in you, Katarina. You're a venomous snake in every place I tread, in waiting to bite me hard with your poisonous evil fangs. Just because you're badly injured doesn't change that."

Suddenly, Katarina grabbed hold of Sue - Ann's ankle and held on, just as Pony stepped into the elevator. Sue - Ann screamed in pain as Katarina's nails sunk into the flesh of her leg. At the same time the elevator doors started closing.

"Then your little brat bitch sister will stay behind with me, Pony! How about that, huh?" Katarina shouted out like a maniac in a state of delirium.

Pony quickly swiveled around on her heels, and in quick move banged the elevator's open button with the gun's buttstock. The doors stopped closing and swung back open. Stepping out, she raised the gun up again and brought it down hard, ramming the gun's metallic, folded buttstock down hard into the right side of Katarina's head and neck joint. Katarina's body went limp, her eyes rolled, and then she became still. Her grip on Sue-Ann's ankle relaxed and the little girl quickly stepped away from her and into the elevator.

"Take a break from being evil, Katarina!" Pony said, glaring at the unconscious woman on the floor. And this time little Sue-Ann didn't wait to ask or be told. She quickly pressed the elevator's close button.

Meanwhile, outside this building and inside the hotel across the street, Ms. Zeal was still observing the situation. Through her spiritual mind zone, she was aware of what was going on between Pony and Katarina and had decided to let the human fight her own battles for now. Afterall, this human seemed to be very good at it, she mused. She now, instead, focused on clearing the path for Pony's exit. Everyone was still where they were as of the beginning when she spotted them, but the guard on the second-floor balcony was looking agitated after he left his guard post to follow up with what was going on inside the building and was now back. Ms. Zeal cocked her ear in his direction, listening carefully. Her super enhanced hearing ability, fully controlled by her thought processor, allowed her to eavesdrop on anything even miles away, as long her mind focused on that target.

She was right. The man was really agitated and as she watched him talk on his walkie - talkie, his conversation in Korean local language was clearly an alarm call, warning the others about what he had just seen inside and asking for reinforcement. Time to shut down his alarm call, and to block the reinforcements, Ms. Zeal decided, as she noticed that the guards in the cars were coming out of, and shifting, their positions.

"Ding, ding, dong. Dong, ding, ding!" she mumbled, smiling broadly and still chewing on the gum in her mouth as she focused the gun's sight on the six, now fully visible, armed individuals. They were all taking positions, facing and aiming at the main entrance of the opposite building. "They really have you cornered, Anna – Maria. You really need some serious help here."

She focused the gun sight back on the guard on the second - floor balcony. He had stopped talking on the walkie - talkie and was leaning over the balcony, making some signs with his hands.

"Ding!" She said and squeezed the trigger. She saw the guard's body suddenly explode into pieces. Something dark, like a ball, went flying up into the open airspace above the street, and then fell to the ground, in the middle of the road. She briefly turned focus on the object. It was the guard's head, a residual of his decimated body.

Ms. Zeal now slightly swiveled the weapon around and focused on another target. This guard had taken position behind the car he had previously been sitting in. His back was fully turned to her.

"Ding, again!" she hissed through the rhythm of chewing on the gum in her mouth. Not only was the guard's body splattered to pieces, but the impact of the projectile mangled the car itself and forced it to roll over to its side.

"Next ... dong!" she mumbled as she found her next target and squeezed the trigger again. This was a sprinter trying to find a spot behind a self-service newspaper stand. His body blew apart together with the newsstand, the papers and some wooden pieces of the stand exploding up into the air and landing back down on the ground in flames and smoke.

The rest of the guards were now very startled. They seemed to have no idea of what was going on or where it was coming from. One of them decided to run back to his car base, doing a zig zag running pattern in what looked like an attempt to confuse his unknown attacker.

"Ha ha ha… ha! Nice try, buddy!" Ms. Zeal seemed to giggle, and then mumbled to herself, "Say, let's try this out. Here we go now. Dong!". She squeezed the trigger again.

Just as the guy got to the car the front suddenly exploded, the projectile shattering the entire engine block, leaving behind a mangled windshield, dashboard, and dismantled front seat area. The impact blew the guard off his feet, thrusting his body backwards and into the middle of the road. A car driving through the street came to a screeching stop as the man's body landed in front of it and pieces of the blasted engine hit the surrounding area of the street like some fiery hail stones.

And then pandemonium took over the street. Pedestrians were running for cover everywhere, and in all directions, on the smoke - filled street. Several cars came to a halt, and then a bus filled with people slammed into the line, bursting up the rear car's trunk. Ms. Zeal watched as people tried to get off the bus, some falling on the ground. Others were running into her hotel. Then she saw one of the remaining guards' grabs hold of a stranded teenage boy, stick his gun barrel into the side of the boy's neck, and drag him across the street and to the other side of the bus, where she couldn't see them.

"Oh… no! How so wicked!" She uttered in dismay, immediately sitting up from her position behind the gun. She knew that the guard man was using the boy as a hostage and or shield to protect himself. Ms. Zeal walked back to the bed and opened the gun case. In it was a rolled-up cloth tool holder. Flipping it open, the holder revealed several gleaming, double-edged knives, some of them with a long pencil thin blade. She didn't even have to touch them, for they floated out of their sockets and into her open hands. She placed all of them into a pocket on her dress. Flipping her fingers, the case closed itself. Then she picked up the car key from the bed and walked back to the gun. Working quickly, she dismantled the gun, stripping it off most of its large attachments until it became the size of mechanical drill, a full machinegun pistol with palm grip, a detachable ammunition magazine and a long barrel. The remainder of the gun at the window was now it's skeletal apparatus. She stuck the machinegun pistol into her waist belt.

She then proceeded to the balcony and opened the sliding glass doors. As she stepped on to the balcony, there was a loud knock at the door of her suite. She slightly turned her head and looked at the door. Her visual scanning ability revealed two men on the other side of the door with nothing in their hands. Ok then, they can keep knocking, she mused to herself. But as for me, I am out of here. She looked at the street below, with its current chaotic situation. Hmmm, it was nothing new to her, this kind of thing. Her missions were always alike, simply chaotic human messes originating from their own bad decisions based on bad endeavors and encounters with deadly forces and unknowns. As the knocking at the door became louder and persistent, she stepped back into the room, then made a dash for the balcony. When her feet touched the balcony floor, she leapt and vaulted over the balcony's guard rail.

The front door burst open, and the two men rushed in, just in time to see her body do the horizontal roll over the top of guard rail and go down. Shocked by the move, the two men rushed to the balcony and peered over the guard rail. They were in time to see her body spin into an upright position and then land, feet first, on the ground below. Straightening up, she looked up, smiled and waved at them, and then they saw her run towards the bus on the street, leap off the ground and jump up high over the top of the bus, and then come down and disappear on the other side. The two men remained transfixed on the balcony, shocked and mesmerized by what they had just witnessed.

Landing on the ground on the other side of the bus, Ms. Zeal stood just a few yards away from where the gun man was standing, still holding on to the teenager, dragging him towards the entrance of the hotel from which Pony and family were trying to exit. His back was turned to her. She flexed her right-hand fingers out in one jerk motion, and one of the pencil - thin bladed, metallic knives in her pocket automatically fell into her open hand. Grasping it, she threw it with deadly accuracy at the gun man. The thin, long blade buried itself deep between gun man's shoulder blades. The gun man's body went limp,

160

his arms fell to the side, the gun fell out of his hand, and his entire body collapsed to the ground. The boy, shaking all over, slowly turned around and stared down at his captor's still body, and then up at her. Ms. Zeal briefly smiled at the teenager, walked up to him and lightly parted him on the shoulder, and then slowly made her way towards the entrance of the hotel.

Inside this same hotel building, the elevator glided down to the first floor and stopped. With her right arm around her mom's weak body and her baby sister tagging on right behind her, Pony raised the gun up as the elevator door automatically opened. She stepped out of the elevator, but then quickly stepped back in when she noticed that a crowd of people wielding long, big knives were approaching the elevator. Upon seeing her, they hastened towards her, but she quickly pressed the elevator's close button and the elevator doors closed again before they got to it.

"Oh boy! Looks like we have hostile company again," she said hastily as she pressed the button that held the elevator in place. Outside the elevator, the people with the knives started pounding on it. Pony leaned downwards and slowly placed her mother on the elevator floor. Her mother winced in pain, her eyes remaining closed.

"It's going to be ok, Mom. I will get you out of here and take you to a hospital. Just bear with me. Hang in there with me for a few more minutes, mom," she said.

"So, what are going to do?" Sue – Ann asked. "We are not going to stay in this elevator forever, Anna – Maria, are we? And I am not going back up there, because I don't want to see your bad friend again."

"Listen Sue-Ann, we have to take mommy to the hospital, or she will die," Pony replied calmly to her little sister. "The way to the hospital is through these doors first and then out to the street where we shall get into our car, and then I will drive you and mommy to the hospital. So, you see, we can't go back up there because it's not the way. But first, I am going to get out of this elevator and talk to those people out there who are now angrily pounding on the elevator door because they want to talk to me. But I must do this by myself. You must stay in the elevator with mommy for a few minutes until I come back for you."

"You are leaving us in here alone? but why?" Sue-Ann asked. "Why can't we just come with you right now, take mommy to the hospital so she can see a doctor, and then we all go home? You can talk to those people after that."

Pony now went down on one knee and faced her little sister, looking her into the eyes. "Sue-Ann, I must go out there by myself to make sure it is safe for us to go through, because not all those people out there are good people. I must talk to them about letting us through without giving us problems. I don't want anyone to hurt you or mommy again. I promise you that I will come back for you. I will knock on the elevator door from the outside seven times so you can know it's me and press the open button to let me in. Ok?"

"Ok," the little girl said, putting her arms around her big sister's neck. "I love you, Anna-Maria." Pony hugged her back tightly.

"I love you too, so very much, Sue- Ann. I promise you I will be back to in no time so that we can get out of here."

Her mother winced loudly again. Pony released little Sue-Ann from her hug and turned to her mother. "You might need this. I picked it up for you from the table in that room," Mom said with a lot of effort.

In her extended, shaky hand was a black, double edged, steel Karambit knife. This Dragon claw was one of Pony's favorite self-defense tools and her late Dad, who had been a united states marine officer stationed in south Korea and in charge of a covert warfare team, had spent numerous hours on and off showing her how to use it. Her mother and mother had met while he was active in the marines, and she was serving as a nurse in the south Korean navy.

"Thanks mom. I think I might indeed make use of it," Pony said, smiling broadly. She hugged her mom passionately. "Love you too, Mom. Please be patient with me, and I will be right back."

She stood up and balanced the weapon in her hand, then stuck the knife carefully in one of the pockets on her pants. The she picked up the gun from the floor and checked it out. Not many rounds left, she noted. "Ok, my people. See you in a few minutes. Do not forget, Sue –Ann, wait for me to knock on the outside of the elevator door seven times before you open."

"Don't take too long to come back, Anna-Maria," Sue-Ann said, as she pressed the elevator "open" button to let her sister out. The doors slowly swung open after that "ding" sound. Pony quickly stepped out of the elevator, and then the doors closed behind her again. The people out there had stepped away from it but were still in the area.

She surveyed the situation.

She was in the front lobby area, and a bunch of men and women dressed in street clothes were milling around in it. She noticed that they all had three things in common. They all had in their hands either a machete knife or machete panga, they all had crazy looking dark sunglasses covering their eyes, and they all wore red bandanas on their head. She counted at least twelve of these people inside the hotel lobby. There was no sign of the lobby attendants or receptionist.

Pony immediately recognized them. They belonged to a notorious Korean killer street gang that called themselves the "Blood for Blood Kkangpae", a Korean criminal gang that specialized in murder for hire activities, drugs deals, and extortion. Their influence was big, extending into North Korea and had mimicking cells in Singapore, China, Japan, Indonesia, Malaysia, and the Nams. They are known to be dangerously ruthless, mindless, and very efficient in their operations. Each branch managed itself, paying special dividend to the parent organization based in south Korea. The principal had used them many times to do outsourced dirty jobs, alongside with the organization's operatives. Pony had encountered some of the gang's contracted people when major Haraabi and herself handled an assignment that also closely involved the principal's operatives. But that was before she and Major Haraabi became intimately close. However, she still never got deeply involved in those operations where this gang was involved, since they were a completely independent organization from hers and were only hired for specific contracts and or assignments.

Pony now realized what Katarina had been talking about. She had brought them in to help kill her and set them up to terminate Pony on sight. And only Katarina would be the one to stop them from doing so. But now that she was upstairs, unconscious, there was no way to pull her dogs off.

"You there, are you the Pony?" one of them, upon seeing her, literally shouted out, sarcastically perhaps, at the same time pointing a double-edged long knife at her.

Pony sensed the anger and craziness in the voice of the man asking the question and braced herself for yet another inevitable fight for, and perhaps of, her life. Her body became so tense that she could feel it in her veins, and every joint in her body experienced that wave of a grinding reaction people experience when suddenly exposed to frigid air. Her bare feet pressed hard into the floor as she slightly spread her legs out in a slow, sliding motion. Her heart rate rose to a faster, erratic beat, and her eyes suddenly felt very dry, feeling like she had just not too long ago consumed several cups of super caffeinated coffee or tea. She automatically leaked her lips, doing it left to right, twice. Placing the gun on the floor mat she was standing on in front of the elevator, she brought her hands together and pulled a thick steel - wired, retainer bracelet all the way down from her right shoulder joint and into her right hand, clenching her fist tight and hence forcing tiny steel spikes to pop out of it. The spikes now lined the entire outer side of clenched fist. She flexed this hand for a few seconds and then relaxed.

But only Pony knew about this reactivating response of her body mechanism. She knew that her body had just flipped into a full-fledged defensive and survival fighting mode. In this mode, she knew she was ready to kill, her brain telling her to fight and kill in order to prevail. It called on all, and beyond, the survival combat training she had experienced at the hands of merciless trainers who had assaulted her body over and over again until it sustained the momentum of stupendous resilience and the deadly level of a mind so void of pain, emotion, and second - thought reactions, that all that was left was the instinct to mercilessly tear apart and destroy with immense speed, strength, and timing capability.

Even her instructors were alarmed at the level of madness she was capable of crossing into when pushed to these levels and had placed her into periodic psychological evaluations. And every one of her psychologists had issued the same warning, and that was to stop pushing her anymore into these variably random, extreme tension modes. Her mind had reached the irreversible levels of deadly or lethal reaction to any potential threats towards her survival and was now a matter of response to any sensed deadly provocation, which they deemed a "hair trigger" balance. Her training then became limited to physical fitness and refresher courses, and only at her own pace, lest it triggered off a deadly outburst or reaction.

"Yea, I am Pony! What's your problem?" she responded in a raspy tone of voice.

"Ok! Let's kill her, now!" the man screamed the order out. His knife wielding cronies responded right away with the same madness exhibited by their commander, attacking from all sides.

Pony lashed out fast, with sidekicks left and right into their body chests and sides, sending two bodies falling backwards and down, and then blocked a machete wielding arm with her hand, grabbing hard at it and at the same time and twisting. As the attacker's body twisted around and forward into her, Pony grabbed at the slender female body, lifted it off the ground and over her head and then went into a squatting position as machetes came down on her. At least four blades cut or were thrust into the body above her head before she sprung up again and threw it back into the attack crowd, sending that group sprawling onto the floor. Blood spluttered everywhere from the slender attacker's badly maimed body.

Spinning around on her heels, she faced another adversary who was swinging at her. She lunged her attack into his body before his big knife came down from the upright, punching him hard into the right side of his neck with the spiked bracelet fist and tearing into his flesh. The man screamed in pain, let go of the big knife and clutched at his neck. Pony hit him with three more hard punches to his mid chest and abdominal areas. Body slamming him out of the way, she picked up his big knife and turned around to meet two knife wielders coming at her with fury. They both chopped at her almost simultaneously, but she was able to ward them off with the big knife in her hand by using its big blade to block theirs. Pony quickly backtracked as she continued fending off their deadly blows, getting them used to that routine, but then suddenly went down into a squat and viciously swiped at their abdomens in one vicious, wide spin, slitting their abdominal walls

open, and then spun back into upright position using both her heels as pivoting points.

As the two attackers doubled over, pony leapt from her position, her feet landed on their backs and then bounced off their bodies, the big manchette raised high. She brought it down hard at the next bewildered attacker's right arm, completely severing it off the body. The limb fell on the floor, the hand still holding a big knife. There was a bone-chilling scream from the attacker as a stream of blood gushed out of his body from the site where the limb was severed off . Then the man collapsed onto the floor, on his knees, still howling loudly and going into massive seizure activity. Spinning the big knife in her hand, Pony retreated, her back to the elevator door again, and assessed the situation. In less than three minutes five of her attackers were down already.

Now the rest of her aggressors hesitated as they too took in the situation. The man who had shouted out the attack order glared at her madly. She stared back at him with equal hostility. The two pairs of raging eyes locked, and it became very clear that they were both prepared to uphold the fierce brawl to the end.

"Attack!" the man shouted.

But before they could respond to the order, Pony jumped forward and swiped at the group with the double-edged machete knife in her hand… right left right left and right again! The movements were so fast they all took a few steps back in an attempt to stay clear of the menacing blade. Good, now that you all have the fear, you are bound to make mistakes, Pony acknowledged in her mind. There was a machete knife laying on the floor next to a still body of one of her adversaries that she had downed. She quickly picked it up, instantly arming herself with two big knives. At the same time, her eyes were darting left and right, everywhere, watching and waiting for any move, perhaps a shuffle of feet…

Someone shouted out something, but Pony was so tense to even comprehend what was said, and then they attacked. They split up into two groups and were again attacking from both sides. Lashing out skillfully with both knives, Pony went into a whirling momentum, effectively blocking off and preventing the multiple blades from reaching her body, ushering in an intense clash and bang of metal that produced fire sparks and went on for at least one minute, and then she changed pattern, suddenly lowering herself down and adopting a frog stance, at the same time lashing out with both knives at several of her attacker's lower extremities. Bodies went down immediately. Vertical, went both blades as she used them for firm points to hoist herself up again and went at it on one side only against a lone figure that had split up from the group following the limb slash. The separated attacker could not hold up to the sudden, fierce double – knife attack that unleashed rapid hard blows on him and in seconds went down, body sliced up into a bloody mess. It was a continuous assault as she attacked a group of four who appeared freaked out by her vicious knife play, and her knives slashed and at all parts of their upper bodies, inflicting deadly injury. They all went down, fast!

But then, as Pony straightened her body up again to face any other remaining adversary, something hard slammed into the left side of her body and sent her sprawling on to the floor, and inevitably causing her to lose grasp of both knives. The blow was very painful, but she had no time to mull over it. Turning over, she found herself face to face with the man who had been shouting out the attack orders, his bloodshot eyes a mockery of the wacky grin on his face.

He had managed to sneak in a flying kick at her left rib side while she was dealing with the last lone adversary and that's what had sent her sprawling to the floor. She was quick to notice that he was wearing a pair of military boots, the steel-toe type, a clear reason for such intense pain from that blow. And now he had this long double-edged blade pointed at, and very close, to her. She, on the other hand, now appeared to be completely unarmed.

This heavily tattooed, well-muscled, lean bodied man looked to be a skilled knife fighter, a relentless killer who knew no bounds. She could tell by the way he handled the big knife and the fierce, blood- curdling look and reactions. And now, with no visible weapon to counteract his, he was bound to slice and or chop his adversary to pieces with ease, a supposedly clean kill. She tried to get up, but he responded by swiping at the attempt with the deadly knife blade.

"Scared now, huh, Pony girl?" the killer said, the wacky grin getting wider. "To tell you the truth, though, I totally hand it down to you, girl. I have never encountered such resistance, such a fight. Look at all my people, hmmm? They are all down, dead, injured or damaged beyond repair. Incompetent, stupid people, I declare them. And yet I brought in some of my best. My client was very right about you. She warned me that she's hiring me because she didn't think she could win the battle alone when it came to you. She told me you are a force to reckon with, that you are one of the best combat fighters in the game, a feared legend in your organization. But look at you now, huh? The great Pony, on the floor before me, eyes full of fear and begging for her life! Oh, what a privilege it is for me! To tell you the truth, I am going to enjoy killing you. I am going chop you up, slice your sleezy pretty body to pieces, every bit of it, until it's all nothing but a bloody, minced-up mess! Wait a minute! I think I will cut your head off and take it back to my boss, evidence that I killed a great one, and that way I improve on my image of greatness. And I think I will also cut one of your hands off and keep it for myself, hang it on a wall in my house as a souvenir, a memory of one of my greatest encounters."

"Then why don't you just shut up and get over with it, huh?" Pony responded with unyielding fierceness in her voice. She was laying on her back now, her arms behind her, supporting the rest of her body. "I think you have fantasized so much about killing me that you have completely lost your mind. Soo much that now you are just a washed-up, delirious, miserable, crazy, hallucinating fool. You have turned into this deranged, soulless boogie man with a messed up, twisted mind! That's why you're talking too much instead of doing what you're supposed to do!"

"What… did you call me?" the man angrily shouted back at her, the wacky grin instantly disappearing. "You, and not me, are the one who's begging for your life now. You're such an insolent little bitch, Pony! Do you even know I am, huh? I am Eddie Jeong, master knife fighter, responsible for hundreds of deaths by simply using this blade. You hear me? Many have died of this blade. It's sacred! You are not going to be the exception, bitch. And just like the rest of those dead people, you mean nothing to me! You all mean nothing to me! So instead of acting like you are the one in control, I suggest that you now prepare to die!"

"You are constantly haunted by those hundreds you have killed. I can clearly see that now. That's why you are so deranged, unstable, and worthless, even before your own god, which is the sword in your hand!" Pony shouted back.

"SHUT UUUUUUUP!" the man shouted even louder, his breathing now noticeably irregular as his chest heaved up and down. He slowly started raising the knife up and his eyes grew wider and redder as he glared down at her.

"Now, or never!" Pony spoke to herself, but inside her mind. She suddenly sprang forward from the floor and landed a heavy left fist blow with an extended knuckle into the mid- chest area of his body. The hollowing, painful, powerful blow or punch forced the man to instantly belch and stumble backwards, losing his balance. Now had it been a regular man off the street, he would have been thrown off his feet or forced to double over in pain by that strike.

But not this master knife fighter! Even as he stumbled, master Eddie Jeong remained on his feet and was able to offensively wield the knife at Pony. But Pony jumped clear, the deadly blade swishing through empty space. Whipping out the dragon-claw knife from pocket, she moved in again, but not without first issuing a fast, crushing flying kick at his knife-wielding hand and sending the big, long knife flying out of his grasp. Side stepping his body to the left, she grabbed at his right wrist with her left hand, raised it up, and then lashed out in an up and down slash with the dragon-claw, slicing half his face, neck, abdominal wall and upper groin areas on the right side of his body open. Spinning around him while using her feet as a pivot and her body crouched, her knife wielding hand went around his front mid-section, and then she rapidly withdrew back to the right, the dragon claw slicing at his waist. Then as she sprung up again, the dragon claw changed positions from right to left hand and then she instantly brought it forcefully upwards, thrusting it into his body somewhere below the right armpit. She then jumped away from him, bringing the knife out with her. As he stumbled forward, now badly injured, she attacked again, striking out again at his neck with the knife still in her left hand, right to left. Rapidly switching hands again, the dragon-claw fell into her right hand as she swung back, slicing at his neck again, left to right. Then she jumped clear and stood still, poised.

In a matter of less than or approximately one minute, she had inflicted so much profound damage to his body!

Master knife fighter Eddie Jeong collapsed to the floor, his body spasming even as the multiple wounds, inflicted upon him by an adversary using a weapon from the same family of weaponry of his professional choice, profusely oozed blood.

"Now you join the hundreds that you have slaughtered with your so - called sacred blade, Master Jeong," Pony said, breathing heavily. "Hopefully you get to be buried with it, because with its master down, the world has no use for it anymore!"

Pony looked around her, assessing the situation. Excluding their commander, all twelve people were down, either laying still in their own pool of blood or injured and crying out for help. Pony loosened her grip on the metallic dragon claw knife and the heavy, metallic, double-edged combat knife fell on the carpeted floor, making a single buffered sound. Holding her left side which was still painfully sore from that kick implemented by master Jeong, she then slowly made her way through the mess to the elevator door, banged hard on it with her clenched right fist seven times, and stood back.

In less than five seconds the elevator opened, and her little sister ran out, instantly putting her arms around her waist.

"I knew you would be back for us," Sue-Ann said, hugging her big sister tightly. Pony slowly rubbed her back, up and down. Suddenly letting go, Sue-Ann stepped back and looked up at her big sister, giving her a sad, worried look. "Anna-Maria, are hurt?"

"It's ok, Sue-Ann. It's time to get out of here now. Let me help Mommy up from the floor," Pony said, smiling grimly at the little girl. "We still need to get her, and you, to a hospital."

She stepped into the elevator, pressed the standby mode button so the elevator won't close, and squatted down before her mother, who was slumped in one corner of the elevator, her eyes closed, her arms on her side. Her face had completely lost color and she was completely motionless. Pony suddenly felt very queasy, the feeling of seeing her mother like this suddenly overwhelming her.

"Mom… mother… please wake up," She anxiously said, gently shaking her mom's still body. "Mother, it's me, Anna-Maria. It's all clear now, and I am going to get you out of here and take you to a hospital. Please open your eyes. Wake up mom, talk to me, will you? I need you to wake up and talk to me!"

But there was no response from the older woman. Pony now became frantic and shook her mother's body more vigorously. But mom remained still. Her heart started beating fast as she placed her fingers on the left side of mom's neck. There was no pulse. She felt both wrists. There was no pulse in both of them and her hands were very cold.

Her mother was gone. Mom was dead.

Pony's left hand slowly went to her mouth and tears instantly filled her eyes. She started sobbing, unable to hold back. But even her sobbing was choked back as she didn't know what to do at the moment. Her brain froze, her heart was skipping beats, and she was beginning to sweat. Gently shoving her little sister to the side, and without saying a word, she straightened up and stepped out of the elevator again. She then instantly started throwing up, coughing and retching as she did so. After an exhausting moment of non-stop gagging, Pony finally turned around slowly and looked at her mother's limp, still body again. Then she looked down at her little sister.

"Anna-Maria, why is mommy not waking up?" Sue Ann asked, looking up at her big sister and putting her arm around hers.

"Mommy is… gone, Sue-Ann," Pony replied, more tears streaming down her face. "There is no more mommy for us, Sue-Ann. It's me and you are now."

"What do you mean?" The little girl asked, her gaze moving from Pony to her mommy and then back to Pony again. "You mean mommy is dead?"

"Yes, sis, our mommy is dead, and I am so sorry," Pony blurted out the words, taking Sue-Ann into her arms. "No more mommy for us."

Sue-Ann started crying, but her tears soon became tears of anguish. She suddenly disengaged herself from her sister's arms, glared up at her, and screamed. "This is all your fault, Anna-Maria! You brought these people to us, and now they have killed Mommy! Your bad friends killed my mommy! You're just as bad as they are!"

"I am sorry, Sue-Ann, I am so sorry," Pony responded. "I am sorry I failed my family, that I put you in harm's way. I am sorry I failed to fully protect both of you. I tried and failed. But I swear to the living God that nobody will ever mess with you again! I will protect you …"

"Like you protected mommy, huh?" Sue-Ann shouted back. "You couldn't protect mommy, so I don't trust you anymore to protect me! I can't be with you. I don't want to be with you anymore, Anna – Maria! I want to be alone!"

With that, Sue-Ann, now sobbing loudly, dashed past her big sister and ran out of the elevator, headed for the main exit, an assembly of revolving doors. Realizing what was happening and what could happen if those revolving doors hit her little sister, Pony ran after her. The little girl was understandably in deep fear and emotional distress, terrified of seeing her mother, all bloody and dead on the floor of the elevator. But then the revolving doors at the entrance suddenly turned and the sole figure of a tall, elegant woman entered the lobby. She stopped when the little girl suddenly bumped into her.

"Aww, hello there, darling… What's the big hurry?" Ms. Zeal asked Sue-Ann, smiling down at the little girl. Sue-Ann slowly took a few steps back and stared up at the tall woman.

Pony caught up with Sue-Ann and raised her right hand, palm up, at Ms. Zeal, and then shook her head quickly as her left arm went around Sue-Ann's shoulders. "Whoever you are, please don't harm us. We just want to get out of here, me and my little sister. I also need to get my mother out of here… she's back there, in the elevator, and she is dead!"

"I am not here to do harm to you and your little sister. I am here to help you," Ms. Zeal replied, still smiling broadly. "Did you say your mother is back there in the elevator, dead?"

"Yes. So, unless you're going to help me carry her body out of that elevator and out of this wretched, evil, building, all I ask is that you please don't interfere with what I must do," Pony replied. "Just stay out of our way."

"You! You are that nice lady who's been talking to me for a long time," Sue-Ann suddenly said to Ms. Zeal, pointing her little finger.

Pony looked down at her little sister, puzzled, and then looked at Ms. Zeal. "Sue-Ann, you mean you know this lady? She's been talking to you for a long time, you just said. How come you didn't tell me about her? When and how did you start talking to her?"

Sue-Ann turned around slowly and faced her sister. "Yes, she's been talking to me for a long time. I have been seeing and talking to her in my dreams."

"In your… what? Did you say your Dreams?" Pony exclaimed, staring at her sister in disbelief. She faced Ms Zeal again. "Please excuse my little sister. She is delirious, probably the side effect of all these things suddenly happening around her the past few hours, and the death of our mother. "Sue-Ann, come on, it's going to be fine. I know mommy is gone, but we going to be ok. I will take good care of you."

"I am afraid all that she's just told you is true," Ms. Zeal said, still smiling. "I have visited with your sister several times and yes, in her dreams, prepping her for this very moment in her life. It's a long and complicated story, Anna-Maria, which I will explain later, I promise you. Right now, I need to take a look at your mother."

Pony took several steps back, dragging Sue-Ann with her, eyes looking like two live electric coils as she glared at Ms. Zeal, and then she said, "I can't believe I am hearing this craziness! Wait a minute, how do you even know my name? I think I am also going crazy. But now, whoever you are, whatever you are, I warn you right, stay away from us. Stay out of our way, or I will be forced to kill you!"

"But she's always been nice to me," Sue-Ann said quickly, and tried to free herself from Pony's arm, but she was no match for her big sister's strength, coupled with the determination to protect her. There was a machete knife on the floor a few inches away from where the two sisters were standing, its long blade smeared with dried red blood. Pony spotted it, and immediately reached out for it. Ms. Zeal did not move an inch, but her eyes followed Pony's every move. As Pony's fingers got to it, the big knife suddenly moved away from her fingers and became air borne. It was as if some powerful magnet was pulling it, and as the two sisters looked on, it floated past them and landed into Ms. Zeal's

173

now stretched out open hand. They both stared at Ms. Zeal, disbelief in their eyes.

"Like I said, I am not here to do you harm, I am here to help you," Ms. Zeal said in a clear, light voice. She dropped the big knife down to the floor, letting it float downwards from her hand like it was stringing down on from a yo-yo. "But first, I need to get to your mother."

"My mother is dead, you witch! And I am the least intimidated by your sorcery tricks! I will do whatever it takes to protect my little sister, for she's everything to me now!" Pony shouted in anguish. She looked down at her bare feet. They were full of cuts, bleeding, and with pain. She was tired and spent. She looked up again at Ms Zeal and continued with her verbal torrent. "Why can't you just leave us alone, anyway? Just go on with your business! Who do you think you are to just suddenly show up and engage us into your whatever agenda you have? Just let us be, so… so… that we can be at peace, so that we can go bury, and then mourn our mother, that's all I am asking of everybody in this world right now!"

There was a blinding flash of light, a vision - blurring flash of lightening before the two sisters, forcing their eyes to momentarily close for a few seconds. When they blinked again, the tall, slender woman now stood several yards away in front of them and had two big white wings attached to her back, all spread out. Her feet were both slightly off the floor. The two sisters stared at the electrifying figure, seemingly dumbfounded yet looking very frightened.

"I am, who I am. Do you believe now? And I am going on with my business as we speak, because my business is you!" Ms Zeal said, no longer smiling or even chewing on the gum. Her voice was deep and hollow. Her big wings were sparkling with a lot of small shiny yellow lights that went glowed on and off. Her eye shades had vanished to reveal pure blue eyes with no pupils. Above her head was a gleaming, yellow halo that emitted a light so bright it lit up the entire room. Her long hair gently floated on her back. For about a full minute, the angel floated above the floor, right there in front of them to see, and then slowly descended back down, wings flapping gently. The sisters stared at her transformation, with their mouths wide open in astonishment.

For the next five or so minutes, the two girls, now holding on to each other tightly, blinked repeatedly, shocked by the sudden revelation. They were clearly shaken to the core. Pony suddenly passed out, collapsing to the floor. It was too much for her mind to handle. Only little Sue -Ann remained up, staring back at the angel. To her, it was simply fascinating, a "wooow" treat. Her eyes still teary, she faintly smiled.

Her big wings flapping gently and creating a gentle breeze in the room, the angel slowly moved forward, walked past little Sue – Ann and Pony's unresponsive body.

"Over here, little girl," she called from behind Sue - Ann. Sue - Ann slowly turned around to see Ms. Zeal standing outside of the entrance to the elevator, smiling at, her mouth swirling around slowly. She was chewing on that piece gum again, her eye shades were back on again, and she now had no wings and no halo above her head. Ms. Zeal then stepped into the elevator.

Sue–Ann turned around and slowly walked back to the elevator entry. Inside the elevator, Ms. Zeal had knelt down, and both of her hands were now on her mommy's body.

"Since you are an angel, can you please bring back my mommy to me?" Sue-Ann asked Ms. Zeal, her voice calm and clear.

That question was none other than an exhibit of the innocence of pure, unreserved faith that only young children can possess.

"Together with your pure faith and love, I think I am going to try to do that," Ms. Zeal said, her voice resonating the same calmness as the little girl's. It was all quiet in the lobby now, the quietest it presumably could have been since it was built. Nothing moved, nothing jiggled, not even someone's breathing was audible. It was like time had come to a standstill. After about two minutes that felt like eternity for those physically present at this interim moment, Ms. Zeal slowly got off her knees and stood up. Her face was now grim as she looked down at the little girl before her, and for a few seconds she stared into Sue -Ann's eyes. Of course, the little girl could not see her eyes, because Ms. Zeal's eyes were completely hidden behind the strange - looking dark sunglasses. Ms. Zeal gently placed right her hand on the little girl's right shoulder and left it there for at least half a minute. Her hand felt very warm and comforting. Then she stepped out of the elevator, looked around the lobby area at the human damage caused by Pony's most recent aggressive interactions, and slowly shook her head. She then made her way to where Pony was still passed out on the floor. She squatted down next to the unconscious woman and looked down at her.

"It's a terrible mess you are leaving behind in this building, Anna Maria, and I wish I could help them," Ms. Zeal said. "But their directives have the heavy presence of the devil's traits, which is not my path. You, on the other side, still have the presence of the light in you, even though this presence still needs to be stronger. I will help you to understand it. That, together with your little sister's unwavering faith in me and the purity of her young soul, together with your repeated pleas to the heavens, has saved your day. For these other people, what happened to them is what happens when you human beings enter a deal with the devil himself. It's a point of no return. Meet me outside when you are ready, Anna-Maria. I will be waiting for you there."

After saying those words, she gently touched Pony's forehead. Pony's eyes immediately opened, and she sat up. The tall, slender woman rose up and walked away, exiting the lobby. Pony did not hear the revolving doors swing, but she could feel that the slender woman's presence was no longer there. Slowly she raised her head up and then saw her little sister, Sue – Ann, standing outside the elevator entrance, looking at her with a big smile on her face.

"See, you were wrong all this time, Anna-Maria," Sue-Ann said, pointing a little finger into the elevator. "Mommy is not dead. Come look for yourself. I think the lady from my dreams, the angel, woke mommy up."

"What… what happened?" Pony asked. She felt fresh, like she had just woken up from a good deep sleep and just needed to stretch. She slowly got up from the floor.

"You fell asleep while standing up and fell on the floor, Anna – Marie. Right after you saw the angel!" Sue Ann said gleefully. "Can you please come here now?"

Anna-Maria's heart skipped as she stared at her little sister, trying to figure out why the little girl appeared to be so cheerful. She took a few strides towards the elevator, then stopped. She felt no pain from her legs or feet. She looked down at her feet. The bleeding scrapes and cuts were completely gone!

She shook her head slowly, perhaps in wonder, and then quickly made her way to the elevator entrance. When she finally stood next to Sue-Ann at the entrance of the elevator, both girls now watched as their mother got up from the floor of the elevator, but only to fall back down on it. She was shaky.

"Mom? You are alive? But I don't understand! You clearly left us! You died! And I was very sure of that!" Pony exclaimed as she stepped into the elevator immediately to assist the older lady up. Sue- Ann joined her and both girls now hugged their mother tightly. "It must be some kind of miracle, and nothing else, for this to happen!"

"What are you talking about? And where are we at exactly? what are we doing here? Why are your eyes wet? Why are you crying?" their mother asked, her voice shaky. "It feels so cold in here. I need a coat!"

"It's ok, Mom, It's now ok. I will take you to the hospital now," Pony said, tears still running down her face. She helped her mom off the floor, helping her straighten up. Her gait was somewhat unstable, but the older woman was able to stay up on her feet with support. She pulled back her mother's heavily soiled, blood-stained blouse to look at the gunshot wound.

There was no wound! It was gone!

Pony stood back in awe. She felt the area with her hand. There was nothing there, not even a scar. It just felt warm to touch. Pony looked around her, then peered into the lobby. There was nobody, of course. She was trying to see if the tall slender woman was there. She slowly shook her head again and taking hold of her mother's hand, she slowly walked her out of the elevator. Little Sue – Ann held on to the other hand.

"I knew it. I knew that the angel would wake mommy up," Sue – Ann said with a giggle.

"And all I had to do was to believe." "Come now, Sue-Ann, let's get out of here." Pony said quietly.

"Anna-Maria, what happened to all these people on the floor in this room?" her mother asked, looking around her with dread in her eyes, as the three of them stepped out of the elevator and into the lobby, slowly making their way to the revolving door entrance, through the maze of bodies on the floor of the bloodied lobby. "Did you beat them up?"

"I stopped them from harming you and Sue - Ann, Mom," Pony answered back slowly. "Sue -Ann, Mom, I want you to close your eyes until we get out of here. I don't want you to look at all this mess, lest it creates everlasting memories. You've seen enough for now. I will lead you out of here. I will let you know when to open your eyes again."

"Who told them to harm us?" Sue-Ann asked but closing her eyes as she held on to her sister's other free arm. The other arm was holding on their mother. "Why would they want to do harm to me and mommy? We didn't do anything bad to them."

Pony suddenly stopped walking and closed her eyes briefly, breathing in heavily. She reopened them again with a sigh, and then slightly turning her head around to the left and looking down at her little sister she then said, "The devil sent them, Sue-Ann. They made a deal with the devil, to harm me, you, and mommy. But I was there to stop them. We're all safe now, little girl, and that's what matters most. Nobody will ever do harm to you and mommy again."

When they finally stepped out of the building and into the warm, welcoming glare of the afternoon sun outside, Pony told the two to open their eyes.

There was hardly any people on the street anymore. Everyone was either hiding somewhere or had run away. A few overly terrified people stood on the sidewalks, some on their mobile phones, some shouting for help, others just looking lost, not knowing what to do. A few cars and other objects were either still burning or had smoldering fire on them. This part of the street, in front of and between the two hotels building, was littered with all kinds of debris, some not easy to identify. Sirens could be heard in a distance.

The big public transport bus, now empty, was still parked in the middle of the street. Right in front of it was a gleaming black jaguar sedan car, with both doors on the driver's side open. Standing next to

178

it was the slender tall woman. She smiled when she saw them. Pony now remembered it all. It was the same car that had earlier come to a screeching halt as she left her mother's apartment block, rushing in response to Katarina's call. She recognized the smiling driver in the car. It was her.

Sue-Ann suddenly let go of her sister's arm and ran ahead, to Ms. Zeal. The latter opened her arms wide, bending down at the knees to receive the little girl. Pony stopped in mid- stride to watch her little sister dash over to this woman she still viewed as a total stranger and hug her tightly. Whatever it was between the two individuals, it was too late for her to intervene, she told herself.

As Ms. Zeal scooped up the little girl in her arms and held her tightly, Sue-Ann giggled and then whispered into her ear. "Thank you very much for waking up my Mommy!"

"You are very much welcome, little friend," Ms. Zeal responded back. "But now it is time to get all of you to a place of safety and where your mommy and big sister can rest and heal more."

Pony finally made it to the car. Her mother, looking somewhat withered and drained, looked up at Ms. Zeal, smiled, but looked down again without saying a word. Pony just stood there and stared at Ms. Zeal.

"You and mom, get in the back seat of the car," Ms. Zeal said, staring back at Pony. "Your sister can ride with me in the front, with your permission, of course. She will be safe I promise you that."

Pony hesitated, then asked. "Where are you taking us?"

"To a place where you will be safe," Ms. Zeal replied. "But for now, I need you to get into the car so we can get out of here before your police arrives here to start their always blindsided investigations. We don't have not time for their interrogations. Time is of essence here, Anna-Maria."

"I don't understand," Pony responded back.

"It's a long story, but I will explain later, I promise," Ms Zeal said.

Mom suddenly coughed, a prolonged cough that sent her body into a heavy spasm. She almost collapsed down to the ground, but Pony managed to hold on tight to her. "Well, ok. But I need some help here, please. Help me get my mother into the car. She is still weak, and I can hardly hold on to her."

Ms. Zeal gently put Sue-Ann down. "Alright little girl, crawl yourself via the driver's seat to the other side while I help your sister get your mommy into the car."

Sue-Ann did what she was told without hesitation. Ms. Zeal now turned her attention to Pony and her mother.

"Here, Anna-Maria, let me take over," she said, holding out her arms. Pony shifted her mom's body into Ms. Zeal's arms. Her mother suddenly became awake and alert and was able to cling on to Ms. Zeal's body. To Pony's astonishment, the tall slender woman easily moved her mom around, like she was weightless, easily and gently getting her into the car, and her mother then buckled herself up. "There you are. Now you can get in on the other side, Anna-Maria."

"Are you some kind of paranormal military force or something?" Pony asked, confronting Ms. Zang directly and staring at the gleaming gun grip that was sticking out of Ms. Zeal's belt. "I see you have some kind of gun on your body. And I have never seen a gun's grip so shiny like that before."

"It's one hell of a gun, I tell you. One that you have never seen or even experienced before," Ms. Zeal said, smiling broadly. "And I am about to use it one more time. Care to try it out?"

"Aaah … I don't know. I am still tired and beat-up, and I don't feel like shooting at anything or anyone right now," Pony replied. "And I thought you said time is of essence, that we need to get out of here quickly. Has that, all of a sudden, changed?"

"Nothing has changed, so time is still vital, but this is something I need to do before we leave," Ms. Zeal said. "It's already been mandated that I do it. And it involves using this gun."

"You are not going to kill us, are you?" Pony said, stepping back.

Ms. Zeal laughed lightly and shook her head slowly. "Really, Anna Maria? And why would I do that? Besides, if I were to do that, I would have done so already."

"Well, lately it looks like everyone wants to kill me, and my family," Pony responded back.

"On the contrary, I am here to protect you," Ms. Zeal said, and then pulled the gun out of her belt. "What I am going to do in the next few seconds is part of what I will explain to you in a few minutes."

She adjusted the safety catch off the gun and then adjusted the magazine. "All ready. You sure you don't want to try it out? It's going to be an out of this world experience for you, Anna-Maria, because my gun isn't like any of yours. This will also give you the chance to end a bad part of your life once and for all."

For some reason, Pony suddenly felt obligated to try it out. It was like something was compelling her to do so. "What do you mean, a bad part of my life? What are you going to shoot at?"

"This building holds a lot of evil secrets and is tainted with the blood of those who died in it at the hands of merciless, human murderers," Ms. Zeal said. "It's been used as the devil's slaughterhouse and has spirits of tormented souls in it that need to be freed. It must be destroyed. Besides, it has your nemesis in it, and she's still alive. Her soul still yearns to kill you, and if she survives today, she will still come after you and your loved ones, wherever you are in this world. You must completely eliminate her before she wakes up and gets out of this building."

"Katarina!" Pony uttered, remembering that she had not killed her but simply knocked her out of consciousness. "How do you know about this building and about her conflict with me?"

"Like I said, it's a long story." Ms. Zeal replied.

"Here, give me the gun," Pony said, stretching her right hand out. "So, all I have to do is to point and shoot at the building, right?"

"Yes, that's all you have to do," Ms. Zeal replied. "Like I said, this weapon is unlike any you have ever seen or used before." She handed the gun to Pony, gun grip first. "Just squeeze off one shot. That's all you will need."

The moment Pony touched the gun's grip and rotated it in her palm for balance, Ms. Zeal mumbled some words and suddenly something came out of the grip and completely wrapped around Pony's entire right arm. In her hand, it felt like a perfectly fitting rubber glove, yet made of some metallic or steel fabric. Pony immediately got frightened and tried to shake it off, but her hand was completely snagged.

"What the hell is going on here? Get this thing off me, now!" she screamed at the gun's owner. She tried pulling with her other hand, but all that effort was in vain.

"Calm down, Anna-Maria," Ms. Zeal said responded, raising both her hands up and confronting the obviously suspicious, freaked out woman before her. "I keep telling you, it's a special weapon, one not of your world. Right now, all it's doing is getting to know you, registering your DNA in its system so it can work with your body system's schematics. That way you can use it. It can't just work with any one or everyone."

"Then how come it's picking on me to use it?" Pony hastily asked, as she quickly and closely examined the weapon in her hand. "I am just like everyone else out there."

"Because I told it to do so," Ms. Zeal replied in a brisk manner.

"You … what?" Pony asked loudly, shaking her head in total doubt and staring at the woman before her like she was unbelievably crazy.

"You heard me," Ms. Zeal responded back. "Now let's get on with it. The Police is about to arrive on the scene in a couple minutes. Let's give them something to think about. You see that small green button on the side of the gun, it's an activation switch. Press down on it gently with one of your fingers from the other hand. The weapon is going to beep, and the green button will turn red. Then the side body will shift upwards like a rolling lever to reveal another button, a red button. Touch the that red button and it will turn green. You will hear a rapid tapping or clicking sound, four times in total. Make sure your legs are apart and firmly planted to the ground, then aim and squeeze the trigger."

Pony quickly followed the instructions, spreading her legs out firmly, pointed the gun at the hotel building, and squeezed the trigger. The gun vibrated, the activity much like an electronic body massager applied to her hand. The sensation systematically gripped her arm and went up and down from hand to shoulder joint and back. Then the muzzle flashed a high intensity spark of pure blue flame, which was followed by a short-lived reverberation as the projectile left the gun. Pony had never experienced anything like this before in her entire military style life! And then just as the first set of police cars pulled up on the street, the projectile hit its target. A loud rambling boom occurred, and the entire front of the building collapsed down. It was as if the structure had just been hit by a big missile!

"Wow!" Pony exclaimed, her eyes popping wide open.

"Squeeze the trigger one more time!" Ms. Zeal shouted out. "We need a total clean out. A complete erosion!"

Pony found herself automatically responding to the order and the same sequence repeated itself. Vibration, her arm tightened, the gun muzzle flashed with the intense blue flame or spark, the reverberation, and boom! This time, before her own eyes, the entire building exploded and then came crushing down, erupting into flames and thick black smoke.

"That's enough! Let's get out here," Ms. Zeal shouted out again. "Get into the car, Anna – Maria, now!"

Pony woke up from her shocked trance and quickly dashed around to the other side of the car. Finding the door already open, she jumped into the back seat next to her mother. The door slammed itself before she could reach for it, like someone was out there waiting for her to get in and close it behind her. With Ms. Zeal already behind the wheel, the gleaming jaguar drove off the street curbside and into the road, speeding off and away from the scene. Pony briefly turned around and looked at the crumbled site. It was now a big, blazing inferno!

"What the hell just happened out there?" she asked Ms. Zeal, turning around and leaning forward in the chair. "That's unlike anything I have ever seen! It's not normal!"

"I know, I know …" Ms. Zeal responded, not taking her eyes off the road. "But I warned you about the experience. I told you it's an out of this world weapon …"

"Stop the car, and pull over, right now!" Pony said to her. She raised the gun and pointed it at Ms. Zeal's head. "Do it or I will pull the trigger and blow you up!"

"Then you will kill us all, Anna-Maria. Put the gun away. Don't be stupid!" Her mother suddenly said, in a clear and loud, strong voice.

"Stay out of this, mom!" Pony shouted back. "I just need answers to all this, now! Who are you and where are you taking us?"

But Ms. Zeal sighed and then pulled over to the side of the road. As she did this, the gun in Pony's hand suddenly unlocked itself from her hold, and suddenly became very heavy, pulling down on her hand. Before she could do anything, it fell out of her hand and to the floor of the car between her feet. Pony stared down at the weapon, looking horrified, and then folded her feet up into the seat.

Ms. Zeal killed the engine and slowly turned sideways in her seat to secure a view of the rest of the car's occupants. She slowly took off her dark sunglasses to reveal a pair of all steel blue eyes with no pupils in them whatsoever. Her adult audience immediately pulled back, already scared. Sue – Ann just stared at Ms Zeal, a look of wonder on her face.

"Don't be scared. I just don't have pupils in my eyes, and that's why I wear the dark shades all the time, so as not to scare you humans," she said, sounding clear and concise. "Ok, Now listen up. I am not human like you, not even close. I am an angel, from heaven above, and part of a group of angels sent to your world to challenge evil and restore God's order. The weapon you just fired off is referred to as an angel blow torch. Its ammunitions are versatile, can blow up anything to a magnitude of unbelievable intensity, but all depending on how I order it. In other words, I control the magnitude with my mind. I was sent out to help you, and that's something I have been doing for some time now, although invisibly."

"Why are you helping us?" Pony insisted, pulling herself back further into the seat, and getting closer to her mother. "Until today, I have never met or seen you anywhere."

"Oh yes, you asked for help. You cried out to God," Ms. Zeal said. "You cried out for protection over your family, which is your mother and little sister. But it all began when you unknowingly decried the evil that was besetting your man friend. You told him that what he was about to do wasn't right and tried to persuade him out of it. And we were listening in. But when he self-centeredly unleashed the evil on you, a decision he heavily regretted later, you knew that your family would be earmarked as a means of both getting to you and retaliation. You pleaded with God in heaven to help you save them. Heaven heard your sincere pleas, and so I was released out of my invisibility to deal with the matter. The difference is, we already knew all this was going to happen before it even happened. So, I started watching over your family through your little sister over a year ago. At the same time, I was listening in to all your thoughts, Anna – Maria. So, you see, I am here to protect all of you, to get you out of harm's way by taking you to a place where you will be safe, a place where the devil or the devil's cohorts can't get to you."

"If that's the case, then why did you let me go through all that fighting in that building?" Pony said. "My mom got shot at, my little sister is traumatized, afraid and worn out, her mind probably affected forever by images of the dead and the injured people in that building. And then look at me, I am all beat up and battered. Looks like you didn't do your job well, angel!"

"Oh yes I did," Ms. Zeal said patiently. "Let me fill you all in on a little secret. Sometimes, we angels, whether it's your guardian angel or a special protector angel like myself, will let you fight, and even conclude, your own human battles. Self-defense is a portion of your human system, fully installed at creation and preset to counter all battles, spiritual or physical. And you were given the free will to modify it in whichever you want. As in your case, Anna-Maria, yours was perfectly modified by other humans to deal with physical combat issues. You're one of the finest human warriors this world of yours has. So, inside that building I simply let you have some fun by letting you do what you do best. I am glad to say you didn't let me down."

"No, you did not!" Pony countered back. "It wasn't as simple as you put it. And at the end of it all, you put the rest of my family in the crosshairs of danger. If you are here to protect us, then explain to me why my mother ended up with a bullet shattering her body. She didn't have to go through all that. Is that what you angels call fun?"

"We allowed that to happen as a lesson to you, to tell you that there is a price to pay when you make deals with the devil," Ms. Zeal replied. "We didn't put a bullet through your mother's body, rather you did. You are the one who put your family in the crosshairs of danger. By the time you realized this fall-out, it was too late. You are very lucky that we responded in time to thwart your demise, Anna-Maria. In reality, even if it appears like it, the devil doesn't play games, and once the fallout begins, it won't stop until you are completely diminished, for you are no longer part and parcel of Satan's plans. And for most humans, it's too late to cross back to us."

"Then how come you didn't let the devil just simply finish me off, that way save my family from all this hustle and pain?" Pony asked. "After all, it's me who made the so -called deal with the devil, not my family."

"The reason is that when we realized that satanic agents had already ensnared you into their deadly plots, we also realized that your demise was imminent but reversible," Ms. Zeal answered back. "And this is because your in-built heavenly element was too strong for them to take you in all the way. You were partially with us and partially theirs. We fought to win your soul back, and finally did. When they realized they had lost, the satanic agents sought you out, and henceforth instigated for your total demise. I was then sent to protect you, but in order get to you I had to go through the innocent being of someone who knew you very well and was part of your genes and blood, which brought me to your little sister. But first, I had to promise your little sister's guardian angel that I will protect her at all costs, especially from the demonic side effects of your deal with the devil. It was I who was inside her when you were held captive in their torture room. I used her to pinpoint, and hence effectively erase the dangerous elements that were about to harm you, using the angel blow torch."

"So, you used my folks as the bait to further your agenda?" Pony persisted. "You put them through all this just to get to me, while they had nothing to do with it. Why? For God's sake you have no right to do that to them. It's ok for you to do what you have to do with me because I am the one who messed up, not them."

"You can call it bait, or whatever your human mind deems it fit to call it," Ms. Zeal answered back, still calm. "The fact is that we are here to further heaven's agenda, and when it comes to that nothing else matters. So, to answer your question as to why we did it that way, it's simply because we can. We do have heaven's mandate to do whatever we have to do."

"Well, your job is done here, thank you very much. we are out of the danger now so drop us off to the nearest hospital so that we can make sure our bodies are fully recovered, and then you be on your merry way out. We can take it from there," Pony said. "Please convey our sincere gratitude to God and all the other angels when you get back to heaven."

"I am not going anywhere with you, Anna-Maria. I am going with her!" Sue-Ann suddenly said, staring at her sister with an angry look. "She's nice and she woke mommy up whereas you could not. So, I am going wherever she goes, wherever she's taking us!"

"That goes for me too," Her mother added without hesitation. "She brought me back from the dead, Anna-Maria, so I can take more care of both of you. I fully owe her my life! She's my angel too! Besides, your friends messed up my apartment before they kidnapped us and now I have nowhere to go. So, I am going to do what she says, as she says it. That means I am going with her too."

"So, you see, you are on your own now," Ms. Zeal said to Pony. "Don't you see it, huh, Anna-Maria? The devil and his advocates are already trying to own you back. And once they get hold of you again, they will carry on with their intention, and that is to completely destroy you. You can only be safe if you come with me."

"Please sister, come with us," Sue-Ann said, turning around in her seat in the front to face her big sister in the backseat. "Don't you see? This angel loves us, I know so because I have known her for some time now and she has already done good things for us. God loves us. Mommy is going to be with us too. Isn't that what you were fighting for all along? Isn't that why you let yourself get beat up and injured? You were protecting us so we can all be together as a family again. So, why don't we just keep it that way then? I don't want the devil to kill you, Anna-Maria. You are my only sister and I love you very, very much!"

Pony suddenly sat up and reached for her little sister, plucking her out the front seat and then hugging her tightly.

"I love you too, Sue-Ann," she said as the little girl started crying on her shoulder. "I love you too, Mom. I now see what this is all about.

187

It's you two that saved my life, not the other way around. It was you two who influenced my mind and led me to pulling myself out of the evil connection with the devil, and for that I am so grateful. So, if you chose to go with the angel, so will I. I cannot bear the thought of losing you again!"

Pony put her other arm around her mother too who, just like her little sister, she was crying also tearing up. Ms. Zeal looked at the trio and smiled. She then turned back around in her seat to face forward. The smile on her face grew broader as she embraced the real gratitude of having accomplished her mission successfully. She now had the full consent of all three humans, assigned to her, to carry out the last part of it her assignment. You see, Human beings have one other privilege installed in their system during creation, and that is the element of freewill. And so even though they never know when, how and why they arrived into humanity, or when they are going to exit it, they have the freewill to decide what to do with their lives and God's Angels have no control or rights to interfere or intervene with that freewill. The Angels will only intervene when they are asked to do so, and that is by the humans themselves or by heavenly mandate.

The Range Rover carrying the principal and the principal's party arrived at the Ripley mansion, in south Britain, late in the evening after they had departed the mansion of incineration. The big iron gates automatically opened after the sensors on the top of the gates scanned a transmitting sensor on one of the ornaments on the principal's fingers. The Ripley mansion, a multi – million-pound sterling private residential complex owned by the principal and the principal's associates, also housed a helipad in its huge compound. There was a helicopter waiting now on the helipad for the principal and the principal's party to take them to their next rendezvous. The Range Rover drove straight up the helipad, pulling up next to the helicopter. The driver, the short, stocky, heavy set black guy, jumped out of the car and quickly ran around to the other side to open the door for the principal. He did, and then stood at ease.

But the principal wasn't getting out of the car yet, because the private line cellphone started beeping with a call coming through. The principal pulled it out to talk. "Is it all done?"

"Boss, that woman, Pony, she escaped together with her family!" the voice on the other side said frantically. "We sent in those killers to get her, and she killed them all."

"What? Katarina failed me? This is unacceptable!" the principal exclaimed with instant anger. "Where is she now? Find Katarina and call me back immediately. I need to talk to her about this."

"Am afraid I can't do that boss," the person replied. "While Pony fought inside the hotel building, we got attacked by someone, or something from the outside. It was crazy, boss, I swear to you! People and cars were exploding to pieces or burning straight up. It was like someone was throwing hand grenades at us, but we couldn't see the thrower. When Pony finally came out of the hotel with her family she joined up with this tall woman. This woman then gave Pony a weapon, a handgun which she fired off at the hotel building. And before my own eyes, boss, the entire building exploded into flames and completely collapsed. Katarina was still inside the hotel. I don't think she survived it. There is no way she could have survived that destruction. It's massive! The Police and fire people are here now and have cordoned off the area."

"Hold on there!? Are you telling me that my entire hotel is destroyed?" the principal asked, sounding irate.

"Yes boss, it's all engulfed in flames now as we speak," the caller replied. "And it's all levelled to the ground."

"Someone's going to pay for this! No one messes with me like that and gets away with it!" The principal raged. "What did this tall woman look like? Was she Korean?"

"Didn't look like it, boss. She was tall with an olive brown skin tone, with long legs and long, silky black hair that fell all the way to the bottom of her buttocks in one long ponytail," the caller replied. "And she had these strange looking sunglasses that completely obscured her eyes."

Without saying another word, the principal got out of the car, angrily threw the phone on the ground and then completely smashed it to pieces with the left heel.

"What is the matter, huh boss? Is there a problem that we can't fix?" The short stocky black guy quickly asked in his deep booming voice. This was not the first time he had seen this kind of reaction from the principal, so that wasn't the real problem. The problem was the aftermath of it all, for when the principal gets rattled, even those on the scene could easily be affected in ways so intense in nature that the moment could unintentionally carry a death sentence with it. The black guy had come to understand that it was the way of nature with his boss, and since he was the one always moving around with the principal, he had taken it to himself to always sooth or appease these situations, so it all does not get out of hand. And now this was one of those situations, for it was clear that the principal was clearly very disturbed.

"Someone just burned down my entire hotel property in south Korea," the principal hissed. "Not only was it one of my most valuable possessions, but it also has a lot of hard money stored in it. We have just lost a lot of money and people. But while we can always get other people, lots of my hard-earned money is almost irreplaceable! Because every penny of it matters to me! But that's not where my real anger is. I am angry that we don't even know who did this to us. I hate to think I am in control all the time yet only to realize that I am not."

"Call one or more of our global connections to help find out who did it," one of the women said. "They always know these things, everything. They always provide you with the answers, promptly."

"Except that boss can't call now," the other woman said, staring at her colleague like she is an idiot. "Because boss has no phone, because boss just smashed it up to pieces, on the ground, with a heel."

"Oh! Sorry, boss, I quickly forgot about that," the first girl reacted back. "You can use mine, though."

The principal's head turned in a full circle without shifting the body and looked at the two girls. The ugly mask was moving up and down due to the labored breathing ignited by the anger. "I have this gut feeling that this time around our global connections won't be able to help us out. I think we have a formidable foe competing for our business. And I think this foe is now out to either stop us or destroy us all together so they can take over."

190

"But you have never had an adversary worthy of being called formidable," the stocky black man said. "So, it now sounds strange hearing it from you. That means this adversary must be one hell of a powerful individual or entity."

The principal's head swung back to face the black guy, completing another full circle pivot on the neck base before finally staring directly at him. "Even I do have powerful adversaries, my friend. I just don't have that many in this world, that's all. But what you just said now resonates with my gut feelings, for I have this one major adversary to always reckon and contend with, and that adversary is not of this world. Maybe it is now this adversary who is trying to get my attention, trying to notify me of their presence."

The principal's masked face slowly looked upwards, staring at the sky. "Always meddling in my business!"

"I still think we can still use our connections too," One of the women insisted. "I have some numbers on my phone contact list. You can use my phone, boss."

"Yes, and we still have powerful connections that we can rely on, the ones that are not so visibly human, the ones I call as a last resort," The principal said. "So, all is not lost yet. But they are not in your phone list, girl. They are exclusively on mine. So now I need to have my phone back."

And with that, the principal leveled the left hand, palm facing down, over the crushed up cellular phone pieces on the ground. Suddenly, the broken pieces sprung up from the ground, upwards and into the hand, hitting it like small pellets. In a matter of several seconds, and while everybody else looked on in awe, the principal had the phone back in its solid form again, right there in the palm of the open left hand. The principal took grasp of it.

"I think I know who to exactly call on about this issue," the principal said in a defiant voice. "They will give me some answers. Meanwhile, tell the pilot to fly us to location B."

While the thick set black guy talked to the helicopter pilot, the two women left the car and boarded the helicopter, followed by the principal who was now talking on the phone and speaking in an ancient language that nobody else understood. Then the black guy himself boarded.

The helicopter with its passengers soon left London, and after some time flew into France. They landed in a small-town east of Paris called Ville de Merles, in the backyard of an old church that bordered an old cemetery. There were two chauffeured black Bentley sedans waiting for the group. The principal got into the back seat of one in which a man, dressed in an all-white ensemble of suit, tie, and a black Homburg hat, sat. The two women and the hefty black guy got into the other Bentley. Both cars immediately left the premises at the same time, the one with the principal leading the way.

"Is La Vielle Reine corbeau ready to see me? I am sorry it's on short notice, but this is rather urgent," The Principal said without greeting the man.

"Yes, she is," the man answered back with ease. "And from what I gather she has been wondering as to when you are going to visit with her. It's been rather long since you last came down here, Diable Incarne."

"I have been rather very busy this particular season, and I am sure you already know that" the principal said. "The two feroce femelle that you provided for my so - called security detail must be keeping you well informed. By the way, Ame de Corbeau, that white suit looks ridiculous on you. How come she let you wear it?"

"Yes, for purposes of blending in, Diable Incarne. Human beings have this stupid obsession of the color white representing purity, so we let them have their way," the man said. "And yes, we are well informed of what's happening all the time. Not only has it been a rather busy season for you, but also a very unstable, disturbing one."

"Do you think she has the answers to my inquiry, hmmm, Ame de corbeau?" the principal asked.

"I don't know, Diable incarne," Ame De Corbeau answered. "As you very well know, she's never been known to provide general overviews. She is always keen to provide specific responses custom tailored to the individual she is dealing with. Just be patient until we get there. I do believe she has the answers, but for your ears only!"

192

"Hmmm… ok," the principal grunted, and then looked away from Ame De Corbeau, staring through the car window at the passing by traffic. There was now this uneasy feeling that all was not ok, the feeling that the answers to the inquiry were going to be mostly unfavorable. The fear was that La Vielle Reine Corbeau was known to predict only the truth, and so if the individual seeking answers was not ready to hear the bad side, then it was better not to go to her at all, but rather just stay on their side and instead deal with the problem as it comes. It was this credential about La Vielle Reine Corbeau that had incited the principal to seek out the old queen for necessary answers needed at this time.

La Vielle Reine Corbeau lived in a big chateau about thirty minutes' drive away from the old cemetery church. The house was tucked away behind big metal gates and inside a high brick wall fence. The gates were electronically controlled, remotely, using high tech electronics complete with T.V circuitry, but all of this was a sham, because the chateau's incumbent was her own security circuitry, keenly aware of her surroundings like the sun is linked to the sky. The big metal gates opened noiselessly, and the Bentleys cruised through with equally less noise. The driveway, lined with thin, tall, bushy and thorny trees on both sides and all the way to the main house, was exactly half a mile long, a smooth ride that revealed nothing much of who lived there. Even as they drove up that half mile driveway cobbled with stone, six crows flying in a unique, side by side straight pattern, followed above the cars until they pulled up in front of the house and stopped. Then the birds separated and settled down on branches of thin trees nearby.

The Principal and the Principal's entourage now got out of the cars and were then led up the wide steps by Ame De Corbeau, through the heavy oak doors to the inside of the house.

The group now found themselves in a huge, well-furnished living room that smelled of stale air. Everything in the living room looked ancient, including the big Zenith television in one corner. The big diamond chandelier hung loosely from the ceiling with several strands of cobweb hanging down from it. The tiled floor looked clean, almost like no one had walked on it for a long time. The one thing that stood out, though, was a sculptor of a big black crow with the human hands and feet. The eyes seemed to move and or blink with their sparkling shiny silver gaze, and its mouth was gaping open, like it was about to speak.

The group was halted in the middle of the room and asked to wait there as Ame De Corbeau went to get their host. He walked towards the big double doors all the way to the left of the room, but before he got to them, they suddenly slid apart and a much older, skinny lady, dressed in neatly pressed dress slacks, a black long sleeved polar-neck jersey, black shoes and black gloves, emerged. Her black hair was long, silky, and went down all the way to the back of her legs, almost touching her ankles, in one long stiff flow. Ame De Corbeau immediately bowed his head in respect, and then turning around, he extended his right arm towards the visiting group.

"Here they are, my most honorable queen, "he said in French, and then stepped out of the way, his head still bowed.

"I can clearly see that, but thank you very much, Lord Corbeau," the old matriarch responded back, also in French. Her voice was very strong and clear, yet she was rumored to be at least over three thousand human years with no sign of slowing down. That, coupled with the mystical powers she possessed but rarely wielded except for consultation or under extreme duress, the old crow queen was highly feared, revered, and respected, a force to be reckoned with. Her consults included, but were not limited to, highly significant political figures and rich people all over the globe, though mostly from Europe.

But she also had a stake in the dark side, for the principal was here not because of her highly acclaimed public status, but because of what the principal represented in the dark world, which is a horrifying possessive power that carefully singles out, selects, and finally takes over certain special human souls and uses them to implement its agenda. Therefore, the old queen knew what was inside the masked body in front of her and knew that she had to tread carefully. So, to avoid the risk of confrontation with this immensely powerful and deadly underworld entity, she had neither the wish nor the intention to influence the masked personality's motives. She was simply playing an advisory role, basing on what she had found out in her astronomic reviews and in-depth, out of this world, research about the principal's inquiries concerning the increasingly troubled business dealings.

The entire visiting group now bowed their heads in respect of the elderly queen crow, including the principal. Then the two girls stepped forward and knelt before her. After lightly placing both her hands on top of their heads, she bid them to arise. The girls stood up and then stood aside to let their boss come forward.

"For god's sake when are you going to get rid of that ugly mask, huh?" La Vielle Reine Corbeau asked, now standing face to face with Principal, though apart. "The possession process has been fulfilled, so you no longer have to wear it. The one you represent is now you."

"Depends on which god you are referring to, Reine Corbeau. The one I serve has recommended that I continue wearing it, and so be it. Tell me, does it bother you in any way, hmmm, Reine?" The principal asked, rather fervently.

The queen slightly raised her eyebrows at the question before replying. "In that case it remains none of my business. Let's stick to what brought you here. Are you ready to hear what I have to say?"

"Good, let's keep it that way," the principal said. "Now, tell me what you have found out for my inquiry."

"Then walk with me to the inside of my private chambers," said La Vielle Reine Corbeau. "These matters I intend to deliver to and for your ears only."

The two individuals now proceeded to walk side by side into the room from which the old crow queen had come, entering a brightly illuminated room with much better, newer and modern furniture, including but not limited to a black grand piano in one corner. The double doors closed behind them. The moment the doubles were firmly closed, the entire environment changed. In the blink of an eye, they were standing outside in the center of a big flower garden, surrounded by miles of neatly trimmed shrubs and carefully tended flower bushes.

The environment was also sustained by a gentle wind that made the flower bushes rustle, like there was something hiding in them and trying to shift positions.

"Why the sudden change in environment?" The principal questioned, sounding suspicious. "You realize I have no time for all these dramatics, right? Just tell me what I need to know, and right now!"

"Be careful how you talk to me, my dear," La Vielle Reine Corbeau said. "As far as I am concerned you are just a possessed soul, still young in this business, while I have been around for ages before you showed up, so I know very well how your show runs. Many have come and gone before you. The change in environment is a matter of security. We are in one of the most secure places on earth. That's how I do my consults."

"Becareful how I talk to you or what?" The principal asked with heightened arrogance. "All I want to hear are your answers to my questions and I will be out of your hair, Reine Corbeau. Or would you rather like me to call on him instead, so I can get what I came for?"

Suddenly the surrounding bushes all instantly withered and then erupted into flames. The brush fire spread very fast and soon they were surrounded by raging ten feet flames. A lot of activity suddenly came from the burning vegetation as thousands of all types of black birds flew out of the flower bushes into the air around them, trying to escape the scotching flames. Some fell back to the ground and into the flames. La vielle Reine Corbeau looked around her, at the same time stepping away from the principal.

"Enough! Stop this madness now or I will have you banished from within!" She shouted. "I used to be his mistress, so I know how he acts. Stop it or I will declare alliance with the holies and then we will see who wins!"

La Vielle Reine Corbeau raised her arms in the air and waved them vigorously at the sky. Thick, black, clouds suddenly appeared from nowhere and filled the sky above them. As she continued to wave her hands, it suddenly started to rain, a flash flood that quickly contained the large flames and quickly extinguished them as fast as they had appeared. But the two individuals remained dry.

"Okay, okay, I get it! Now, can we talk?" the principal quickly said, stepping close to the old queen. "I am sorry about messing up your private place, but my lord happened to be nearby and so when I

196

mentioned that I can call him in, he simply showed up. But now I see that he's backed off . I still need answers to my inquiry."

"Such acts of barbarianism have gravely affected my relationship with you and your master and will continue to do so for years and years to come," La Vielle Reine Corbeau said, sounding angry as she looked at the hundreds of dead fowl all around them. "You have destroyed my garden of peace because of your impatience and arrogance. Yet I brought you here because I wanted you to hear what I have to say in a peaceful, quiet environment, because I thought you would digest the consult news and advise much better. Instead, you made it worse for yourself. But I am not surprised, because your master knows no peace, only anarchy, evil and treachery. He thrives in chaos. Either way, that won't change my message to you because it is what it is, and that's what you came here for."

"Ok, Reine Corbeau, I am sorry about all this," the principal seemed to cower down. "And yes, I still need to hear the answers to my inquiry. Please. You are the only one who can help me. I really do apologize for being so impatient and arrogant."

"It is not you, Diable Incarne," La Reine Corbeau said. "It's that which is in you, that which possesses your soul. I am very much aware of his intimidating tactics, but I am no longer afraid anymore. I have already made the alliance and it has made me stronger. He can't touch me. Never again!"

The principal slowly turned away from the old lady, looked around, and then slowly turned back around to face the old lady. The two faced each other for at least two minutes without saying anything. The environment was now calm with no more rain. The flourishing green vegetation had quickly grown back to its previous normal.

"Satisfied?" La Vielle Reine Corbeau said, her face expressionless.

"Yes, indeed I can see that now," The Principal replied. "But how did you do that? My master tells me he owns this universe, and so he can do whatever he wishes to do in it, be wherever he wants to be."

"The place you are right now is one of the many illusions of my mind. All I have to do is make them real, but because it's in my mind, I chose who to let in and who not to let in. That, my dear, is the reason why you are here, and he can't be here," The older lady replied. "Now, are you ready to receive the answers to your problems?"

"I have been ready the moment you accepted to do this service for me, after I contacted you for help," The Principal replied.

La Vielle Reine Corbeau cleared her throat. "Yes, you are under attack right now from a vicious force unlike any other. And this is because the extremely ambitious, and radical, and deadly project you are trying to undertake has caught someone else's attention. They do not like what you intend to do, not at all. They intend to stop you, and are already here to do so, at any cost."

"Who is it, or them? and how did they get to know about my business? Please tell me that you already know who it is," The principal responded back, appearing to be agitated by the fact that someone on this planet was trying to interfere with the business project. They would have to be dealt with in the same way as others have been. "Is this human competition? Because if so, I will definitely crush it! Perhaps a government or government agency? Or just some unknown enemy that has sprung up from nowhere? That is why I terminated that military man, major Haraabi. He was sloppy with his work. He failed to eliminate that Texas billionaire and hence maintain the secrecy of my project. Now the Texan has leaked it all out. Either way, I will deal with it squarely. I just want to know who they are."

"You eliminated the wrong individual. Major Haraabi tried to do exactly that, eliminate the billionaire for you, and he wasn't sloppy about it. He failed because he didn't know that the American billionaire was already under the protection of your antagonist," La Vielle Reine Corbeau replied. "I am here to tell you that this is no ordinary human force we are talking about here, Diable incarne. It is one hell of a force to be reckoned with. The thing is, they are not interested in taking over your business, nor your money. They are just concerned the nature of your business. They don't like what you are about to do and will stop you from doing it. And for that reason, and with what I know about this force, I suggest that you abandon this project immediately."

"That is definitely not an option, old woman!" the principal exploded in an angry, stentorian voice tone, and suddenly turned away from the old lady again. When the Principal turned around to face La Vielle

Reine Corbeau again, the mask had changed color, from black to deep crimson. "Tell me who they are, right now, and the rest will be up to me. I fear no man, no organization, no government, or other. This is my business, and anyone who dares to stand me in my way will be uprooted and destroyed. They will face the full wrath of our retaliatory powers!"

La Vieille Reine Corbeau's face became grim and tight, and then stepping forward to where her face was inches away from the masked face, she scoffed at the principal. "You are right when you say you fear no man, no organization or government. But you better fear this one, because it's the master of the heavens that you have angered. It's his war angels who are down here, all the way from heaven, to stop you. That is why all your recent actions to thwart your purported enemies have inevitably ended up as failures. The holies are here, Diable incarnate, sent by the almighty himself. It is a war you won't win. That is why I am advising you to abandon this project immediately. That is why I allowed you to see me at such a short notice, because I then had to personally let you know about the danger involved. You have the right to know!"

"Well then, bring it on. It will be a war between the evil and the holy, as it is always claimed to be by the humans!" the principal said. "I will not stop what I have started because someone from nowhere does not want me to do it. I will now consult with my master. Thank you for your consult, and advice. We shall take it from here."

"I plead with, and for you, to please listen to me, devil incarnate," La Vieille Reine Corbeau said, raising her arms up and placing both her hands on the principal's shoulders. "Even your master shies away when it comes to heavenly intervention, particularly when the lord of the heavens is himself involved. He won't be there for you when the final phase of heaven's wrath is unleashed on you. For yours and your people's sake, let it go, please …"

But the Principal roughly shrugged off the old lady's hands. La vieille Reine corbeau felt an extreme burning sensation run through her hands, like she had touched something very hot. Sparks of fire came off the principal's shoulders where her hands had touched.

"My master has ordered me to do it and I believe in everything that my master says, so do not try to persuade me anymore with your intimidating rhetoric!" the principal snapped back in a deep, menacing voice. "With him I am untouchable and unstoppable, I will fulfil my own destiny! With his help I will destroy everyone and anything that dares to stand in my way, starting with you, Vieux Corbeau!"

The principal suddenly lashed out with both hands, which suddenly turned into open wolf paws, at the old lady. The mouth immediately and suddenly transformed into an open rattle snake mouth with fangs and a red slithering snake tongue which was in the form of a full grown, double headed centipede. This was complimented by a shrill, nerve chilling, ear piecing, angry scream.

But the principal grabbed at empty space, for there was no La Vielle Reine Corbeau anymore, and neither were they still standing in a bushy flower garden. The principle was instantly back in the first living room with the old, stale furniture. There was no sign of Ame De Corbeau either, and all side doors were now sealed off with a cement sealed brick wall. The only people in the room were the principal's entourage of three people. The principal immediately transformed back to normal. But the mask still retained its crimson color.

"Treacherous, ragged old crow!" the principal hissed angrily. "Let's go, right now! We have a lot to do and less time to do it!"

The group immediately walked out of the stale living room and into the compound. The cars were also gone. There was nothing that suggested the existence of any life in this area except for the trees and the birds on them. And then the moment they stepped onto the grounds, the entire entrance to the building also sealed itself off with a cemented brick wall. The building had fortified itself into a totally secure castle!

"So now we have no transport…" one of the girls started saying, but she was cut off.

"That won't be a problem!" the principal said, raising both arms up. This was complemented by a torrent of loud words which, again, no one else understood. By the time the arms came down, the throttle of a helicopter could be heard overhead, and soon became louder and louder as the machine came closer to where they were. It soon landed right in the middle of the crow compound. The principal immediately walked up to machine and looked at the pilot. He was dead, looking grotesque with his neck broken in two places. The principal turned to the stocky, heavy set black guy. "Fly us out of here and take us to Charles De Gaulle airport, now!"

"Right away, boss," the black man responded immediately. Going over to the pilot's side, he opened the door and yanked the pilot's body away from the controls, then out of the seat, dumping him on the ground. "Poor bastard. I wonder what happened to him. But if he's already dead, how the hell did he fly the helicopter from there to here?"

"I methodically got rid of him, because I didn't want him to witness our ways, which the master warned me about. He was one of them, a believer in heaven and its master and prophets," The principal answered back. "From now on I strictly prefer having only those that I trust around me, and since he's not part of us, we had no use for him anymore. He died a good death, anyway, because he didn't see it coming, nor did he know what hit him. I deployed our invisible forces, just like other invisible, and visible, forces are now at play against us. Our invisible forces brought the machine over to us."

"Wow!" the two girls exclaimed simultaneously as they boarded the helicopter. The black guy raised his eyebrows and smiled broadly.

The principal looked at the women and briefly nodded. "You two girls shouldn't be surprised by anything like this at all. You have been around me long enough to know that strange things do happen around me all the time. That's what we are, that's how much we're empowered to do by our master. After all, as vicious guard dogs disguised as humans, you yourselves are abnormal, vicious creatures from the dark world."

"We didn't say we are surprised, did we?" one of the women asked, staring at the principal questioningly.

"We are just simply appalled at how so efficiently things are happening and being handled," The other woman added.

"Well, I hope that's the case, because now is the time to let you know that we are officially at war," The principal said. "Basing on what the old queen crow told me, and I hate to be the one to say that she's never wrong, there are forces out there actively working against us, interfering with our business. This enemy is very powerful and will stop at nothing to bring us down. So, we'll have to fight back. We shall use everything we have got. Master has promised to help us fight back, because he wants us to carry on with this project, he wants us to succeed! So, under no circumstances are we going to stop. His powers and resources are now at our disposal. We are now way much more powerful than what our enemies think. But we must now move quickly. There is no time to waste."

As the helicopter took off into the air, the principal got on the phone again. When the recipient picked up, the principal issued the following orders. "Do all it takes, at whatever cost, to eliminate the Texas billionaire. Double the force if necessary. And from now on, I am directly in command of the project. You now report directly to me. Major Haraabi is no longer with us. Do you understand?"

There was positive acknowledgement from the other side of the phone.

"One more thing," the principal said. "Prepare for my arrival on the Turikai island. We are on our way now!"

The battle for the Seventh Dimension had now begun.

# Chapter Eight

## THE WORLD'S GREATEST ARMY

*B*ut heaven's war angels fully raging on earth now wasn't the only problem for the devil incarnate. Another force was quickly assembling itself to combat the evil entity and its intentions. The outcome of Pony's data output alerting the world about the devious project, while on the plane to North Korea, to several of the world's big security agencies was also beginning to materialize. For even though they have their own indifferences, mistrusts, and misunderstandings, the matter at hand seemed to highlight a clear and present danger for everyone. At least that was exactly the way Pony's brief, but intense, well written message, indicated it. That a fatality of a massive destructive nature, and at a global scale, was about to be unleashed. It called on these world agencies to act fast and prevent it from happening.

But the facts about this message were both confusing and maybe hard to distinguish between hoax and reality, and at the same time difficult to dispute. This is because the situation became even more complex when totally unexpected, and unlikely, sources showed up in the picture to support the message.

You see, the revelations at Namugongo, in Uganda, to the local leaders of three of the world's most vibrant religious groups were directly but secretly revealed to their respective regional heads who, though unsuccessful in obtaining more open disclosures from Mother Edina due to her presently unclear minds, took the matter as not only fascinatingly divine but also serious, taking it further up the top of the hierarchy of their respective religious faiths. As a result, word about the divine revelation and warning of an impending global catastrophe finally reached the ears of the imam of the Grand Mosque in Mecca, Saudi Arabia, the Archbishop of Canterbury in England, and the supreme Pontiff in the Vatican.

As it was meant to be.

Due to the divine nature of these messages, it was very important that the facts involved were properly and carefully investigated in order to protect the sanctity of the world's biggest and most important religious spiritual venues. It was thus very important that these necessary investigations be conducted in utmost secrecy, and without having to disturb the old lady's peace. As a result, several secret meetings were also being conducted during the investigations and in different locations, all discussing the reality of the issue.

This now led to the leaders of the different world faiths, which expanded to the leaders of the Tibet monks, the eastern European orthodox, and representation of the joint supreme leadership of India's Hindu sect, which sent a high-profile representative, all coming together as one, not as divisions. After determining that the findings were worth further attention, it was decided that the matter be forwarded to the respective political heads of state, who had the power and resources to investigate deeper into the issue.

This coming together of the world's religious leaders, regardless of their differences, is also supposed to be.

Pony had not exactly named the place from which the deadly project was being set up or could be launched, but had given the numerical coordinates, and this was mainly because both the principal and major Haraabi took it as a precautionary measure not to mention the exact location by name, only communicating using coordinates about it. And as thus that's all she ever really got to know, after quickly perusing major Haraabi's notes while he was sound asleep on one of his less - intensive days. Aerial survey pictures indicated it was in a little-known island country, somewhere off continental Europe. Nothing much else was known about the place, even though it could be accessed by boats, helicopters, and cargo planes. Satellite pictures, however, revealed that there was suspicious, ongoing activity on the island.

So, when Pony's message hit home with the world's biggest security agencies, the matter became more bizarre when, at the same very time, the religious groups issued their memorandum, largely because the two sources appeared to be relatively unknown to each other. It raised eyebrows from different corners of the world.

The United States C.I.A chief Leah Durapree got in touch with several of her major international counterparts from all over the world, citing secrecy for fear that if this was true, the aggressors would hear about the leak about their deadly project and would hasten their progress and or change their schedules or location. There was no one to trust, but a united, collaborative, and well-coordinated effort to conduct a thorough investigation and reaction was needed, and fast. She suggested that since this was a global concern, a joint commando force should be set up and sent out to the island to investigate and if warranted, destroy whatever danger they find. The Europeans wanted in on it. and so did the Chinese, Canadians, certain African nations, the Saudi Arabian kingdom, India, Israel and even Cuba.

And as thus, Special commandos from these nations, all fluent in English, were carefully but also hastily selected and then sent to a secret military training camp in Arizona, United States of America, for quick training and briefing. Pony's message had indicated urgency, and so there was no time to waste.

The twelve - man, one-woman team, led by navy seal commander colonel Wilson Carkenbo, assembled for the first time inside the soundproof, air-conditioned secret bunker turned conference room in the training camp on a Monday morning, one and a half weeks after the Leah Durapree virtual meeting had adjourned and the different heads of states had signed on. The one woman on the team was from China.

Colonel Carkenbo, dressed in a green military outfit befitting a private, was a surprisingly short, but sinewy, bold headed, beardless black man who preferred to talkless and instead emphasized on action. He briskly matched into the room where the rest of the group was waiting for him and took his place at the head of the long table. On his heels was a female soldier holding eleven folders. The group stood up upon his entry and saluted, standing at ease. He nodded back at them briefly.

"Thank you. Please sit down," he said. They all sat down, while he himself remained standing, his hands resting on top of the table in front of him, legs slightly spread apart. His voice was deep and grave. "Please introduce yourself, name and country. You have five seconds each to do that."

"Jiang Hong, People's republic of China," The only female in the group stated, raising her hand briefly, a faint smile on her face.

"Frederico Santiago, Cuba." The next in line said.

"Peter finch, Great Britain."

"Yassin Al Sabani, Saudi Arabia."

"Benjamin Moshe, Israel."

"Phillip Bhekumbuso, South Africa."

"Otto Mueller, Germany."

"Jack Caron, France."

"Aahan Aghosh, India."

"Andrei Sokolov, Russia."

"Liam Johnson, Canada," The Canadian concluded the list.

"Good! Now that we all know each other, I am Colonel Wilson Carkenbo, United States Navy seal commander of operations, and I am in charge of this mission," the colonel introduced himself, taking a glance at his watch. "Now, listen up. First of all, let me say this, that when I look at you' all, I don't see any differences. I don't see Indian or Chinese, Russian or Cuban or Canadian, French, German, British, African. Hell, I don't see Arab or Israeli either! I see the world before me. I see the world's greatest army, assembled here, in one place today, and about to fight for the good of, to defend, the world. Our world. We have no time for emotions, cultural, political, geopolitical, language or religious differences. I don't see rank among us, I see structural responsibility. We are here to save the world from a catastrophic, manmade disaster, an evil threat that needs to be stopped! We are it, soldiers! Now, I know you are all seasoned soldiers, that is why they selected you for this mission, but for the next six days, we are going to conduct a series of intense drills and simulations that will orient us to the situation and therefore our mission, and how we are going to go about it. The next six days are going to be intense, physically and mentally demanding. After these six days, we shall by all means be ready, like it or not, for this mission. For now, my department secretary will give each of you a manual about the drills for you to read over tonight. We start tomorrow. Report to this room at O600. Any questions?"

The female department secretary started passing out the manuals. When she was done, she turned around and nodded to colonel Carkenbo. Nodding back, the navy seal commander patiently waited to see if any hands came up, but none did. No one had any questions. "Alright then, see you all here tomorrow."

And just as he had briskly matched into the room, Colonel Carkenbo briskly matched out. The members of the world's greatest army had already each been oriented to their living quarters, which were twelve tents set up in an open yard not too far away from the briefing room.

And as he said it, the training began the next day at 0600 sharp. Members were up by 0500, courtesy of an inbuilt tent wall alarm that sounded off with shrill sounds of explosions that triggered off instant alertness with each occupant of a tent. Bathroom visits, cloth change, hygiene checks and other personal issues were all conducted within that hour. Breakfast, which included boxed eggs, enhanced orange juice, and a super nutrition bar, was hastily served and eaten in a small open tent and then members joined the colonel in the briefing room, which had completely been transformed. There were no chairs or desks this time. Members had to remain standing while facing a huge digital map that showed actual aerial views of the area of operation. The colonel was able to significantly zoom in on the area to the point where activity on the ground was visibly clear, and items of interests like gates with guards, perimeter fence wall, and entrances to the main building, a vast, white-washed castle, were significantly earmarked. There were a few helipads inside the area's walled in compound, with helicopters on them.

Day one of training began, with area studies and discussions, colonel Carkenbo letting members weigh in on the situation before introducing a draft plan. He warned members that his introductory plan of operation was a draft model for security purposes and was subject to

change. This day ended in 1800 and members were dispatched for supper which included dried fish with enhanced watermelon juice, boxed potato, and nutrition bars.

The members never saw the conference room again until after the sixth day of training. Those five days were spent outside, simulating attacks, mock ambushes, and demo explosive demolitions. The training was hard and rigorous with air jumps, roped wall climbing, mile long belly crawling and rolling, cat and mouse, approaches, fire jumps, tactical approach based on geological appeal of area of mission, weapons and tools orientation, teamwork and response, to mention but a few. These simulations were repeated over and over again. The demolitions were loud, ear piecing explosions that created dust and smoke, even though stealth approach was emphasized. Members were even introduced to attack dogs and other animals and summarily showed how to ward those threats off. On the sixth day, a Saturday, members were introduced to an arsenal of weaponry, and were able to experience with these tools on open range and close quarter encounter simulations. These weapons and gadgets were some of the most powerful and sophisticated military stuff anyone had ever seen. Member were impressed. But they were also reminded of the simple fact that any given, available item could be transformed into a weapon for survival in a life-or-death situation. It was until 0700 on Sunday morning that members were released from training and allowed to self-evaluate with weapons and tactics. But by noon that day everything was shut down and members ordered to rest.

Monday morning the group met again in the original conference room and received the final briefing from Colonel Carkenbo. And as he had promised, the final draft was different from all other plans. Things like routes, logistics, and timing were completely changed around, but the tactical assault plan remained the same. According to the plan, no military uniforms were to be used, as the target area was encompassed by a remote village and the team did not want to cause a local commotion which would in turn alert the target. Instead, a special attire was issued for each that had a computerized format attached to it. Call it a smart uniform. On this day, too, members were each issued their backpacks which contained the stuff they needed to complete the mission.

"Remember, soldiers, that in this situation we are the unknown. We're the uninvited guests," the colonel said. "So, we are unlikely to be received with open arms. So, we've only got us because we identify to each other, and although I want each one of you to remain on full alert all the time, we are to watch out for each other's backs. We move in as a team, do the job as a team, and get out as a team. Not only is that necessary for our survival, it's the best and only thing to do. Understood?"

The members all nodded. "Any questions?"

No one raised their hands.

"Alright then. Welcome to Operation global life support! We meet here tomorrow promptly at 0600," the commander reiterated.

"We have a plane to catch!"

On that same Monday that the world's greatest army was departing for the mission, U.S Senator Mitchell "Barry" Binion, vice chairman of the senate intelligence committee, returned to his rented home in Washington D.C early and locked himself in his study. His wife Gretel Ruth Binion wasn't home this week as she had travelled out of state to visit with an ailing aunt. He pulled out his wallet and extracted a small piece of white paper from it. The small paper had a series of numbers, thirteen to be exact, written on it. He pulled out his cellphone from his jacket pocket and tapped in the number with a right-hand finger. It was immediately answered.

"Hello?" the soft, female voice responded.

"I am at home now. You can come over," he said.

"What about your wife. Isn't she at home?" the female taunted.

"Oooh, come on. You think I would ask you to come over here if that bitch is at home?" the senator asked, sounding impatient. "Listen, just get your cute butt over here as quickly as possible. I have a bottle of your favorite wine here with me, all chilled. I wanna share it with you, mew mew. But hurry up and be here before it gets warm."

"Ok, I am on my way. What are we eating? I am starving, babe," the female said.

"Dammit, Marija, I am not even thinking about eating any godamned food. All I care about right now is eating you," Senator Binion replied impatiently. "We shall think about what to eat after the make – out. You are my food, and I am starving right now. I hope you understand what I mean. I just can't help it. You're so damn beautiful and sexy!"

"Ah, ah, aaaah, big boy. We don't mention names on the phone, remember?" the female said, adding a giggle. "But for what you have done for me, and for what you mean to me in my life right now, I understand what you mean, and I will head out right away. See you in a few minutes, big boy."

"How many minutes?" the senator asked anxiously.

"Aaaah, let's say about fifteen, Barry," came the reply.

"I thought you said we don't mention names over the phone," the senator retorted. "Why then are you using mine?"

"Tit for Tat, big boy. You said mine first, so I wanted to make sure you remember that part," came the reply with another giggle. "See you in fifteen. And be ready to go when I come in."

Before he could say anything else, the line went dead in his ears, indicating she had hung up.

Her names were Marija Savnik, twenty-eight years old, third-year chemical engineering student at the university of east Washington. They had met at an event at the university where Senator Binion was the main guest speaker and Marija was one of the school's presenters. Her beauty, plus her display of passion for the subject of her presentation, caught the eye the fifty-three-years-old senator, and he had asked to speak to her. After that initial conversation, they had exchanged numbers and soon after that they started communicating to each other frequently to the point where it was on a first name basis.

It was also during that time that Senator Binion was having problems at home with his wife of twenty years, Gretel, a schoolteacher. She was getting frustrated with his not being at home that much anymore, always coming back home late due to senate business meetings which, actually, was the truth. This wasn't the case when he first became senator.

But then the situation became worse when he became vice chair to both the intelligence and foreign affairs committees. Arguments over his increased absences at home ensured, and eventually climaxed to where Mrs. Binion asked him to resign both posts or she was going to file for divorce. He had told her flat out that wasn't going to happen in the nearest future. He loved his job, and although she was frequently at his side during his public campaigns, bringing him packed meals and fresh clothes, he had solely worked very hard to get elected for senator. And so, he wasn't about to quit just because she wanted him to be at home early to watch television with her, and certainly not for a wife who couldn't even cook him dinner anymore but insisted on eating out every evening.

She didn't divorce him, but things started getting bad at home. She refused to sleep with him, frequently locking him out of the bedroom. Or if he came back home late there was no warm dinner waiting for him, the dogs were not fed, all the house windows were open, and he was mainly ignored. Mornings were the same, she would leave without saying a word to him or at least setting up any breakfast for him.

Then she started being absent herself. And when government work increased, forcing the Binions to rent a house in Washington, she declared she didn't want to be in Washington and so she was frequently away from the house, always having reasons for not to coming with him for senate dinners or government functions and other ceremonies. Gretel Binion had resigned her job as schoolteacher when he became senator to support him in his official capacity, and since they had no children, she was free all day. She kept flying back to their home state to take care of business with her parents or relatives, leaving the senator alone in Washington. Soon he had to fly to the home state every week and sometimes midweek just to check on her and her folks, and then check on his folks too, even though all could be done over the phone. The situation became so tense that he didn't know what to do anymore.

And that was when he met Marija. Soon the senator and freshman student became very close and started having an affair. The sex was sizzling, and fully satisfying for the semi – separated senator, and in exchange, a lot of personal expenses and issues were taken care of for the very attractive and much younger woman who was in the United States studying on a scholarship. A lot of these interactions were done away from the rented residence, for even though she was rarely at the house or even in town, the senator's wife could show up anytime and unannounced.

But today was exceptional. Greta Binion had called her husband this morning to tell him that her father had suffered another stroke and was in the hospital on life support. Although she wasn't crying, she sounded disoriented and alone, which on one hand senator Binion did not understand because Gretel Binion had two siblings and a few stepbrothers and sisters, her parents having both come from previous marriages which had children. However, senator Binion listened to her talk with an open mind, tried to comfort her with kind words of strength, and promised to be there as soon as possible.

That meant, too, that she wasn't going to be in town at all today, which was nothing new, and therefore wasn't going to show up at their house, unannounced. The house was free and open for his philandering with Marija. He badly wanted her today that just the thought of her coming over made him feel so horny already. He wanted to intimately interact with her before he left for the home state to comfort his sorry wife.

Senator Binion immediately jumped into the shower after talking to Marija and washed up. He put on a pair of boxer shorts and then after spraying a little bit of one of the cologne sprays that Marija had bought for him, he wrapped himself up into a cozy house bath robe. He then went to the kitchen, opened the wine fridge and took out the bottle of vintage wine he wanted to share with her. Picking up two wine glasses, he put the entire ensemble on a silver tray and proceeded to the bedroom. Marija had this weird thing with fast – paced classical music, especially before and during sex. She claimed that it turned her on in a big way, just like drinking a big bottle of a potent energy drink. And it really did, he had taken note of that, for she was one hell of a wild one in bed and could go on for long sessions after that. The girl had some skills, he gave it to her. And she was as much fun and creative as she was wild.

"Alexa, play "Dance of the two wolves" at a low volume please," he verbally signaled to the satellite service. "Play it continuously for the next three hours."

212

Alexa positively responded, and the music, channeled through premium sound Bose cube speakers, started playing. He then carefully placed the tray with the wine and glasses on a bedside table and proceeded to pull back the covers on the bed. He then looked around. Everything seemed to be in place...

Except for that picture of Gretel smiling grandly and staring back at him. For some reason, that picture always freaked him out, and he always avoided looking at it. Yet he wouldn't dare move it, or he would hear about it for the months. Moving it would culminate into a lifetime of verbal abuse, a series of headache inducing, blood pressure raising, nerve wrecking cries and reminders of how much he doesn't love her anymore. But tonight, it had to go, lest he could lose his erection by just looking at it. He walked over to the nightstand where it was, picked it up, and threw it in one of the dresser drawers, slamming the drawer shut after that.

The doorbell rang. Senator Binion felt his manhood immediately rise, and quickly adjusted the front of his bath robe to where the tenting wouldn't be so obvious. He then made his way from the bedroom and to the front door and opened it.

Marija stood right there, dressed in a pretty floral dress, looking so pretty and a little taller in her high heeled shoes. But she didn't have that pretty, inviting smile on her face that she always puts on every time they meet. She instead looked frightened and was holding her purse in front of her with both hands. Surprisingly too, she didn't do that usual spring forward leap that always landed her in his open arms. She just stood still in the doorway, her blue eyes blinking nervously and her lips quivering.

"What's the matter, mew mew...," Senator Binion started asking, getting concerned immediately, his arms still spread wide open to receive her. She was about to say something when she was suddenly and roughly shoved forward, forcing her into a stumble which would have made her fall hard on the floor if he hadn't been there to grab her, and making her drop her purse. Then two tall, clean - shaven men walked into the living room after her and slammed the door shut behind them. One was black and the other white. They were both dressed in suits and ties with that professional downtown business personality outlook.

213

They both had black gloves on their hands and dark sunglasses covered their eyes. Marija clung to him, her body shaking like a loose leaf in a frantic wind.

"You crazy bastards!" Senator Binion exploded in anger. "What did you do to her? She's a harmless woman, for god's sake! If it's money that you want, I can write you a check or I can give you the cash I have at hand. There is fifteen thousand dollars in that nightstand drawer over there. Take it and get the fuck out of my house!"

"We don't want your money, sir," the black guy said, smiling.

"Do you people know who you are messing with?" the Senator asked angrily. "I am a United States senator with a lot of responsibilities, so all I have do is to make one phone call by speed dial and people you've never seen before will be here in minutes. They will arrest you and lock you up or shoot at you. Now, with all that being said, this is my private time with my girlfriend, so take the money and scram! And I won't report or call anyone about this incident."

"Oooh, we very well know who you are, Senator Mitchell Binion," The white guy replied. "Masters Harvard law and business, special permanent advisor to the President's office on global intelligence systems linked to American foreign policy. You, however, have another master's degree in criminal justice, homeland security option, and have been very influential and successful in organizing vital and systematic counter terrorism strategies."

"You are married to Gretel Ruth Binion, a retired schoolteacher and gospel enthusiast," the black guy added, grinning. "No children, just pets, two dogs to be exact. You have two siblings, Lou and Leo who both now live in Texas. Your parents both live in Montana, and we know where all these people live, Senator."

"We also know about your secret affair with your pretty little mistress here, Marija," The white guy said. "We have been following both of you for some good time now. Poor Gretel Binion, she has no idea of what's going on right under her nose. You are cheating on your wife, senator! That's not good, not at all, especially that we have pictures and videos of you two being intimate. You really don't want Gretel Binion to see them, nor do you want your political opponents to get hold of them. They will be all over the tabloids!"

214

"So, you are here to blackmail me, huh? Is that what this is all about?" Senator Binion asked, sounding defiant "Well, let me tell both of you something. Your little scheme isn't going to work. I don't care if Gretel gets to know about me and Marija. I and my wife stopped being close long time ago. And as for my colleagues, many of them are not exactly innocent either, and maybe with the same reason as me, just because their wives are a pain to live with. So go ahead with that too, I won't be the first, and neither the last one to do so!"

"You are a rare smart character, Senator Binion," the white guy continued. "You always find your way around issues. Although we shall get back to that later, that's not why we are here. We are looking for certain important information for our clients who know that you have access to this info all the time. Our clients sent us to get it from you."

"What information? You idiots know I work for the government, right?" Senator Binion asked, frowning deeply. "Now if you think I can just dish out to you vital, classified United States government info I am sorry to say you have come to the wrong man."

"Then we shall kill everyone and everything that is linked to you if you don't give us what we want, senator," the black man said, sounding indifferent. "Starting with your little bitch here." As he said that, he retrieved a handgun from inside one of his external coat pockets, then retrieved a long piece of metal from the other. He attached the long piece to the handgun, making it a silenced weapon. He then pointed the gun at Marija, who was still clinging tightly to Senator Binion. "Then you will also have to explain why you have a dead woman in your house, a woman who appears in intimate photos with you."

The white man did the same thing. He soon had his silenced gun out and ready.

"Wait! You don't have to do that!" senator Binion said, hastily raising his hands in front of Marija. "I wish I can help you on that, but I cannot access classified information when away from my office. I don't have the authorization to do that."

"Yes, you can, and will, senator Binion," the white guy insisted. "You have a laptop computer that you carry with you when out of office and from which you can log into government systems for your department. You always keep it with you inside your house. It's in this house. Get it out now and give us what we want, or we shall kill her. Like I said, you are a smart character, senator Binion. Smart enough to understand that no government secret is worth your loved one's life. It's up to you now to save her life or even those of your other relatives."

"I just told you, I can't access classified info when away from office," Senator Binion insisted. "I am not allowed to do that. I don't want Marija to die either and I will do anything you want to save her. I just can't do that."

The two men looked at each other, nodded their heads and then once again pointed their guns at Marija. "Then you leave us no choice but to waste her, senator Binion," the white guy said.

"Wait, please don't kill me! I know where he keeps the computer," Marija said quickly, and suddenly detached herself from senator Binion. "I can get it for you, and even start it. All he must do is to log on into the government system."

"Well then, what are you waiting for? Go get the damn computer out now!" the black guy snapped. "I am personally beginning to lose my cool with you fools. Your boyfriend here seems to think we are here to fool around!"

Marija rushed into the bedroom and went straight to the enclosed walk-in closet, much to the surprise of Senator Binion. One of the men followed her. She pulled the carefully arranged suits aside, one by one, until she revealed a whitewashed wall section that had a small switch on it. She flipped the switch up and the wall unfolded, revealing the front of an inbuilt safe with a small screen on which there was an array of numbers, symbols, and letters.

"Come over here, babe. Now! I need you to type in your credentials in order to open this safe to get to the computer," Marija shouted out at senator Binion.

Senator Binion sighed, slowly stood up, and walked back into his bedroom. He stared at Marija in surprise disbelief. "Marija, what do you think you are doing? How did you know there was a safe there?"

"Do what she says, Binion!" the black guy, who had followed Marija into the bedroom yelled, making the senator flinch. "Open the damn safe!"

216

"Stand aside then, woman," Senator Binion said to Marija, but before she did, he roughly shoved her out of the way. Using his fingers, he touched several letters and numbers on the touch screen and then a small camera hall on top of the screen began flashing red.

"Please focus both eyes on the camera on top of the screen," the digital instruction voice command said. Senator Binion placed his face squarely in front of the camera. The computer then issued a low sound chime and then the locks of the safe clicked open. Marija stepped around the senator and pulled the safe door back, revealing an inside shelf which contained a blue laptop.

"There it is," Marija said. She picked it up and handed it to a bewildered senator Binion. "Please babe, do what they say, or they will kill both of us. They already killed the gate guard."

Senator Binion walked back to the living room without saying another word and sat down. He opened the laptop and a short red line prompt showed on the light blue screen. He typed some words and numbers on the keypad. The red line disappeared and then a small square box below the keypad lit up in red. He gently placed his right thumb on top of the red box and then did the same thing with the left one. There was a loud blipping sound which repeated itself 3 times and then the screen lit up to reveal another blue page with a U.S department of homeland security logo on it. A series of warnings flashed up on the screen warning the user not to go beyond this step if not authorized to do so. He typed some more stuff on the keypad and then the screen changed to another site with different links and word menus.

"Ok, we are in. What do you want?" He asked the two intruders, looking up at them.

"We want all the data about Operation Life Support. We want all the plans on it, the schedule, and who is on it," the white guy said.

"Operation life support... hmmm so then it's true. The whole godamned thing is real. There are bad people out there who want to toxify and destroy this world, and all in the name of what? money?" Senator Binion said, sounding disgusted. "You're all some cruel, relentless, murderous human bastards, the devil's very own, I dare to say! Do you realize how deadly this is going to be if it is unleashed? Do you realize that your own families and friends would be affected too?

Your very intended actions, if implemented, could be a destruction of mankind's physicality and spiritual standing. If you're part of this, I pray, don't do it. It's totally preposterous!"

"Shut your pie hole, Senator!" the white man said. "Like we mentioned earlier, we are here to get the info for our clients. Whatever they plan to with it or why they need it is not our business. We are professional collectors and or enforcers, if all that makes sense to you. Too bad if doesn't, because we don't care if does or not. So, once again, give us the info we need so that we can get the fuck out of your house, and you and your bitch here get to stay alive. Those are very simple instructions, man. What, exactly, in all that don't you understand?"

"Well, I hate to tell you that the people who sent you have plans to release a deadly virus which would cripple the world while they benefit from the antidote that they themselves created," Senator Binion persisted. "What you are being ordered to pick up are plans to stop this from happening. We here in America got tipped off by an anonymous source about this evil project, and we in turn secretly alerted not only our allies, but other key figures on the world stage about it. And now we are sending in an allied, elite team of the world's finest commandos to investigate the issue. If they find it, our commandos have orders to destroy the entire setup and then the world moves on. In other words, if you are not part of them, you are aiding a bio terrorist, and if this thing happens, you will have to live with the guilty conscious for the rest of your lives!"

"Like he just said, we are paid to collect, enforce and deliver for our clients. We don't care about what they do next after that," the black man responded. "Just give us what we ask of you, now! Save all that crap about guilt for yourself. After all, who do you think tipped off our clients about your plans to attack, huh? It's someone, some people, somewhere in your government that talk too much or are also part of this that tipped off our clients about your planned response. People who also know that you are the key planner for this operation and sent us after you. So, you see, you people in the so - called governments all over the world are equally guilty. You can't trust anyone anymore these days, especially where money is involved."

"I can't believe what I am hearing!" Marija exclaimed. "Is this really true, all this about a bioterrorist plan to release deadly bacterium into the world and then turn around and sell the antidote?"

"According to the anonymous tip, yes that's what's going to happen if we don't stop it," Senator Binion. "You can look at it for yourself. It doesn't make any difference now. I am compromised already. It's all in this file."

The black man produced a flash drive then said "Here, download the whole file onto this drive, Senator. Now!"

"I can't do that! This is classified material and a download would signal breach, which will be tracked back to me!" Senator Binion said. "I will have to explain why I did that to a team of national security experts. I could easily face potential treason charged if I don't have the right answers."

"That's not our problem, Senator," the white man said. "Just do it! And this is the last time we ask."

"Alright..." Senator Binion responded, shaking his head slowly. "I am an American to the core, and patriotism is at the center of my heart. There are times when I even believed I could die for this country, do anything to protect it. By doing what you are asking me to do, I am exactly doing the opposite. With this case, it's beyond patriotism to nation, it's a failure to humanity, because human life that's at stake. But I also realize that under these very circumstances, I have no choice but to do it. On the other hand, maybe I shouldn't, hmmm? Because either way, do it or not, you are going to kill me anyway. My wife was right, I shouldn't have put myself into all this government stuff, it's too risky."

"Don't be stupid, Mitchell!" Marija said abruptly, prompting Senator Binion to turn around and look at her with total disbelief again. It was also way back in their relationship since she last called him by his first name. "Your plans to thwart the bioterrorist's deal were compromised long time ago by someone within your own government, and perhaps your peer group, those senators who work with you. Don't you see it? They're also part of this whole bad thing. So, it's not your fault that you find yourself in this predicament. Someone let you down! Are you sure you want to die for someone else's sins? Give these men what they want and whatever happens after that happens! The world will take care of itself, or God will take care of the world. God made it anyway. I just don't want to see you, or even myself, die. Not for this, Mitchell!"

Senator Binion stared at her for about ten seconds, and thereafter turned around and repositioned the computer. He typed some stuff quickly and the screen flashed with different colors. The computer released a series of blips and then a download menu showed up. He then directed the file copy to the flash drive. His finger hit enter, and the data started flowing. The room went quiet as this was happening. There was a single blip sound when the download was completed. Senator Binion pulled the flash drive out of the computer and offered it to man closest to him. "There you go, people. That's all of it on that drive. Now if you are going to kill me, let's get over with it."

The black man again pulled out something from inside his coat. It was a small portable, computerized phone tablet. He pressed a few numbers and waited.

"We have the Data you wanted," he spoke into the gadget. "what's the next step?"

The voice on the other end was quite audible. "Plug the flash drive into your slot and hit transmit. I need to see it first before I send it over to my boss. Standby please. You're going to have to kill the senator immediately if this is not the right stuff. Don't forget to kill the woman too. She knows too much already. We don't need her anymore anyway!"

The black guy plugged the flush drive into the bottom of the gadget and then tapped something on its screen. At the same time, both men raised their silenced guns and pointed them at Senator Mitchell and Marija, who was still standing next to him. Senator Mitchell slowly shook his head again, and then closed his eyes. He could clearly hear Marija's heightened breathing.

"Ok, we are good. Please standby again for a minute while I transmit your money," the voice said. "There! Five hundred k! Thank you for doing business with us."

"Wait! What do you want us to do with the senator and the girl after all this? Still want us to kill them?" the black man asked.

"That's up to you. Do whatever you want to do with them," The voice said. "We got what we wanted, so we don't need them anymore.

220

But if I, were you, I wouldn't waste the senator, especially one with his kind of credentials. Too much heat for nothing. Chances are that they would be on you in no time. Perhaps waste the girl, because like I said, she already knows too much. It's your call, guys. Goodbye!"

The phone tablet beeped once, signaling the end of the connection. "We got our money, partner?" the black man asked his colleague.

"Yep! It's all in the account," the white man said.

Marija sighed with relief, and Senator Binion opened his eyes to see both men lower their guns.

"Alright, listen up," the black man said. "We are not going to kill anybody this evening. But I caution you, senator. Any word about this meeting and its outcome, or if we get a call from our client that your "Operation Life Support" schedule has been changed in any way from the original plan you just provided, you shall hear from us again. Be warned that we know where your parents and your siblings exactly live, and we will go after them. We will kill your wife Gretel and your two big dogs too. We shall kill them all. That's how this whole business runs."

Senator Binion slowly turned around and stared at Marija. His eyes teared up. "And you, how could you betray me like that? The voice on his phone mentioned that you should be killed because you already know too much. That means that you are part of them. It means that this whole affair with me has been a sham all along, just to get to me and set me up for this day. No wonder you knew where that computer was stored. You have been part of this act all along. Maybe you deserve to be killed for whatever reasons they deem fit. I don't feel sorry for you anymore!"

"Please, babe, let me explain…" Marija started to say, but Senator Binion raises his hand at her. He definitely didn't want to hear it.

"I really loved you, Marija," Senator Binion said. "Very much. I fell in love with you the moment I saw you on that stage at Washington's, when you were doing that presentation. You were the perfect replacement for the void in my life, ever since Gretel disengaged herself in our marriage. I was lonely and sad, and you made me whole and happy again. I was lost, you helped me find myself. You healed my sick soul. Besides, I cannot get over making love to you, it is wonderful and thrilling. You made the man I should be again. I swear by God I could have done anything, everything in my power, to keep you forever with me. But now that you have so much betrayed my love, and my trust, I have no choice but to give up on all of it. It was all just a dream! It's over now, Marija. Just go away, now!"

"Listen to me very carefully, Senator Binion," the white man said, taking a step forward to directly confront the senator. "The real thing is that we hired miss Marija way before you two started seeing each other. Her job was to get on to you or any one of your colleagues and salvage as much data as possible about the American intelligence system and how it currently operates. The only way to do that, of course, was to turn herself into the object of your desire. But when this deal came in, we wanted to be able to get us into your house so we can get what we want without having to kidnap a high - profile U.S senator, which she easily did. But there is more to that than what really you know, because it got personal."

"Ye, Senator. She's the reason you are still alive after stretching our patience so thin," the black man cut in. "Marija, why don't you tell the senator yourself what the real deal is."

Marija cleared her throat. Her eyes were full of tears and her body was trembling like she was experiencing seizure activity. But she wasn't having seizures for sure. She was just so scared of what his reaction was going to be, now that he had established her betrayal.

"I am pregnant with your child, Mitchell," she said in a shaky voice. "It was not supposed to be that way at all, basing on the criteria of my job. People like me just use other people to get what's needed by our bosses. We are trained to offer our bodies to our intended victims if necessary. Your case wasn't any different, but then something came over me. I fell head over heels in love with you. This has never happened to me before, but I found myself unable to resist these feelings. You're a great person, Senator Mitchell Binion. You're kind, gentle, and very caring, and very handsome too. These two men are my field directors, providing all the support they could. We have worked together for some time now, and since I am much younger, they are like big brothers to me. And so, I confided in them that am pregnant and then begged them not to kill you. I also promised to ease the burden of kidnapping you by bringing them straight to you to get what they want. I want to be part of you, Senator Binion, even if you're married. I want to have your baby, to provide you the child you have never had, or was never going to have."

"Senator, her job was to seduce you and get you to us, not to fall in love with you and even get pregnant," the white guy said. "We give all our women operatives special contraceptives to prevent this from happening, but your girl here decided not to use them, for the obvious reasons, of course. She fell in love! She's now pregnant, a no in our line of business. But like she said, she's like a baby sister to us, and since she's determined to keep the baby, your baby, we decided not to punish her, but instead support her. It's now up to you, Senator Binion. It's your woman, with your kid, and we ask that you find a way to take care of the situation. We have done our part."

"How about my wife?" Senator Mitchell asked, nodding his head again. "Do you know what this means? If I am named as the father to her baby, it means marital infidelity, and as a high-level member of the senate, I would be on every newspaper and tabloid news in this nation. Marija and the baby would never have peace either. Influential people and connections that I know will immediately alienate themselves from me. I will lose my constituency's trust, and hence my job. People everywhere will be calling me a scoundrel, a cheater, a bad man. It will be the end of me. The damage is done, Marija, and largely thanks to you. I am sorry, but I won't be of any use to you or your baby."

"I think we have something for you in our possession, Senator," the white guy said. "We carried this small package with us as extra insurance to get to you, and since we already got what we needed from you, we won't be needing those anymore. So, whatever you decide to do with the contents is entirely up to you."

The man placed a brown, medium sized envelope on the table, in front of senator Binion.

"I don't need anything from people like you," Senator Binion responded quietly. "There is nothing that can be done now to bring my life back. You scumbags just destroyed it. So, take your stuff and get out of my house, now! And take the woman with you too. The very sight of her now sickens me to the core!"

"Marija? Are you coming with us? You heard the man. He doesn't want you anymore! He doesn't want his kid either!" The black man said. "He is too concerned about his political career to understand what else is at stake here. That is why you are instructed, during your training, never to get deeply personal with a target. That's why those very expensive contraceptives are given to you. To avoid bad or terrible situations like this."

"No, I am not coming with you! You can leave, the same way you came in, but without me. I am going to stay here and talk to him about this!" Marija replied, sounding more determined than ever.

The two men looked, and then nodded, at each other. They pocketed their guns, and then left without saying another word.

"Mitchell, please hear me out," Marija started to say, laying her hand on his. But senator Binion stopped her by yanking his hand away and instead raised his other hand to her face again.

"Please… just go, okay. Get the hell out of my house. Right now. Like I said, just the sight of you makes me sick to the stomach!" he said, glaring at her. "I don't want to ever see you again!"

"But I have your baby growing inside me, Mitchell. Made out from our passionate love for each other," Marija pleaded, in between sobs. "I love you too, Mitchell, so much. That is why I kept it. Even if you don't want it, I am going to keep it and raise it anyways, because this will always remind me of you and me together. You may not know, but girls like us come from far, and we are forced to do things like this for survival. They provided me with the money for my education, but also told me that at any given moment they are going to need me for special tasks and that I must always be ready to do what they want or ask me to do for them. And if I refuse, I was told, they will stop my education funding, and would also kill me and my family. That is how I got involved with you, because they noticed how close me and you had become. I am sure that envelope contains photos of me and you kissing or something, leverage they were going to use against you, to blackmail you, just to get what they want. I didn't even know they were doing surveillance on us and taking photos."

"Marija, I didn't get you into these problems. You put yourself in it knowingly, so deal with it!" He responded. "I repeat, I am done with you. Just get the hell out of here and out of my life, now! I am tired of repeating myself!"

With tears running down her cheeks, Marija picked up her purse from where it had fallen on the floor and slowly made her way to the door. She opened it and stepped out of the room without another word. It was raining outside, a steady drizzle that showed no signs of letting.

"Goodbye, Mitchell," she said, her voice already hoarse, wiping her tear-soaked face with the back of her hand. She turned around to look at him one more time and then closed the door quietly behind her. And then she was gone.

Senator Mitchell remained seated, in front of the computer on the table. He suddenly burst out in tears, covering his face with his hands. He had lost everything, just like that. What was he thinking, he asked himself? Maybe he should have listened to Gretel when she urged him to resign his positions on these high-level committees, to refrain from being too involved with the government. If he had done what she had asked him to do, maybe he would have gone on with a better life. But now, he rarely saw her, except when she needed something, mostly money, from him. He hardly knew her anymore as his wife, all because he had become too ambitious with his career, something he had honestly thought would benefit both of them greatly now and in their future together. And now he was about to lose his job too, because of downloading all that sensitive, so - called classified information in the privacy of his home, but more so because he got himself hooked to a woman with bad intentions. The investigators were going to want to know why he did that data download, and what he did with it.

There was a knock on the door, a soft knock. Senator Binion looked at the door for a moment, wondering what it was this time. The knocker was not using the doorbell, which was by itself abnormal, except for Marija, who always knocks on every door before coming in. She had once told him that she loved the old-fashioned knock and considered doorbells an annoying way of announcing oneself. Besides, doorbells were too public, whereby it could be anyone, whereas knocking on a door could be personalized by both the knocker and the knock's recipient, thus eliminating the element of surprise, she had claimed. Fascinating personality, he had presumed, at that time. But now all that had just gone down the drain.

He slowly got up, walked over to the door, and opened it without asking who it is. It was the security man, and he was holding the back of his head.

"Douglas... well, I thought you're... never mind." the Senator reacted instantly, because he had been told that the two men had killed the doorman and his dog. "Come on in, don't stand in the rain, man. Are you ok?"

"Good evening, sir... yes, I am ok. Just a badass headache," the doorman replied. "I don't know what happened, but when your... aah other madam came by with two guys to see you, I was still booking them in when I suddenly blacked out. That's all I remember. Maybe it's the madam's perfume, because she was standing close to me, but I also think something was sprayed into my face before I blacked out. That's all I remember. Your lady just woke me up now as she went through from my post where I had slumped over... Never mind, sir, I was just checking to see if all is ok with you."

"You passed out... fainted, maybe?" Senator Binion said, sensing that Marija and her group had probably sprayed some chemical into his face that had made him pass out. "Perhaps you may need to check out the situation with your physician, make sure everything is fine in your system. Or I can find you a physician who can check you out. I will take care of the bill."

"I will, sir," the doorman acknowledged. "Alrighty, I will get back to my post then. Have a good night, Senator."

"Good night, Douglas," Senator Binion replied, and closed the door. He went back to the table, folded and picked up the laptop computer, and was about to make his way to the bedroom when he noticed the brown envelope that the two men had left for him on the table. And right on top of it was the flash drive the men had given to him to download the classified material. Now that he was by himself, his total curiosity was suddenly aroused. Marija had mentioned that the men could have taken photos of him and her together to use as leverage to force him into giving them what they wanted. He decided to look just

226

to see what they had on him. She was right. The envelope contained a bunch of print outs of digital copies of two people kissing and making it out in the most erotic and intimate postures, and at several different places. Some of these places he very well recognized. But the pictures were not revealing the senator and pretty Marija having their best moments of intimacy. Instead, the pictures showed Greta Binion with another man. The digital copies even had the dates printed on them. Senator Binion carefully examined the pictures over and over again. He didn't know the man in the photos with his wife, but for sure she looked very happy in the man's arms.

Senator Binion suddenly felt alive again. He was now most certain that one of his major problems was about to be solved. For as long as Greta has found happiness in another man's arms, and there was evidence of it, then it would be a happy send off, one not likely to be full of extra drama. Senator Binion got up and made his way to his bedroom and to where his cellphone was on dresser. He may damn well lose his job for downloading sensitive material, but not because of scandal on his part. That way he gets to keep the woman he had so much fallen in love with and his baby. He picked up his cell phone and tapped in a number from his memory.

"Yes…" it was clear Marija was still crying.

"Where are you right now?" Senator Binion asked.

Marija hesitated before replying. "In a cab, on the way back to my apartment," she finally replied.

"Marija, turn around and come back to my place. You and I, we need to talk. I just realized that there is no sense in letting you go, not like that. I love you, and I now want to be with you and our baby," senator Binion said decisively.

She hesitated again, not sure of what he meant or what was going on. "Do I have your assurance that all is well, Mitchell? That you won't give me any more hell over what happened today? I am very tired, very hungry, and very stressed right now. I just can't take it anymore."

"Yes, you have my assurance. All is well. Just turn around and come back to me," he replied.

"Ok, then. Let me tell my driver to swing me back. See you in a few minutes," she said. Then they both hang up.

The principal received the information about Operation Life Support within the hour after the two men left Senator Binion's house.

"Good job, my people," the principal reacted, sounding pleased on the phone, looking at the data on a secured interface screen on an iPad. "We shall be ready for the human force when it comes around. We shall give these commandos a great welcome party. Make sure the folks who made this possible get their monetary reward. What other good news do you have for me? have you found that Haraabi woman?"

"Not yet, boss. She seems to have vanished into thin air, together with her family," the caller said. "But we are looking everywhere. As soon as we find them, we shall kill them immediately, and then update you."

"Very well. Now proceed with our plan for the Texas Billionaire," The Principal said. "And people, do not play with this one. Make sure he is completely erased, him and his family. He must pay for his betrayal. He's the one who linked the Americans and the others to us. And my people, only call me back when the job is done and done well. Failure is not an option on this plan of execution and if you fail me, then consider yourselves dead. We shall come after you, and your entire families too. You will all be killed mysteriously in a matter of time, guaranteed. That's what happens when people fail me."

"Yes, I do know about your intolerance for failure, but we shall not fail you on this one, boss," the caller replied. "Consider that rich Texan and his family a damned, dead deal."

The principal hung up the phone without another word, then looked at the pilot of the Jetstream plane the group was now travelling on. "How many hours left to reach our destination, captain?"

"Three and a half hours left, boss," the pilot replied.

"Try to make it faster than that. Make it in two, at least, or I will decease your soul and fly the damn plane myself!" The principal responded back.

"I will try my level best, boss." The pilot said.

The principal looked around the inside of the plane. Everyone was wide awake and alert. The two women were watching their personalized television unit shows, while the stocky black man had a headset on his ears and staring out of the plane window. Good deal, the principal concluded. It was a rule that none of his escorts were to fall asleep while their boss was awake. Sleep was the sole command of the principal, and until that command was issued, no one dared to do so, or they would find themselves dead! The only other two people on the plane were the pilot and co-pilot.

The principal walked past the three and entered the self-contained, executive passenger cabin of the plane, closing the door. The cabin was top of the line luxury, an airborne super comfortable suite with all amenities a busy executive would desire in it, including a birth tub and a twin-size bed. It was on this comfortable bed that the principal finally decided to rest, content that everything was going to be fine and as planned. After all, there were only a few loose ends left to be tied and then all would be clear. But there was no way to tell if the bed's occupant was really sleeping or just merely relaxing. That remained a secret behind the mask.

# Chapter Nine

Texas state trooper Gregory Walker the fifth, was parked on the side lines of Texas highway 820 west, quietly listening to National public radio news in his patrol cruiser while he observed the highway activity. He had noticed that lately the number of heavy transport trailer trucks, also commonly known as eighteen-wheelers, had increased on Texas highways, especially at night. He always wondered why there was such an increase in road haulers and was always eager to know what was being transported in those trailers and or their containers. He randomly stopped some of them, asking their operators to open the back of those containers, but so far, no luck. He had found nothing illegal or suspicious. He fantasized on finding a container loaded with illegal weapons, Or counterfeit money, or tons of drugs. Or a trailer full of illegal immigrants. While all those would be a good deal for his department, it could also mean a promotion for him.

But personally, though, there was nothing else he hated so much as those immigrants, illegal or not. All bull Shit, baloney stuff, you know, letting all these foreigners in! In his view, these people are simply invaders, a bunch of people draining national or state resources, taking jobs away from local, born and raised, Americans! In addition to that, these immigrants create a spike in the crime rate and then to add insult to injury, they even bring about interracial marriages too. Disgusting, heinous, crossbreeding mannerisms and practices that are slowly but surely changing the face of this great country. Why, it was now evidently happening in his own home state, the great state of Texas!

In fact, that was one reason why he had stopped talking to his youngest brother. Why? because that fool married a black woman! The woman was no doubt very beautiful and hardworking, and they already had two beautiful kids. But that meant nothing to him, because an abomination deed had been performed. The walker blood was diluted, corrupted, diseased, broken, and would never ever be the same again!

Their great Grandfather Gregory walker the second, had insisted on, and in fact decreed, that such a thing must never ever happen in the family. According to his grandfather, great grandfather had repeated over and over again that the walker family was to stay Walker with no glitches, which meant same race line, and largely Texan at heart. That son of a bitch of a brother had even left Texas and settled down in California with his family, leaving him, as the oldest in the family of eight, the entire responsibility of holding up the entire Walker clan which includes their old ninety-eight years old grandma. He blamed his brother for breaking the family regulations, disrespecting his now deceased great grandpa, his grandpa, and the entire family. And so, for those reasons, he had shut his brother and his mixed breed family out of his life and had not spoken to him for at least five years. In the beginning, his brother had tried calling him several times, trying to reach out to him, but he kept ignoring the phone calls. Those phone calls stopped after some time. He figured out that his brother had gotten the message finally given up, which was perfectly ok with Greg Walker.

He had brought this issue up to his wife, Lori. But Lori walker, herself a white native Texan, had hastily brushed it off, saying that it was all God's will. If that's the woman God had granted to her brother-in-law for a wife, and as long as they loved each other and maintained, peace, harmony and respect between and for each other and for the rest of the family, then so be it. The rest of the walker family, including her husband, should also respect and love this brother and his family for who they are. She added that Grandpa Walker's stipulations were foolish and of a different era and should be completely disregarded and

discarded. Greg walker, totally surprised by his wife's response, decided not to ever bring the issue up with her again.

But back to the highway problem, maybe it was exactly how one of his work colleagues, David Wyatt, had tried to explain it to him, that the boom in internet business had in fact boosted a boom in intercontinental transport and delivery of merchandise. He still didn't understand the connection between the two, but oh well! As a law man, the more activity he sees like this at night, the more the chances are that something unlawful is going on and it's his job to find out, and geeks like Ed Nguyen just didn't understand that. They were too busy locked up in their so-called high tech lives, and behind their desks, to understand the business of the real world. Other department colleagues had avoided discussing these issues all together, simply telling him that it just didn't work that way these days, and that the Texas law department did not subscribe to such issues. Maybe you should keep those thoughts to yourself, right Greg? Then they would just suddenly walked away from him.

He heard a buzzing sound, and instantly became alert. Shit, it was his phone going off . He pulled it out from the bottom of his lunch bag and looked at it. It was his wife calling. Now why was she calling him at this time of the night? In fact, what was she still doing up at 12: 30a.m? Yet she was supposed to be up at 5:30 am to start preparing school materials, breakfast and other necessary stuff for their six kids, ages ten to seventeen, before they got up. Very crazy woman, he thought, as he picked up the phone and answered it.

"What is it now? You know that you are supposed to be sleeping at this time, woman!" he said.

"We are pretty much out of drinking water and milk, trooper Greg," she yelled in his ear. "That's why I am calling. This is the only time I was able to be free to carry out stock on what we need, when they're all sleeping. So, get us that stuff on your way back home. Bye! love you, Trooper Greg!"

"That's it?" he asked.

"Yeah, that's it, for now," she replied, after hesitating for at least fifteen seconds.

"Alright. Will do," he said.

He then hung up before she said anything else. He tossed the phone over and into the seat next to him. He hated it when she called him "Trooper Greg". And now he had to stop at a grocery store to get not less than ten gallons of water and six gallons of milk minimum. There goes my morning, he acknowledged to himself. For by the time, he got all that stuff out of the grocery store, took it home, unloaded it and put in the fridge, then get himself washed up and then take a nap, it would be way past midday, because in addition to all that, Lori would create other errands for him to do.

But Lori was not just a simple Texas wife. She worked hard to support the family as an admissions nurse at one of the state hospitals in the city of Fort Worth, and as a full-time mom when off duty. She barely had time for herself and or her husband. With six kids, all enrolled in school activities and all to be supervised, fed, and monitored, her hands were full. That's why he loved and respected her so much, and always gave her a break when she made him angry. Frankly speaking, he didn't know what he would do without her.

The phone started buzzing again. He reached over and looked down at it. It was Lori again.

"Now what is it again?" he asked, sounding annoyed.

"I have a question for you, Trooper Greg," she said. "Why is it that every time I tell you that I love you I never get a response back? It would be nice to hear it from you, you know, especially after putting in a long day. It's reassuring for both of us as we go through our daily struggles and or challenges together, like raising and taking care of our kids. By the way, you used to do that when we first met, even after we had our first one or two babies. You bought me flowers at least once or twice a week, and I loved that so much. You used to call me several times in the day just to check on or chat with me, and that always made my day. You used to come home and hug or talk to the kids, pick them up from school and take them to Macdonald's. All that has suddenly changed. No hug, no "howdy my honey", no goodnight sweetheart, nothing! You don't call unless I call you. These things are very important in a family, you know. I wonder what happened, what has changed. I want to know, Greg. What's up with you this time around? If it's the job, we need to talk about it and maybe find you something else to do. Hell, you don't have to always do what your Papa or grandpa Walker did. It's our life, you know, and we shall live it on our terms, not theirs! So, we can always change things around. I just want you to be happy, you know. Life is too short not to be happy. And we are in this together, remember? Please talk to me, Greg. Talk to me, before it's too late. I really want to talk about this. I am damn sure that together we can fix whatever problem."

It was at that moment, during the few seconds of him being quiet as he tried to comprehend what she was exactly saying, and her waiting for his response, that a series of black vehicles sped past his patrol car. His speed monitoring machine instantly registered over one hundred and twenty miles per hour with a warning vibration on the dashboard. And none of the cars had their lights on except for the lead vehicle. That, alone, was enough to heighten his senses.

"Lori… listen, I gotta go, right now! Duty calls!" he said quickly, and then pressed the shutdown button on his phone. He then immediately started his patrol car, drove it out of the dark ditch on the side of the freeway where he had parked out of sight, and set pursuit, all lights flashing.

There were five black sports utility vehicles all following each other, a mysterious convoy consisting of four Chevy Tahoe hybrids and one Chevy suburban which was in the middle. As the patrol car fast approached, the driver in the lead car echoed off a warning to the rest of the cars behind him.

"Oh, oh. Do you guys see what I see? Looks like we've got company in the form a fast-approaching police car with all lights flashing," the driver of the lead vehicle said through his hands-off communication set which consisted of a complete headset over ears and mouth.

"Yeah, we see that. And now he's turned on his sirens too," the rear vehicle driver said.

"What do we do now, boss?" the lead driver asked, maintaining his speed.

"Just pull over to the side of the road, now," someone in the suburban replied. "Let's find out what the damn officer wants."

"Got ya boss," the lead driver said, and immediately eased foot pressure on the acceleration pedal, slowing down the vehicle and then pulling off the road. The order from the suburban had been heard through all communication headsets of the people in the other cars, so all the other drivers did the same thing.

Inside his patrol car, trooper Greg walker started calling in the report as the convoy slowed down and then started pulling over to the side of the road. "This is Patrol unit TSHP44 pulling over a mysterious convoy of five black SUVs that was heading west on 820 at a uniform speed of over one hundred mph, with all the lights off except for the lead vehicle. Might need back up on this one as soon as possible."

"Acknowledged, Unit 44," the dispatch officer responded immediately. "Standby, 44, while I activate other units in the area towards your location. At this moment, do not engage, unit 44. Repeat, do not engage, until the other units arrive."

"Got ya. All target vehicles have now pulled over to the side of the road," Trooper Greg Walker replied.

"Got three highway rapid response units headed your way now, trooper. ETA is about five to ten minutes," the dispatcher responded back. "Good luck, unit 44!"

"Thanks," Greg Walker said, and the line went dead. He turned on the full beam spotlights on the bilateral sides and on top of his patrol car that fully illuminated the row of cars in front of him. He then sat back and waited.

"What's next boss?" the lead driver asked.

"Looks like the officer is chilling, taking his time getting out of his patrol car. I wonder what he's doing," the driver in the rear car said. "We have no number plates on our cars for him to run a check so why's he not getting out of his car?"

"He's probably waiting for back up," the voice from the suburban, a male's, came in loud and clear. "Ruma, get out of the car and go to the officer. Ask him what this is all about."

Ruma, a beautiful blond female in her mid-twenties, and one of the passengers in the rear vehicle, acknowledged and stepped out of the car. The over tattooed female, with multiple facial piercings and a close-cropped hairstyle with different colored strands sticking out, was dressed in green military cargo pants, a tight-fitting, sleeveless leather jacket over a bright red bra with a small black square marking the location of each nipple, and sleek black military boots. She pursed her lips and then quickly unbuttoned the front of the leather jacket, exposing her entire cleavage on which, strangely enough, a small, twenty-five carat gold, gleaming cross rested, attached to a white cotton string. That cross had been bestowed on her by her mother who, after taking note of her daughter's unusual psychotic behavior patterns, had given it to her as a means of protection from Ruma's own devilish acts. Mother had told his daughter to always wear it.

When trooper Walker saw her coming out of the car, he immediately responded by turning on the patrol car's external communication system and ordering her to get back into the car and not to come out again until she's been asked to.

"Don't stop. Continue walking towards the patrol car until I tell you to stop," the voice from the suburban ordered her through the earpiece in her right ear. "Mobile force two, four and five, arm up now. We are about to give him a war if he starts any trouble!"

"Roger, boss," a voice from one of the cars responded back.

Seeing that the person wasn't responding to his orders, trooper Walker repeated it. But Ruma continued walking towards him.

Trooper Walker quickly got out of his patrol car, drew his weapon, and pointed it at Ruma.

"I said get back into the car and wait for further instructions," He repeated. "What part of that don't you understand?"

"Tell him you are transporting a highly sensitive government program and he need not to interfere," the command came into her ear from the suburban. "If he refuses to understand, which is most likely what he's going to do, tell him that if he wants to see his family again, he should back down and leave immediately."

"Yow, officer, we are transporting a highly senthitive federo governmento program, so dis ain't your show. In other words, you need not to interfere!" Ruma said, sticking out her tongue that had a small metallic ring attached to it and which made her speech sound junky as she continued gyrating towards Trooper Walker.

"That doesn't matter to me," Trooper walker responded back immediately. "I said get back into your car and stay put until I ask you to come out. I am not going ask you again. Consider this your final warning!"

"Yow Officer, do you have a family? Wife, kiddos? Perhaps a side bitch?" Ruma asked. "Because if you do, and you wanna see 'em again, me strongly suggest that you back off, get back into yaw fuckin' police wheels and drive away."

"And what if I don't, huh? Are you threatening a Texas peace officer? Well let me warn you that it's a felony to do that, you godamned nasty piece of shit!" Trooper Walker verbally responded, sounding aggravated by both Ruma's open cleavage and her seemingly adversarial verbal responses to his warnings.

"Ruma, stop right there. Retreat to the car, now!" the voice from the suburban said through all connected headsets. "Activated units, get ready to attack."

"Me wanna take part in dis too, Daddy. Can me join the party?" Ruma asked.

"Definitely, if you feel up to it." The response came back.

As she got close to the trooper, Ruma suddenly stopped, turned around and walked away from him, headed towards the line of cars. As she opened the car door to get in, another order came through her earpiece, loud and clear. "Alright Guys, light that fucker up!"

Ruma reached inside the car and grabbed hold of a gun, a fully automatic assault rifle, from the floor of the car and corked it ready. At the same time, the doors of convoy cars number three, four and five simultaneously opened and closed. Three men stepped out of each car, all armed with full auto .50 caliber tactical assault rifles. As they crowded the middle of the freeway, Ruma straightened up and faced trooper Greg Walker again. She levelled the gun at him.

"Sorry, officer, but dis galla be yaw last fuckin' ass day!" she quipped at him.

Unfortunately for trooper Greg Walker, he didn't get the chance to respond.

The entire group of nine people, together with Ruma, suddenly opened fire on the trooper, shredding his body with .50 caliber bullets and killing him instantly. But at about the same time, two of the three activated back up trooper units arrived, pulling up right into the blaze. Several members of the convoy advanced forward, creating a sort of front line, and opened fire on the newcomers. The backup troopers had no time to pull back or retreat and got fully hit by the heavy gunfire. The windshields of their patrol cars were completely shattered to pieces as the heavy bullets hit the vehicles and then hit the targets inside. The group advanced further, surrounding the still rolling highway trooper vehicles.

Those troopers never knew what hit them. The tires on their police cars were completely ripped and flattened and headlights shattered. The engine hoods flipped open as the latches blew apart, creating an intense, smoky arena. Ruma raised her fist up and the shooting stopped. She quickly walked over to each of the backup patrol cars, gun poised, and peered inside. All occupants' bodies looked very bloody and unresponsive.

"All done 'n' clear," she communicated through her mouthpiece, immediately turning around and walking back towards the convoy. As she walked past trooper Greg Walker's bullet riddled, motionless body, she stopped and looked down the dead trooper. Shaking her head slowly, she said "Nasty piece of shit, isn't that wha' you called me, huh? Well, looket you naw! Yaw fault, cop. We asked that you back off and go home, but you didn't heed to our warning. Too bad, because naw you dead as shit!" She spit down at his still body, and then walked away.

"Ok, everybody, good job. Now retreat to your vehicles and let's hit the road again," the order came in from the Chevy suburban. "We still have a job to do. We have a fuckin' billionaire and his family to kill, and time is of essence. So, let's get going!"

With Ruma leading the way and without saying a single word, everyone retreated to the car they had come out of, and the convoy left the scene.

Five minutes after the killer convoy had left, the third and last of the backup highway patrol cars responding to trooper Greg Walker's call pulled up on the scene, and quickly checked it out. What they found was really gruesome and shocking, especially with trooper Greg Walker. Immediately blocking off that section of the freeway, the two troopers called for immediate help which included the need for several emergency ambulances.

It was in an average of fifteen to twenty minutes after their call, the entire area was filled with, and surrounded by, police and emergency personnel activity. Six ambulances were on the scene, at least twenty highway patrol cars with all their lights flashing had arrived, with more on the way. There were two helicopters hovering around in the sky above the scene, and one managed to land close by. This helicopter was from a nearby trauma hospital and was picking up the only sole survivor of the slaughter, a relatively young female rooky patrol officer who was still on orientation and had volunteered to ride along with the backup team in the second patrol car in response to Greg Walker's call. She had pretended to be dead in the patrol car, which was all dark in the inside, and so the shooter, Ruma, did not see her breathing. But the bullets had hit her in the left shoulder, arm, abdominal wall, and thigh. Despite all the bleeding she had suffered, the trooper was still alert and oriented. Everybody else was dead. Six Texas highway state troopers, including trooper Greg Walker, ruthlessly gunned down!

Unacceptable in Texas! The killers just messed with the wrong State! Texas was totally pissed off and was going to do everything possible to hunt down the killers!

In a matter of time, police roadblocks were being set up in the surrounding areas on and linking to the highway, with orders to shoot if any drivers refused to stop or resisted the search. More Helicopter surveillance was also being set up.

But the killer convoy had already gone past the search area, vying off into a side road that would eventually get them to their destination in the next hour or so. The man in the suburban, who was giving all the orders, was a U.S Marine Commando turned private gun for hire operative, called Woodrow Brinks Crane. The seasoned veteran had been around for some time now, and his organization was well respected in the underground circles as one of the best, well connected "cleanup" assassination group on the planet. Based in the United States, Crane, whose outfit was commonly referred to as WBC GUNS (for hire), had numerous connections globally that enabled him to operate anywhere in the world. That, coupled with funds out of the immense fortune he had built from these illegal contracts over the years, had made him powerful, relatively untouchable, and somewhat invisible. He simply was one of the very best in the underground business of killing people, individually or group. He had even toppled some governments, directly or indirectly, and supported junta establishments, with his guns. He had undertaken bank heists in several nations, did gold and diamonds heists in places like the Congo, traded or sold deadly weapons to the best buyer, and helped rescue captives from hot places like Mogadishu, Libya, and Yemen. He had helped clean out entire troublesome gangs in hot areas in the United States and other developed nations. And all this was in addition to numerous individual assassinations, political and non-political. As long as his fees were met and paid, he made sure that the job was done, and done well.

There was only one main difference between Woodrow Brinks Crane and a person like Major Haraabi, and that is that Woodrow Brinks Crane was a very bad man, naturally. His methods of operation were totally unorthodox, ruthless, and brutal. He was known to use extreme means in situations where it was not necessary to use them, and collateral damage was never his concern, like wiping out an entire stadium of innocent people just to eliminate one individual. He was known to behead his targets and carry the head back as proof of his good work, or brutally eliminate a client's entire family, including friends, if his full dues were not met after the job was done. He had once shot his father in the leg after the two got into an argument, and shot this one guy in the face, killing him, for threatening to dump one of his daughters after getting her pregnant.

But he had this one daughter, Ruma, who he had taken over by force from her Filipino mother when she threatened to take him to court for support and restraints. Not only did he kill her lawyer, but he threatened her family, sending people out to beat up Ruma's grandparents, an endeavor in which all the family pets were killed and one of Ruma's maternal uncles was brutally beaten and maimed. Ruma's mother was forced to give her up, and all court proceedings pertaining to the issue were halted and eventually dropped. And as such, Ruma was incorporated into the WBC organization, her father personally taking over her training. Although he had several other children from different women, none of them were as involved in his business as Ruma was, because as much as he sent money out for their support, they hardly saw their dad or even knew him that well.

But Ruma was different. Special. In her, he saw himself. She displayed his ragged side, was generally not scared of anything or anyone, and rude as hell. She had the ability to be tough and unyielding and was always eager to learn and engage. She had caught on very well with the training with guns and knives, clearly showing that she wasn't afraid of using them. The girl, now in her early twenties, seemed to have done it all. Although he didn't understand her bisexual nature, he knew that in her he had found his heir apparent, for at sixty - eight years old he felt that he was getting old and that aging was catching up with him to where, very soon, he must hand over to more capable brains and versatile minds. He now let her handle small jobs, now and then, and she had done very well on those. He was beginning to rely on her more and more, though taking his time to do so.

Recently, he got this phone call from one of his main agents, a seemingly complex friend of his who always showed up with small, but sophisticated, well paying, clean - up jobs. This guy never showed up unless he was very sure of the job's availability, and always personally put a guarantee on it. He also made sure that whatever Crane asked for in respect of the job being done was promptly provided and without any questions. Everything was always discussed and finalized before Crane accepted the job, including all expenses and pay outs. Because once WBC accepted the job, it was considered done. Failure was no option for Woodrow Brinks Crane and his outfit.

This was considered to be his last job where he would be directly involved, and then after that he was going to retire and let Ruma take over the show, running it together with his assistants. He was planning to remain in the background, though, but mainly as a consultant or advisor.

241

The agent had a job to eliminate, or assassinate, a billionaire and his family. He had stressed to Crane that the client badly wanted this done well, once and for all, so there was to be no tolerance for any mistakes. The client was willing to foot any cost for the job to be done, and since Crane was known for always accomplishing the task, applying whatever it takes to do it, however complex it was, the agent felt without any doubt that Crane was the best candidate for it. They had met at a remote place, inside one of Crane's houses, as Crane had no trust in doing business in public places like hotels and discussed everything. He had Ruma sit in on it too, so she could have hands - on, first class experience on arranging deals. Woodrow Brinks Crane was even more pleased when his terms of payment, that being half down, half after the job was done were met, especially at the price he asked for. The money was wired to a private account that very day and the deal was signed up with the agent.

What Crane didn't know was that he had just made a deal with the devil, and that those kinds of deals seldom come without deadly consequences.

After the agent left, Crane summoned in the rest of his crew and the group had sat down and had an in-depth discussion of the project and how to best handle it. They had a timing of one week in which to have it done. One of the things he had learned from his experiences with such jobs was that with big money also comes top notch problems, like dealing with top-of-the-line security details for multi - million targets, or secured, high-end political ones. To deal with such, he had figured out, one had to hit hard and big, with no mercy, because a billionaire's or high-end political figure's security group had no problem enclosing their client within their physical network, and if you dare to step into it without proper authorization, you would be very dead meat. Therefore, incoming external adversary, which in this case is Crane and his team, must study or analyze, and then find a way to go around, the physical security network first in order to break into it and then move in fast and hit hard, in order to get the job done.

They had one advantage on this assignment, though, and that was that they knew that their target is in an isolated location, and although this wasn't always a problem for Crane, they did not have to worry

242

about killing any innocents during the attack. The target in this case seemed to be self-contained.

But the agent had also cautioned him over and over again that the billionaire may not be as easy a target as it looks, that for some unknown reasons, some other groups had already tried and failed. The billionaire seemed to have some kind of sophisticated protection of his own and that, the agent had said, was the main reason why he had come to Crane, because the Crane group was one of the very best in this business, the cream of the crop, not only in the region, but worldwide. One of the best in the silent world of assassins. But the agent had also added, in a single verbal statement of notification, that the client had warned him that there could be consequences for both himself and Crane if they failed, even though he did not mention what he exactly meant by consequences. Crane didn't like being threatened, and could have easily declined the assignment, but the money was too good to be declined. With the down payment immediately paid upfront, the job was worth a shot.

So now Crane had carefully assembled his team, armed with powerful weapons like never used before, getting them ready for a massive assault on the billionaire's dwellings before stepping in and implementing the kill. They had even rehearsed the moves over and over again and henceforth establishing a firm routine.

Earlier, in the past couple of days, he had sent over a small team of his people to scout the place, and their feedback had confirmed that the Billionaire and his family were indeed there. Using his connections of the people he knew, plus those that worked for him, like network engineers and programmers, he had tapped into the billionaire family's telephone network and listened to every conversation that came from that house. That's how he got to confirm that the billionaire had indeed set up a new security detail, separate from his usual personal one, which a friend of the billionaire's had strongly recommended.

So today, Crane and his crew, were on their way to do the job. Two of the vehicles in the convoy carried the massive arsenal of portable weapons, and that is why he would never let that trooper, or his cronies get near them. If the trooper had eye-balled these weapons, his attention and suspicion could have been immediately heightened and there was

243

no telling where it could all have ended up. More so, Crane could not afford the delay. This operation, much like the rest he had undertaken in his second career in the world of human target elimination, had a timing on it. Crane felt that it was much better to completely erase the trooper nuisance and or risk than play merry– go–round with it.

"Does anyone see what I see?" the driver of the lead vehicle suddenly, and once again, said via the wireless ear communications network. "Ahead of us, in the sky. What are those things? They seem to be headed in the same direction we are going."

"Yeah, I see them. Looks like some big birds flying to some place," someone replied from a different vehicle. "And they seem to be moving fast too."

"Thowse can't be birds, turd!" Ruma came through with her messed up speech pronunciations. "They're tow big to be birds, and on toup of that, 'em things have a bright yelloo ligh' showing on them. Tel' me, anyone ever seen any huge birds like that flying aroun' in the sky with a yelloo' ligh' on they head? Don' thin' thow! Bite me if such a thin' even exists! Only in fairy tales, maybe."

"Probably the U.S military conducting tests on some of their new crazy toys like aircrafts or drone weapons. They usually do them at night," Crane weighed in. "Not our concern, guys, so please focus on the mission ahead of us, will ya? We have fifteen minutes to get to our destination."

"Got ya, boss," the lead driver responded, but his eyes remained focused on the sky ahead too while he drove. The mysterious flying things finally disappeared below the horizon line. Boss was probably right, he told himself. They were probably drones or aircraft traversing a night sky with a pale moon.

Fifteen minutes' drive away from the fast-moving killer convoy, tucked away in his ten thousand square foot, beleaguered mansion with his family, billionaire Bernhardt Vonsberg sat alone in the main living room, in front of the fire place, a tall glass of sweet red, table wine in his hand. Feeling sleepless, tossing and turning in his bed, he had decided to come downstairs in fear that he will wake up his wife, Myra, who was sleeping soundly next to him in their king size queen Anne bed. His mind was not at ease. He felt very restless.

244

Unknown to Myra, her husband was restless because of the ongoing situation of threats to his life, which was very frustrating because of its sudden impact on him and his family's life, yet he still didn't know who was behind the threats, why this was happening, or even how to stop it. All he knew, and felt, was that his life was suddenly in danger, under maximum threat from an unknown or invisible enemy who had already boldly signaled that he was after him and possibly his family.

The fact that he almost got killed by the estranged driver from that meeting at a faraway island place, plus the telephone call from his hometown chief of police, together with his trusted friend Greg to tell him that a group of his would - be killers had turned up at his house, had cemented his fears.

But their story also clearly mentioned a mysterious individual who called himself Zeal, and that this Zeal guy had single handedly turned his would-be killers away. They sounded terrified by their experience with this guy but were also somewhat excited about it. On request from Zeal, they had refrained from discussing what had exactly taken place with anyone else. Zeal had requested that they only talk to Bernhardt Vonsberg about it. No one else, not even their very next of kin, was to be told yet!

Was this the same Zeal that had come to his rescue on that island? Or the same one that had called him via the pastor's mobile phone back at the house in Southlake?

But the Chief of police had sounded off a warning that there was a need for tighten security from now on and until further notice and had recommended a well-known security specialist firm that could handle the billionaire family's needs very well. That very morning after they had moved into the mansion and after hearing from Greg and the chief of police, Bernhardt Vonsberg had contacted the firm and they had immediately come over, spending many hours at the mansion setting up a security perimeter. They had advised that for the first week nobody leave the premises, and that anyone who came to the mansion had to go through thorough scrutiny before being let on to the premises.

Which had turned out to be very frustrating for the entire Vonsberg family, especially with the fact he had not yet told them the reasons these changes were happening. That very evening, after the security firm had set up the security perimeter and their personnel moved on board by setting up surveillance and routine monitoring units around the big house, Bernhardt Vonsberg was forced to hold a family meeting to explain what had happened on his business trip, about his first engagement with the mysterious Zeal, and the personal phone call he had received from him via the pastor's phone.

The entire family of wife and kids, plus the sister-in-law and his own sister, listened quietly as he narrated the story, all the way to the end, not excluding the story phoned in by his Greg and the police chief himself. But he could sense that all that stuff was confusing to them, especially when it came to the Zeal part. They were silent, signaling a tense sense of being in fear of, like him, the unknown, but more for them because they themselves had not experienced the events firsthand. He could see the doubt on their faces. They were finding it hard to believe what he was telling them.

And so, it was no surprise to him when his son Barret paused the question that seemed to be on every one's mind.

"Ok, Dad, we hear you out, and I will be the first one to admit that this stuff you are telling us is compellingly scarily, and weird too!" the young Vonsberg said. "The question I have for you is when is this going to end? Are we going to live our lives like this forever?"

"Unfortunately, Barret, I don't have the answers to that yet," Bernhardt replied with a sigh. "This whole thing has come to me suddenly and unexpectedly. My whole world has been suddenly compromised by these developments and I am still trying to figure out how to deal with it all. I am just asking all of you to hang in there with me until I eventually find a solution to the problem. I hope it won't take long to do so."

Barret Vonsberg had then stood up and came over to where his father was seated, facing all of them. He put his hand on his dad's shoulder and said, "Dad, you are one of the richest people on this planet. You have a lot of money. Surely this money can buy us back our freedom, ward off all these threats, and get us back to our normal lives. It shouldn't take time at all."

"It's not that easy, son. Money is not a means to everything. Besides, we don't even know what we are facing yet, so we cannot stop it," his father replied. "We need to know what we are facing, and the source of it, in order to eliminate the threat once and for all, so that it doesn't come back to haunt us. The enemy has all the time in the world, and will patiently wait until the security is lax, and then strike. You can have all the security you want in the world, but somewhere there will be a flaw, a breach in the system, and then the inevitable can or will happen."

"That's all bullshit, dad!" Barret exploded. "You just don't want to spend the money, that's it! But I swear to God I can't live like this, people! You don't get it man, do you? All you care about is your money, and your shitty business friends and crappy deals. You don't give a crap about your family! You're being inconsiderate and selfish! But I miss my friends, my school, and the world out there. This needs to end as soon as possible, otherwise I am going to go crazy on you. All of you!"

"I say watch your mouth, Barret!" his sister, Benita, suddenly yelled at him, almost hysterically. "And you may not address or shout at daddy like that or using such words. Are you even paying attention to what he's saying? Or you are too busy thinking about yourself, as usual? What he's just told us is not bullshit, it's very real. Otherwise, he wouldn't be sitting here himself telling it to us. He said he's working on it, and asked us, his family, to hang in there with him while he does so. And I fully believe him, because he's already taking measures to keep us safe. So as of right now, what he needs is our unwavering support. Now more than ever, and that's what we need to do as a family. All of us, because we are all affected. So why don't you quit acting like a spoilt brat and do exactly that! I suggest that if you have nothing positive to contribute, then just sit down and shut your big mouth!"

"And what if I don't, little bitch sis? What are you going to do about it, huh?" Barret fired back, glaring at his sister with visible anger.

"Barret… please ease up there, will you, son? No need to get angry and using such words. Can we please keep this a civil discussion?" their mom, Myra cautioned the two siblings.

"Then I will be forced to shut it up for you!" Benita replied with equal ferociousness. As she said this, she stood up and walked over to where her brother stood, now in the middle of the living room, between her father and the rest of the group, confronting him directly. "You want to try me out, huh, "big ass" brother? I suggest you don't, because I will not hesitate to mess you up. I am just about tired of your whining, and your disrespect for daddy and everybody else here!"

"Oh really, huh? So why don't you show us how you're going to do that. Show us now, little bitch...," Barret responded back, but he didn't get the chance to finish whatever else he was going to say to finish his sentence, because the five-foot nine height, eighteen years old, one hundred fifty-five pounds Benita suddenly lashed out and struck her six-foot five height, two hundred and forty-two pounds, twenty-two years old brother in his face with her clenched right fist. The blow was hard enough to instantly daze him, causing him stumble backwards and almost lose his balance.

"What the hell...." Barret exclaimed in utter surprise, and then she hit him again, this time on the left side of his neck, below his left jaw, with her left clenched fist. Bum! This time, Barret lost his balance and fell on the floor, leaving his sister standing over him like a triumphant boxing champion who had just knocked out his opponent. Her actions were lightning fast too!

"I said back down, Barret, or I will be forced to hurt you again!" Benita shouted at her brother, shaking her clenched fist at him.

"Children, stop it! Stop it, right now!" their mother suddenly shouted out hysterically. It was the highest voice pitch that any one had ever heard from her ever since she started falling seriously sick two and a half years ago. It was an eerily, high pitched wail that went deep into everyone's consciousness.

The other two women then quickly intervened, standing in between the two warring siblings. Adalicia Vonsberg, Bernhardt's sister, pulled Benita back and away, while his sister-in-law, Wendt, jumped in between her fallen nephew and his sister. There was blood dripping from the right side of Barret's mouth.

"Alright, that's enough, Benita! Now Back off!" Aunt Adalicia shouted at her niece.

"Now I am going to kill you, you little bitch!" Barret also shouted out, anger welling up in him. I don't care if she is my sister. I am going to kill her!"

"Now don't you all mind all that talk. He doesn't know what he's saying right now. It's all anger or rage, coupled with that stupid, youthful vigor," Aunt Wendt said quickly. "Calm down now, Barret dear, calm down!"

"Oooh no, you won't!" Aunt Adalicia sounded off immediately after her sister in law's utterance. "Maybe you don't know this, but your sister has been taking private lessons in mixed martial arts for the past three years and now has a black belt. I hate to tell all of you this, but she's fully capable of defending herself and very able to take you on, Barret. Wendt, please take Barret upstairs and fix him up. We don't want this happening anymore."

Aunt Wendt helped her nephew to get up off the floor. He got up without saying another word, and the two left the living room, with Aunt Wendt holding her still dazed nephew's hand, and slowly helping him make his way upstairs.

"Bern, did you know about Benita taking fighting lessons all along?" Mayra Vonsberg asked her husband in between labored breathing. That sudden, high - pitched reaction was already taking its toll on her.

Bernhardt Vonsberg slowly shook his head, trying to comprehend the turn of things. "Yeah, I know about it. I recommended it for her, because as a girl, she needs to know how to defend herself."

"And you didn't sign up her brother on it? that's not fair, Bern. You are showing favoritism for one of the children. You are fostering a split between the two. Shame on you!" Myra Vonsberg said sternly.

"It's actually you who's being unfair, mom!" Benita said, freeing herself from her aunt's hold and turning around to glare at her mother. "You let Barret get away with everything, with a lot of nonsense! But you know what, I don't care. He's your son, so he's yours to mess up. But I will be damn if I let him talk to Dad like that! He needs to learn how to respect his parents and other grown-ups. Daddy doesn't deserve that toxic, noxious attitude from any of us. Not even from you, mom!"

And with those final words, Benita strode out of the living room, running up the stairs. Everyone heard her door slam with a heavy thud.

"Well maybe if he didn't spend too much of his time acting brat with his mama, we could have made it happen!" Aunt Adalicia jumped in, facing her sister-in-law.

"Please stay out of this, Adalicia," Myra snapped back at her. "This is an internal problem. Stay out of it!"

"Oh really? So now I am not part of this family?" Aunt Adalicia responded back to Myra's statement with animosity. "You better have an answer to that question, or I will make sure you hear it for the rest of your life!"

Myra Vonsberg grimaced, then sighed, and then said "I am so sorry, Adee. I really didn't mean to say that… it just came out that way. Please forgive my sickened mind. I love you to death and I appreciate you being here with me as I go through this dreadful illness."

"Ok, people, enough!" Bernhardt Vonsberg suddenly shouted. "Stop all this squabbling. You are all frustrating me more now. I have a major problem on my hands now to solve, and that's, by itself, already too much. I don't need any more additional problems to deal with!" Aunt Wendt returned from upstairs.

"How's Barret doing, Wendt?" Myra Vonsberg asked immediately.

"He's ok. He just needs to wind down," Aunt Wendt replied.

"Ok. Now help me get up. I need to go back to the bedroom," Myra said. Her sister helped her get off the couch, and together they made their way upstairs, one step at a time, leaving Bernhardt Vonsberg with his sister Adalicia alone in the living room. But she didn't stay long either.

"Sorry about all that, Bernhardt. This shouldn't be happening now, or even at all," Aunt Adalicia said, walking over to where her brother was seated and gently parting him on the shoulder. "I know you have a lot to think about now. I am going to go upstairs too. Do you need me for anything?"

"No, thanks. I am ok. Thanks for stepping in and stopping the kids from fighting each other," he said to his sister. "I think all this is affecting them tremendously."

250

His sister also left the living room. He stayed longer, watching television for a while, and then decided to go back to bed. But not after updating himself with his new security detail. He did that by communicating through a special computerized interface that allowed him to view the entire premise and see where the armed guards are. Everything looked good, the report came back. He then called, and spoke to, his oldest son Brennon, who was currently living in Europe. The twenty-six years old was wrapping up a master's degree in international business and also managing his dad's business there. Brennon had expressed concern at what was going on and had quickly set up a private security detail for himself. His father, however, did not tell him about his siblings' altercation. He didn't want to bother him with that.

But Bernhardt couldn't sleep and kept turning and tossing. The disturbances within his family were a sure sign that all was not well now, and he felt that this was because of the ongoing problems. Everyone was stressed out, unhappy, and disturbed. That's why he left the bedroom again and was seated alone again in the living room with a glass of wine.

Unknown to him, other things were going on elsewhere on his premises. Something with wings suddenly came out of the clouds, riding the wind gust that had suddenly picked up in speed, and landed quietly on top the mansion's tiled roof. It was an adult man. The wings folded back up behind his back, and then retracted themselves into the sky, fading back into the space above. Squatting on top of the house, the man reached inside his black coat and pulled out a cell phone. He said something to the phone, and then waited.

A minute or so later, inside the house, Barret Vonsberg came bounding down the stairs and into the living room. He had his cell phone in his hand. "This is for you, Dad. It's a guy's voice, and he asked to speak to you. I don't know who it is, and I don't know why he is using my phone number to get to you."

Bernhardt frowned, and then took the phone from his son. "You, ok?" he asked his son. Barret nodded in affirmation. "Hello ..."

"Hi, Mr. Vonsberg. This is Zeal. I am outside your house now ... Well, I am right on top of it," the caller said. "In a few seconds I will come down to the ground and I will knock on your door. Will you please let me in? and by the way, tell your son that it won't be necessary to call the police."

"What? You can't be serious!" Bernhardt Vonsberg said. Reaching over, he picked up a small link on the surveillance monitor screen that remotely enabled him to switch views from the surveillance cameras outside. He switched to full Arial view.

"Dad, look at that. There is someone standing up on top of the house, talking on a phone," Barret, said, pointing at the seventy-inch screen, flat panel, visual monitoring system set up on one of the living room walls by the security company. "Should I call the police?"

Bernhardt Vonsberg stared at the screen, and sure enough, there he was. He zoomed in on the figure. It was Zeal, the man he had encountered on that island's airport, the one that saved his life that evening. He had no idea how Zeal happened to be on top of his house, or why he had showed up here in the first place. He looked at his son and shook his head. How did Zeal know Barret was going to say that?

"No, son. No need to call the police. We have enough private security already. And he's talking to me right now, via your cellphone," he said to Barret, with a surprised look on his face. "How did he get your number? You two know each other already?"

"I don't know him at all, Dad," Barret replied. "I don't even know how he's able to call and talk on my phone because it's supposed to be totally out of charge. It had totally shut itself down just a few minutes ago and I was looking for my charger to plug it up when it suddenly lit up and indicated an incoming call. The phone rung, dad, even though I had it in vibration mode!"

As they both stared at the screen, the figure suddenly vanished. In the next few seconds, there was a light knock on the door.

"Barret don't leave yet. Stay right there," Bernhardt Vonsberg said. Handing back the cell phone to his son, he got up and walked to the door, and for some reason, he opened it without hesitation. The man who called himself Zeal was now standing right there, in his doorway. How he had come down so fast from the roof top to the door was itself a mystery of its own. He stood aside to let him through.

"Thank you for letting me in, Mr. Vonsberg," a grinning Zeal said, stepping into the house. "It's a little bit nippy out there, guys. I now really appreciate the cozy warmth in here."

"Wow! How the heck did you do that? In one moment, you are on top of the house, and in the next second you are at the door…" Barret asked, a look of surprise on his face.

"Hi, Barret. It's nice to meet you, I am Zeal," the man, slightly shorter than Barret but way much muscular, said. "Sorry I had to borrow your phone. I Couldn't use your father's because its upstairs in his bedroom, at the bedside, and I didn't want to disturb your mother with its ring. She's sleeping soundly." He took off his hand gloves, that looked like they had spikes on them, and offered his hand. Barret shook it, though hesitantly. Though Zeal's hand felt very warm, that was the tightest grip that Barret had ever felt in a handshake, and it was over in about two seconds. It felt like Zeal's hand faded out of Barret's hand, like it had turned into air.

"Barret, I would like you to meet the mysterious Zeal, the man I had told you about that saved my life at that Island's airport and had also suddenly called me on the Pastor's phone," Bernhardt Vonsberg said. "I don't know how he does his stuff , but I have learned not to doubt his abilities lately. You have just experienced, first-hand, the mysteries that come with him." "Have a seat, Zeal. Would you like a drink or something to eat?"

"Thanks, but no to drinks or food, Mr. Vonsberg," Zeal said, sitting down in one of the single chairs in the living room but immediately leaning forward. "Listen, we have no time. I want you to do something for me and I want you to trust in me. I want you to call off your security people, now. Tell them to vacate your premises."

"You want me to call my security guard detail off? But, why?" Bernhardt Vonsberg asked with suspicion, raising his hands and voice. "I need these people at the moment to protect me and my family from impending danger out there. And you are asking me to call them off, when they have just been here for less than two days?"

"That's right," Zeal replied.

"I don't think so. That's crazy, dad. Don't do it!" Barret said.

"You're asking me to do something very difficult," Bernhardt Vonsberg said. "I mean, if I do so, who will protect us then, huh? If you can prove to me that you have the means to protect us, then maybe I will call them off. But until you do so, they are staying put."

"Listen, I wish I can tell you how this is going to work out, but unfortunately, some things are not meant to be explained or exposed.

At least not yet," Zeal said. "You just must trust me and do what I am asking you to do. We are fast running out of time too, so I need you to make a quick decision here."

"Look, man, you can't just suddenly walk in here and tell my dad what to do!" Barret said, stepping forward. "You heard what he said. He's not taking the security detail off , and I agree with him, because it doesn't make sense. End of story!"

Zeal slowly turned around and stared at the younger Vonsberg. He still had the grin on his face when he said "You're really a pain in the rare, for sure, young man. I got the vibes about your nature before I came down here but ignored them. Now I see the problem. Nonetheless, this is a matter your father needs to handle, not you, and I would appreciate that as you standby and bear witness to these events, don't talk. So, Mr. Vonsberg, come on, all you need is a little faith in me, but a lot of faith in God."

Bernhardt Vonsberg hesitated, slowly shaking his head. "Like I said, if you can prove to me that there is another way you are going to protect us, I am afraid I will remain a man of little faith at this time."

"But you said earlier on to us, and then repeated it to Barret a few minutes ago, that this very man, known to you only as Zeal, mysteriously saved your life back there on that island, right daddy?" another voice joined the verbal exchange. It was his daughter, Benita. She had come downstairs when she heard her brother making his way back downstairs. "Then he called you via the pastor's phone, again warning you to get away from dangerous people who were coming for us. That was also mysterious, given the fact that pastor didn't know him at all. Then you told us that you got a phone call from Mr. Green and the chief of police to tell you that a man by the same name had saved them from gunmen who had come to our house in Southlake wanting to kill you, right? Now he just called you on Barret's phone which has no charge and had totally shut itself down. Don't you get it, Daddy? He's not your normal, regular kind of human being. He's a special, unique individual, maybe an angel, and he's trying to protect you, something he has done before. That's reason enough to make you do what he asks, however vague it feels."

They all turned around and stared at Benita. She was now standing at the bottom of the step, in her pajamas, looking at them.

"Benita, you've been listening in on us all this time?" Bernhardt Vonsberg acknowledged his daughter's presence.

Zeal strode over to where she stood and offered his hand. "Hi, I am Zeal," he said.

But Benita's hands did not move, remaining tacked away inside her pajama pockets. The angel's hand remained suspended. However, she smiled briefly at him, looked up at her father and said "Daddy, call the security detail off, now. Just do what he asks of us. We will be ok. Just do it."

Bernhardt Vonsberg stared at her daughter for a moment of about ten seconds, and then walked over to his leather recliner, reached into one of its side pockets and withdrew a small gadget that looked much like a cellphone. It had a big red button in the center which he pressed down with one of finger and held down on it while he spoke into it.

"This is fox one. Please vacate premises immediately," Bernhardt Vonsberg said. "I repeat, vacate premises now! I will notify you as to when to resume your coverage."

"What? What seems the problem, sir? Can we talk about it?" a voice echoed back from the gadget's speaker.

"Everything is fine. There is no problem. I just want you guys off the premises for now, and immediately," Bernhardt Vonsberg repeated.

"Mr. Vonsberg, this is a strange order and equally dangerous," the man outside lamented. "Perhaps I can have you talk to my boss, or I can come in and we discuss this more…"

"Mr. Vonsberg, please, we have no time left on this. They need to get off this property now," Zeal cut in as he withdrew his hand back after it was rejected by Benita and staring earnestly at the frustrated billionaire.

"Dammit I said leave my premises, now!" Bernhardt Vonsberg shouted into the gadget. His two children stared at him in surprise. They had never seen their father this way. "I don't want to discuss anything with you or your boss. Just do what I am ordering you to do, or I will cancel the entire contract. Do you hear and understand me?"

"We hear you loud, and clear, sir," the response came back quickly. "Give us about five minutes or even less and we shall be out of here."

Zeal sighed in relief. And as they all watched on the big surveillance monitor, at least twenty men emerged from areas surrounding the house and made their way down the driveway to a big, well demarcated guest parking lot where half a dozen dark green Hammer trucks were parked. Zeal looked at his watch, and in a few minutes shy of five, the guard vehicles drove out of the well illuminated compound, through the double wide gates which opened with remote access that the owner had given to his hired guards and disappeared into the darkness beyond.

"There, it's all yours now. Our entire lives are in your hands now, Zeal!" Bernhardt Vonsberg said. "I hope I have not made a mistake I will live to regret for the rest of my life. Because if anything bad happens to my family, I will not allow myself to live anymore, for I will not be able to bare the pain. Mark my words Zeal, I would be better off dead than face that pain or grief. And so, to spare me from all that, please tell me or show me what this is all about."

"I can't believe this. So just like that, huh, dad?" Barret suddenly spoke up again. "A guy jumps off the top of your house, then you let him in, and then you suddenly put our lives in his hands! What kind of thinking is that dad? Or is it because you don't trust anyone else in this family except your karate wielding daughter here? Oh, now I get it. Because she now has a black belt in martial arts, she has totally worn over your heart. Totally ridiculous, this is!"

And with that, Barret Vonsberg shook his head and then immediately left the living room, making his way back up the stairs. His sister had to quickly step out of the way as he almost bumped into her. But neither did the two other individuals in the area acknowledge him or turn around to look at him as he departed the scene.

"Your faith has come a long way, Mr. Vonsberg," Zeal acknowledged as he faced the billionaire and his daughter, Benita, who had now come closer. He winked at her. "And for that we are very grateful, because that's all we need in order to be activated. Faith in God. Let me assure you that you will not live to regret anything. You and your family are safe with us. We are going to protect you, just as I protected you at that airport. Now, as I speak, a group of hired human killers are on their way to here to kill you, to finish you and your family off for good. They are coming with a lot of sophisticated, heavy and light firepower that your security detail would not be able to match, especially given the element of surprise. These killers plan to suddenly attack and hit hard with their firepower, and no one on your security detail was going to survive it. After that, they were going to match into your house and make sure that you, and every member of your family in this house is dead! We are here to stop them from doing that."

"We? I only see you here, Mr. Zeal. Where are the rest of the "we"? out there?" Benita asked coming closer to Zeal.

"And how did you get to know about all this, Zeal?" Bernhardt Vonsberg added to his daughter's barrage of questions. "How do you know that there are people on their way to kill us?"

"Just as I knew that you have a security detail before asking you to send them home. I also know that you have powerful beam lights set up in those trees surrounding your estate," Zeal said. "I know that your security team had carefully set them up to completely illuminate the enemy's hiding places in those trees. Am going to ask you to turn them on in the next very few minutes. And miss Vonsberg, I asked your father to send the security personnel away to get them out of harm's way. I now ask that you be patient, both of you, for what you're about to see will completely change your lives forever, and perhaps help explain and answer all your questions about the 'we', and perhaps help explain my mysterious ways."

A few minutes away from the Vonsberg hideout residence, Woodrow Brinks Crane and his crew were still driving on a wide two- lane road when a series of utility vehicles sped past them, going in the opposite direction.

"Security detail vehicles, I know the type," Crane said. "Good thing they are headed in the opposite direction. Wouldn't like them headed in the same direction we are taking."

"Would them people pose a problem to us, daddy, if they were goin' to whe'we are goin'?" Ruma asked. She was now chewing hard on a strip of beef jerky, the smacking noise coming through the entire communication system. The gunning down of that highway police officer had somewhat unnerved her, and the hard chewing helped her calm those nerves down.

"Not really, especially with this project. Nobody dares to get in our way on this or they will face the fire. But they would be a godamned pain in the rare," her father replied. "And Ruma, would you please make sure you aren't gnawing on whatever is in your mouth while communicating? It's very annoying, that noise you're making with your mouth. Otherwise, I will be compelled to stop this convoy just to come out there and pluck it out of your mouth with my combat knife!

A brief period of silence prevailed on the communication system for a couple of minutes before Ruma came back on again with "Ok daddy. Sorry daddy, will spit it out now." She was always afraid of her father, and although she knew he wouldn't really use his knife to pluck it out of her mouth, he would probably knock it out of her mouth with his fist. Her father didn't play games with her at all, or with anyone else on his team for that matter. At least, with her, not in public. To her, he was just a flat-out badass man with a very bad attitude most of the time. But he still let her play sassy around him. She knew that regardless of the meanness, she was his favorite thing in the world. He adored her more than anything else in his life and he had himself said it so.

After that, nobody said anything until they made a right turn off the main road and drove up a winding sloppy drive way that finally ended on the outside of what appeared to be a high fence of metal poles held up by a thick, complex looking maze of barbed wire, the type that would electrocute any flesh bearing body, be an elephant or just a fly, with thousands of high voltage electricity upon contact, and make that entity sizzle like a pork patty on an overheated grill. The winding sloppy road, however, led them directly to a pair of high, completely opaque metal gates. There was no way to see inside, because even on the other side of the high fence was plenty of foliage made of numerous, closely planted tall and skinny, trees. The convoy came to a dead stop at these gates, waiting for further instructions. All engines went dead, and all lights were turned off on the cars.

"Keener, get going on those gates, boy," Woodrow Crane ordered. "Rivers and Burt, support him with lights and balance. You all know what to do. The rest of you, start getting your weapons ready. The operation will begin any moment from now!"

Keener, his electronics infiltration expert, had already scouted out the double gates and seen how they worked a week ago, taking pictures and videos of them from a distance and using a drone to study the gates' outlook up close. He even found out the manufacturer and downloaded the design and functionality of the big, electronically controlled metallic doors. He then got to figure out how to hack into their control system, which he surprisingly found easy. Armed with this knowledge, he now knew what to do as he walked up to the gates and pointed an infrared ray of light to the left side where there was a tiny, small box with a red light on it. He carefully opened the small box, which, surprisingly, was not secured, and plugged something in it. Asking one of the other guys to hold his flashlight in place, he then walked back to the car and got on the laptop computer again. After rapidly typing for about two minutes, he pressed the "enter" key with a hard tap using his middle finger on his right hand.

The huge gates noiselessly glided open, all the way to reveal a two lane, two ways well paved driveway bordered by more trees plus what looked like fancy statues of things not so clear in the moon light.

"Bingo!" Keener said, sounding overjoyed with his success. "Good job, son," Woodrow Crane acknowledged. "Drivers, take us in. This driveway will lead us to a vast compound with a huge parking lot, but we are not going into the lot, because it's definitely guarded. We are stopping midway to set up the firepower gear. Hernandez and Jermain, you will get the mortars out first and set them up. You have two minutes to do this. Marko and Chen, get the rocket launchers and prepare for assault. Jeff and McConnell, prep up the grenade launchers. Envilo and Kizito, roll that 50g submachine gun out on top of number car three and have it ready for assault. Keener, you know what to do with those drone guns. I want the mini tank bomber on the road facing in the direction of the house. Backa and Singh, get on the remote controls for car number four, make sure it's loaded with the load of C4 and set it ready to detonate once the self- auto driver gets the car close to the front of the house. Big Vladimir, is the sniper rifle ready for knocking out any fleeing figures? You know what to do. The rest of you, have your assault rifles out ready and put on your gas masks. I am about launch the self-propelled nerve gas cannisters. This is it, guys. The operation is on. Let's go earn those ten million dollars!"

Doors flipped open and everyone disembarked from the vehicles and quickly started assembling their respective equipment. Everyone, except Ruma. Clinging on to her assault rifle, she remained seated inside the car, staring blankly out of her door window. Someone suddenly rapped hard on her window glass pane, making her jump! It was one of the guys, Kizito, the tall, lean-bodied, muscular guy from Africa with a heavy accent. She stared at him angrily, but then smiled. Of all the guys on the team, she liked him most. He was less talkative, polite, and came across as very caring. Her dad liked him too. Just for curiosity and adventure, she had slept with him, and boy, what an experience! He had burst through, and made his way, deep into her hole like some hungry, angry beast, making her want it again and again. He mentioned to her that she had passed out a few times during the intercourse. They had bonded after that, but casual remained the tone of things. Even with that, and despite the fact that she had tried them out too, each one at least once, it still made the other guys on the team jealous of him, maybe because she had made him the main deal. They isolated themselves from him most of the time. And neither did he care much. He kept to himself most of the time too, anyway.

"You not coming with us, Princess?" he whispered to her after she rolled the window down. He knew, just like the rest of the team, that this was her first direct, hands - on experience in the field. "No need to be scared. I will protect you. Come out, it's all gonna be fun."

"I naw, and thanks Kiz, but I jus' suddenly feel under the weath ah, like I am fixin' to be sicko something'," she replied. "it's ok, you guys can go on. I will catch up wid y 'all in a few minutes."

"Alright then," Kizito whispered back, and then went back to his vehicle, now enhanced with the 50g machinegun rifle. He was going to man it, and was ready, only waiting for the command from Woodrow Crane.

Woodrow Crane made a roll call of all his operatives, confirming ready or not. Everyone confirmed ready, except Ruma. He called out again to her, but she remained quiet.

"Hey, Ruma, have you suddenly developed cold feet?" someone whispered through the communication network, which was instantly followed by chuckling.

"Oh, come on guys, give her a break!" Kizito came through. "We all know that this is her first time on a live operation."

Harnessing his gun over his shoulders, Woodrow made his way to the car in which his daughter was seated, still staring blankly out of the window. She rolled down her window pane after he tapped on it.

"Is it true that you are suddenly scared of participating in this operation, huh, girl?" he asked quietly. "I thought you said this whole thing was going to be just another adventure for you."

"I know but I jus' don' feel good about the whole thing anymore, daddy," she replied. "I suddenly have a bad feeling about it, like something bad is about to happen to all of us. I think we should pull out immediately, daddy. Get us out of here! Let's go home, before it's too late."

"Well, it's too late to pull out now, girl," Woodrow Crane said, shaking his head slowly. "I just can't cancel an operation when we're right in the doorway, more especially if the main reason is based on one of my operatives developing cold feet. For that matter, just sit back and watch while me and the boys finish this off."

With that, Woodrow Crane walked away from her. He gave the order for the convoy to advance forward, towards the main house. His plan was to move quietly further into the compound, closer to the house than they were now, stop and then launch the ravaging assault. After that, they would go in and comb the place for any signs of human life. And if any, gun them down. He planned to take a souvenir, the billionaire's head, as proof that he had completed the job.

"Aaaah, boss, I think we have a problem," the lead driver said suddenly, after clearing his throat. "I see something standing in our way, just ahead of us."

"What are you exactly seeing, Josh, that's standing in our way?" Woodrow Crane asked as he made his way to his control vehicle.

"Looks like someone sitting on a horse, boss," Josh, the lead driver, answered. "And they are slowly moving towards us."

"Yeah, I see it too, boss," someone else said. "And that horse... never seen anything like that before. The thing is fuckin' huge. It's like a beast of some kind."

"Hey guys, do you see what I see?" Kizito came in. He too was monitoring his way ahead through his night – vision – abled binoculars as he stood behind the 50-caliber machinegun on top of his vehicle, through the open sunroof of the SUV. "At least three more people have shown up out of nowhere and are standing next to the one on the huge horse. And they all have some sort of creepy bright yellow light around their heads. I don't like this boss, but I am already to blast these guys down and out of our way. Just give the word, boss."

"What the fuckin' hell is going on?" Woodrow Crane snapped. He was beginning to wonder that just like his daughter, Ruma, his men were beginning to freak out on him too. Yet he had never seen them act this way before, talking shit like seeing people on horseback or people with yellow lit heads appearing from nowhere. He had worked with these men for a long time, and they were not the kind that got intimidated easily or even at all. They were hardcore fighters and assassins who had already proven that they will stop at nothing to get a job done, and this included putting their lives on the line. That's why he made sure they were paid very well. So now for them to start seeing and saying strange things like this was out of their world. He adjusted his night vision gaggles and focused on the trail ahead.

Nope, his men were not hallucinating. What they were seeing was actually there. It was real. And now the figure on the big horse was dismounting. The dismount seemed to be with a lot of ease, like it was being done in slow motion. The person did not even grab at the reins or at the horse's neck for stability. And then the moment this individual's feet touched the ground, a brief gust of wind enveloped the area, making the leaves on the trees all around them rustle. The other individuals did not move.

"Josh, turn on your full beam overhead lights. Let's see who these guys are," he ordered via the communications system.

"But boss, won't that give us away?" another voice, that of Singh, came through immediately. "I thought we are to remain unseen until we spring the attack."

"Just do it!" Woodrow Crane responded back.

Josh turned on his headlights, all in full beam. Suddenly, there was a cracking sound, that of breaking glass. All the headlights on his vehicle self-shattered, exploding to pieces and blacking out.

"Boss... did you see that?" someone said through the communication system.

"Hey, what the hell just happened?" Josh shouted through the communication system. "My headlights just went out! But none of those folks in front of us even raised a finger."

"Calm down, Josh. Hey fellas, do you think we have a hidden sniper?" someone else's voice, Envilo's, came through. "I think we have someone sniping at us, fellas."

The yellow lights around the top of the heads of the people ahead were now glowing brighter, creating an eerie brightness around them.

"Wait a minute, those lights look familiar. Could those be the things we saw flying ahead of us in the sky?" someone else asked. "The ones that boss said could be government military stuff..."

The individual from the big horse suddenly spoke. The voice was clear and strong from where they stood yards away, like a megaphone was in use. It was more on the feminine side. It also came out in multiple tones, like more than one person were speaking at the same time.

"Woodrow Crane, I am going to say this only once," the individual said. "Get your people out of here, off these grounds, and take them home. That way, your souls will be spared. Do it now before it's too late!"

263

"How the fuck does she know my name?" Woodrow Crane's voice echoed through the communication line in form of a whisper. It was obvious that he was talking to himself.

Inside the Vonsberg mansion, in the living room, Zeal turned around and faced its owner. "Mr. Vonsberg, I want you to now turn on all the security lights in the compound, so you can see clearly what's going on."

"Sure, Zeal, if you say so. Everything is on this square panel in my hands," Bernhardt Vonsberg said. He located the digital button marked "Remote exterior lights" and touched it with one of his fingers Suddenly, the entire compound was flooded with bright light. Zeal gave a thumbs up to Bernhardt Vonsberg, then opened the door and stepped out on to the balcony. He stopped at the guard rail and then beckoned to father and daughter to join him.

Then Beret suddenly came bounding down the stairs, so fast that his two kin folks turned around quickly and stared at him. "Dad, there is a horse out there, a huge horse! Right here in our front yard! And a bunch of people and cars too!"

"Something is going on, Barret," Benita said responded before her father did. "And I think Something is about to happen. Come, he wants us to join him on the balcony."

The trio stepped out of the living room and joined Zeal on the balcony. The view below was spectacular. It was like watching a movie on a huge screen but being inside the show itself.

And now the different parties in the front yard were able to clearly see each other. On one side were four individuals and one big beast of a horse – like animal. The individuals were each clad in an attire similar to that of roman emperor generals, complete with shiny metallic sheath around their arms, legs, and chest front and back, and a gleaming, yellow helmet on their heads. Three of them held a gleaming, golden yellow shield in their left hand and a long blade in their right hand of same similar outlook. The fourth individual, standing in the fore front and right below the big horsey beast, did not have a shield, but bore two brightly gleaming golden objects in each hand. The big animal itself was clad in armor. It had one other feature that distinguished it from a regular big horse. It had two big, gleaming, golden yellow, front facing horns.

On the other side was several human individuals, clad in what was clearly paramilitary gear, complete with black berets and body vests. The ones on the ground were all armed with what looked like, to the people on the balcony, assault rifles, while the ones on top of the vehicles had handheld bombard weaponry except for one who sat behind a machine gun. Their guns were all aimed at the mansion and the group that stood between them and the big house.

"Daddy, please listen to me, dis ain't normal stuff we're seein' here. Git us the hell out of here, now! These people, or things… they're gonna kill us all, Daddy! Please!" The communication system exploded with Ruma's wailing, frustrated voice. "I can feel it! Dis ain't for us! Dis ain't good at'all!"

Silence followed. Obvious tension, everyone waiting for a decision that could ultimately alter their fate. It was obvious what Ruma was saying. They were facing an adversary that, for some reason, didn't seem to be of this world, from their outward appeal to their fierce approach. The warning to vacate the billionaire's grounds didn't sound like a request either. It had come across as a command, and a warning. And despite being faced by powerful weaponry, the adversary group wasn't budging at all!

On the other hand, colonel Woodrow Brinks Crane was never the one to give up that easily, and always followed through at all costs. And this job had big money locked in it, money that could change everyone's life. The connecting agent himself had said it. This deal was so big and full of money they would all part ways and retire from their killer lives. And a two and a half million-dollar fee had already been paid upfront as a down payment. But it was his call, he's the boss. The other guys always followed his decisions, followed him to the core. Whatever he says is always the final decision for them.

"It's not an ambush, guys! The billionaire has his own defense, remember? We can work through them. We have enough firepower while they look like they're ill prepared. So, No retreat, no surrender. We have a freakin' job to do, and we're going to see through!" the boss exploded back through the communication system. "Ruma, I shall deal with you later after this, you freak! The rest of you, let's show these motherfuckers what we're made off! Go weapons hot, people, full blast ahead! Get these jockers out of my way. They're the only things standing between us and your money!"

And that was it. Kizito corked the machinegun again, combining the ammunition belt to the gun, and opened fire. The machine gun fire was like a rapidly repeating crank of heavy manufacturing machinery. Not hesitating, the rest of the team followed suit, their silencer rigged weapons sounding like multiple opening fireworks mixed with popping corn sounds! Kizito's car started advancing forward, the others following.

"You wanna stay alive, huh, Rob? then don' drive forward!" Ruma snapped at her driver, pointing her gun at his head. "I will blow ya' fuckin' head off and take over this truck me theft if you do! instead, prepare to rol'it backwards at my command. Let those moo'therfuckers die if that's what they wanna do! For your info, I just ain't ready to die today!"

The cold touch of Ruma's gun barrel and the accompanying click of the gun's safety catch coming off was enough to convince Rob the driver that she wasn't kidding around. He stepped on the breaks, making the car come to a dead stop.

The quartet in front of the advancing fiery front-line also changed. Their partial body armor suddenly changed to a complete wrap up, their entire bodies disappearing inside the new shell. After this happened, the quartet stood their ground as the Woodrow Crane team's heavy volley of bullets simply ricocheted off their bodies. On the balcony, Zeal raised both his hands in front of him and a wave of heated air, like that coming off a hot tarmacked road, came between the balcony and the compound. The Vonsberg felt it and took a step back.

"Sorry guys, just making sure no stray projectiles get to us," he said, maintaining his stunt.

After at least several minutes of serious gun shooting, someone shouted out the obvious through the Woodrow Crane communication wave – length. "I am afraid our fuckin' ammo doesn't seem to be hurting them at all, boss!"

'Mako, Chen, Jeff and McConnel, cut those canons loose on them, now!" came the order on the wave – length.

Almost instantly, a rocket launcher went off, first with a booming sound, and then a swishing sound, aimed straight at the lead figure of their adversary, the one standing in front of the big horse. And almost as instantly, the individual grabbed at the flying rocket as it hit home, just like a soccer goalkeeper grabbing at a flying ball. There was an explosion, followed by a big ball of fire, and then smoke.

Another series of rockets and grenades were released, but the same thing happened as the other members of the quartet jumped forward and warded off the bombardment with their hands. A stray rocket crossed the line and into the compound, then exploded on contact with Zeal's invisible barrier. The group on the balcony saw it coming, and the human group screamed and tried to duck down! Only Zeal remained upright. There was a display of a huge fireball, a slight shaking of the balcony, and then the blast evaporated into lots of black smoke. The people on the balcony didn't even hear the resulting sound from the balcony at all.

The smoke started fading away, revealing to the Woodrow Crane team the prevailing upright figures of their adversary. The bombardment hadn't phased them out either.

Then the adversary group began their move forward.

Their leader suddenly sprung forward, leaping up into the air and flying over the Woodrow team's heads and landing smack down, feet first, on top of the Josh vehicle's engine hood. The landing came down with so much force it was like a massive, heavy stone boulder had been dropped on the front of the car. The engine stopped running, instantly shutting down with a winding noise and both front tires crunched down to the ground as they deflated like punctured balloons, their metallic rims breaking into pieces. As Josh looked on, he saw the figure spin around in a crouch and then a gleaming, big bright yellow knife came swinging down, slicing through half of the windshield from the right side and completely severing and separating his body into two parts starting from below his left breast line and then through the rest of the windshield, ending on the left. His killer paused for a couple of seconds, and then leapt again.

267

Then the big, beastly horse charged, its head lowered, and its horns curved toward Kizito's machinegun - bearing vehicle. The gleaming horns smashed into the front of the car with full force, the impact hurling the car completely off the ground and into the air. The car landed several yards away on top of a set of small, bushy trees, completely crushing the plants flat down and hitting the ground upside down with Kizito underneath it. His body was completely mangled underneath the car, like a heavy object crushing down on an empty beer or soda can. The other three members of the quartet's human looking individuals spread out, two going to the left and one to the right. One of these individuals reached the side of Chen's vehicle in the blink of an eye and a leg lashed out at the car. The vehicle bounced off its four wheels and rolled on to its side. The attacker then leaped on to the vehicle and thrust the long gleaming blade of his yellow knife through the rear window space of the overturned vehicle, shattering the glass and going through Chen's chest. The part of the blade that was inside him speed rotated inside him like a rotating electric wood - saw blade, instantly shredding the contents of the inside of his chest. The attacker withdrew the blade and leapt off the vehicle. Spinning around, he raised his blade bearing hand and brought it down hard on the car, slicing it into two separate halves. The move completely amputated both legs off Chen's partner Marko, from the above the knees downward. As Marko screamed in horrifying pain, the attacker raised his knife again and thrust it into his mouth. The blade tip popped out from his scalp, rotated and split - blast his skull, before being yanked away again, splashing the contents of his skull all over the place.

The other attacker went for Jeff and McConnell with their grenade launchers. The attacker, using his right, blade free, shield wielding hand, smashed the shield into the car's rear left window, completely shattering the glass and hitting Jeff on the left side of his rib cage, below his armpit. The blow delivered a hefty smash at his left heart wall that blew blood out of his body through his mouth, nose, and ears. Instantly withdrawing the hitting arm, his attacker then lashed out again with the shield at an incredible return speed, smashing into Jeff's shoulder blade. This second blow completely crushed and severed the entire left limb off Jeff's body. The arm and its supporting fleshy parts were instantly tossed into the air. Quickly stepping back a few yards, the attacker leapt off both feet, somersaulted over the top of the car in one flip, and landed on the other side of the vehicle where McConnell was. The attacker then smashed through the car's door window with the shield wielding right hand again. The shield split like a receiving baseball glove and latched on to McConnell's right neck as he slumped to duck down, and yanked McConnell's body outwards with full force. At the same time, this attacker body slammed the car, causing it to roll over. McConnell's body was force pulled out of the car, crushing through the car's body and tossed like a rag doll into the air. As his body gravitated downwards, the attacker wielded the now long, gleaming, golden yellow blade into the air, wielding it from side to side with incredible speed and slicing McConnell's body into three separate parts before it hit the ground.

Even before McConnell's three body pieces slammed into the ground, the attacker spun around on both heels and rushed back to the car again. He apparently wasn't done with Jeff yet. Grabbing hold of the vehicle's side with his right hand, he pulled. The car slammed back into position on its four wheels. The attacker then thrust the blade in his left hand through the driver door. The blade went through the left side of the driver's body, coming out on the right side. Pulling back the blade and out of the already dead driver's body, the attacker then grabbed hold of the door and yanked it off its hinges. He threw it away into the nearby bushy side of the road and then popped his head into the inside of the vehicle, beyond the driver's dead body. Jeff was seated slightly upwards, leaning on his severed, bloody side where his left limb had been. In his right hand was his gun, a tactical shotgun. The gun's mouth met with the lower part of the attacker helmeted head.

"Go to hell, motherfucker!" Jeff shouted out and pulled the trigger. Boom! Boom! The gun went off, twice. The close-range impact caused the attacker to stagger backwards, but not falling down. "Got ya, motherfucker!"

But as Jeff looked on, the attacker simply stepped back into position, and then the helmet unfolded, revealing the face behind it. It was the face of an adult human, male or female, he couldn't tell at this time, but just that it had all the human features, except for the eyes, which had no pupils. The attacker then smiled, the mouth opened, and spit the two bullets fired from the shotgun out of it. His attacker's right hand suddenly lashed out, hitting Jeff on the side of his neck with the now clenched shield before he could fire again, instantly rendering him unconscious. As the gun fell out of Jeff's only hand, his attacker thrust the blade of the golden knife into his chest, the blade rotated inside, and then pulled it out, all in a matter of seconds. After that, the attacker immediately turned around and walked away.

Meanwhile, Hernandez and Jermaine levelled their mortar guns and using the digital target markers, they unleashed the portable smart bombs on their attackers. Hernandez aimed at the big horse as it turned around in their direction, and hit home, completely knocking the big animal off its feet and down to the ground. There was an explosion of course, but then, just like a playful puppy dog, the big beastly thing rolled right back up onto its four legs and started to vigorously pound the ground with its fore hooves, raising them up in the air and bringing them down hard to the ground. And every time those hooves hit the ground the impact made the ground tremble like a mini earthquake.

"Shit, man, I hit the damn beast with a mortar, and it fell down, but got right up!" he shouted out at Jermain. "What the hell is that? Dude, that's not alright! It's fucking insane! I say it's time to scram out of here, now, man!"

"Let's see he can handle another one!" Jermain shouted back, resetting the shoot arrangement of his weapon to bazooka mode. He quickly levelled his sights and aimed. But instead of seeing the horse, he saw something else. It was the big horse's rider standing in between them and the animal now. The figure stood there, hands flung to the sides, legs wide apart.

"This wasn't meant for you, fucker. But ok, you want to take it instead, be my guest!" Jermain mumbled under his breath and fired off the weapon. There was a swishing sound as the missile left the weapon and took its short journey to its upright target. As the two looked on, the armor-clad figure suddenly leapt forward and grabbed at the flying missile before it hit home, the hands rolling it around like a basketball player rounding a ball in his hands, spun around in mid - air and threw it back at the two men. Dunk! The bomb landed on top of their car which exploded into a massive fire ball as the bomb materialized it to

270

pieces, and with a big boom! Both men were completely maimed, and their bodies torn to pieces as they got flung in different directions by the ordinance's close-range impact.

Everyone was shaken by that explosion, but more so by the rather volatile, violent end of those team members. Woodrow Crane stared at the burning remains of the vehicle, and suddenly anger welled up in him. He quickly looked around him. Everything looked to be so messed up already. There were only three cars left, and one had his daughter inside it. The other two, one his command post, the suburban in which his close confidants Backa and Singh were still seated, together with his tech advisor and support, Keener. That car also contained the C4 load, but for now he didn't see how he was going to use it, for he wasn't about to detonate it here. That could be committing suicide. The three of them were still waiting for his orders to launch the electronic weapons. In the third car, it was Big Vladimir, with his big, fifty Cal assault, sniper rifle, and his driver, ready to roll. These people were like his sons, always standing by him during impossible moments.

But if there was one thing Woodrow Wilson was known for, it was his ability to follow through with his assignments, at any cost. Even as a commander with the fearless, world renown United States Marines, he always led the way, never once flinching in the face of the enemy. Hell, he got a medal for his fierceness and upholding of the marines' core values. And he wasn't about to change that either. His only concern now was conservation of his legacy, and the only way to do that, he declared, is to protect his daughter, Ruma. He needed to get her out of here safely and to safety. After all, and for her own unclear reasons, she had asked to go home, didn't want to be part of this anymore. He should have listened to her, let her go. He now felt that he had let her down, as a father, by refusing to pay attention to her plea. She obviously wasn't made for this stuff , wasn't probably ready to take over his mantle. He had made a big mistake by getting her involved.

As for him, he still had a few men left to continue with the fight, the chance to earn those millions. The thing to do now was to get her out of here, and then for him and his guys to continue with the fight.

"Rob, can you hear me?" he quickly said through the microphone attached to his mouth.

"Aaaah... yes boss, I can hear you loud and clear!" Rob replied, slightly hesitating. Ruma still had the cold gun barrel on his neck.

"Get Ruma out of here, now!" he ordered. "Take my daughter as far away from here as possible. Go, now! The rest of you guys let's finish this off. The Battle is not over yet until I say so!"

"Yes sir," Rob replied and immediately started the vehicle.

"Hold it there, Rob," Ruma said. She suddenly opened the door and jumped out of the car. She sprinted over to where her father stood and took hold of his arm. "Daddy, don' do dis. Let it be now! Them people, they aren't really human, no! We've seen enough of what they are capable of doin', so I beg of yow, Daddy, please! We have enough Moonie to live on for the rest of our lives. We can give some to them guys left, and then move on. I don' wanna lose you, Daddy, I don'!"

Woodrow Crane turned around angrily and shrugged his arm free of her hold. His face was glistering with sweat and looking grim. "Now listen to me carefully, you freak!" he shouted out at her. His voice was hoarse. "This is my business, and I made a terrible mistake getting you involved in it! I want you out of here, now, and that's an order! I suggest you get back into that fuckin' car and let Rob take you wherever before I change my mind and kill you myself!"

The look on his face and his tone of voice was enough to convince her that her father had crossed the line out of reasonable thinking. He was determined to do what he had to do and there was no turning back. And at this point, she quickly realized, it was the time to do as he said and get out of here, basically to save herself before it became too late. Ruma suddenly stepped forward and embraced her father, holding on to him tightly for at least five seconds, and then with tears in her eyes, she turned around and ran back to the car, jumping in and shutting the door behind her.

"Rob, ge' me out of here, fast!" she said to the driver as she wiped the tears off her face. Rob started the car, put it in reverse mode, and stepped on the accelerator. The car jumped backwards, and he managed to swing it around to face the gates. He started driving forward at instant accelerated speed.

272

But they didn't get far, for suddenly, his headlight picked up this figure standing right in their pathway. He stepped hard on the breaks, suddenly bringing the big car to a dead stop.

"I said ge' me out of here fast. So why are yow stoppin'?" Ruma, who was still turned around in her seat, trying to get a last glimpse of her father, asked.

"It's one of those guys, Ruma, and he's standing right in the middle of the way!" Rob replied. Ruma quickly turned back to look and saw the armor-clad figure with the yellow light around the head standing a few yards away, in front of them. The legs were spread apart, the left arm hanging down, holding the gleaming shield, while the right hand was raised mid-way up, palm facing them. The figure was signaling at them to stop.

"Well, too bad for him, ain't stopping no more!" Ruma said. "Keep going, Rob. Run 'im down, Rob. Crash an' grind that fucker down, hard!"

"Hey, I… I can't," Rob responded, sounding alarmed. "I have never run over a human being before. Not even an animal. I just can't do it!

"Then get away from the wheel, Rob. I will do it myself!" she snarled at him. "Move it, now!"

As Rob quickly shifted himself into the front passenger seat, Ruma opened her door and jumped out of the car, ran around to the other side and got into the driver's seat, slamming the door shut behind her. Rob grabbed at the dashboard, looking terrified, as she released the parking brake and shifted the gear to drive.

"Now here I come, fucker! Let's see if you will hang around long enough to be banged up and run over!" she hissed, and then jammed her foot down hard on the accelerator. The big car, with rear tires squealing and engine raving, moved forward with all force.

But their adversary did not move out of the way, and it felt like ramming into a concrete barrier! And yet the front of the car did not even slam into the full body, but rather only their deterrent's stretched out right hand and legs. The engine raved and the rear tires screeched, making the back of the car dance around left and right like it was on a super slippery road surface. As Ruma's foot pushed down harder on

273

the accelerator, their adversary suddenly leaned forward and started pushing the raving car backwards, against its own advancing force, using the right hand only as the leverage point.

"I'll be damned!" Rob shouted out those words as he witnessed the sheer robust strength of the opposing force. Thinking quickly, he grabbed hold of Ruma's tactical assault rifle, and instantly aiming it at their adversary, he pulled the trigger. The blast completely shattered the car's windscreen, the heavy, repeating, grinding sounds of the weapon's rapid output an assault to their ears.

"Rob, noooo..." Ruma screamed, fearful of what was likely going to happen due to his gun attack on the dreadful thing. The weapon's output was useless against their adversary and Rob was definitely going to be killed, just like those before him who had dared to use their weapons against them. But it was too late. Rob was beyond recall, screaming at the top of his voice like a maniac, as he squeezed the trigger with all his strength and directed the full blast at the enemy in front of him.

Without shifting position and still pushing against the car using the right hand, and as the bullets bounced off the armor-clad body, their adversary raised the left hand that bore the gleaming, golden shield and pointed it at them. Ruma ducked downwards, hitting her head on the steering wheel as she did so, and her foot releasing the accelerator at the same time. As she peered up, three balls of extremely heated air hit Rob's body, and that force blasted his body and the entire passenger seat section backwards with such force it rammed through the seat behind him, and then the next seat, until it blasted the lift gate off the back of the car and into the outside. Ruma never knew where Rob's body ended up, but with such a blast, she knew he was no more.

As she cowered down in the driver's seat, not knowing what was going to happen to her, it downed to her that at this point there was only one thing to do, and that is to surrender. There was no other choice, nowhere to run or even hide any more. Using her right hand, she reached for the key in the ignition and switched the engine off.

"Okay, I... I... I give up. Whoever yow ah, I... I surrender!" She shouted out at the top of her voice, her lips trembling so much she could feel her teeth chattering. "I... I am gonna com'out now, I have no weapon with me, an'… an' then yow can do whatever yow wanna do wid me, jus don' kill me, please!"

A brief, approximately one minute silence followed. The only sounds now were coming from the action several yards away from where she was, where her father and his aides were still engaging their adversary

Ruma was beginning to pull herself up and out of her hiding place when suddenly the driver's door was ripped off the car with such brutal force the rest of the structure shook. The sudden rip - off noise was sharp and piecing to her ears and made her feel like her heart was about to jump out of her chest. Then a hand, all gleaming in some form of shiny, sparkling metallic material much like foil paper, suddenly grabbed her by the back of the neck, just like the way puppies or piglets are sometimes handled by seasoned farm hands, and pulled her out of the car. This move, however, was done slowly, with ease. She was then dropped on the ground.

"Move!" the command came in form of multiple voice tones. "I… I… can't," she replied, raising her head up to try and look at her adversary. It was then that she was hit hard on the side of the head. That blow completely blacked her out.

On the other front, several yards away from where she was, the fierce fighting was raging on. Woodrow Crane still standing at the frontline, confronted by three of his foes. But now they were out of formation, one each on the far side of their leader, who now stood just yards away but directly in front of him, with the big horse. The leader, appearing tall and elegant in the shiny body armor, was now clearly visible with right hand resting on the lower left side of the beastly horse's neck, left hand on the side with legs slightly apart. But the glowing, yellow ring of light around the top of their Adversary's heads made it even more fascinating, because neither him nor his crew had ever seen anything like this before. It created an aura of total mystery, of something unimaginable but yet real, a sense of being at loss because of not knowing exactly what is what, or who is who, that they were fighting. He was so focused on this figure that he didn't notice one of the four foes splitting from the group and go after Ruma and Rob as they sped away from the scene in the big sport utility vehicle. His two standing men did notice the move but remained unresponsive to the action, too mesmerized by how fast this foe suddenly dashed off after the car to even mention it to him. To say the least, the individual just moved a few steps forward, then leapt off the ground and towards the direction of the getaway vehicle before vanishing into the air.

"Backa, Singh, get your guns ready and join me out here on the front line," Woodrow Crane finally issued the order through his mouthpiece. "Vladimir, cover us with your weapon. Keener, on my count, launch those drones. Backer, Singh, I want all fire directed at the individual with the big horse. No exceptions. I think if we break him, we break the rest. Vladimir will take care of the other individuals if they engage. And guys, I may not be able to use this communication network again, so these are my last orders as of today. I only ask that you give it all you've got. Thanks for supporting me always. Now, let's do this. Good luck and Godspeed! Ready guys?"

"Hooyah!" came the feedback through and all over the communication network.

The two men got out of their vehicle and quickly took their positions on his side, Backer to his right, Singh on his left. The two looked at each other, grinned, and issued each other a thumb – up salute. They had their assault, tactical, fully automated guns poised and ready, plus some other military stuff on them. Vladimir's driver started the vehicle and slowly edged it closer, with big Vladimir poising firm through the opened sunroof.

But then the other two adversaries returned into formation again, moving closer to their purported leader even as Woodrow Crane issued the orders. It was as if they had read Woodrow Crane's mind.

"Boss, do you see that?" Backer said quickly, addressing Woodrow Crane directly. "It's as if they heard your orders before you voiced them."

"Good. That means they are afraid of what's coming for them and are moving to protect their leader," Woodrow Crane replied. "Standard loyalty, they're ready to die for him. Die they will, then. Maintain the focus as planned."

But then, the purported leader of the adversary group slowly raised the left arm, and as this happened, the gleaming tool in the hand faded

276

out. The entire five fingered hand was now clearly visible. Woodrow Crane sighed in relief. They had human traits, after all, and that made the enemy as much vulnerable to him and his men as they were to them, he told himself. He had begun to wonder if he was up against a space alien force of some sorts. The arm remained up, palm facing them, and then the lead adversary spoke, and it was in the same deep, multiple voice tones as before.

"Put your weapons down and surrender, human warriors, and your lives and souls will be spared," the subtle warning came. "If not, then you will all perish. Surrender now or die."

"And why should we be the ones to surrender?" Woodrow Crane shouted back in response. "Who are you people anyway? You think we are intimidated by your fancy body suits, yellow heads, and flashy hands? Nope, we are not, and therefore shall not surrender. You guys do it! Surrender and then get out of our way. Do so now or die!"

"We are part of a battle group from heaven above," the adversary leader replied with left hand still up. "We've been sent down here into your world to find, expose, and completely destroy the evil amongst the occupants of the seventh dimension, which is here. We are here to save humanity, remove the chaos, and restore God's order and peace. We intend to restore it to God's standards, and we have the mandate to destroy and decease anything or anybody who stands in our way."

"And you think I am going to believe all that bullshit you are telling me about heaven and God?" Woodrow Crane shouted back. "Nah! Go sell that fake mambo jumbo to somebody else. Now you listen to me carefully as I tell you this, because I am going to say it only once. We were trained by one of best fighting, battle - ready forces on this planet! You ever heard of the U.S Marines, huh? I don't know about your force group, but out here we are taught to fight back against the enemy with all we've got, not just to simply surrender. And so, I tell you, get the fuck out of our way or get ready to face the full consequences!"

"Surrender now, or by heavenly mandate, you shall perish!" the lead adversary repeated, the multiple voice tones suddenly becoming louder in unison. This warning sounded to be an angry, final warning. "If you surrender, I shall let you walk away with your lives, and your sins will be forgiven, Woodrow Crane. Heaven will grant you amnesty, a fresh start. My offer is an indication of peace, an olive branch offered to even the evilest amongst humanity. Let it be with you, today and now, Woodrow Crane. Just simply lay down your weapons and walk away."

Still outside on the balcony, now standing next to Zeal who still had both his arms raised to sustain his protective shield, the Vonsbergs looked at each other. They had witnessed the first tango of the two warring factions in their front yard, but were now perplexed by what looked like, from their point of view, an apparent moment of cease fire.

"So… what's happening now? Is the fight over?" Benita asked, looking intently at Zeal.

"By all means it's not over yet," Zeal replied. "You humans are too stubborn to understand the wisdom of God. Despite the warning that heaven is involved, the people out there are willing to give it all up to fulfill their goals, and that is to kill all of you and get paid for it. Their leader is determined beyond recall getting that monetary reward, at whatever cost, his or other human beings. He knows no boundaries, no rules but his own. Yet he forgets that only God makes things possible, from birth to the end, and that one will be held accountable for the evil done to others. This is because God gave us life, and he's the only one who decides how and when to take it away. So, what this human is trying to do is only in his human dreams. It's never going to happen, and him and his team may never see another day beyond today. Because we carry heaven's mandate to thwart evil, we won't let them do it."

"Does this mean that you and your group are going to kill them?" Benita asked, still not getting the gist of the entire story. "I don't get it. You mean we are all just going to stand here and watch two warring factions destroy each other, instead of intervening and preventing this tragic event from happening? And on our premises? You should go out there immediately and mediate between the two groups. If not, then I will do it!"

"No, you will not!" her father retorted, sounding angry. "This is not your war, Benita, so stay out of it! Just be glad that these folks came out here to protect us. Only God knows what one of those groups was going to do had they gotten the chance to get to us. So, we're going to let them fight it out to the end and get over with it. We are lucky that we at least have Zeal on our side. Right, Zeal?"

"Yes, that's right. Besides, I won't let you go out there anyway, young lady," Zeal said. "Because if you do, you will be caught in the crossfire, and that, young lady, will make your parents very sad. Thank you so much for the offer to mediate, but heaven declines your offer."

"In other words, Benita, simply just stay here with us and watch!" her brother added, staring at her. "Do it for all of us, sis. We cannot afford to lose you, and for that matter any of us. But more especially you! You 're cherished by everyone in this family, myself included. So, if anything happens to you now, this family will be forever damaged."

Benita stared back at her father and brother, her face expressionless, slowly shook her head, but said nothing.

Out there in their front yard, Woodrow Crane decided enough was enough.

"You talk too much!" he angrily shouted back in response to his lead foe's dire warning. "Ok, guys, let's go weapons hot on these fellas!"

"No! Walk away, human. Walk away!"

For a moment, maybe a full minute, everyone held back. For this time, it wasn't the lead adversary talking. That warning came from the big, beastly horse. The animal had indeed talked, its voice sounding hoarse but loud and clear!

What in the hell …

The miracle of a talking animal should by itself have been enough to tell Woodrow Crane that this wasn't a normal group he was fighting, enough to make him think twice about risking a confrontation with this paranormal adversary, because they weren't the usual worldly show everyone was used to. But the devil had his tentacles already sunk so deep into Woodrow Crane's soul that he was completely blind to this sign. He was hell bent to confront his perceived enemy!

"Bullshit! Let's give it to them, boys!" he shouted out, at the same time yanking communication set off his head.

All hell broke loose as Woodrow Brinks Crane and his men unleashed it on their adversary with their guns, advancing forward as they did so. From inside one of the vehicles, Keene unleashed his toys, a series of armed small drones that flew out of the back of the car and faced the enemy. He pressed the red button and their double-barreled front guns fired off bullets in rapid succession from the center, while the others on the sides fired of mini rockets.

But instead of rebounding, the three adversarial group sprang into action too. Suddenly adopting a crouching position, right hand letting go of the big horse's side, their lead foe dropped both arms and then quickly raise them up again. And when those hands came up, there was a loud, noise, more like an explosion, accompanied by a sudden gust of wind which instantly became still. It was like that sudden gush of air became frozen in place.

And that was it. None of the ammunition fired from Woodrow Crane and his team could penetrate this invisible barrier. Their bullets simply bounced off.

"This is some godamned freakin' shit! Use your Grenades, boys!" Woodrow Crane cried out, and unhooking one of his, he yanked the pin out with his teeth and threw it at the enemy. The grenade exploded somewhere in midair, causing what looked like a small fire bubble, and then died out, leaving nothing but black smoke behind. The grenades from his men also suffered the same fate. When the rockets from the drones hit home, they bounced back, repelled and spiraling out of control and landing into the surrounding bushy areas where they exploded.

The big horse suddenly did its dance again, squealing loudly as it raised its big front legs up in the air and brought them down with a heavy thud on the ground. Reaching through the invisible barrier with both arms, the adversary's leader stretched them out, pointing both hands into the space beyond and above. Two gleaming hand weapons were now in both hands, spewing bursts of bright red fire balls that went flying at Keener's drones. Keener watched as his flying machines got downed with rapid, remarkable precision, and in just a matter of less than ten seconds, all the drones were completely out of service, having been blown out of the air by the adversary's rapid, fiery projectiles, which completely shattered them into small, fiery pieces in rapid succession.

But keener sent another round out, this time sending them not in a line up formation, but all over the place. The drones, with their deadly firepower, where like a swarm of displaced bees. They unleashed a blistering shower of small smart bombs that could normally have completely shattered through a moderately-protected ground defense system and downgrade it to nothing. But the invisible wall held up against the deadly attack, until Keener directed the drones higher up, left and right, predicting the invisible wall's range of coverage to be just as wide as the user's intended protective margins, and then recalled them back in a rounding detour.

The bombs exploded behind the walls, blowing up a series of cars parked in the private family parking lot and whatever was within the surrounding vicinity. Some of the drone fire came to hit very close to the balcony where Zeal stood with the Vonsbergs, but Zeal's protective barrier actively repelled the bombs, downgrading them to smoke explosions and rendering them harmless to the house and its owners.

A small victory for Woodrow Crane and his team, but also a move that appears to have taken the adversary group by surprise, causing them to quickly rethink their battle strategy. This change in battle strategy was also the tipping point of this battle between the two warring factions. The adversary's change in strategy became more aggressive, and things for Woodrow Crane and his team started going bad.

The wind suddenly started blowing normally as the adversary group's leader suddenly dropped the shield and advanced forward towards Woodrow Crane and the remainder of his group. Each of the adversary leader's hands still held on to the gleaming yellow pistol – like object which appeared to come out of the very hand that held it. In just a few seconds, the leader shot down all of keener's second round of drones from the air using the firepower from the pistols with pinpointing precision, despite the drones flying around without formation. The small machines, when hit by the small projectiles from the gleaming weapons now simply exploded into numerous sparks of bright fire upon contact from the fiery ammunition, and then evaporated in midair, living nothing but small clouds of black smoke and no residual falling on the ground.

At the same time, the other two foes did the same thing their leader was doing, using similar weaponry but focusing their attack on a totally different target. Their total output, which looked like numerous, small oval pods of hot lava the size of large chicken eggs, rained down nonstop on Keener's vehicle, the source of the drones, and with Keener still in it. The ammunition exploded upon contact with the car's body, completely burning and or melting down the car's entire structure to the core in same way fresh, molten volcanic lava engulfs and destroys anything in its path. The overpowering stench from the resulting searing effect on the car's fabric immediately hit the air, complicated by that of burning human flesh. Keener didn't even get to scream out his terror and pain, because his body was hit and completely disintegrated by a series of hot molten lava pods from the attacker's ammunition in the midst of the disintegrating vehicle. The rapid, spewing and swishing downpour didn't stop until the entire framework of the big car was a flat mess on the ground, metal, rubber, glass and all.

Seeing this happening, big Vladimir threw his big, assault sniper rifle to the ground below and away from the vehicle he was in and then he himself jumped out of the car, staying clear, fearing that he would be targeted next with the deadly heaters. Landing on the ground on his legs, he quickly scooped up the big gun and reopened fire on one of the adversaries who was still spewing his gun's output on Keener's already downgraded vehicle. The heavy bullets hit home, forcing the shooter to stop, but the foe himself remained upright, like a stalled robot.

Suddenly, another figure appeared behind him from nowhere. He saw the movement from the corner of his eyes and quickly turned around, but it was too late. It was the fourth foe, the one that had gone after Ruma and Rob, that had suddenly reappeared on the scene, dragging Ruma's body by holding on to back of her waist belt on her khaki pants, just like carrying a guitar case by the handle. Seeing what big Vladimir was doing, this individual fore let go of Ruma's unconscious body, dropping it down to the ground, and confronted him. As big Vladimir turned around, he was body slammed hard on the left, and then in one swift move the gun was aggressively yanked out of his hands and tossed into the nearby bushy area like it was a plain stick. The body slam made him stumble sideways, but he didn't lose his balance.

Now one thing was plain certain with him, and that is no one takes away his favorite toy and stays to laugh about it. If it happens that the offender doesn't get killed, that person would surely get a very bad, and or, rough whooping! He automatically decided that this individual certainly wasn't going to be exempt from the punishment, and since this was a battle ground now, he was going to kill this enemy, not just whoop ass!

As the battle of weapons raged on a few yards away from them, the two individuals faced each other. The one in the metallic looking body armor with roman – emperor kind of helmet had arms spread out on the side, fists unclenched and legs slightly apart, while the other one, in green military fatigues, complete with a black beret and steel toe boots, had both arms raised and gloved fists clenched with legs spread wide apart.

"I don't know who or what you motherfuckers are, but at this point I really don't give a damn anyways!" the six foot eight, two hundred and eighty-pounds, muscle packed Russian hissed. "The one thing I know is that I have come to hate you so bad I am going to mess you up like hell never did before to anyone! You wanna dance, come on, let's dance, motherfucker!"

Without saying anything back, his foe took the first steps forward, moving towards him in quick short strides. A wide, forward swinging right was thrust at him, aiming at his neck, but big Vladimir parried off the blow with his left hand, stepped into his fore's space and implemented a series of swift, rapid power punches into his foe's upper abdomen and chest areas, finalizing the counterattack with one hard blow to his foe's chin. His fists hit on a solid, hard metal surface, but he felt some shifting with the blow to the chin of his opponent, making him think that he could dislodge the helmet and or even the entire body armor that way. Stepping back to create some space, he lashed out with a flying kick to the same area, bam! The helmet shifted, and his foe stumbled backwards from the impact of those blows. Big Vladimir then leapt high off the ground and into the air, spun around in midair and landed another hard, left flying kick on the right side of his adversary's neck. This time, his adversary completely lost balance and hit the ground with a thud.

Reaching into one of the pockets on his cargo pants, he pulled out a big, fully automatic military pistol, systematically flipped the safety off with his thumb and then holding the gun with both hands, he fired it off at point blank range at his foe, aiming at the head. Sparks appeared as the bullets hit and bounced off the helmet on his foe's head, causing it to jerk sideways left and right as a result of the heavy bullets hitting home at such a close range. Big Vladimir emptied the gun's entire magazine on his opponent until it clicked empty. No time to reload, he decided, and threw the piece away. But his foe appeared to have withstood the deadly gunshots and slowly started getting up from the ground

"OK, motherfucker, I can see now that you're too scared to fight it out in the open. That's why you hide behind fuckin' body armor!" he growled. "Why don't you just come out of your shell and face the beat up with in a fair, open body fight like me, huh?"

Thrusting both his hands in his cargo pockets again, he pulled out two double edged combat knives with blades made of titanium blended metal and flexed his muscled hands. Not only did big Vladimir possess a ninth dan in Taekwondo, but he was also very skilled in combat knife fighting.

His adversary came up off the ground without using arms for support, an upright rising powered by both leg muscles folding straight up. Big Vladimir's taunting challenge seemed to have been heard, for the moment his foe stood upright, the body armor suddenly dislodged itself, helmet and all, and now what stood before him was a woman, as tall as him, with flowing, silky long hair, dressed in a white robe with long arm sleeves, the robe tied together and held in place at the waist by a shiny yellow rope. She was both barehanded and barefoot now. Even through her robe, he could not only see that her feminine physical attributes were well pronounced, but also somewhat enhanced, though still with no big difference from a physically well- endowed female athlete. The only unique features were that her eyes, with no pupils, were two twin, sparkly shiny yellow oval features that blinked on and off, and then the thin, bright yellow halo that still surrounded the top of her head. Big Vladimir watched as his female foe rolled her neck as she looked straight at him.

"Stand down and surrender, son of man, or you will be swiftly executed and with no mercy, just like your defiant friends," the woman said in a calm but clearly audible voice.

284

"I can see that beating wasn't enough for you, bitch!" he retorted, staring right back at his foe and poising for the next attack. "I am definitely not standing down, not after what you motherfuckers did to my friends. Those people were my buddies, you feel me, huh? On the other hand, why don't you, yourself, stand down, huh? Why me? You can just carefully walk over here to me so I can give you a kiss on your fuckin' cute lips, give your bottom a fair spanking, and then you and your buddies can get the hell off my planet and go back to where you came from. Or are you scared of being spanked?"

The woman did not respond to his rhetoric, but instead started walking towards him in quick long strides, her arms still down on her sides, chin slightly lowered.

"Alright then, let's dance!" he hissed, flexing his knives.

The woman suddenly flexed her arms outwards, flexing both hands repeatedly with fingers unclenched. Big Vladimir, carefully balancing the knives, lightly swiped at her body, tensing his body for an opportunity to strike a deadly blow in the right place. But his foe quickly proved to be good too, blocking off all his knife jabs quickly at his wrist level, ducking her body back and forth, fast but also with unmatched ease. That opportunity to strike came, however, when he managed finally jump at his foe and thrust his right-hand knife right into her face!

But it was like thrusting the deadly metallic weapon into air. There was no flesh to pierce into, just empty space. His hand was thrust back at him in a strong, bounce back, pop up motion.

"What the hell!" he exclaimed loudly.

Then she stepped into his space and lunged at him with rapid left and right fist jabs into his face, bam bam! Her fists were surprisingly solid and heavy for a female, and made his head jerk backwards, causing him to stagger. He felt the sharp pain come through, making him somewhat dizzy. Big Vladimir suddenly spun around and lashed out with a low hook kick, a side rib blow to his foe, but she did not even wince, stagger or lose balance. Then he did a spin around, went down and tripped his foe to the ground. She hit the ground with a thud but bounced right back up like she was on a trampoline. Big Vladimir

straightened back up in a matter of seconds, only to find her already there, waiting for him.

Now facing big Vladimir again, she suddenly lashed out with a left fist swing. Vladimir saw it coming and responded with a right. His knife wielding right hand was blocked by a rock-solid fist and then a chop followed. He withdrew his arm before the chop hit home, becoming just a skin glaze, but the power in that block punch knocked the knife out of his hand. He felt some tingling, like an electric jolt, which caused a shot of pain in this hand. As he shook his hand in pain, his adversary came at him with a kick at his legs, but big Vladimir skipped high and away from it. He landed well, but looking up, his foe was already too close again for him to have that two - second brain action plan flash. And so, he lashed out blindly with a swinging left hook fist at his adversary's face. But his foe quickly grabbed at his hand and wrapped a tight grip around his wrist. That second knife now fell out of his left hand. He now realized that he had been effectively disarmed. As his foe did this, big Vladimir threw in a right hook punch, hoping to destabilize the adversary and free himself from her tight wrist grip. But to his surprise, his right-hand wrist was also quickly grabbed and locked in a tight grip like the left one.

Then the pressure started building around his wrists as his surprisingly and immensely strong female opponent squeezed his wrist hard like a wet hand towel being wringed off its water. Big Vladimir groaned in pain as the grips became even tighter, sounding like a wounded lion or big beast. As he tried to vigorously free himself, lashing out with forward front kicks into the front of his foe's body, he suddenly noticed the change in color of his foe's arms. They were turning bright red, the color rolling down both arms from the elbows downwards until it reached both hands that still held him captive. Then the glowing, bright red color reached Big Vladimir's hands.

That glowing redness was a searing heat that immediately started burning through his flesh until he himself smelled the stench of his own charred flesh. This time around, big Vladimir squealed like an infant in acute pain, and his efforts to squirm out of his foe's grasp increased. But it was all useless. Vladimir fell to his knees as the intense heat went through both of his wrist bones like a welder's metal- cutting torch. His eyes almost pooped out of his sockets when suddenly both of his hands were broken off his arms in single side twist actions and thrown away, left and right, into the surrounding bushy darkness.

"What did you do to my hands, you godamned piece of shit?" he cried out in pain as he looked at the two stumped arms that were so charred on the ends that just a little blood was dripping down.

Without replying to that question, his foe now lashed out with a swing up kick, like he was a penalty ball, hitting him hard right below his navel area. The shattering foot blow sent his big body vaulting into the air and landing again on the ground a few yards away. As he tried to get up, his legs wobbly, his mouth was suddenly filled with warm fluid, forcing him to cough and splutter. Blood gushed out of his mouth, running down over his thick moustache and dripping to the ground. Big Vladimir collapsed to his knees, unable to remain upright anymore. His stomach was tightening into very painful knots, and he felt like he was about to faint. His foe now strode up to him, stopped a couple of yards away, legs spread out and hands akimbo, and looked down at the agonizing man. She nodded her head slowly, from side to side.

"Is… that… all you've got?" Big Vladimir mumbled, staring back at his adversary with mockery, trying to smile.

"Yes, and I think that's enough," the reply came back in a low pitched, calm voice from his foe. She then turned around and walked away from him, stopping only to pick up Ruma's seemingly unconscious body from where she had dropped it to the ground in order to confront big Vladimir. She carried Ruma in the same way she had handled before, by grabbing the back of her trousers. Her body armor suddenly retracted, rewrapping itself around her entire body until she was shelled in. She started walking towards the three remaining human figures.

What this she didn't realize, though, and that is it really mattered to her, was that Ruma was already awake, and had watched, in horror, the entire time big Vladimir battled with his foe, and his final demise. As she was carried away like a small sack of potatoes, she saw big Vladimir's body tip forward and hit the ground, staying still. Tears started rolling down her eyes and dropping to the ground, not just because what she had just witnessed was so horrifying and frightening, but also because

she didn't know what they were going to do with or to her. She didn't want to die.

Several yards away from her and her captor, Backer turned around and watched the fiery, bright orange pods shoot out of the adversary's hands, fly above and past him to hit Keener's vehicle. He watched as the car literally melted down to the ground, with Keener's body first writhing vigorously and then completely disappearing inside the hot mess. That was the most terrifying ordeal he had ever experienced in his life, and at this point, it simply signaled his defeat and or surrender. He didn't want to fight these people or things anymore. Terrified, Backer threw his gun to the ground and took off running in the opposite direction, away from his team and his adversaries.

Singh saw Backer suddenly drop his weapon and run away from him and Woodrow Crane. Then as he looked on, a pair of fiery pods hit Backer, one at his legs, the other in the back. He heard Backer's high-pitched scream as the heated pods hit him and basically cremated his lower body. The remaining chunk of his body, mostly shoulders upwards, fell to the ground. Now also becoming more terrified by what he had just witnessed, Singh suddenly raises his gun above his head with both hands, signaling he was ready to surrender, and started walking, but not in the opposite direction. Instead, he strode towards the adversarial group.

"Don't kill me... I surrender, I surrender...," he shouted out at the adversary, at the top of his voice. He then strangely started walking in circles when he got close to the adversary team.

"Singh, come back here, you son of a bitch!" Woodrow Crane shouted out after him, but it was too late. A fiery red pod hit Singh's upper body, separating it from the lower part. Both parts got blown into separate directions, falling on the ground. Woodrow Crane watched as the separate parts of Singh's body burned in flames, his lower torso twitching vigorously. At the same time, small chunks of wet flesh spluttered his face, forcing him to immediately spit. Then the feeling of overwhelming nausea took over. Bending down, he retched up a big stream of vomit. After a few minutes, he slowly looked up, sweat dripping down his face and neck. He saw the leader of his adversary group now walk towards him, the big horse closely following behind him.

Woodrow Crane threw his weapon to the ground, glaring angrily at his advancing fore. He slowly withdrew his big commando knife from its sheath on his right hip. He was going to go for the leader up close, slash at or thrust the big knife into the exposed area of the front of that helmet. He decided he was still going to die fighting. He wasn't going to cowardly give up or surrender like Barker and Singh. Nope!

Because that wasn't his style of doing things. But the adversarial leader stopped a few yards away from him.

"Look behind you now, Woodrow Crane!" the leader said to him.

It sounded more like a command than a request or notification.

Panting, Woodrow Crane slowly turned around. Standing a few yards away from him was one of his foes, and dangling from this foe's right hand, was his daughter, Ruma. She was dangling from her pants' waist belt. His face went crimson red when he noticed that it was her in the foe's hold, and he started breathing heavily, his chest heaving up and down. And as he looked on, her captor foe let go of her and her body dropped to the ground with a light thud. Ruma's body suddenly shifted, first in a slow, writhing movement on the ground, and then she slowly sat up.

"They got me, daddy," she sobbed loudly like a small baby. "But they kill ever 'body else. Please save me from 'em, daddy. I don' wan' die!"

Woodrow Crane Slowly turned around, glaring again at the adversarial leader. He threw his big commando knife to the ground.

"There, I now completely give up," he shouted out. He fell down to his knees and started sobbing loudly. For the first time perhaps in his life, Woodrow Brinks Crane felt physically, emotionally, and maybe spiritually broken. "You can do anything you want with me, but you must let her go. She's innocent of everything, I am the one who led her astray and into all this mess. Please don't kill my daughter. Take me but let my daughter live. Please, let her go, I beg of you."

For the next couple of minutes, none of his foes responded back to him. He looked around him. He was now surrounded by all four, including the big horsey animal. They all just stared back, and down, at him.

"Are you hearing me out, you 'all dummies?" he shouted again, hysterically. "Let her go, she's young and innocent!"

"Before I commit your soul, is there anything else you want to say to us?" the leader finally broke the silence. The multi – toned voice was harsh and grinding to his ears. "Maybe ask for forgiveness of your sins in this life? You might find solace, and therefore mercy, on your soul in your next life, but it all begins here, in this one."

"Spare me the humor, will you? I will not seek solace, pity, or mercy over my deeds, good or bad, from that which is unknown to me," Woodrow Crane replied. "You claim to be heavenly dispensed, but I don't see that here. Look at what you have done to me, to us, huh? So as far as I am concerned, I see barbaric space aliens or, perhaps, technologically advanced and or enhanced forces, or robots, hired to protect a rich man, a billionaire. And you did your job well, I will give you that. But all that has nothing to do with my soul or heaven or humanity. So, once again, all I ask is that you to let my daughter go, and nothing else."

"Even in your downfall you still sound so defiant!" the adversarial leader responded. "I gave you the chance to redeem yourself, but you threw it away because of your unquenchable greed, just like a lot of other humans do. But very well, we shall spare your off spring, but shall definitely take your soul. The bad deeds that you have so horrendously done in your lifetime shall not go unpunished, because they greatly outnumber your good deeds. But most of all, you have openly or privately defied God and the heavens in some of the most terrible ways ever known in the life cycle of humanity. You presumed yourself untouchable and mighty, the glory of both only preserved for the almighty God in heaven. And in doing so, you have inflicted pain, turmoil, and death to humanity, which has raised concern from heaven. Now your day has come too. Your soul shall be doomed to hell's tormented bases forever. But before I commit your soul, I will allow you to get a glimpse of the unknown, starting with the ones standing before you."

With those words, the leader's arms slowly went up until the open hands were above head. The glowing yellow light, which this time was being seen as a foggy shade of vaporish glow above each of the four adversaries' heads, suddenly turned into a glowing golden ring, brighter than a halogen light. So bright was it that it brightly illuminated the entire areas like the lights used by roadside construction or repair teams at night. Then the shiny protective, metallic armor on their bodies, including the helmets and footwear, disappeared, dissolving inwards into their bodies to reveal female human bodies dressed in long flowing, shiny, long sleeved white robes, held in place by a shiny, golden rope at the waist. Their partially braided, silky hair was floating around the front and back of their bodies. Even their robes themselves were alive as if they had a life of their own, for at this moment, there was no breeze in place around them, yet they kept moving around bodies wearing them.

It was difficult or impossible to define their skin color or tones, or areas of origin, because their facial, hand and bare feet features revealed nothing short of a mulatto appeal that also glowed in the light. But the most distinct feature on their very pretty and beautiful faces was their eyes. Each eye had a sparkling bright yellow, diamond - like twinkle in the center. Each of them also had a shiny metallic silver - looking, bracelet on their right wrist that too, kept glowing. Their bare feet barely touched the ground below them, making them look like floating apparitions.

The four females were so beautiful that both father and daughter blinked in total awe, and the angels stared back at them with faint smiles on their faces. And now their feet suddenly rose further off the ground as giant wings, like those of a blue jay bird in flight, evolved out of their backs and spread out in a spectacular show of mightiness. Even the huge horse now had wings.

"Now, earthlings, behold our presence before you," the lead angel said, her voice now plain and smooth but with a gentle wail in. "Do you believe now?"

"Kneel, Ruma, please kneel down!" Woodrow Crane suddenly cried out, sounding like a deranged man, and turning around to look at his daughter, whose captive angel had now moved away from her.

But Ruma remained seated on her bottom, arms and legs spread out, with hands on the ground and shoulders slightly hunched forward, staring upwards. She was completely transfixed, mesmerized and or hypnotized by the glory of their appearance. Realizing that she wasn't even listening or paying attention to him at all, he quickly turned back around to face his captors, who had now formed a semi- circle around both of them. He fell to his knees and bowed down, placing his forehead to the ground.

"Please… please spare me. I now do believe. Forgive me for all the bad things I have done," he cried out in sincere despair. "I repent. I promise to completely reform and denounce all my badness and madness, and my disrespect of the divine."

There was no response to his pleas, and when he looked up again, there were two tall muscular men standing in front of him, one bright and the other dark skinned, both clad only in flaming blood red buggy trousers, pointed red shoes, and a red cape held in place by what looked like an iron collar around their necks. They each wore a bronze like helmet that completely obscured their faces and necks. From Ruma's viewpoint, each of these individuals had a long tail attached to the bottom of their backs that was swooshing back and forth. Each man also held an object in their hands that looked like a long metallic spear. These two individuals now completely obscured his view of the female angels and their horse that had, a few seconds ago, stood before him in the spectacular revelation of themselves.

"Now who the hell are you guys?" Woodrow Crane asked loudly, sounding deranged again. "I don't need to see you. I still need to see and talk to those bombshell beauties with their wings. So, you guys get the fuck out of my way, right now!"

The two men turned their heads and looked at each other. Ruma could easily swear that she saw their heads rotate completely around in a complete circle just to face each other. Then she saw them nod their heads at each other, rotate heads back into position, and then they suddenly thrust their spear - like objects into her father's chest. And as the metal heads sunk into his chest, Woodrow Crane bellowed out in agony, a one time, most horrendous, bone – chilling outcry that lasted for at least half a minute before his body stiffened and arched backwards until it was almost bent into two halves, facing upwards. They lifted him off the ground using the spears inside him. With his eyes wide open and looking like they were about to pop out of their sockets, Woodrow Crane's mouth suddenly gaped open, and a form of visible dark blue vapor burst out of it until it formed itself into an agonizing human silhouette. Ruma could tell that it had the complete shape of her father's physic, complete with bulging eyes and mouth still open. It was like it didn't want to get out its physical body. But the two muscular, tail wagging men let go of the hold on the spears in his body and quickly grabbed at the writhing vaporish form by its arms. In a matter of seconds, they sank into the ground below them with it, completely vanishing. At the same time, Woodrow Crane's body dropped back to the ground with a thud, right in front of her. Ruma screamed loudly, completely terrified by what she had just seen and heard. She jumped back and away from her father's body as it now lay still on the ground, looking so pale it had the color of ivory. Surprisingly, the two spears were no longer stuck in his body. They, too, had mysteriously vanished. She could now see the glorious angels again, still floating off the grounds in the splendid shiny robes, wings flapping up down in almost slow motion. The lead angel was the first one to come down to the ground. After her bare feet touched the ground, she made her way towards Ruma, her stride a gentle walk. When she got closer, Ruma could see that the angel's entire body, though opaque, was full of the yellow light that flowed down from the golden halo on top of her head. Scared, Ruma tried to move away, but she was now so petrified that her muscles froze in place, rendering her completely still.

The beautiful lead angel then spoke. When she opened her mouth, the air from within her body engulfed Ruma's entire body like a fresh breeze, and the smell was that of freshly cut roses. Her voice was a gentle, clearly audible, and soothing whisper, like someone trying to calm down a crying infant. "My child, you have witnessed so much already of what has happened here today and in your fragile life, so much that your mind, which is the face of your soul, has been damaged all the way to the core. Your Soul has been corrupted by the evil your father had fostered into you. But fear not anymore, for I am going to mend your soul for you. I shall wipe away the spate of sorrowful and sinful memories and replace them with fresh gentle ones that will forever dominate your soul from now on. This means that the old you will be gone, replaced by a new you that I will send on a mission of goodwill, representing part of me here in your world. Are you ready to be the new you? Are you ready to become a part of me?"

Still completely petrified, all Ruma could do was to nod her head quickly in agreement. She could not only hear, but also feel the gentle voice of the angel reverberating through out her entire body. She suddenly felt, and she didn't understand why, intense chills take over her body and started shivering. She was experiencing extreme feverish symptoms, with goosebumps engulfing her entire skin like a rash. Her teeth started chattering and her lips quivered. She could now feel her heart beating very fast in her chest. She felt rumblings in her stomach and another intense feeling, that of nausea, took over and made her feel like she was going to pass out. She saw herself reeling, and then collapse sideways to the ground.

But then she suddenly woke up and quickly sat up, like someone suddenly awakened from a bad dream. The fresh, rosy breeze that blew on her as the angel continued talking suddenly made her feel like she had just taken a fresh, rose – petal perfumed bath. She saw the angel stretch her arm out and then her hand, made of yellow light, gently touched her forehead using one finger. There was a flash of light, a high-pitched noise that rang in her ears, and then a total black out.

It was like an immediate, instant change when she opened her eyes again, finding herself seated alone on a roadside bench on an empty street in a downtown area. Looking around her and ahead, she recognized the street and then the city. She was in downtown Fort Worth, Texas, on a street known as Magnolia. There was nobody in sight on this street, and a few cars drove by. Across the street, from where she sat was a brightly illuminated two - storey building with a huge bright cross on top of it. There was a wide, clear sign below this cross and just above the building's main door on top of the steps that read "Sisters of The Holy Ghost Convent".

Ruma felt the strong urge to move forward, but only in one direction, and that was towards this convent. It was like this inner will strongly urging her towards it, like something was strongly asking her to stop whatever she was thinking and just go knock on that door. She looked around her. The was alone, cold, and hungry. And so, just like an American zombie, Ruma got up from the bench and started walking towards the convent. She didn't stop to look left and right as she crossed the four - lane street, nor look around her. A speeding car honked twice but she didn't even seem to hear it. She just walked straight over to the other side of the street, then up the wide steps that led to the door. She then knocked hard on the door, seven times to be exact, and stopped. She didn't know why she knocked seven times, she just did it.

The door opened immediately at the end of the seventh knock. Four fully cressed nuns stood on the other side of the door, inside a brightly illuminated room. One of them, the one who had opened the door for her, had a small flashlight in her hand which she now turned on, shining it in her face. Ruma blinked and tried to shield her eyes from the bright beam of the flashlight by lowering her head.

"Raise your head up, child," the nun said to her in a gentle voice. "I need to see something."

Ruma slowly complied, her eyes blinking rapidly in the strong beam of light.

After that, the nun turned off the flashlight and faced the rest of her colleagues.

"As expected, timely! She indeed carries the mark on her forehead," the nun said. She then joined the rest in the lineup against the wall to make way for her to come in and said "Do come in right away, my dear. We've been expecting you all day."

Ruma did not even hesitate. She slowly made her way to the inside, walking past the nuns without looking at or saying anything to them. She just stared straight ahead. It was warm and cozy inside this building, and she instantly felt good. She then heard the door close behind her. The door to her past was now permanently closed.

But the night wasn't over yet for the Vonsbergs. As their compound got rocked by gunshots and explosions, the rest of the Vonsbergs, the three women, left their bedrooms in panic, not knowing what was going on and came downstairs. The frail Mrs. Myra Vonsberg, who was assisted out of her bed by both her nurse sister Wendt and her sister – in - law Adalicia, remained on the couch in the living room.

She was too weak to remain standing up and she couldn't bear the wind blowing outside on the balcony. But she could hear the noise from the outside very well, and just like the other two women, she was scared. But Adalicia and Wendt joined the rest of the family on the balcony, and that was the time when Keener and his technology loaded vehicle was totally destroyed and erased. From their view point the explosion was spectacular, seeing those golden pods stream through the air and hit Keener's vehicle which rather seemed to rapture than explode, then completely melting down to the ground. When the resulting illuminating flush finally died down, they all saw more of the fiery pods flying around and then strike the two men down.

A period of about five minutes of quietness, and everyone caught their breath. And then suddenly, half of the compound was illuminated by a light brighter than the security lights. This was the time the four angels and their beastly horse shade their armor and opened their wings to reveal themselves. It was the most unbelievable, most stunning, and glorious sight ever to behold by the Vonsbergs, collectively and individually!

Though they didn't fully understand what exactly was going on, the Vonsbergs also partially witnessed the extraction of Woodrow Crane's soul from his body by hell's two messengers. Partially because the four angels had made a semi-circle around the site of extraction, spreading out their wings and obscuring most of the view. And so, what the humans on the balcony saw coming from within the semi – circle of wings was a flush of bright light, like a spark of lightening, then a puff of black smoke ascending into the air and fading away. Only Zeal knew what had just exactly taken place.

After this, the angels seemed to be doing something to what looked like another human being on the ground, and then they looked up at the sky, then separated, breaking up the semi-circle. Flapping their wings, they rose off the ground and then glided to the middle of the compound, a move that brought them closer to the balcony. The angel's leader was back on horseback. As their bright white wings slowly flapped down behind their backs simultaneously in a slow- motion maneuver, they made a line up in front of the big house, facing the balcony.

What a spectacular sight for the Vonsbergs. The glowing yellow color around the angels, and the halos on top of their heads that emitted this light that illuminated the area, far brighter than the compound's security lights, the bright sparkling pair of yellow eyes on each face, and their continuously flowing robes made this one show they would never, ever, forget in their lifetimes!

Zeal, who had already put his arms down after the complete demolition of Keener's vehicle, now turned around and faced the completely awe struck Vonsberg family. None of them could believe what they were seeing, and everyone was speechless at the moment.

"I warned you earlier, Mr. Vonsberg, about what you were going to see, which is never meant for any human to see. But this is a special occasion, so we made an exception for you, a special family. And now your lives have been touched, and forever changed. You all will never be the same again," Zeal said, a smile on his face. "For what you have just witnessed, and what you are looking at now, is a simple revelation to mankind that we are here and that we are real. God has just blessed this family to be the first to witness one way in which some of heaven's simple battles can be won. Yet this is far from the real thing, for when the mightiness of heaven's battles happen, mountains will crumble, seas and oceans will rise, and the stars in the sky will hide in fear, all this in response to God's fury. What you have just witnessed today is a mere warning to mankind that his wrath can reach every corner and nook in your world, and that no one can hide from it. It also establishes our presence on earth. We are here to clean up the vermin that has overcome God's seventh dimension, vanquish the evil, and protect the faithful."

Nobody responded back to him. The entire group of five human beings on that balcony had their eyes and minds transfixed on the four angels and their giant horse standing several yards away in the middle of their compound, facing them on the balcony.

"Oh! I won't blame you for that. The life changing effect has already begun," he said, and then walking around them, he walked back into the living room where Myra Vonsberg was laying down on the couch, eyes wide open. He offered his right hand to her. "Mrs. Vonsberg…"

Myra Vonsberg stared back at him, a look of suspicion on her face. "Who are you, and what have you done with my family?" she asked, her voice sounding shaky and weak. She didn't offer her hand to him. Like mother, like daughter. But this time around, Zeal's arm remained stretched out in front of her, his hand open.

"I am Zeal, and I am here to protect you and your family," he said, still smiling. "Your family is out there on the balcony, and they are all safe."

"Are you sure?" she asked, her lips quivering.

"Yes, Mrs. Vonsberg. You're all safe and out of danger now, for good and forever," Zeal replied. "There will be no more safety concerns from now on. Never again, thanks be to God."

"Are you the same man who saved my husband at that airport he was talking about?" She asked. "He told us that someone was about to kill him after he came out of his business meeting, but then another man came along and saved him. He said that the same man later called him back using the Pastor's phone."

"Yes, that was me, Mrs. Vonsberg," he replied. "But it's all over now, and like I said, you and your family will remain safe, intact, and blessed, from now on. Just remember to keep up with your faith in God, and to worship and praise the almighty God in heaven every day of your life."

Myra Vonsberg then slowly lifted her arm and placed her feeble hand in his. He went on and placed his left hand, too, on top of her hand, completely sandwiching it in both of his. "Oh my, your hands are so warm and comforting, Mr...." she said. She had not mentally grasped his name yet, and he fully understood that. But Myra Vonsberg also experienced something else. The warmth from Zeal's hands seemed to warm up her entire body, and it felt really good.

"Yes, they are," he responded back in a calm and gentle voice. He then, without asking, helped her seat up straight on the couch, for which she thanked him. "I am afraid I must leave now, Mrs. Vonsberg, for my friends are waiting for me outside, and I don't want to keep them waiting for a long time. It was a pleasure meeting with, and talking, to you."

And with that, he gently let go of her arm and then left the living room. The same thing happened again as before with Barret, and that is she felt his hands just completely dissolve off hers. Once he got outside again on the balcony, he didn't stop, but walked past the still shocked and or mesmerized group five people and hurried down the steps, hastily joining the angel group in the compound. The Vonsbergs now watched as he hugged each one of the angels. Then the one on the big horse dismounted and hugged him tightly. A thick mist or cloud suddenly descended from above and surrounded Zeal and the angels. Now only their heads and the top of their shoulders and wings were visible. They seemed to be talking, but no one on the balcony could hear what they were saying. After a period of about five minutes, the occupants of the balcony saw a single bolt of blue lightening come from the sky above and its lower end touch the cloud, disbanding it to nothing. And gone, too, were the four angels and their big horse. Only Zeal remained. He slowly made his way back to the balcony.

"I must leave now. My job is done here, Mr. Vonsberg. There should be no more security concerns for you and your family," he said after a heavy sigh. "You' all take care. Peace be with you from now on. Remember, put the holy spirit first, and keep your faith high."

"Zeal, what about the mess in my front yard? What do I do with all the cars and human remains?" Bernhardt Vonsberg asked, facing Zeal. "I don't know what to tell the police, or the Sheriff, should they come by to investigate the bright, fiery explosions and loud noises on my premises."

"Don't worry about that. It will be taken care of," Zeal replied. "Just do two things for me. One is that make sure none of you goes into or near that battle ground until come day light. Do not, and I repeat, do not set foot beyond this balcony until daylight. Your compound, Mr. Vonsberg, is technically ours for now and is tainted with live, non – earthly matter that will completely devour nondivine material on contact. The other is that immediately after I leave, turn off all the lights in your entire compound, including the light on the balcony, and close up all your blinds. Do not even attempt to peep through, or you will go blind forever! Our cleanup crew, if I may call them that, prefer to work in the dark, totally unseen or unwitnessed. By daylight, your compound will be clear."

With that, Zeal shook hands with every individual on the balcony, smiling and acknowledging with a brief node. He shook Benita's hand last, and then turned around to leave.

"Wait!" Benita said loudly, sounding urgent and grabbing at his right-hand jacket sleeve. Zeal turned around briefly, a look of surprise on his face. Benita then hugged him tightly, holding on to him for several seconds.

"I want to see you again, Zeal," she whispered in his ears. "Promise me that you will come back to see me, and then I will let you go." Zeal gently hugged her back, lightly patting her back.

"My missions are many, miss, and I barely have any time for anything or anybody else," he whispered back. "But ok, I promise that I will come back to see you."

Smiling widely, she let go of him and stood back with the rest. Zeal again nodded his head at the Vonsbergs and then made his way back down the balcony steps and into the compound, to the exact spot where he had stood with the other angels a few minutes ago. He then spread his arms outwards. As the Vonsbergs looked on, something big and bright came flapping down from above, just like the way a butterfly flaps its wings, and attached itself to his back. It was a huge pair of bright white wings, just like an eagle. Zeal turned around one more time, waved at them, and then with his massive wings flapping, he rose from the ground, going higher and higher until he disappeared into the sky.

The Vonsbergs remained on the balcony and watched him until he completely disappeared amongst the clouds in the sky. Several yards away from them, down the driveway, things still looked broken, tone up and or damaged beyond repair. The small trees that lined the driveway were all completely bent down, and some were uprooted.

The flower bushes were no more, completely shriveled and or destroyed. The small statues of mighty, ferocious jungle animals were all either broken down and shattered to pieces. And the remains of damaged and destroyed cars, and dead human bodies, were visible in the shadows. There was only one vehicle, the Chevy suburban further down the driveway, that had remained intact. Woodrow Crane's mobile command post seemed to have survived the onslaught. Elsewhere in this front yard, some debris was still smoldering.

Nothing moved out there. Only a gentle wind prevailed, fueling the burning smell of things in the air. Bernhardt Vonsberg slowly shook his head. Like the rest of his family standing around him, he was still shocked, and even terrified, by what he had just witnessed, and not just only the battle in his compound, but the presence of the winged beings. It was like a dream for him, yet this had all been real. He slowly turned to his equally shock - stricken family and led them back into the house. Everybody was still speechless. Only Benita Vonsberg faced her dad with a strange, faint smile on her face, linking her hand into his. She had that distant look of excitement in her eyes, but she too remained silent. He put his other hand around Barret's and then led the two children back into the house. The two women followed behind.

The small control gadget was still in his hand. He touched the "off" button on the touch screen and the entire compound was suddenly plunged back into darkness. He then closed all the blinds, tightly.

"Well, about time everyone came back inside to me! Whatever you all were doing on that balcony must have been so good that everyone forgot about me!" Myra Vonsberg said in a strong, clear voice. There was no sign of trembling or delay in her speech at all. And now she was standing in the middle of the living room with no support and feeling up a big glass with orange juice from the juice fountain attached to a beverage machine.

Now everybody stopped dead on their tracks and stared at her. The change was definitely clear. For Myra Vonsberg, and not too long ago, was too weak and frail to even stand on her two feet, later on to be able to hold a filled-up glass of anything. She could not even hold and put a light plastic cup up to her lips. Someone had to hold it for her while she took small sips of the drinks. She couldn't endure the big sips because a large volume of any liquid, running down her throat, even water, was too painful to swallow and it would take forever to finish the drink. Now everyone watched as she placed the glass full of juice to her lips and gulped down its contents until it went empty, all in a matter of seconds!

Her two caregiver sisters rushed to her side, but she shrugged them off . "It's ok, and thank you so very much, but I am perfectly fine, my dears," she said. "I feel good all over, with no pain anywhere. It's been long since I felt this good. I am just hungry. I feel like I haven't eaten for days. Wait a minute, where is that nice young man with the warm hands? Did he leave already?"

There was silence in the room. Everyone just looked at her.

Another speechless moment prevailed again.

Now the moment Bernhardt Vonsberg switched off the compound's high density security lights, plunging it into total darkness, things started happening. Inside Woodrow Crane's Chevy suburban was his mobile phone, tacked away in a compartment on the dashboard. This mobile phone suddenly started emitting a buzzing sound, indicating an incoming call. The buzzing went on for several minutes as there was no one to answer the phone. But then, the green "answer button" pressed itself.

"Hey, I have been trying to reach you for a long time. Why the hell were you not picking up, huh?" the caller yelled. It was the death broker, the agent or middleman who had hired the Woodrow Crane team to assassinate the billionaire on behalf of the incarnated principal.

"We were busy!" the recipient of the call said, the voice sounding strangely hollow but yet clearly understandable.

"Is the job done?" the caller asked quickly. "I have to report back to the client, because he wants to know. You told me it would be done by this time. We are actually way past the time you had guaranteed to me that the job would be done and over with!"

"No, the job has not been done and it will never be over with," the recipient of his call replied.

"What? What do you mean by that? You don't even sound like Crane, so who's this? I need to speak to Crane right away, right now! So put Crane on the phone!" the caller said, suddenly sounding very angry and anxious.

"Woodrow Crane can't talk to you right now," the recipient replied. "In fact, he will never talk to you again, ever! And that's because he's dead! Everyone is dead, do you hear me? They are all dead! So, listen to me carefully. Go tell your client that we are aware of what's going on and we are not going to let it happen. We are now done with Crane and are now coming for your client. And if you don't want the same fate as Crane's and his team to befall you, I suggest you better run and hide, far away. Do not look back and don't ever do what you have been doing again! Don't you ever, you hear me? Consider this your final warning!"

"What? Are you out of your freaking mind?" the caller started to say, his voice shrilled. But the line suddenly went blank. The recipient had terminated the call.

Inside the Chevy suburban, Woodrow Crane's cellphone suddenly burst into a bright, single flame of fire, but which quickly self-extinguished. That single burst of fire completely disintegrated the whole machine without damaging its surrounding area.

On the other side of the spectrum, the caller, Rashid Rahman, a thirty something black guy, stared at the phone in his right hand for a moment, then slowly put it down on top of his computer desk, which also served as his office table, in one corner of his small living room. He mostly worked in self-solitary confinement from his luxurious, one bedroom apartment home in Dallas Texas. He only left when he had to set up a plan of action with his contracts, the men and women he brokered on behalf of his clients who wanted death deals done. He was always the middleman, the man with the connections. His philosophy was that hey, as long he didn't order it, or do it himself, he was intact. He simply brokered the deal between both ends, handled the money transfers, of which he took a percentage as his fee, and then made sure that it all happened. And most of these deals always went through, with both ends getting their sides done. As long as everyone was happy, and as long as he got his brokerage fee, everything was always fine. Until now.

For the first time ever in his ventures as a death broker, he felt very nervous. And he didn't know why. But it all started with the moment his phone call to Woodrow Brinks Crane a few minutes ago, was answered. Not only did he feel strangely terrified by that voice, but it

303

also felt like the voice was inside him, like his mind was talking back to him. It was also right at that very moment that his body experienced a chill, like he had suddenly developed a feverish cold. Still trembling from the chills, he got up and walked to his bedroom, where his coat closet was. On his way, he checked the thermostat. The temperature read at seventy-seven degrees inside the house, a temp that he's usually very comfortable with.

He selected a jacket, the winter type with light wool in it, and quickly put it on. On his way back, he raised the room temperature to eighty degrees heat on the thermostat. Then he went back to his desk, picked up the phone again and pressed the redial number. He was calling Woodrow Brinks Crane again. He wanted to know who the person was that had answered his call. It buzzed three times in response after it redialed, and then he got back a message telling him the number he had dialed is no longer in service, and that if he felt this was an error, he should check the number and then try again. He didn't recheck the number, because he knew it was the correct one, but he redialed it again. This time around, it didn't do the repeated beeping sound that indicates ringing on the other side. It simply beeped once and then repeated the message. He redialed again, feeling frustrated already. It beeped once, and the line instantly got disconnected. Feeling even more frustrated, he dialed it again. This time around, it didn't beep. Instead, his entire phone system shut down. He had to restart the phone! What the hell! He tried again after that, and the same thing happened, his system shut down again. He had to restart the phone again. Tired of doing that, he gave up and put the phone down for the moment.

Now he had to call his mysterious client, the one who had told him that failure was no option on this job. This same client had warned him that should he fail on this deal, he will suffer the ultimate consequence himself, that of death.

Rashid Rahman suddenly realized that he now had two warnings from two different entities, and they both had similar attributes. The one who hired him, and the one who answered the Woodrow Crane cellphone. Both were invisible and mysterious, in that he had never met or seen the individuals behind the voices. Both seemed to have interest in the same deal, although he couldn't figure out how. And they both came across as forceful, their very words compounded in threats. But Rashid Rahman, who had studied psychology to a masters' level, also realized that there was antagonism involved here. His client wanted him to do something that the other side did not want him to do. His client had threatened him with death if he failed, the mysterious person behind the voice on the Woodrow Brinks Crane phone had threatened him with the same if he carried on with the deal. But the later had one extra, and better, option for him, and that is to run and hide and that as long as he stopped what he was doing, all would be good.

For some reason, Rashid Rahman saw that as a second window or chance, and perhaps a better choice. Not only was he going to run and hide, but yes, going to get out of the death broker business for good, because with this last job, it just didn't feel right anymore. He had way enough money saved up to enable him to venture into another business and this time he wanted to be on the normal side of things.

The cellphone on his desk suddenly started vibrating, bouncing the machine around on the table. The heavy, noisy vibrations also jolted him out of his current deep trend of thoughts. He looked at the number. It was the client calling. He stared at the machine for a moment, letting it continue vibrate for at least a minute, and then he pressed the digitalized answer button, at the same time putting it on speaker.

"Rashid!" he said, his usual way of answering business calls.

"Is the job done?" the caller asked. It was the same strangely haunting, growling and chilling, deep voice that had prevailed right from the beginning of the whole deal. It now also had a snap in it, which added a menacing grip to it. Even though he had never met the caller in person, Rashid Rahman always felt like this caller was in the room with him, causing him to have goose bumps all over. He hesitated before answering back. He was figuring out the best way to answer that question.

"Yes, or no?" the caller prompted again.

"They couldn't do it. The billionaire seems to have very good protection," he finally replied. "The guys that I contracted were the best on the market. They are all dead now. They died trying to do it.

There is nothing else I can do for you now, my friend. I can, perhaps, refund your money..."

"The money doesn't matter to me right now," the principal responded back, already sounding angry. "What's important to me is to know that you and your friends failed me. And for that reason, you will pay the ultimate price. You are going to die, just like your friends. You can run and hide, but we will find you. It's just a matter of time!"

"Listen to me, you son of a bitch. You don't scare me, huh!" Rashid Rahman shouted back into the phone. "You came looking for me, I didn't look for you, and now you are threatening me? Your job deal didn't work out as expected. I had no control of what happened, don't even really know what happened out there. But so what? I am telling you now that all I know is that the people that I hired to do it were the best, and if these guys couldn't do it, then no one else in this world can. So instead of threatening me, why don't you just take back your money and find someone else to do your job for you? If not, then perhaps shove it up your ass! Forget about me! I can't help you anymore. Otherwise, you go to hell yourself!"

"Hell is where I come from, my friend. I just don't intend to go back there yet. There is so much to do up here," the principal responded. "But I am going to send you to hell, and have you imprisoned there until I revisit. Then I will punish you, and a lot of others, for failing me!"

"I don't know who the fuck you think you are, or even what you really are exactly, but oh no, you aren't taking me anywhere, asshole!" Rashid Rahman snapped back. "Just take yourself to hell, and perhaps stay there for good! Now if you think you're Lucifer the devil, then I have some bad news for you. This is our place, devil, and you can't just come up here and claim citizenship. God banished you from heaven, and we don't want you here either!"

"What did you say?" the principal asked menacingly.

"You heard me!" Rashid Rahman shouted back, and then shut the phone off. His mind was so rattled for him to repeat himself. He was done with the whole thing. He threw the phone on the floor, stood up, and crushed the machine to pieces with the bottom of his bare right heel, several times until it became a tattered mess.

And yes, he was going to run and hide. He already had a contingency plan in place for moments like this. He knew all along that a day like this would happen, where everything suddenly gets to go wrong, or down. And in his line of work, retaliation was the paramount risk. He had a plan to go into hiding until things cooled off, and that is if they ever cooled off! He then walked back to his bedroom and opened a small leather bag that was underneath his bed. He took out another cell phone, which was already on and speed - dialed a number. The call was answered in a few seconds.

"Oh, oh!" a female voice answered. "Is it that time?"

"Yes, Misty, it's that time. We've got to go." he replied.

"Ok Babe. I will be there in a few minutes." She responded back.

Even though they each had their own place of residence, Rashid Rahman and Misty Munro, a hospital nurse, had been dating for a long time. They had met at a topless strip club, where Misty, a white girl in her early twenties, was then working at that time. Her obvious natural beauty, even if not so glamorous, caught Rashid Rahman's attention as she worked the pole and he sat in the audience, alone at a table and sipping water from a water bottle. He then wrote the words "let's meet and talk" on a small piece of paper that had been his transaction receipt on entry to the club, together with his phone number, and attached it to a ward of a few one hundred-dollar bills. He then walked up to the pole and stuck the money into the elastic band of her panties. She didn't respond right away, so he came back after a couple of day and did the same thing, adding an extra bill to the amount. She finally responded after five trials in two weeks of his now almost daily visits to the club and agreed to meet with him at a local diner.

When they met inside the diner, she totally looked different from her the way she appeared at the strip club. She was all dressed up and looked flaming beautiful, way more than he last saw her! Yet she still maintained the natural appeal, with no makeup or anything else extra fancy. Rashid Rahman introduced himself as a businessman, and immediately asked her what she really wanted to do with her life. She told him she was saving money to go to nursing school. He made her a preposition. He told her that he was ready to finance her nurse education but that she had to stop what she was doing now so she can focus her school stuff .

She couldn't believe what she was hearing, and for that kind of thing, she was willing to quit the club. The next day, she put in her two weeks resignation notice while she figured out if his preposition was real. It was, for in the next few days, she enrolled into a private nursing institute, all paid off by him, and began her studies in within the next month. He also found her a better place to stay while going to school and paid all her bills and bought her a newer vehicle to start her new school life with. After a few years, she graduated on top of her class with a bachelor's degree, and they became soul mates with some limited benefits, which increased as time went by.

But soon she started wondering why he wasn't popping the question. She was ready. She would marry him in a heartbeat, she told him, and it didn't have to be anything big or fancy. She didn't care about all that stuff. She viewed herself as a down to earth, no nonsense, homegrown, backyard Texas girl who was determined to make it in life on her own terms, do whatever it takes. She had no time for whinnies and sissies. And now all she really wanted was him. She wanted to keep him to and for herself, forever. She saw him as her angel come out nowhere who graciously helped her realize the pinnacle of her dreams. To her, marrying him and bearing him a child or two, or whatever number he wanted out of her, was one way of showing gratitude for his being so good to her.

On his part, when asked by her as to why he came out of nowhere to that particular job place, picked her out of all those other girls, and did all this for her, his answer was that he didn't know why either. He confessed, though, that he saw real beauty in her, and that the attraction had happened instantly. He also said that he felt like something was urging him to go get her and not anyone else, and that it felt like an urgent urge to such a calling as he had never experienced before. He had stated that maybe God was leading him to make that choice for a reason. A reason that remained to be seen yet.

After pestering him for a long time to a point where it was getting into the way of their relationship, Rashid Rahman finally explained to her that his business was complicated and even dangerous, and that if he got married to her at this time it would complicate their relationship by involving her in the dangers associated with his business. In fact, he told her, on any given day and at any given time in the future, things could go so crazy per his business that he would have to quickly pack his bags and leave. He told her that he had everything set up for that moment and had showed her his quick move baggage. It was safer for her at that time not to be married to him.

She had listened and agreed to that, but made him promise that someday, somewhere, they would get married. Also, he wasn't going anywhere without her, she had told him, and had set up her own quick exit bag. She told him that she was ready to drop everything, including her life, for him. So, he gave her a cell phone, all red in color, and asked her to make sure it was always fully charged, and to carry it on her wherever she went. The point was that if she ever received a call from that phone, she would know that it's bad news, and it is time to go. And so for a long time they viewed themselves as best friends, with benefits and had remained loyal to one another.

And now after a decade plus, the bad news day was finally here.

Misty Munro got the phone call while seated at the nurses' station at the hospital where she worked. She felt the vibrations in her left pocket of her uniform pants, against her hip and immediately pulled out the phone and answered it. After she spoke to him, she went straight to her supervisor and told her she had a terrible emergency and had to leave immediately. And no, she had no time to explain anything, she had to go! Just the way she was acting was alone enough to tell the nurse supervisor there was no stopping her.

Her apartment was about fifteen minutes' drive from her job location, and the road was clear, so she got there quickly. Her heart thumping, she jumped out of her car, slammed the car door shut behind her and rushed to her door of her ground floor apartment. She opened it hastily and rushed straight to the closet in her bedroom. Inside that closet was a stand-alone standard size leather backpack, which she immediately grabbed and then dashed out of the bedroom. She stopped in the middle of her small neat, well-furnished living room that she had carefully set up to match her spinster life status, slowly shook her head, and then left the apartment, closing the door behind her but not locking it.

Once she got back into her car, she drove fast, sometimes going above the speed limits. Misty Munro felt rather excited, not afraid, about what was possibly happening or going to happen. She was not scared of the unknown, but more so, was ready to face anything with, and for her man. She couldn't wait to get to him and stand at his side to face whatever was coming at him. Her Puerto Rican mother, more than anyone else, had taught her to always be fierce and fearless, and to always stand by her husband, stand by her family. That was the main reason why she wasn't afraid to run away from home when she was barely twenty to face the world on her own. Her father, a native white Texan, had joined the U.S army after high school and was trained to be a sniper. But he subsequently died in one of those never-ending wars in the middle east.

Her father was also a big fan of the second amendment and loved guns. And so, he had taught her a lot about one thing: guns! He had a passion for guns and shooting, and he passed in on to his daughter at her tender age. By six years of age, Misty Munro could handle and fire a pistol. By thirteen years old she could handle a rifle very well, from assembling it to shooting. At sixteen she was an expert shooter with both small firearms and bigger guns alike.

But then her father died. He left all his guns to her. Her mother, a nurse at a local hospital, remarried three years later, stating she was tired of living alone. Mother sold their house, stating the house reminded her a lot of Misty Munro's father, and relocated from San Antonio to Dallas Fort Worth with her new husband, and soon became pregnant.

But Misty Munro didn't like her new stepfather, and soon there was a fall out between her and her mother over that. Her stepfather didn't quite appreciate her free-spirited attitude, she didn't really give a damn about what he said, and soon ran away from home, with the dream that one day she could go to nursing school and become a nurse like her mom. She sold all her father's guns so for solo startup money, keeping only two pistols which were her father's favorite and with which she had trained a lot. She used the proceeds to rent her a low level, one-bedroom apartment, then went hurting for a job. Any job. A friend she had met at church introduced her to the topless strip club. She told her that she had a good body shape and a cute smile, so she can get the job.

It also paid well, especially the tips from satiated customers. The owner agreed and hired her. About seven months later, Rashid Rahman came along, and her world changed forever.

Misty Munro always felt that she owed him her life and could do almost anything to repay that debt. She felt that this may be the moment to do exactly that, to be there for him like he had been there for her. She was playing one of her favorite songs from a selection on a compact disc, called "Ride on time" by black box as she drove to his place, which was about thirty minutes from her place. Her father used to love that song and played it all the time.

About five minutes before she got to his place, her phone rang. It was him calling.

"Hi babe. You … ok?" she asked immediately.

"Misty where are you?" he asked. He sounded anxious. And he rarely called her by name. It's always baby, moon love, or desert flower. "We need to go!"

"I am about five minutes away, babe," she replied quickly. "Just give me five minutes only, and I will be with you, I promise. Can you do that for me? Please, honey boo."

"Ok. But not more than five minutes." He replied, and then hung up the phone.

In another place in the world, the principal placed the phone on the nearest table after talking to Rashid Rahman and stared down at it for a moment. Raising both arms in the air, the principal mumbled a series of words which also included the names Rashid Rahman, for three full minutes. After that, the arms went back down in place, and then the principal walked into the passenger area of the jet, where the girls and the stocky black guy sat. They were all in their individual seats, asleep. The principle walked past the trio and into the cockpit. As expected, the pilot and his assistant were both wide awake.

"How much time left to get to our destination?" the principal asked the pilot.

"We are landing in less than thirty minutes, boss," the pilot answered quickly. "I suggest you get back into your seat and buckle up. We are experiencing sudden strong turbulence in the air."

"Hmmm, I don't need to sit down!" the principal growled, at them. "I created that turbulence,"

The principal looked at the three aides. They were all asleep. Placing a hand on each side of the masked face, the principal mumbled some words and the three suddenly woke up, sitting forward all at the same time, like they were collectively coming out of a bad dream. Their respective seatbelts jerked them back down into their seats. Unknown to them, the principal had used telepathic powers to scream with high intensity into their heads, just to wake them up.

"You all are supposed to be awake and guarding me, not the other way around," the principle growled again at them menacingly. "You need to get ready, for we are about to land, and as soon as we do, we immediately head out to our primary destination. There is no time to waste anymore."

"Why is the plane shaking so bad?" one of the women asked, holding on tightly to both of her seat's armrests

"Air Turbulence," the stocky black guy said. "It can be crazy sometimes. Some occurrences can sometimes shake the plane in a really bad way."

"It's me who created the turbulence," the principal said. "So, calm down, it will soon be over."

"You did? Why?" the other woman asked. "It's so strong, and quite scary."

"I hired someone else to eliminate the billionaire for me after the other groups failed to do so," the principal answered. "But he failed me too. He failed to kill the billionaire and his family and so, he has to be punished for failing to do his job. I therefore summoned our underworld agents and together we created a messenger of death to go after him and carry out the punishment. The presence of the underworld agents is what created the strong turbulence."

"Ewe, I am glad I am not him!" the stocky black guy said.

"But it's beginning to look like no one can get rid of the billionaire," one of the women added. "Something is not right. Maybe that's what that major guy was trying to tell us before we killed him. Whoever is protecting this billionaire human is way stronger than we think. What do you think, Kimbi?"

"Yeah, he tried to warn us, but we did not listen. But sure, as hell that billionaire must have some… sort of out of this world protection," Kimbi replied. "Maybe you should have sent us to do the job instead, boss. I've been wanting to visit the U.S, and specifically the state of Texas, for a long time anyways. Freakin' cowboy country! I hear it's beautiful out there. Could get me some cowboy meat too."

"Then if what major Haraabi was trying to tell us is right, then consider yourself lucky that I didn't send you there," the principal said. "Because you two could have failed me too, and then I would be forced to kill both of you for that reason. I do not tolerate failure from any of my workers, hired or from my inner circle. You fail me, you face the ultimate punishment. You die! That is why I sent the death messenger to eliminate the man I hired to do the job after he told me he had failed at his assignment. He even called me names and insulted the master! My personal messenger of death will make sure he pays for his incompetence!"

It was still dark when Misty Munro drove through the gateway that opened up to the interior of Rashid Rahman's apartment complex, and then followed the winding car pathway that is bordered with several three - story apartment blocks. She knew her way through very well, of course, having come here to visit with him numerous times. As soon as she arrived outside his block, she packed the car in a visitors' parking area. She opened her backpack and pulled out the two pistols, all well loaded, looked at them briefly, and then put them back, but in the zipless pocket, for quick access. Then she quickly got out the car, closed, clicked the remote lock, and then took off running towards the steps at the front entrance of the building, with her backpack in her hand. She rode in the elevator to the third floor, which was his floor, and was soon outside his door and knocking loudly on it.

"Who's it?" he asked loudly from inside. "It's me, babe…" she shouted back.

After a few seconds the door flew wide open. Rashid Rahman had a gun in his hand, a snub-nosed, semi – automatic pistol which he quickly placed on the kitchen countertop close to the door and then they crushed into each other's arms, hugging tightly for a moment. After a brief, passionate kissing moment, they both stepped back.

"I am finally here, and I am so glad to find you still intact," she said, kicking the door shut with a backward flip of one of her feet. "You sounded so frantic when you called me that I panicked, thinking that something terrible had already happened to you! What's going on, babe?"

"I am ok for now, and very happy to see you, but I am afraid that if we don't get out of here now something is going to happen. I can feel it," he said.

"What do you think is going to happen, babe? I don't see anybody or anything else here or out there," she said quickly. "I have never seen you like this before. You're already freaking me out!"

"I will explain later," He replied, catching his breath. "We just need to get out of here, now!"

"Ok. Can I use the bathroom? I just need to pee, that's all and it will take me only seconds to do," She quickly said, already moving towards it.

"Ok. But please, hurry!" he replied.

Placing her backpack down on one of the small dinette chairs, she rushed to the bathroom, and without bothering to close the door, pulled down her scrub pants and underwear, and quickly sat down on the commode. She now felt stressed, because of his nervous behavior, but also still felt, in some strange, now heightened way, excitement. But deep in her mind, too, she quickly said a prayer to God for all to be okay.

Outside the bathroom, Rashid Rahman resumed his nervous pacing, his heart racing, as he waited for her to come out. Then a thought came into his head. As she came out of the bathroom, he rushed into his small bedroom and picked up his leather - jacketed Koran from the bedside table. The holy book had been given to him by his father as he was about to board the plane at the international airport in his country to come to the United States to study engineering. He was told it used to belong to his grandfather.

Picking up his pistol and sticking it under his belt, then pulling his sweater down over it to conceal it, he headed for the door as Misty Munro picked up her backpack and followed close behind. He opened

314

the door and then instantly jumped back, almost knocking her off her feet. A loud hissing sound came from the doorway as they both looked up again and found themselves face to face with a big, fully upright poised, king cobra snake with its hood fully flared. The hissing animal looked very menacing, and without going down, it made its way through the doorway and into the living room.

"Oh my god, what the hell…" Rashid Rahman shouted out as the snake suddenly made a lunge at him. He managed to jump clear, finding himself next to her. "It's after me, Misty!"

"Step back babe!" Misty Munro shouted, and quickly shoved him out of the way, placing her herself directly in front of the big snake. Quickly reaching into her backpack, she pulled out a pistol. It was one of her two guns, a Walther P99 semi – automatic, ready to fire. She aimed it at the animal.

But then, and to their shocking disbelief, the animal opened its mouth and spoke! Its voice was a slow and heavy, deep throated output similar to that of an elderly human male. "I am not here for you, woman. It's him that I am after, so get out of my way or I will kill you too."

"It's talking… it's talking, Misty!" Rashid Rahman shouted out, sounding very frightened. "What… what is this? Please tell me I am not dreaming!"

"Shit, no you won't!" Misty Munro replied back to the ferocious talking serpent, appearing not to be spooked by a talking animal. She had watched too many fairy tales movies during her little girl age phase which featured talking animals and had always mentally delved into the possibility of seeing one upfront. So maybe this was it. She squeezed the trigger. Blue and yellow sparks flew out of the gun's barrel accompanied by bullets and loud ear-piercing blast sounds. The big snake suddenly swayed sideways, causing the heavy bullets to miss its target and instead shatter the wall and part of the door behind it. As it dodged the bullets, it edged closer to them. But they too backed away, only to find themselves in one corner of the room. As they did so, Misty Munro dragged her backpack with her. Noticing that they were cornered, the animal hissed louder and opened its mouth, revealing its massive fangs. Its hood was still fully inflated. Even as it dodged the bullets, it was getting ready to strike.

"Oh really...," Misty Munro said as she acknowledged the animal's moves. Still randomly firing the gun in her right hand, her eyes staying focused on the animal, her left hand dropped the backpack on the floor, then reached down into it and withdrew another gun, an exact replica of the one in her right hand. Her Dad's favorite guns. Both guns now started blazing at the snake, as she skillfully fired them in a twisting, wavy pattern using her hands, quickly adopting to the snake's movements. Suddenly, the serpent lunged forward, swinging sideways and then swooping upwards to strike at the right side of her neck. But she was too focused on, and tuned to, it's movements to miss a thing. A slight twist of her upper body brought her face to face with the gaping mandibles, and then...Bang... bang, bang... bang!

The first two shots hit the serpent straight into the mouth, shattering the roof and splitting the back of its head. As the force of those shots thrust the serpent's head upwards, the next two shots hit it below its hood, the last one completely severing its shattered head off the rest of its body. Misty Munro stopped shooting and jumped back, landing into place next to Rashid Rahman. They both stared in shock as the rest of the headless serpent danced around, still upright, it's severed arteries spraying black blood all over the place. Then it slumped down onto the floor, wiggled around like a hands-off pressurized water hose for a few seconds, and then the whole long thing slithered itself out of the room, tail first, through the open doorway and disappeared in the outside darkness beyond. When they looked at the rest of it remains on the floor, the split, mangled head parts were all strangely dried up and had turned into white bony structures. Even the blood from the animal was completely dried up, turned into plain black stains.

"Come on, babe, let's get the hell out of here!" Misty Munro said as she threw one of the guns back into the open backpack, at the same time withdrawing a fresh magazine for the one in her hand. Instantly ejecting the near empty one from the gun, she plugged in the fresh one, then zipped up the bag and wrapped its thick straps around her shoulders. Turning around quickly, she reached out to Rashid Rahman with her free left hand. He in turn grabbed it and yanked himself up from the corner where he had been all crouched up in fear. He still held on to his Koran book all this time. He then grabbed his own backpack and together they stepped out of the apartment, watching carefully where they stepped and where they were going.

The elevator was around the corner and as they got to it, it opened, and two people stepped out of it. When they saw Misty brandishing a gun in her hand, they quickly took off running in the opposite direction. Misty and Rashid quickly got in it. She touched a numbered button on the control panel, the doors closed, and the elevator rolled downwards. A few seconds later the doors swung open again on the first floor. They rushed out of it and then ran through the empty hallway that led to the outside.

"Which car, mine or yours?" Misty asked quickly once they got out of the building and into the parking lot.

"This way!" Rashid replied and led the way to carport where his C7 corvette was parked.

But they stopped dead on their tracks when they suddenly realized that the car was surrounded by a park of four vicious – looking dogs. Misty recognized the breed immediately, because her stepfather kept two of them. Big, black rottweilers. Their eyes, pure red with no pupils, glowed like live coils in the shadows of the carport. The growling dogs now came out of the shadows of the carport and advanced on the couple. The dogs split ways, three going to the right side, advancing on Rashid, and one taking on Misty.

"What the hell…," Misty exclaimed. But the two humans didn't get the chance to retreat and talk about it. There was no time to contemplate about this new development, for in just a matter of seconds after they came out of the shadows, the menacing dogs attacked. Misty instantly raised her gun and fired at the already airborne animal as it pounced on her. The shot, fired at point blank range, tossed the animal sideways and to the ground, away from her. The animal hit the ground with a thud and its body started shaking like it was experiencing a grand mal seizure and then went still. It didn't look like it was going to ever get up again.

And as the other three growling dogs pounced on Rashid, he stumbled backwards, fell on the ground, dropping his backpack but holding on to, and covering his head with, his Koran book in his hands. The three growling dogs all landed on top of him.

There was a big bright flash of white light, which was followed by a thunderous explosion, both lasting about three seconds, total. Even the ground shook within that time frame. Rashid felt this high heat in his hands and instinctively his fingers released the holy book. At that very same moment, the three vicious dogs fell off Rashid, slammed onto the ground away from his body, stiff and dead. Their mandibles were stretched wide open, teeth bearing out, their nostrils flared outwards, and their eyes popped out of their sockets. The explosion also set of a series of alarms on several cars in the parking lot.

"What... what happened?" Misty asked, screaming out the words, sounding scared. "I mean, the flash, the explosion! And look... look at the damn dogs!"

"You're asking me? I don't know!" Rashid shouted back. Reaching down to the ground, he picked up his holy book. It still felt very warm in his hands.

Suddenly, a man appeared from nowhere and started walking towards them at a very fast pace. From Misty's viewpoint, it appeared like he came out of the air. Misty saw him first and her gun wielding hand came up again, fast.

"Stop, don't move any further! Or I will shoot!" she shouted out at the man. But the man continued moving towards them.

Misty pulled the trigger. As the shot rang out, the man fast ducked, his upper body bending sideways all the way down to the left while both his hands remained folded up on his chest. The bullet missed him, and in a flash moment he was upright again, resuming his fast-paced walk. In a matter of seconds, he reached Misty and in one quick, hand move he smacked down at her gun-wielding hand, knocking the gun out of it. Misty felt a sharp pain in her hand and winced loudly, bending down as she did. It was like being hit with a heavy concrete block. The acute pain in her hand was instant.

"Crazy humans and their guns! You're all too trigger happy to think before you shoot, yet you're supposed to be mindful of the consequences!" the man exclaimed in a deep, commanding voice, and then quickly turned around to face Rashid. Both Misty and Rashid were now able to look at the man closely. He was well dressed in a black suit and shoes, white shirt, no tie. His skin was of a glowing bronze color, and he had no hair on his head or face, except for eyelids and eye lashes. Misty, her hand painfully throbbing, stepped back and away from him.

"Those demonic animals were sent here to kill you, not her," the stranger continued, finally standing still and pointing a finger at Rashid. "But since she was getting to be in the way, she was bound to suffer the same fate!"

"Sent? How, and by who, and why?" Rashid asked as he quickly got up from the ground. Stepping over the dead dogs, he walked over to where Misty was, putting his hand around her waist. They then both faced the man directly.

"That information is irrelevant to you at this moment. I don't even think it matters anymore!" the man replied immediately. "Now listen to me very carefully. I want both of you to get into the car that's parked seven spaces away from your car to the left, right now, and immediately drive away from this place. The ignition is ready. Go now, and do not look back! And never, ever, come back to this place again! Go!"

The man sounded very resolute, his face very tense and or grim. Reacting to his command, Misty quickly picked up her gun and put it in her backpack, while Rashid, still holding on to his Koran with his right hand, scooped up his backpack with his left and together they quickly walked to the car, a gleaming black Jaguar Sedan, which was, as the man said, parked exactly seven spaces to the left of his Corvette underneath the carport. The doors were already unlocked, and they got in, shutting the doors immediately. Rashid handed over his stuff to Misty who placed everything in the back seat. Coming from out of their chair sides sit buckles automatically wrapped around their waists and across their chests. After hesitating for a moment, Rashid placed his hands on the steering wheel. The car's entire dashboard lit up, and the car started itself. As he looked up, the rare view mirror automatically adjusted itself to his eye levels and seeing nobody ahead of him, he pushed the gear to drive position. The car rolled smoothly forward. He spun the wheel around, making the car face the exit gates, and stepped on the accelerator. The car glided forward smoothly and quickly again. Even the headlights had already turned themselves on. They could hardly feel the roar of the engine. As he drove forward, he looked behind him one more time, through the rare view mirror. He could see the silhouette of the man who had come to them, standing close to where his car was parked, legs apart, hands hanging down to his sides.

In a matter of seconds, they were out of the apartment complex and onto the street, driving away from it. A couple of police cars, their sirens blaring and lights flashing, sped past them. Someone in the apartment complex had probably called the police after they heard the shots fired by Misty.

For the next hour or so, no one said anything, as each individually pondered the horrifying, terrifyingly mysterious, events of the night, from the sudden appearance and attack of the talking serpent to the sudden attack of the vicious, red eyed dogs and then the sudden appearance of, and engagement with, their last acquaintance, the fast- approaching, fast - talking man. All happening in a time frame of not more than thirty minutes, these events were very difficult to contemplate in their minds individually.

"Where are we going from here?" Misty suddenly asked, breaking the silence.

"Anywhere far away from here! For starters, Corpus Christi. I have a small two-bedroom beach front house there," He replied. "We shall stay there for at least a week or two and then from there, God willing, maybe fly out of the country to Israel, where my older brother lives with his wife."

"I need to go to a hospital now, babe," Misty said, looking at her now swollen right hand. "I don't know what it was, but that man's slap on my hand, which I think was his attempt at disarming me, really crushed my hand. I think it's broken. I can hardly do anything with it now, and it's hurting like hell!"

"Is it that bad? That's very strange, baby" Rashid said. "I saw him hit at your hand, but I swear it looked like a mere slap on it. I don't think it's broken. Can't it wait until we get out of this area, much further away from it? Then we will use the car's travel place locator to find the nearest hospital."

"Believe me, babe, it was as if he slammed my hand with a concrete slab or brick," Misty said. "It can't wait, babe. Otherwise, I am about to pass out on you because of the gut-wrenching pain."

"Ok then, baby. I will look for a hospital around here. Help me look for it. We can use the car's place locator." Rashid replied. Just like himself, Misty was very technologically savvy, a thing with the new generation x.

"Sure," she said, and immediately started working on the place locator buttons. "Man, this thing is complex. Wait a minute. I think it's voice oriented. Let me see… there it is. The button for voice command activation."

"Welcome to divine pathway global locator, or DPGL," the system said clearly after she pressed the button. "By reading your mind channels, I already know what you're looking for. The closest hospital is The Greater Western General hospital. Basing on your current speed, and if you follow my voice prompts, you will arrive at this location in twenty minutes. The highway is free of traffic."

They both stare at each other, their mouths open.

"I will be damned!" Rashid voiced his obvious thoughts.

"Things are getting more and more bizarre by the minute!" Misty added loudly. "But looks like for the better, I guess."

They arrived at the hospital in the exact time mentioned by the DPGL and walked into the emergency room, which wasn't so busy at the time. A Stat x-ray of the hand revealed that indeed her right hand's metacarpal bones were shattered. The doctor recommended surgery intervention as soon as possible. But Rashid insisted they had no time to do it here. After he told the doctor where they were going, the doctor said he had a contact at a main hospital in Corpus Christi, a surgeon who would fix Misty up. He gave them the contact's number, gave Misty a shot of strong pain medicine plus some pills for later use, and soon they headed out again after Rashid paid the hospital bill with one of his cards. It didn't take long before Misty fell asleep, which was a side effect of the pain medicine. Rashid quietly drove all the way to their destination, nonstop, and as advised by their previous acquaintance in the apartment parking lot, never looking back.

On the other side of the spectrum, in another place in the world far away from Texas, and as the plane prepared to land, the principle suddenly exhaled air heavily, stumbled backwards, and then collapsed on the floor of the passenger walkway. This was at the exact time moment that the three vicious dogs on top of Rashid Rahman experienced the flash of light and explosion that ultimately rendered them dead on the ground, in the apartment parking lot all the way in Texas, united states, in another time zone. A few minutes before that, the principal had experienced a sudden throbbing headache, followed by tightness in the chest, and had retreated to plane's executive rest chamber to take an aspirin. The sudden headache and chest pain happened at that very moment in time, again far away in Texas and in a different time zone, that Misty Munro blew the talking snake's head off its body.

Now, the three subordinates, though taken by surprise due to the fact that they had never seen anything like this happen to their mysterious boss, responded quickly, unbuckling from their seats and rushing to their master's side. For a moment, the principal was unresponsive. The three aides, now anxious and or petrified by the sudden occurrence, couldn't arouse the masked figure. One of the women rushed to the cockpit and rapped hard on the door with her fist. The door opened and the co-pilot stepped out. He looked young and handsome. He had strange eyes. Instead of having the normal oval pupils, the brown part in the center of his eyes were vertical. Kimba quickly eyed him all over, like he was a slice of medium - rare, cooked meat.

"Hello. I am the co-pilot. We are preparing to land at this time. What seems to be the problem now, Miss?" he asked, a frown on his face.

"Boss is down. Just suddenly passed out. We need help, now!" she screamed at him.

"Ok, let me notify the pilot," the young co-pilot said, and turned around to leave. But Kimba grabbed at his left arm tightly, preventing him from leaving. His face became grim. "Hey, I said let me go get the pilot. He's a trained paramedic, one of a kind. Now Let go of my arm, miss. You're hurting me!" He added grimly.

"You better hurry up!" Kimba said, at the same time letting go of his arm.

The co-pilot quickly disappeared back into the cockpit, looking frightened and holding his left arm with his right. And he had reason to. The area on his left arm, where Kimba had gripped him, was totally numb, already severely bruised, and very painful.

The pilot stepped out of the cockpit in the next two minutes, after letting the young co-pilot take over the controls of the plane. Unlike his assistant, he was tall, looked much older, and exhibited a big burly body frame. His thick arms were all very hairy. He had a thick, grey moustache, and a long, receding forehead hair line, balding in the middle of and all the way to the back of, the scalp. The Hair on both sides of head appeared wispy. He stepped forward and his towering form bore down on Kimba. The big, grey eyes, overlapped by thick grey patchy eyebrows, focused on her. They had the intensity of an animal in them. But Kimba did not flinch. She stared back into those dark gray eyes with the same intensity.

"What seems to be the problem, child?" the pilot asked in a surprisingly very gentle, soothing voice.

"We need help. Our boss just collapsed on the floor right before our eyes. Boss is completely passed out and we're unable to arouse boss back!" she replied quickly. "Can you help? Please!"

"Let me see," The pilot said. Looking past Kimba, he took one look at the masked individual on the floor and then slowly looked away. He faced Kimba again. His face had the same dopey look as when he first appeared out of the cockpit. "Hmmm, Come closer child. I want you to whisper these six words in your boss's left ear, slowly, one by one. And whatever you do, do not in any way let any part of your body, not even your cloth, get in contact with your boss's body or the mask. It's very important that you don't."

Kimba slowly stepped forward, corking her head to one side. The pilot, bending down a little, placed his lips to her ear and whispered the six words to her. Then he straightened up and took a few steps back.

"Go on child, do it now," he said nodding his head at her. "The rest of you, I bid you to stand clear."

Kimbi and the stocky black guy both now stepped back, giving way to Kimba and watching her intensely. Kimba, her body shaking like she was experiencing a fever, and obviously frightened, slowly made her way across the aisle to where the downed Principal lay. She slowly went down to her knees, lowered her face to the left side of the principal's left ear, and remaining in whisper mode, recited the six words, one by one. The devil incarnates chest suddenly rose up, stayed there for about five seconds, then went down again. This sequence repeated itself six times and then it was followed by rapid heaving of the chest several more times before finally getting down to a much normal, regular pattern. Then the Principal suddenly sat up straight. Kimba fell back, pulling herself away from the principal. Her eyes, all watery, opened wide as she slowly stood up, a smile on her face. Kimbi's eyes opened wide too, and she mumbled something in awe, more of in a triumphant way, her hand going to her mouth to suppress a scream of joy. She embraced Kimba tightly. The stocky black guy said nothing. He just nodded his head slowly as he stared down at his newly reawakened boss.

"What happened? What happened to me?" the principal asked quickly looking around. "Why am I on the floor? what am I doing down here?"

"We don't know, boss. You just suddenly passed out and collapsed on to the floor!" the stocky black guy replied. "Here, give me your hand. Let me help you up."

"Thank you, but no need to," the principal said. Without effort and not holding on to anything for support, the legs flexed like an actively revolving conveyer belt, and the principal's body rose up straight from the floor. "Who brought me back?"

Kimba's hand slowly went up and then she said. "There is this guy, from the cockpit. I think he's the pilot. He told me what to do and immediately after I did it, you woke up."

Her hand was pointing in the direction of the cockpit. But the elderly, burly pilot had already retreated back into his cockpit. The principal slowly walked over to the cockpit entrance, the trio giving way to their boss, opened the door, and peered inside.

"Hmmm. But there is only one person in the cockpit, a youngish looking man, and it doesn't look like he's even controlling the plane," The principal said, closing the door to the cockpit and then looking back at his aides. "You all get back in your seats and buckle up. The plane is already landing."

"But… we saw the pilot, and his boyish assistant," Kimba said. "They both came from in there. What do you mean there is only one person in there? Where did he go?"

"Come look for yourself, Kimba," the principal said. "There is no one in here except the young fella. The plane appears to be on auto pilot and running smoothly. And the flashing sign on the dashboard indicates that we are landing."

"Kimba, it's complicated. Everything about boss is complicated, to a level that you and I can never comprehend," the stocky black guy quickly said to her in low tones. "And boss dislikes aides who don't immediately believe in what is said to them. So, if you still want to be with us, just forget about it. Just take your seat, buckle up, and be quiet. Then all will be good, sweetheart, all will be good!"

Kimba looked at Kimbi, who was facing her, her chest rising and falling quickly. Kimbi winked at her in affirmation. So, Kimba did as she was told. She sat down in her seat, buckled up, and kept quiet.

Sounding weak, the principal spoke again. "Good! Now listen up. We must now hurry. There is no time to waste. As soon as we land, we head out. The enemy is drawing closer, trying to stop us. I am now convinced that we have a very powerful, formidable force to reckon with, and they are not waiting. It's this same force that's protecting that American billionaire and thwarting all my other efforts. Now I want all of you to unlock your war modes and be ready to fight for, and protect, me at all costs. We cannot, and shall not, fail when it comes to this project. It's very important to me. Are we clear?"

"Boss, we're always ready, and will die for you if it comes to that. So, we hear you loud and clear!" the stocky man acknowledged. The two women quickly nodded their heads.

Without saying another word, their masked boss walked past them and disappeared into the executive wing of the plane.

The challenges ahead had suddenly and finally become very clear after the Devil incarnate physically experienced the soul - depleting

defeat of the devil's dark forces sent to Texas to bring about the demise of death broker Rashid Rahman. And this was just the beginning.

# Chapter Ten

Two specially chattered planes landed within the territorial neighborhoods of the Island republic country known as the Turikai, one at Libya's Mitiga international airport, another at Italy's Reggio Calabria airport in the early hours of a Tuesday morning, three hours apart from each other. Both planes were directed to private hangers especially suited for their occupant's arrivals, and although they arrived at different times and at different locations, these parties were all headed for the same destination immediately after landing, without having conclusive evidence about each other's agendas. It was all speculation at this time.

The first plane arrived at Mitiga international airport and the principal with the three assistants deplaned and immediately boarded a helicopter that flew them to a Turikai city private airport. This airport, though big enough to handle big jet planes, was off limits to international flights. Only designated flights, mostly cargo planes that delivered essential stuff or people, landed on it. Visitors to the island had to fly into international airports in neighboring countries and then either catch a boat to the island or fly in via helicopter.

A convoy of cars which included several black Land rover cars and Toyota crew cabin pick-up trucks loaded with heavily armed guards was waiting for them at the airport when they landed. One of the cars, a cross country Mercedes Benz and the only Benz brand in the entire fleet, was parked close to where the helicopter landed. As the principal and the three assistants got off the helicopter, a man came out of the Mercedes and slowly made his way to meet them. Several armed guards followed him. His name was Piajohnney Moongoo, the current President of the Turikai republic.

"Good to see you, Principal, your highness," The President said, offering his hand to the principal. "Although I was expecting to see Major Haraabi today, and not you, at this time. I was scheduled to meet with you at a later date, when the product is fully ready for deployment."

"Change in plans, Mr. President," the principal replied, shaking the president's hand briefly with a gloved right. One of the fascinating things about the masked individual, the President had noted during his few encounters with the devil incarnate, is that there were six fingers, not five, on each hand and which made the handshake rather complicated. "I gave major Haraabi a leave of absence, a break from his duties. He worked so hard and needed a break. On top of that, I wanted to oversee the final process myself, speed things up a little bit. Thank you for letting us use your country and resources for this project. It has allowed us to do our work with minimal interference, if any."

"Don't mention, your highness. I am part of it, remember? This is my contribution to the business," the president said. "It's a pleasure doing so."

"Yes, I know, but still much appreciated. And I promise you, it will all pay off greatly. A lot of money will soon be in your coffers and or bank," The principal said. "One other thing, Mr. President. I think we are expecting some uninvited guests. They are coming from America and will attempt to meddle with and or destabilize our business."

"What? The Americans? How did they get to know about it?" The President asked, frowning. "That's a legit concern, your highness. You know how nosy they are. They will stop at nothing to unveil the unknown, even beyond their own boarders. I don't want them in my backyard. Not in their secret mode capacity, especially."

"Someone among us let us down," the principal replied. "But no worries, Mr. President. Let's say we also have our own powerful people all over the world, even in America. Among the rich and powerful in America are some of our own. These friends of ours got wind of the

Americans' little secret, a plan to sabotage my business, and warned me about it. We now know every detail of their little operation to try to stop me, and we are effectively going to stop their intrusion instead."

"But how is that so? Nobody notified me about these people coming to my country without proper authorization!" The president said, sounding furious. "I am going to put my military on high alert. So, don't worry. They won't even get close to the castle, because the moment they pop in, we shall nab them and hold them in custody. Then I shall launch a formal complaint to the U.N. I will present the U.N council with the evidence."

"Relax, my friend," the principal said. "Let our friends come all the way through. We shall be ready for them when they arrive, and after we capture them, we shall interrogate them for more info using out of this world, extreme methods. And when we are done with them, they will return to their homes in body bags. Or even never go back to their homes at all."

"Alrighty, if you say so, your highness," the President said, sighing in relief. "We shall look away, let them come to you. We will let you do your job. Just do it well, make us all filthy rich!"

At first, a slow head nod from the principal was the only acknowledgment the President got back after this particular statement. But then the principal suddenly verbally responded back.

"Hmmm… I just don't get it with you human beings," The Principal said. "For example, look at you here, president Piajohnney Moongoo. You have everything most humans wish they could have in their lifetime. You're a successful businessman who is already wealthy beyond normal. You have a great, prestigious job as leader of a nation and well connected globally. You have a beautiful wife, children, and a great extended family surrounding you. Even your health is great for your age. Yet here you are, asking me to make you, and the rest of your cronies, filthy rich. But tell me this, what more are you exactly looking for, huh, President Moongoo? Are you not satisfied with what you have already?"

"Naaa, it's just business as usual," the President replied, shrugging his shoulders while raising his eyebrows. "Life is all about achieving more and more. Life is one big deal, and I have been doing deals all my life."

"Is that so? I hope you haven't forgotten that business comes with risk," the principal responded back. "And with risk comes the possibility of losing it all, everything you've worked so hard for and achieved in life. My business proposition is no exception to this rule. Are you willing to lose all you have achieved just because you still want more?"

President Moongoo hesitated for a moment, slowly shook his head, and then looking straight up into the masked figure's face, he said "Now you listen to me very carefully. Don't worry about me, or what I have to lose or whatever. It's none of your business, ok? Just worry about getting us there. I have done my part, and I am sure others have too. Now do yours, will you?"

And with those words, President Piajohnney Moongoo turned around and walked back to his car, his flock of bodyguards following closely. Once he was inside, one of his guards closed the door behind him and his convoy left the scene.

After the president left, there were three cars left. An army-green colored range rover and two black, military type jeep wranglers with just a handful of armed guards in them. They were just a handful of guards because the principal wanted it that way. It was all cosmetic, for the principal didn't really have the need for them. The President had no idea what the devil Incarnate, and the three assistants were really capable of. The group of four was its own security.

"Ok, let's get going now," the principal said, nodding to his group. "We have no more time left to waste!"

The group got into the army – green range rover, the two women sitting in the back with the principal, while the stocky black guy sat in the front with the driver. They left the scene with one jeep car leading the way and the other tailing the range rover.

The forty minutes' drive led them through downtown Turikai City and took them to the West side of the country, through a dusty village that looked medieval, and then to a small town called Tapsakesei. In Tapsakesei was one big attraction, an old castle, which was once the seat of power for the island's long-gone indigenous rulers. The current regime's friends had bought the castle from the Turikai government, despite protests from the minority group of the Island country's ethnic people. With the help of President Piajohnney Moongoo, who made sure that the deal was carried out without much opposition from the country's senate by threatening members who didn't agree to the sale with death to them and their families, the principal had bought and secured the old castle.

Once the old castle was passed on to its new owners, it was closed to the public due to reconstruction. It was modified to suite the principal's project. Machinery was flown in and set up, followed by all other necessary materials needed for the project. After the modifications were done, the contracted people who set up the machinery, air conditioning and other stuff were all rounded up and told to go home. The Contract was over. Only that they didn't make it back home. They were all killed, shot dead the very night they were discharged from their contracted work, during a farewell party for them. Their bodies were buried in a mass grave right somewhere on the island and not far away from the old castle. The principal wanted to make sure that new secrets of the castle's interior was never leaked out to any one on the outside, lest they suspected something and voiced it out, hence attracting unwanted attention.

Then contracted scientists were brought in and instructed on what to do exactly. Before they realized what was going on, they were surrounded by armed guards, a lot of them. They were given beds and prepackaged meals and told that they were not allowed to leave the compound, meaning they were not leave the premises at all until, perhaps, the project was over. No phones, no internet, absolutely no contact with the outside world. Anyone who tried to leave was to be shot on site. A few impatient, but clever minds had tried to escape, despite the death threat. But with the top-notch security apparatus surrounding the premises, plus numerous, prowling, armed guards, designed and led by a top notch, ex -military, security expert known only as the major, they were quickly spotted, rounded up, and summarily executed. From that time onwards no one else tried to escape again.

That was exactly six months ago. But a month or so ago, Major Haraabi, a.k.a the major, had to suddenly leave the castle, leaving his assistant in charge. Rumors circulated amongst his subordinates and others within his circles that he had a special, secret meeting conducted in another small town not too far away from the old castle, and that after this meeting he had then disappeared. No one knew where he was, except his assistant, whom he stayed in touch with via phone daily.

But for a little over a week now, the assistant had not heard from his boss at all. He contacted a high-ranking officer at the country's military headquarters, since most of the guards, except himself, were Turikai military. He wanted to know why Major Haraabi had suddenly broken off communication, knowing very well that he practically managed the facility. The officer had promised to look into it and get back to him as soon as possible.

Two days ago, that military headquarters official had called him back and told him that changes in management had just been made, effective immediately. He was told that major Haraabi was no longer in charge of the facility's security, and so he was not coming back, and that he, major Haraabi's assistant, was now the officer in charge. He was also asked to prepare the facility for a special visit from the overall owner of the facility who was to arrive in forty-eight hours. And now, he had just received a phone call that the owner had arrived in the country and was on the way to the facility. Everybody was already gathered in the big mess hall. The scientists were separated on one side of the hall, all dressed in their white coats, while the guards were lined up in rank and file.

The assistant's names were Jacques Kakra, a retired military officer from the respected Italian Carabinieri, and was specifically employed for the job of facility security assistant by Major Haraabi himself. They had known each other for years, both orphan children partly raised in the same orphanage. They had both decided to join the military at the same time, but while Kakra had joined and stayed on with the Carabinieri in Italy until he ranked captain, Haraabi had gone on to join the European community commando academy, and thereafter trained under various top military organizations. But then, and suddenly, Haraabi had resigned his top rank military job with the United Nations peace corps and started working as a private military advisor, consultant and contractor. They still stayed in touch and their close friendship flourished even after captain Jacques Kakra, who was about eight years older than Haraabi, retired from the Carabinieri. And so, when his friend, who he considered as his own brother, called him

332

out of retirement to come help him manage a high tech, militarily supervised medical facility in the Turikai republic, Jacques Kakra jumped to it and accepted the job, which was also high paying.

It was Jacques Kakra's military management training that had kept the operations of the secretive project in line, since Major Haraabi was in and out of the island country most of the time.

But nothing in his career, or even in his entire life, could have prepared him for this day. He had experienced strange times, been in strange places and seen a lot of strange things, by the time he retired from military service, and he was pretty much grounded. But today's events changed that. This was different. He was standing outside with at least thirty of his armed guards, all in green military uniform and black berets, with himself in an all-black, military police attire, when the owner's three - car convoy finally arrived. Now, he had expected to see a suited figure, perhaps with a tie, one of those corporate management stereotypes, or someone in plain civilian clothes since they were coming to an island, come out of one of those vehicles. Or even a shady military type, one of those crazy ones with dark sunglasses and a menacing face. Or perhaps a mad, bespectacled scientist in a long white coat, since the project he was guarding was basically a sensitive scientific operation.

But it turned out to be none of those. The owner turned out to be uniquely different and yes, scary!

When the main gates to the compounds were opened, the three- car convoy rolled in and came to a dead stop in front of the main entrance after crossing the lowered moat bridge. Armed guards from the two jeep wranglers quickly jumped out of the cars and poised themselves with guns ready, like they were ready to react to at an impending attack. Then the front passenger door of the green Range Rover opened, and a short, stocky, hefty looking black man got out and approached him. Captain Kakra did not flinch, turning around to face the significantly shorter, heavy-set man without changing his demeanor.

"You in charge here?" the black man asked, without so much as uttering any greetings and staring up at the six foot five, lean bodied former military officer with a grim face.

"Yes." Captain Kakra replied.

"Ok. I hope you are ready for us. Now listen up, man," the black man said, moving closer. "The big boss and two very beautiful female assistants are about to step out of the range rover. I am cautioning you now man, that whatever you do, try not to stare at the boss's face for a long time. Its best that you don't!"

With those words, the black man turned away from the captain and faced the range rover. He nodded his face briefly. Both rear doors of the range rover simultaneously opened and two very beautiful women, one black and one white, dressed basically in black, sleeveless T shirts with a picture of a human skull on the front, tight black cargo pants and black military boots, stepped out with ease. They too lined themselves to one side, keenly taking in their surrounding environment. When the principal stepped out of the car, captain Kakra looked at that masked face once and immediately looked away. Not only was it one of the ugliest, frighteningly menacing masks he had ever seen, but also the most hideous one that made him feel dizzy and or nauseated. The mask seemed to instantly have an intensively chilling, hypnotic, dizzying and high pulse - setting effect on him. As the Principal slowly approached him, captain Kakra issued a stout salute, staring straight ahead.

"You must be my new head of security," the principal said in a deep throated, growling voice. "What are your names, soldier?"

"Captain Jacques Kakra, at your service, sir!" he replied.

"I am only known as the principal to all my workers and enterprises. You seem to be very focused on, efficient at, and dedicated to, your job, Captain," the principal said. "I think I shall claim you for my own. You will be part of us from now on."

After saying that, the principal reached out with the right hand, and placed the palm on Captain Kakra's face, completely covering it up. Captain Kakra, taken by surprise, tried to step back, but it was too late. The gloved handheld on tightly to his face for about ten seconds and then was suddenly withdrawn. The captain breathed in heavily once, then exhaled slowly. A small tremor went through his body and then, still at ease, he slowly turned his head to face the masked Principal. He was no longer afraid or affected by the hideous mask. The principal's three assistants looked at each other quickly but said nothing.

"Thank you, boss. And I will always be of service to you anywhere, and at any time, boss," He reiterated.

"Good. Now lead us into the inside of the building. I want to meet the rest of my workers." The principal said. At the same time, the hood on top of the principal's grey medieval cloak raised itself up and draped itself over the principal's head, obscuring most of it the masked face except for the mouth.

"As you wish, boss," Captain Kakra responded. "Please follow me."

With the captain leading the way, the principal and the three assistants made their way into the building. There was a podium already erected in the mess hall. Before the Principal could get on the podium, Captain Kakra went on it and made a brief introduction.

"Alright listen up, folks. Today we finally get to meet the overall owner of this facility, the person who pays us to be here. Please give a standing ovation to our big boss, the principal," he said. Himself clapping, he stepped down from the podium, nodding to the principal to take over.

As the audience of more than one hundred people in the hall, majority of them armed guards, stood up and clapped, the principal got on to the podium and waved back with a gloved left hand at them. The principal finally got to speak when the clapping died down.

"I am here today to take over and personally oversee the administrative and functional duties of this facility, with immediate effect," The principal said. "There is going to be a rapid change in schedule. I want this project's work accelerated and completed much earlier than scheduled. I know that most of you want to go home, so the earlier we finish the better. Captain Kakra here will remain as my head of security. The rest of you should return to your regular workstations. Do so now!"

"Hey boss man, are you aware that we have been kept here against our own will for at the past six month?" someone in the audience stated loudly. "I don't know about anyone else here, but frankly speaking, I don't want to be here anymore. I am very exhausted, and I want to go home, now!"

"I wasn't aware that you were kept here against your own will," the principal responded back without change in voice, and briefly turning around to look at captain Kakra. "Please step forward now. I would like to clearly see the person who's talking to me."

A tall, elderly looking, bespectacled, averagely built man in a white overcoat made his way through the audience and to the front. He was one of the scientists.

"So, my friend, let me get this clear. You're telling me that you're being held here against your own will and that you're so tired you want to go home. Now. Is that right?" The principal asked, still standing on the podium, a uniquely sinister, shadowy figure.

"Yes sir. I am very tired, and I feel that I am done with this place and its work. I want to go home, to see my family and friends, to sleep in my bed with my dear wife, whom I miss so much," the man said, staring up at the podium. "And I am ready to walk out of here, right now, with or without your permission!"

"Hmmm, I see. No problem. I can help you with that," the principal acknowledged. And with those words, the principal's right arm slowly went up, until the hand was directly pointed at the scientist. The principal then clenched the right hand into a fist, slowly at first and then tighter.

The man at the front of the audience suddenly grabbed at his neck and started grimacing as his face suddenly started turning pale. He started gasping for air. The principal slowly raised the clenched right fist further upwards, and the man's body suddenly rose off the floor, feet dangling in space, as he continued to tightly grasp at his own neck with both of his hands. His eyes grew wider and wider, almost popping out of their sockets, and his tongue suddenly popped out of his mouth. It looked purple and very swollen. Finally, blood started oozing out of his eyes, nostrils, and both ears. The rest of the workers in the mess hall quickly stepped back and away from what appeared to be a self-dangling, self-strangling man, instantly terrified and not knowing what was going on or what to do with their grimacing, obviously choking, colleague.

The principal suddenly made two jerking movements with the clenched, fist, to the left and then to the right. In similar response, the man's neck and head jerked itself to the left and then to the right. Everyone heard the snapping sound from his neck bones. The principal then unclenched the right fist, snapping the right hand open, and the scientist's body dropped to the floor with a thud! Now laying on the floor with his neck in a grotesque position, everyone in the audience could tell that the man was already dead. A puddle of blood started forming under his head.

Everyone in the room, except for the principal and the three assistants, looked at the dead man on the floor in shock. They were so shocked they remained frozen in place. Captain Kakra faintly smiled, dutifully.

"Now does anyone else have something to say about being held against their will? Or, better still, is there someone else here who is in a hurry to leave my facility simply because they're exhausted and want to go sleep with their spouse?" The principal asked in a heightened, growling and menacing voice. "This man was in a hurry to go home, so I helped him get there, fast! Any other volunteers?" Nobody said anything, no one responded back.

"Didn't think so!" the principal said. "Now, you all get back to work, now! Lest I change mind and strangle all of you! Captain, take me to the production room. I want to see how much work has been done, and what is left to be done. I want to see who's in charge of the laboratory!"

The workers left quickly, disappearing through different doors on the sides of the mess hall. The castle, or facility, consisted of three levels of operational space. The first level, or sublevel, was predominantly underground, and that's where all the secret work was being done. It was a labyrinth of rooms and corridors that all led a central area that acted as a hub to other areas. But only one door connected this hub to another central room where all the technical work was happening. This room had its own elevator that led to the second level, which was considered the main or central level because that's where all outside business was conducted, mainly for supplies or medical visits. It also contained the main entrance to the building. All elevators started and ended here. The third level, or living level, was on top of the central level and contained all the living quarters for everyone in the building.

Everyone convened to this level after completing their workday. That was where all social interactions took place. It also held bridged corridors to guard posts on the outside. Only the guards were allowed into and through these corridors and on the three guard towers on the outside. The three guard towers were manned by armed guards on a twenty-four-hour routine. The second floor also had a twenty-four-hour armed guard system that patrolled both the inside and, on the grounds outside, with dogs.

"As you wish, boss. Follow me please." Captain Kakra replied. "You, and you, clean up this mess!"

He was directing two of his soldier guards to remove the dead scientist's body and clean up the area.

He then led the principal with the 3 assistants to an elevator. The entire group got into this elevator which quietly glided down to the sublevel floor. Once they arrived there, Captain Kakra quietly led the group through a well illuminated hallway, and that was after crossing a big, also well illuminated open center space that was similar to the mess hall on the floor level above them. Unlike the mess hall, this space had no chairs or tables. It was just a plain hub space where doors opened and closed to different hallways. The illuminated hallway led to the double – door laboratory entry, which was guarded by armed men on both sides. These guards immediately went at ease as the captain, the principal, and the principal's entourage approached. The doors automatically slid wide open because Captain Kakra, as head of security, had remote access in form of a tiny smart gadget he wore on his wrist like a watch. All he had to do was to raise his arm, point the round surface of the gadget at the doors. He was the only one who had it now, since Major Haraabi was no more. Everyone else had to punch in a personal, special code and or place right hand on a digital panel in order to go in or come out.

The laboratory, a combined, modern state of the art testing, creating, and manufacturing center, was the busiest area of this old castle turned scientific facility. Machines where humming everywhere, and busy workers, dressed in clean white coats, gloves and masks were everywhere. Test subjects, which now included humans, were locked up in clear glass cubicles, sedated or otherwise. Robotic arms were being used to reach into these testing areas and implement injections and clean ups. As the entourage walked through, a dead human test subject was being wheeled out through a side door to the cremation room. Captain Kakra led them to a small office where a tall, skinny man was bent over a sophisticated looking microscope, examining a specimen on a slide plate. He was the microbiologist in charge of the laboratory. He didn't look up when they entered his office, too focused on what he was doing. The principal turned to Captain Kakra.

"Leave us!" the principal told the captain.

Captain Kakra nodded, and stepped out of the office, closing the door behind him and leaving the principal and the three assistants inside. He remained standing nearby, in one corner. Inside the office, one of the women tapped the seemingly busy scientist on the arm. He literally jumped, like had been pierced by a sharp object. His eyes grew big when he saw the small group of people in his little office. But then he quickly regained composure of himself. The principal looked at the scientist's name tag. "Ning Pei Pei. MD", it read.

"Yes, what…," he started to say, and then stared at the masked principal, his face going grim. "What… can I do for you people?"

"Dr. Pei Pei, I am the owner of this place, the one who pays all you people's salaries," the principal said in a delayed, word by word pattern. "I am your boss!"

"I gather you're…, I mean, I already know that. I can feel it!" Dr Ning Pei Pei, a specialist in microbiology, responded back.

"Good. Now listen to me carefully, Dr. Pei Pei," the principal continued. "I want you to tell me something. Do we have the master strain ready?"

"Yes, and no, sir. We have the original ready, the one that major Haraabi has a sample of, together with the antidote for it," the microbiologist replied. "But I have redeveloped the strain, made it more deadly than the original. I am working on the antidote now."

"So, are you saying that you haven't duplicated it yet?" The principal asked, taking a step closer to the scientist, the growling back in his voice. "Please tell me that you already have something processed. Something in stock for me to see."

"Yes… yes, yes, yes," the scientist responded quickly. "We have already duplicated the original virus and have multiple phases ready to for distribution to wherever you want it to go. We have both the strain and serum antidote. It's the new, much deadlier strain that I need to duplicate now. I just completed working on it and now I need to duplicate it, plus the antidote. We are supposed to start work on that tonight."

"Then hurry up and do it!" the principal snapped at the microbiologist. "We have run out of time. I am giving you eight hours to do it, or I will kill you. I want copies of both the strain and antidote for the original and new developments delivered to me today, by or before midnight. No exceptions, no excuses. Do you understand?"

"Yes, yes sir," doctor replied quickly. "I will deliver the masters to you myself, this evening, sir. We are going to work extra hard to prepare and finish the duplicates on the new strain before midnight. All will be good and timely, sir."

"Good!" The principal acknowledged, turning away immediately from the scientist to get out the tiny, stinky office. The stocky black guy opened the door for his boss and the women, then he himself followed. Once out of the tiny office, they noticed that Captain Kakra was busy talking on his mobile phone and was frowning.

"What is it?" the principal asked immediately, automatically feeling Captain Kakra's troubled mind.

Captain Kakra hangs up the phone and then faced the principal. "I have just been told that an American – led commando team has landed in a neighboring country and is headed our way with specific orders to search and destroy, boss. But I won't let that happen!"

"Good. Let's go get ready to meet them. I want them captured and brought to me alive" the principal acknowledged. "We are going to teach the meddling Americans and their buddies a lesson they will indeed never forget!"

A specially chartered American transport plane landed at Italy's Reggio Calabria airport in about three hours on that same Tuesday morning after the principal and the three assistants had landed at Libya's Mitiga international airport. The plane was directed to a special private hanger in which the operation Life Support team, led by U.S navy seal commander Colonel Wilson Carkenbo, disembarked with

340

their gear. Once they were done with unloading, they made their way to the outside where they were met by an Italian military official, who was waiting for them with five non - military vehicles. The Italians had been told that the American led team was coming in, but only a few in the government knew what it was all about. As far as the Italian military official was concerned, the American led team was here for an expedition on the Mediterranean Sea. They were not even dressed in military uniforms. They just had a lot of baggage. He, however, had to make a phone call to one of his superiors to notify him that the group had arrived. After that, his only remaining duty was to simply transport the expedition group to a location somewhere on the Italian Mediterranean Sea coast, some miles away from the airport, and leave them there.

After he dropped them off and drove away, the world's greatest army started assembling their gear, which included the assembling of three small, four – piece, silent small engine military stealth canoes capable of carrying six people at a time. They quickly assembled the three special boats. The third boat, slightly bigger, had a heavier engine designed to help tag extra baggage in the water while controlled by one operator. It took the team roughly an hour to assemble everything and then get them into the water, their engines humming silently as Colonel Carkenbo led the way towards the seashores of the Turikai island republic. It was heavily misty and cold out there on the sea, but each team member was wearing special vision equipment that allowed them to see through thickened environments like this and special "at sea" thermal navy costumes that defied high wind sea surf and intense surface of the sea insect swarm attacks.

Approximately forty minutes later they arrived on the Island's shores and quickly pulled their stuff of the water, unloading their gear from the waterproof baggage that they had towed along. In just a matter of minutes, the team transformed itself into a group of shadowy warriors armed with portable assault weaponry which ranged from combat knives to short, silencer rigged, high tech submachine guns with marked night target finders, and miniature explosives. Everything was designed to outfit a modern, portable, mobile covert stealth force, including Gravity defying, all weather, all terrain shoes. Each team member's backpack had a special bottle filled with a special hydration liquid that lab scientists had created to accomplish a single sip, thirst quencher dose mixed with thirty milliliters of super energy fluid. The bottle had a thin, elastic rubber straw protruding from the backpack and that is attached like an antenna to the fluid filled bottle which is inside the backpack. All the users had to do was to pull on it and suck in one single sip, let go and the straw self-retracts back down. The liquid comes out but can't go back in. A hygiene safety measure.

"Tapsakesei village town due north approximately three and a half miles from here," colonel Carkenbo announced, looking at the small, Camera - like device in his hands. "GPS readings indicate no hilly terrain, only straight road bordered with vegetation. The island is famous for rare but also very poisonous species of crawlers and rodents, so watch your step. Let's go!"

They started walking, employing an emphasized, quick, semi jog pace. It took the team roughly another forty or so minutes to reach the village, which was primarily the residing area for the remaining, and dwindling, original population of the Island's indigenous people. The village town had an overwhelming stench in the air of dead marine life, even though the entire area seemed to be emitting smoke from burning wood. That, mixed with the heavy mist, created a hazy environment.

"Whatever these people are cooking here smells terrible," one of the team members acknowledged, covering his nose with his arm.

"I was actually reading about the Turikai island republic history while on the plane, and they actually mentioned the stench," another team member added on it. "The writer states that the indigenous folks living here deliberately create the stench as a way to keep the nonindigenous folks out, to discourage them from coming to this area. They want to be left alone and want none of this new culture that is being imposed on them and which is replacing their own. The writers stated that it actually works, and that central government workers rarely came down here except on special assignments like specialized research studies, military expeditions or national medical interventions!"

"Don't mind the stench. Focus on the mission ahead!" Colonel Carkenbo advised.

The heavy mist was still in place, but there were people walking around on the dusty road, occasionally stopping to look at the strangers who just suddenly appeared from nowhere and were walking on their Sand covered road, in their village street. Most of them, though, avoided the strangers by either looking in another direction or quickly walking away from them. The colonel noticed an old man seated by himself on a wooden stool outside a small brick house, smoking a pipe. The old man stared at them as they walked by, following them with his eyes. Unlike the other folks, he did not look away and neither did he move. Colonel Carkenbo suddenly stopped, reached into one of the pockets on his cargo pants, and pulled out a small gadget. It was a pocket voice translator. He turned it on and verbally issued instruction into it.

"English to Turikania. How are you, sir? Please show me the best and easiest direction to the old castle," he stated into the machine. The machine beeped, and the search blinker came on and rolled on the screen for a few seconds.

"Ready to translate. Touch button on right side of screen to proceed," The machine said when the search cycle stopped.

Colonel Carkenbo turned back around, walked back to the old man, smiled, and after cranking up the volume, he pressed the button on the right side of the machine's screen, holding it near the old man's ear. The old man did not budge an inch. The translator echoed back the translation, loud and clear.

But the old man did not smile back. His face grim, he raised his hand and pointed in the direction they were going with a finger. His hand remained stretched out, straight. Then he waved two of his righthand fingers in front of the colonel face, put his hand down, and looked away. Colonel Carkenbo slightly bowed his head at the old man, and then walked back to his group. One of the team members had his own pocket, digital Gps machine out in his hand, looking at it closely.

"Says here we about two miles away from a landmark building, south of here," the team member said.

"Yep! Just like the old man indicated with his fingers," the colonel acknowledged. "Straight on, two miles. Let's get moving again."

The road was exactly straight, as indicated by the old man, a narrow path that developed into a sharp slope. On top of the slope, the team was able to look down the incline, and to finally lay their eyes on the

343

splendid, majestic white castle which was where the road ended. The castle was seated at the bottom of a valley, surrounded by a low level, hilly topography, and one could see numerous roads all ending outside this structure. This made it easier to understand certain facts about the castle, such as the fact that why the old, beautiful and majestic building used to be the main seat of government for the ancient rulers of the island and its surrounding regions a few centuries ago. This was the center for everything, for everyone, until the invaders came in, conquered and took over the Island, subsequently pushing the indigenous people out of the way. The imperialistic invaders then created and built their own city, and then relocated the seat of government.

"The old castle, a type of square stone keep, was built in the seventeen hundreds. But it quickly became a relic establishment after the new groups took over, and now is the only monument left of historical significance to the indigenous Turikai people," Colonel Carkenbo told his team. "The Turikai do not believe in, or even subscribe to their new rulers. They still believe that inside that castle are their true rulers, in spiritual form, and until not too long ago when the new rulers suddenly took over the castle, closed it off, and denied public access, the Turikai indigenous continued to visit it with gifts and food. Some of oldest Turikai lived in it, some living for as long as one hundred and twenty years of age, counseling and advising their people. The last Turikai elder who lived there died several years ago at the age of one hundred and twenty years, and was succeeded by his only son, who was seventy something years old already."

"So where is this oldest son now? living inside the castle? I don't want to kill him," a team member asked jokingly.

"Nope. The new rulers offered him a parliament seat on the ruling council to represent his people, while he still remained recognized as the paramount leader of the Turikai, referred to as his royal highness the king," The Colonel elaborated. "He's also the vice president of the nation, but both titles are primarily ceremonial and of no real significance to the new rulers. According to recent history I was given during the briefing, he had no choice but to join the new group, which is quite powerful, otherwise they were going to kill him and abolish the old establishment and its traditions all together. Although it sounds like betrayal, I can't blame him for it. You can't beat them, perhaps join them. But he still kept his offices in the old castle, still meeting with his people, even if they were not too happy that he joined the new rulers. When he suddenly died, and nobody knew what killed him except that it was a brief illness, his youngest son took over, both as king and vice president. The son is now in his late fifties. Then about two years ago, the new rulers decided to take over the castle, and offered the new young king a brand new, modern brick mansion with all kinds of amenities in it, in exchange, and lots of money. Against the wishes of his people, the young Turikai king conceded, moved into his new house in the modern city, not far away from the new modern white castle, the residential seat of the current President of the Turikai Island republic. He abandoned his people, leaving them in poverty while himself and his family live a luxury life."

"Such an old castle. What do you think the government is doing with it?" another team member asked. "It doesn't look idle at all. I can see from here some blue smoke coming from it."

"That's what we are here to find out," the Colonel said with a sigh. "According to intelligence reports, this is where the purported danger to the world is being set up. As you all know, we're here to infiltrate the old castle, locate the danger if it's there, and destroy it all together. All right everybody. Check your gear, make sure it's all ready for the show. You all know what part you're playing. But remember, we stick together. We are a team." They all acknowledged simultaneously.

Even as the world's greatest army team advanced on the old Castle in the small, isolated town of Tapsai Kesei, the heavy mist experienced by Colonel Carkenbo and his team while on the Mediterranean Sea continued to encroach on the mainland, slowly making its way inland like some thick vaporous silver blanket. Even the natives had never experienced this kind of heavy mist on their island, and on this part of the Mediterranean Sea, visibility almost reached zero. The islands of Malta and Cyprus became invisible in the mist while motorists in coastal cities like Tunis, Tripoli, Rome, Athens, Alexandria, Jerusalem, Beirut and even Damascus had to turn on their vehicle headlights in order to navigate their way through the mist in their cities. It was gravely darkish in these cities. All boats and ships in the area were

345

ordered to dock as soon as possible and not to go back to sea until further notice. Flights were halted as all airports were shut down due to visibility issues.

But the heavy mist engulfing the island republic and the vast part of the Mediterranean Sea surrounding it wasn't the only bizarre change going on in this area of the Mediterranean Sea shared by several countries. Thick, dark grey, and black clouds developed from nowhere and slowly engulfed the region. The vast cloud coverage was seen over most of Tunisia, Northern Libya and Egypt, southern Italy, most of Greece, most of western turkey, most of Lebanon and Israel, and over Jordan. Other parts of Europe were affected, too, by this dark cloud coverage, even though not as bad as the Mediterranean region close to the Turikai island. The vast clouds even encroached on some areas of west Africa. It was like a vast storm was brewing above the region but with heavy mist engulfing the areas below first. And as the vast clouds became darker, flashes of rampant lightening with no thunder became evident all over the covered area. The airport administrators in the lightly affected areas began issuing warnings to air crafts that were still airborne to either land immediately to avoid being caught up in an impending storm or avoid flying into the region all together until the storm is over.

Then as if these elements were not enough to create a commotion, turbulent surface winds of over thirty miles per hour developed over the area, causing unstable sea waves, some high, to roughly swap the coastal areas, even rocking some of the docked big ships. Smaller boats were dangerously being shaken up and or tossed around as the surface waves rocked the areas.

An air traffic controller at Mitiga international airport put down his headset and beckoned at his supervisor to come over. "I see something that's not like aircraft moving very fast on the radar, coming towards us, and I can't identify it. There is big airplane engine sound, but I see no plane, sir."

The supervisor came over, looked at it, and frowned. "It's probably a stranded plane, man. What else could be out there coming towards us, huh? A meteor, perhaps?" the supervisor said, staring at the screen. It was a small blip on the controller's blue screen. "Hmmm, I see it now. Transfer the image and sound to central vision. Let's take a closer look."

Central vision, a giant digital screen that highlighted the entire area's aircraft activity, was used by joint chief air traffic controllers to analyze and identify closely developing issues in space above the region's airports. Unlike the basic flight controllers' screens, this big, satellite-controlled, imaging screen covered the entire Mediterranean region and could magnify aircraft in space so they can be identified and even studied. Every airport in the Mediterranean region now had one, and all of them were interconnected to each other.

But this particular image was not easy to identify, because it was flashing on and off on the radar as it moved south over the area, much like a shiny blinking light, not an object. It disappeared and then reappeared at least every ten seconds on the giant screen. The chief air traffic controller picked up a communication set which consisted of a headset and microphone and echoed off a warning.

"Unidentified aircraft, please slow down and identify yourself," he said through the mike, hoping to get a response back. "I repeat, slow down and identify yourself. We cannot allow you to land on our airport unless you identify yourself."

But all he could hear back was intervals of crackling sounds. "Switch sound to central coms, please," he instructed another member of his staff. Central coms, used to super boost transferred sounds from an air traffic controller unit to overhead speakers, makes the sound from outa space much clearer. It was usually used in conjunction with central vision.

Sound was transferred to central coms. It was a relatively distant, but noticeably booming, roaring sound, just like that made by a big jet plane preparing to land, and it was getting louder.

One of the wall phones rang. It was a yellow connecter telephone used by chief air traffic controllers at different airports to communicate to one another, especially if there is a confusing problem or issue in a joint air space like this one over the Mediterranean Sea. The chief air traffic controller quickly scooped up the receiver.

347

"Salim, this is Giuseppe at Reggio Calabria," the caller said. "Do you see what I see and are you hearing what I am hearing?"

"Yeah, I am looking at it right now," Salim answered. "It's not very clear and at the moment it doesn't look like an aircraft to me, but it's moving fast. Wait a minute, it's now slowing down."

"But if it's not an aircraft, then what is it, Salim?" the caller, the chief air traffic controller at Reggio Calabria airport asked, sounding quite frustrated.

"We don't know what it is either, Giussi," Salim replied to his colleague. "It sounds like a plane, though. A big plane. I have already asked that they identify themselves, but I got nothing back. No response except static noise. Well, it has slowed down, and it is entering your space now."

As Salim said that the thing, still completely camouflaged by the thick dark clouds, entered chief air traffic Controller Giuseppe's airport space. Giuseppe and his staff stared at the shiny thing as it floated by, slicing through and in between the thick black clouds above them, a shape shifting, glassy mirage with jagged yellow edges and flashing strips of bright red fire sparks coming off its body, perhaps an over visualized, complex and unstable, self - reacting fata morgana in the sky. And with it came this dynamic, mesmerizing, incredibly heavy, roaring or booming sound, just like a big jet plane slowly floating through space or preparing to land. The booming sound was so incredible that the entire building shook, the furniture rattled, doors self-slammed, and all alarms in the area were triggered off. All the airport pole lights, and ground runaway plane guide lights went out as their bulbs and shells shattered. It felt like an earthquake was going through the area. Then it went past them, and all became quiet except for the alarms still going off. After it was gone, all electricity power suddenly went off, instantly plunging the entire airport into near darkness. But within a few minutes, power generators kicked in and power was temporarily restored.

"Salim, it's coming your way now!" Giuseppe said, sounding frightened. "And Salim, I don't like this… thing! Whatever it is, it is very powerful, and it is quite terrifying. I think we should notify our national air military defense immediately!"

348

"Alright, let's see what this really is. I still think it's probably some big plane lost in the wilderness of thick black clouds and…" chief Salim started to say, but then it arrived. Chief Salim turned back to the central vision computer keyboard and rapidly typed a command that enabled Central vision to act like a three hundred and sixty-degrees periscope sweep, modifying its vision status to a three-dimensional model. As the booming "thing" rumbled past and heavily shook the building, Chief Salim looked closely at the big screen. There was nothing on the screen at all now. He quickly typed in another code, reversing the model back to normal. Now even the blipping thing, the shiny flashing light was gone! The thing had totally become invisible on the digital screen! This meant that it was obviously non - detectable by the defense radar system!

Then came the incredible, booming sound, so big it rattled the desks and chairs even as staff members clang to them. The glass in the windows instantly cracked and then completely shattered. Then all radar computer screens, including the giant central com screen, went blank and then cracked. Smoke started coming out of them. All Stuff on the wall fell down. Empty chairs tumbled down to the floor. Open doors slammed themselves shut so hard that glass doors were completely shattered to pieces while wooden ones developed cracks. Faucets in the rest rooms and breakroom areas turned themselves on, with sinks and commodes cracking and splitting, and water sprayed everywhere as pressurized pipes shattered and or burst. Part of the ceiling caved in. The big, incredibly supersonic, thunderous boom followed by constant bright streaks of lightning, was so overwhelmingly deafening that Salim and his staff were forced to cover their ears with their hand and fall down on the floor.

And then, suddenly, the sound ceased, and the thing was completely gone. And for several minutes, everyone in the building remained quiet and very still, inevitably and completely stunned!

"Chief… I think… one of my ears drums has been blown!" one of the traffic controllers said, suddenly breaking the icy silence. "I think I can only faintly hear from one ear only."

"I am… bleeding from both ears, chief," another person stated. "And I can hardly hear!"

Chief Salim, who had lost his balance when the boom hit home, slowly got up and walked over to his desk. He punched down hard on a red button with his right-hand palm. The red button was supposed to activate a red alert in form of a sweeping loud siren over the entire perimeter and beyond. It would also activate a military alert used for warning about invasion at vital entities like airports and others.

But nothing happened. The alarm had, too, ceased working, totally disabled by the fly by, unknown thing with its heavy, thunderous boom. Chief Salim now picked up a red phone, also on his desk, a direct line to the minister of defense. But it did not have a dial tone. Not working either.

"The alarm is not working, and all phones are down!" he announced, ignoring his staff's change in condition. "Laenat Allah ealaa dhak! We under siege and we can't even communicate!"

He walked away from the desk but stopped when he noticed that all his staff members were down on the floor and holding their heads in their hands, and most of them were dripping blood from either their ears, nose, or mouth. He shook his head slowly, feeling dizzy and giddy. He then slowly made his way to the door that connected to the outside, holding on to the walls. Although it was cracked and loose on its hinges, he managed to open it. A man dressed in police uniform was trying to make his way up the steps and coming towards him. It was Ali Hassan, the airport's chief of police.

"Oh my god, we saw it, Salim! We saw it and we ran and hid in the building's basement!" Ali Hassan rather shouted out at him.

"You... saw it? What... what was it? Where did it go?" Salim asked, supporting himself by holding on to the guard rail beyond the entrance to his offi ces.

"Salim, it's shiny, with no clear shape, and with bright sparks of yellow and red fire falling off its body!" Ali Hassan answered quickly, and then added. "It just disappeared into the heavy mist on and above the sea!"

At this point, though, chief Salim couldn't hold on to himself any longer. The heavy dizziness and or nausea finally overwhelmed his system, and the tall, heavy-set man with a potbelly stumbled forward and fainted, his body flopping over the steps with terrific, repeated thuds.

As soon as Colonel Wilson Carkenbo and his team left the area, the residents of Tapsai Kesei village, men, women, and children, all together quickly came out of their shanties and gathered around the old man with the smoking pipe. The old man was the village's most senior elder. Nobody knew his real age, but it was rumored that he was way past one hundred years old. They scrambled to him, wanting to know what one of the men from the group of strangers wearing strange looking clothes, carrying strange looking bags on their backs and strange looking hand tools, had told him. The man, a gentle and patient authoritarian, attempted to calm them down by waving his arms up and down, but no one seemed to be paying attention to him at the moment. So, he simply kept quiet until the last talker was done. Then he spoke.

"They came out of the sea, and I believe they are here to destroy the old temple," he said slowly, using the term temple to refer to the old castle, as it was generally referred to by everyone in the village. "They are also going to kill everyone in it."

"That's our temple. We need to stop them from doing that!" one of his grandsons, a fierce looking, forty something years old man said, and everyone altogether applauded.

"They can't just walk into our village and do whatever they want to do without asking permission from us, right?" another person shouted out. "Besides, the temple will lose its sanctity if people are killed inside it!"

"This is the time to fight for, and get back, our temple!" yet another man shouted out. "Maybe we should call them back and ask them if they need help from us. We can fight alongside with them. That way if they try to destroy the temple, we will be there and instead, we kill them!"

"Let me bring out our weapons. You and you, come with me," the old man's oldest son said, pointing at two teenage boys standing in front of him. "I want all men in this village to assemble here. We will be leaving shortly!"

"Silence!" the old man suddenly snapped, raising his voice.

Everyone stopped talking immediately, surprised, or perhaps shocked, by the old man's sudden uproar. In this village, no one had ever seen the old man raise his voice that way. He was always quiet and gentle with everyone, young and old.

"Forgive me, most venerable father," the oldest son said, turning around to face the old man, and making a slight bow before him. Now everyone did the same thing. "What would you like us to do, father?"

The old man cleared his throat and said in a deep, hoarse voice. "Look around you. Do you see this mysterious, thick mist? I can hardly see. In all my years of life, I have never, ever seen this kind of mist on our land. I have seen mist, but not this kind. Look, it has almost turned midday into night. Now, look at the sky. Do you see the thick, gray and black clouds? If you were paying attention like I was, you would have noticed that these clouds just rapidly appeared from nowhere. And then there is the distant lightning and thunder that has been going on for some time now, yet no rain or storm has shown up."

Everyone looked around them, like they had just noticed the thick mist. Others looked up at the sky. The usual blue sky was now completely obscured by the thick, gray and black, clouds with bright, repeating streaks of lightning in all over.

The old man raised his right hand and with a finger pointed at the darkened, lightning - filled sky.

"My dear people, there is no need to fight anymore!" he said, his voice, though still deep and hoarse, suddenly becoming shaky. "The answer to our problems is not with these strangers. The answer is coming from up there and is about to happen. I strongly believe that's exactly why we are having this mysterious mist and dark clouds."

As he said this, they heard the sound of distant thunder, which had now become exceptionally loud and heavy enough for the gathered villagers to feel the rumbling in the ground they were standing on.

"Most Venerable father, what do you want us to do now? Go back into our houses and wait for the answer?" a woman, with a child on her back asked. "It's suddenly gotten cold out here too."

"Don't you all hear and feel it?" the old man asked, his eyes opening wide. "Because I can now hear and feel the greatness and power of what's in the sky. I even feel it beneath my feet. No, my daughter. I want all of you to stay where you are, get down to your knees and raise your heads and arms up towards the skies. Do so now, to welcome the messengers from heaven, for they are coming to protect and liberate us from the evil on our lands."

His oldest son, an older man himself in his early seventies and who was still able to do a lot of things for himself, began thinking that his old man was losing his mind. The cold, fast breeze was becoming too much for some people and they needed to retreat to their homes and sit by a fire with their children, regardless of what was happening or going to happen. Even then, and as far as he was concerned, his people had been waiting for over centuries to see supernatural changes, had called on to their gods for help, and nothing has ever happened. Instead, for him and others of his generation, they had helplessly sat back and watched as their lands were ravaged and or taken over by cruel, fierce, strangers, and their tribes dwindle into extinction. And that was because, he always reiterated to his friends, they spent too much time listening to old, senile old men like his father, who kept worshiping invisible, non – active gods and spirits, instead of themselves taking action. He was in favor of his own son's ideas of action, and that is why, at this moment, he wanted all this "elder" craziness to stop. After all, he was going to be the next leader of this village after his old man passes away.

So, he stepped boldly forward, bowed briefly, and then faced the old man. "Venerable father, with all due respect, I think the people should return to their houses. What you are telling us to do does not make sense at this very time…" he started to say, but he was cut short.

"Just do as I say and do it now!" the old man interjected, raising his voice and staring at his son angrily. "Now is the time, boy! NOW IS THE TIIIIIME!"

The tone his father used was again enough to convince him to obey the older man's commands. "Just this one more time, old man, just this one time!" He said in his mind. There won't be another time like this again! Enough of this foolishness! Next time around, he would urge the people to ignore the elder's orders. The older son now immediately turned to the gathered villagers, whose numbers had grown, and uttered a loud command for everyone to get to down to their knees, raise their hands and faces to the sky.

The entire village community seemed to be present, and they all responded to the village leaders' call. Man, woman, children, all went down to their knees, raised their arms and faces to the sky. Only the old man stood up and remained on his feet, the smoking pipe now extinguished and laying on the floor. His own sweaty face was now, too, fixated to the darkened sky above. And for the next five minutes, nothing happened. Five full minutes of quite speculation and raised arms to the sky! Some people, especially the little children, put their already tired little arms down.

And then it started happening, an unprecedented spectacle that would forever change, and remain, in the lives of this indigenous, locally marginalized village community. A spot in the darkened sky above suddenly opened, the dark, thick clouds parting to reveal an oval, very bright spot in between them. The spot was so bright that the observers felt an overwhelming strain to their eyes as they continued to look up. The same spot in the cloud also flashed with a lot of lightning, complimented by heavy, grinding, thunder. Something protruded out of the overbright spot, and fully aligned itself vertically. Numerous glowing Sparks of bright fire were falling off this thing and flying in all directions. At first it was small, but then started growing bigger in size as it started to slowly descend towards them. As they soon came to see, it was in form of a human being, sustained in the air by massive, flapping golden yellow wings that blazed with fire. The glowing sparks of fire were falling off these wings, and as the winged figure descended, hands crossed on chest, streaks of staccato lightning came down with it.

But as the winged being got closer to the ground, it slowed down more, and the fire and its sparks faded out of the wings. At approximately seventeen feet away from the ground, the winged figure unfolded its arms, and then, with one leg fully stretched downwards and the other leg crouched up, the figure suddenly stopped moving, remaining suspended in the air. An extremely strong, rotating wind engulfed the ground below like a mini tornado, causing all types of stuff to be sucked off the ground below like in a strong vacuum machine, and spiraling this stuff into the air around, and then the sucked-up stuff instantly got burned into total nothing as it was rotated around the figure. This suspension in air stance lasted for about two full minutes, and then the descent continued.

The Archangel's feet finally touched the ground, with the stretched-out leg foot first, and then the other leg unfolded to simultaneously allow for both feet to touch the ground together. Small splashes of fire blew out of both feet like a welding blow torch, scotching the ground around and below both feet, and then faded out. The Staccato lightning completely faded out too. The big wings flapped heavily at least three more times and then gracefully folded themselves behind the angel. Up in the sky, the thick clouds moved back into place, completely concealing or closing off the overbright spot. The thunderous activity continued, making the ground rumble, but when the Archangel's left hand rose up, with ease, the rumbling thunder in the sky stopped. The hand then slowly went back down again.

But at this moment the community gathering, which at first was transfixed by the mesmerizing debut of the Archangel, now lost control of themselves, suddenly scared of the phenomenal revelation, and pandemonium took over. Everybody for themselves, with the old man's oldest son at the front, they ran away in all directions except towards the archangel. So eager were they to save themselves, some mothers left their children behind. Some of the children cried as they were pushed over by the adults, but most of them remained quiet, staring blankly at the imposing figure before them that was in a full, gold plaited body armor suit. Above the figure's head was a big gleaming golden ring that kept glowing on and off and emitted a bright yellow light. A golden halo. A few fearful mothers remained in place with their children, clinging to them tightly, too terrified to move. The other person who remained still was the old man, who slowly lowered his gaze from the sky to the ground when the Archangel was finally fully descended.

But the gold body armor suddenly opened up, and self-absorbed or retrieved itself into the body inside, exposing the mighty archangel to the earthlings. The halo extinguished itself by slowly fading out. And

355

there before the few who remained, stood the most stunning, elegant and perfectly poised, bald headed, light skinned, human female with a lean body and unbelievable muscular attributes. In the modern world, she could be described as light skinned, a pure mulatto. Her eyes were completely emerald, green but had no pupils in them. When she slightly opened her mouth, like in a snarl, all golden teeth were revealed, but there was no tongue in place.

She was now clad only in a black, high waist, long, flared vintage leather skirt, the bottom edge just falling short of the ankles, held in place by a tightly knotted golden sash, and a matching leather bra that covered her perfectly shaped full breasts but appeared to have no straps holding it in place. Her flat, thick metal soled, iron- edged, iron strapped, over the knees, laced up thigh high, low heeled boot shoes covered up her legs all the way up to where a girded tunic stopped, her brown thighs minimally revealed through a slit on both sides of the garment. Her right forearm was covered by seven thick, shiny golden bracelets, while the left bore seven shiny metallic silver ones. These ornaments didn't appear to shift in position at all even when she lowered or raised her arms. Though not long, her perfectly shaped fingernails looked like red metallic buds. Tattoos of strange looking objects were all over the rest of her uncovered body. She held a gleaming golden thing that looked like a big, four – way or cross car tire lug wrench in her left hand.

The Archangel looked down at the women who stayed behind, and who were still on their knees, with their children sitting on the ground. She then looked up at the old man with his lowered face.

"Old man, the almighty father in heaven gave you a lot of years of life so that you can continue the role of preservation, spiritual guidance, and leadership of your people, just like those elders before you," the Archangel stated in a clear and gentle voice. "But you are not supposed to make them kneel down on the ground like this!"

"Please forgive me, Holy one, forgive me," the old man replied timidly. "It is our way of showing great respect, in this case respect of your coming to or appearance before, us. Look at us, filthy and ragged. I don't think we are even worthy of your presence among us, holy one, or being on the ground you're standing on."

"We only kneel down before the almighty father in heaven, and no one else. So not even before us his angels, should it be done," the Archangel said. "I shall overlook the punishment for you for this deed today, old man, but must it be noted again, expect no clemency."

The old man did not respond back this time, for fear of offending the Archangel with any more of his words. He simply remained quiet and still.

But the Archangel had already turned her attention back to the women and children. Looking down at them, the archangel smiled broadly, her face lighting up, once again revealing the perfectly lined golden teeth. Her eyes opened wider and a sparkling, yellow pupil appeared in each eye like two bright, shiny, dazzling sapphires. One of the babies mumbled something, in a funny way, and then to everyone's surprise, all the toddlers pulled away from the adults and started making their way towards the Archangel. Some crawled, some hobbled, and others dashed their way toward this unknown entity, and without hesitation. The adults, on the other hand couldn't, for some unknown reason, refrain their children from going towards what they themselves were afraid of.

"Arise, all of you. No more kneeling," the Archangel said, waving the four – way ornament at the women. As the women slowly stood up, still looking fearful of what they had never seen before, she went down to one knee, stretched out her hand to one of the children. It was this boy child, making his way ahead of everybody else, towards her. This one simply stood out. The angel put her ornament down on the ground and picked up the child. The two smiled at each other.

"Oh, how right he was. The kingdom of heaven indeed belongs to the children. Hear me out, old man. The next leader of your people has been chosen. Behold, this child will lead your people into the next generation after you," The Archangel said, which made the old man quickly look up.

"What about my oldest son?" the old man asked, a bewildered look on his face. "For centuries the Turikai people have held the tradition that a senior tribal elder shall only be succeeded by his or her oldest child in all duties, upon his or her passing. In addition to that, my

oldest son has been schooled for this leadership role since he was a child."

"Well, I tell you now, your traditional law has now been rewritten and overruled by the heavens, old man," the Archangel said, putting the child down. "Your line will end with you. This child's destiny has been now altered and he will be your people's next overall leader. He won't need any schooling for that. We have already set him up. He will rise to lead your people back to independence and freedom. He will rise to liberate your nation back from the people who stole it and from those who sold it out. And so, from today until his rise to mature age and prominence, this child is henceforth under our protection."

Seeing the archangel looking more human and talking to those that were left behind, the rest of the run–away community started to slowly come back. But the old man suddenly stood up, and facing the Archangel directly he slowly said, sounding very tired. "Praise be to the will of God, and since I am no longer needed, I think I can now go back to my house and rest peacefully for the rest of my life. My work is done here. I have lived with, and for, this moment of your coming to us in my dreams for a long time. It wasn't easy, I can tell you that, because it always came to me as a terrifying vision. And just as I did, this world's evil ones also knew of your coming and have been patiently waiting. They are ready to rise against you. I kept seeing, in my dreams, your fight against a terrifying serpent with multiple heads, which are always hissing loudly and trying to bite me. Believe me again, this was very frightening. That's why I kept it a secret from all my people for all these years, because whoever I would have told would then, too, start suffering from the same burden of bearing the curse of those terrifying dreams like I do. But now that you're finally here, it is all over. So go on, holy one. Go now and start your war of cleaning up this world's filth, and I hope you came well prepared."

The Archangel smiled at the old man. "Yes, you can go rest peacefully now, and yes, I came well prepared, old man, for I come bearing a mandate from heaven, decreed by God. And I am starting here, today. Goodbye, old man."

Nodding his head slowly, the old man picked up his pipe from the ground near his feet, bowed down before the archangel, and then slowly star-ed walking away. The people in the now reassembled community gathering made way for him, wondering what had happened to make him finally move. The old man had stayed sitting on his stool, outside on the street by the roadside for the last six months, only getting up to go use relieve himself. He ate and slept in the same spot, smoking his pipe, most of the time his eyes fixated to the sky.

As he walked past his oldest son, he said in a quite audible, clear voice. "You're no longer my successor. That boy, over there, is now the chosen one."

The old man pointed a finger at the toddler, who was now standing up and in front of the Archangel. The toddler, his mother, and the rest of the infants had their eyes fixed on the archangel.

"And how is that so, most venerable father?" the oldest son asked, frowning as he looked in the direction of his father's finger. "It is the law of this land that an elder will be succeeded by his oldest child after he passes and joins our forefathers. That is a traditional law that cannot to be altered by anyone, and with all due respect, not even you!"

"Certainly, and of course, it's not been altered by me. But by her, over there!" The old man said with a faint smile, raising his long, withered face in the direction of the Archangel, who was turning around to leave after hugging each and every child that had come to her. He was the least troubled about the changes anyway, because over the years he had developed dislike, distrust, and eventually total discontent for this son because of his insolent mannerisms towards the people and his unreasonable, mostly mindless, and generally ruthless ways of dealing with issues. His son's uneasiness around his own people was already bringing about social unrest within the community. The old man's hierarchy of respected elders, who had held the people together, was now being questioned because of his son's behavior, and talk about change to a different family line of elders was becoming loud. And with those words, the old man resumed his walking, entered his little house, and closed the door behind him.

Now angered by his father's words, oldest son turned around and loudly beckoned at the Archangel. "Excuse me, you over there, maybe you won't mind reminding us again, who are you and what brings you to our village?"

The Archangel slightly turned around and her open, gentle eyes locked with the oldest son's bloodshot, cynical eyes. A brief smile crossed her face.

"I am Cephia. I bear good news for your community, that from now on, rest assured that all is not lost. All that was taken away from your community will be returned. It's all part of the mandate given to me by the almighty God, the holy spirit, who is seated in heaven," The Archangel replied. "And as for you, an original, older son of the Turikai people, you should right away stop your habit of over - intoxicating yourself with alcohol because you are just a few extra glasses away from instantly dying from it. In fact, it's too late now. Stopping now will only buy you a little extra time, just a few months, of your life. I suggest that you use that time to reconcile with your family and those members of the community that you have offended, and to put your life affairs in order. It's most unfortunate that you won't be able to enjoy the blessing of a wonderful long life like your ancestors before you."

Everyone now turned around to look at the old man's oldest son. Looking scraggy and unshaven, he was well known for his long time, die-hard relationship with alcohol. The oldest son stared back at them briefly, and then his eyes slowly turned to the ground, like a person who has been publicly shamed and then shunned. He then turned around and walked away from the gathering, disappearing into a sloppy wooded area. It was the last time the village community saw him, for he completely vanished, and his body was never found.

The Archangel now slowly stretched her arms out, and suddenly, her big, white wings reappeared. With one big flap of the wings, she rose off the ground, flapped again to steady herself as she hung in the air, smiled at the village people one more time, and then flapped herself further up and away into the air, rising higher and higher until she faded into the thick mist.

"Did you see that?" One member of the "operation life support" team, Jiang Hong, said looking up and pointing at the sky. It was at the time when the archangel was descending from the sky.

"Yeah, a bright spot in the sky, with lightning flashing from it," another team member acknowledged. "I think the dark clouds just momentarily parted a little bit to reveal some bright sun rays from a concealed sun. Nothing unusual, right guys?"

"I swear I saw something come out of that bright spot and fall downwards, very bright like a comet, or something like that," Jiang Hong added. "The only difference between this occurrence and a comet is that this was a straight-line, vertical descent. And I have never heard of, or seen, a comet doing that. I don't know if it's only me feeling that way, but I think strange stuff is going on around here, on this island. It kind of feels eerie!"

"Probably just an effigy of your imagination," yet another team member said, taking a sip from his special water reservoir straw. "What could possibly come out of the sky like that, all clear to the human eye, yet we didn't hear it crush or something? On the other hand, if you say it's awfully humid out here, that I can agree to."

"I concur with you, Jiang," another member said. "I saw it too when I happened to look up because of the weird bright lightning and heavy thunder that had suddenly showed up in the sky. And if you also noticed, whatever it was descended straight down in a non − stop, vertical stream for several minutes."

"I was about to say it's kind of strange to see lightning and thunder in a state of heavy mist or fog like this," another member said. "I see very dark, thick clouds up there, looks like rain clouds to me, but yet not a single drop of rain has shown up. And the wind, it's suddenly went very still, compared to how fast it was going when we first landed. No wonder it become so humid."

"Hmmm, maybe I shouldn't be the one saying this, but I have the same gut feeling like Jiang telling me that something is not right around here," Colonel Carkenbo said after they had walked on further for a little while. The team was now less than a mile away from the old, whitewashed castle, now visible through their special night vision mist penetrator eye gear that could also be adjusted into binocular mode. They were about to get off a sloppy terrain and get on to a flat sandy road that led directly to the big gates at the front of the castle, which was its only entry and exit point. "Take a closer look at the old castle. I see nobody in sight, yet satellite imagery transmitted less than twelve hours ago showed armed guards with dogs manning the gates and the castle's look - out towers. Intelligence reports also clarified that this is supposed to be one hell of a heavily guarded place. Yet we are now not seeing any guard activity going on."

Everyone turned their attention to the structure and zoomed in on it closely using the binocular mode of their special eye gear.

"Maybe they are all inside doing something," one team member said.

"Probably staying away from the intense humidity, and the fact that the entire environment is shady because of the heavy mist or fog," another team member said.

"Which is to our advantage. We can sneak in on them without too much disturbance," Yet another team member added. "We should be able to climb up those brick walls and silently land inside, cut some opposing throats on the other side of the wall, if any, including their dogs and then make our way into the inside of the structure."

"I don't take things for granted, soldiers," Colonel Carkenbo said, sounding a little grouchy. "What if the people in there have been tipped off by someone about our coming, huh? We're not the only ones who know about this operation. There are other people, in our respective governments, who know about it too. A lot of other people are involved in the discussions about its planning and implementation. We could be walking into a trap of some kind. It feels so quiet to be ok. Here is the logic. Guards don't back off because of mist or humidity issues. They do what they're supposed to do regardless of the conditions. Their absence here makes it feel very strange to me."

"That Italian officer who drove us to the coastal front, he got on the phone the moment we showed up at the airport," a team member acknowledged to the colonel's thinking. "It was like he was notifying someone about our arrival. He did it so immediately, like there was someone, somewhere, who was eagerly waiting to know."

"I didn't like him at all," another team member added. "His entire attitude sacked!"

"I think we are going to implement plan B before we go in," the Colonel said quickly. "We shall throw in those smokeless sleep gas bombs first. Everyone, switch on your earpieces now, because from now on it's imperative that we stay fully connected. I need feedback immediately if anything comes up that you don't understand. Then I want each one of you to run around the perimeter of the castle wall, which has a clear path around, circumference approximately one mile, and throw a sleep gas bomb canister over the wall every four hundred meters you run. Before you throw it in, attach one timed firebomb device on the wall, then throw another one over the wall and into the inside perimeter, just like you did with sleep gas bomb. The fire ones are all already set to explode in forty minutes after timer is started. You each have three differently colored smart bomb or grenade canisters. Blue, red, and black. The blue one is the sleep gas, which will release its sleep gas content in fifteen minutes after it's time is set. Attach the black one to the outside wall and throw the red one over the castle wall fence. They will automatically explode fifteen minutes apart. All you must do is to press the small, tiny button on it by firmly pressing down on it for five seconds. It will blink red once, indicates its set. Check all your other portable weaponry, make sure it's all set right before we go in. You all have a special pill in your left shirt pocket, take it out and swallow it will nullify the sleep gas effect on you. Without that pill, the sleep gas, a neuro toxin, will knock you out just like anything alive on the ground out there. You all meet with me again at the front, which means the castle gates. I want first runner to go the moment we get to the castle, then next one follows in sixty seconds, until we are all dispersed. When you're all done, we will have enough destructive power to destabilize the immediate outside of the castle, which will also serve as a distracter to their security manpower. All of you except Jiang, who is coming with me to rig the gates. Now let's test out the communication. One two three… all receiving me loud and clear?"

All the team member now plugged in their super bluetooth earpieces and confirmed connectivity. Then every team member opened unzipped their cargo pockets to have access to the tiny bomb units inside. Silencer rigged guns were all set ready. Each also found their pill and swallowed it, including Colonel Carkenbo. The team then made its way down the sloppy terrain and into the sandy road and started running in fast-paced jog mode towards the castle, which was about a quarter of a mile away now and did not stop until they got to its perimeter wall.

"Remember, guys, we have only sixty minutes of time to get all this done and then get out. The sixty minutes start now!" the colonel said. "Alright, first runner, go!"

A team member took off, disappearing into the mist. After sixty seconds, another one followed him. The sequence continued until all eleven men were gone. Now colonel Carkenbo and commando Jiang quietly made their way to the castle's main entrance, characterized by two big iron metallic gates that were operated electronically from inside.

Back to the first commando runner, he ran the path alongside the castle's perimeter wall and after sixty seconds, stopped and reached into his pockets, pulling out three tiny canisters. Quickly unplugging the top off each one of them, he pressed the tiny button on top, waited five seconds, then threw two over the wall after attaching one on the outside wall. Then he started running again.

But suddenly, and without warning, someone or something stepped out of the thick mist and bumped hard into him, forcing him to stagger sideways off the path and into the concrete wall. Before he could react, a barrage of fist blows hit his body, so fast and hard that he was pinned against the wall. His attacker slammed a knee into his middle, and as he bent over in pain, a blow that felt like a sledgehammer hit his head. He blacked out instantly. His attacker quickly picked up his limp body like it was a big fluffy doll and threw it into the invisible space engulfed by the thick mist, away from the path. His body landed with a thud. The attacker then stepped back and faded into the mist again.

The second commando runner followed in exactly one minute after the first commando then left the team and ran on the path for ninety seconds, then stopped and did the same thing the first one did with the three canister bombs. Then he took off again. But he didn't make it to the gates either. He was too suddenly attacked, and like his colleague, he didn't get the chance to fight back. He was knocked out and thrown off the path and into the dark, thick grey mist. The same fate befell the rest of the next nine commando runners. The common feature here was that they got attacked by surprise and were hit hard, yet no one got the chance to know who or what hit them.

The last commando to do the run was Otto Mueller, the big, tall, and muscular German hunk of three hundred pounds of solid muscle, known to his peers back home as one hell of a mean, killing, war machine. Otto Mueller had already had his share of covert operations, and he came out of all of them ok, living behind a pile of dead enemies. But now, for some unknown reason, he stopped briefly and looked around him, rolling his neck and shoulder muscles, while peering into the fog. Maybe it was instinct, a rare seventh sense. Then he heard something, like a rustling of leaves. Instinctively, his hand moved to his side, but not to pull out the bombs. Instead, he pulled out a big, double edged commando knife. Man, or animal, whatever it is, he was ready to slice all of it up. He poised himself, peering closer into the mist...

"Whoompshh", came the noise from the air, and not the ground, instantly followed by something coming down on him. But all he saw was a pair of legs showing suddenly and then the feet hit him hard in the chest, sending him to the ground. He landed on his bottom with a thud, his back smashing into the brick wall behind him. Now that took the wind out of him, but with the big knife still firmly in his hand, he wasn't giving up yet, and started getting up.

"Stand down, or I will decease you," someone said in a chilling, menacing, ghostly sort of voice. He looked up to see the silhouette of this tall, masculine figure touring over him.

"In your dreams, nutzlose kacke!" The German commando growled back, leaping to his feet. He had just called his attacker useless shit!

But then as he did that, the silhouetted figure moved too, and was way much faster, like a dash! Whoom! A movement of hot air hit him in the face and then a heavy sledgehammer type of thing hit him "Poom" below his chin, sending him back to the ground again. He was still reeling with dizziness when the big knife was smashed out of his hand with brutal force, sending the heavy blade flipping into the air and falling further away somewhere in the misty surrounding. It must have hit a stone or something hard, for he heard its clattering sound as it hit the ground somewhere. Another heavy blow hit him in the face, slamming his head hard against the brick wall. As his head bounced back from the wall, another heavy blow him again in the face, making him very dizzy. To him, these weren't normal hand blows smashing into him. Rather, it felt like a big, heavy rock being used to bash his head! Then, something like a pair of big metallic pliers grabbed at the back of his neck, yanked him forward like he was weightless, and then another heavy thing smashed into the back of his neck. Otto Mueller, like the rest of his colleagues, blacked out without knowing exactly what or who had attacked him.

"I told you to stand down!" the deep, ghostly, menacing voice from the silhouette reiterated. The figure then moved in closer, picked the big German commando off the ground with ease, and threw his limp body into the heavily mist – engulfed, surroundings of area. His body made a heavy thudding noise when it landed somewhere in the pale darkness beyond.

The silhouette figure turned around on the path and moved away, fading into the mist again.

At the outside of the castle's big gates, Colonel Carkenbo and commando Jiang finished rigging up both sides of the castle's big gates with explosives and then again crawled on the ground to get out of the blast range. They had to crawl their way to and from the gates so as not to be detected by any cameras, even with the presence of such heavy mist or fog. They didn't want to take chances of being seen or even motion detected. After crawling across the front to the opposite gate post, the two Operation life support team members stood up and leaned their bodies against the brick wall. The colonel looked at his watch.

"Caron should already be here by now," he said, referring to the first team member to run the castle's perimeter, French commando Jack Caron. "I wonder why he's not here yet."

"Want me to go check him out?" commando Jiang asked.

"Let's give him a couple of minutes. If he's not here by then, you go check up on him, and perhaps the others too," the colonel replied.

Silence. Tic tok, tic tok, tic… toc… toc! Those minutes passed by, and nothing happened. No one showed.

"That's it, Colonel. Two minutes over!" Jiang Hong said. "I am going to check on Caron and the rest."

"Yeah! Go for it," the Colonel responded back.

Commando Jiang Hong took several steps forward and then stopped. She slowly retraced her steps until she was standing right next to the Colonel.

"What is it?" Colonel Carkenbo asked quickly, his hand immediately going to his gun.

"Do you see what I see? There, that shadow! And now… it's turning itself into human form…" Jiang Hong replied back, cutting off her speech as they both witnessed the transformation. The figure that transformed itself from its silhouetted, shadow form in the heavy mist and into a full human form stepped forward and faced them.

"Don't bother. They won't be able to catch up with you now, and not soon either," The new arrival on the scene said, arms hanging at body sides. The voice was strong, menacing, and yes, with a ghostly taunt in it. Yet they could sense the feminism in it. The individual looked completely unarmed.

The two commandos looked at each other for a moment, and then looked back at her again.

"Who or what the hell are you, and what are you talking about?" commando Jiang asked in response.

"I am Cephia, an archangel from heaven above, sent down here to your world by God, to deal with your vermin, to extinguish all evil," the individual replied. "Your friends are not coming soon because I silenced them, though temporarily. Now listen to me carefully. The devil, through his incarnate, already knows you're here, that you're coming to destroy him and or his deadly project. But he's too powerful for you to handle and will kill all of you! And that is why I was sent. I am also here to stop you from engaging in any battle with him, to save your innocent lives. At this moment in time, the devil will stop at nothing to get his way. I am the only one who can stop him, because I come with heaven's mandate to do so."

"Did you say… God? What God?" Jiang Hong, asked quickly sizing up the figure before her. A female, slightly taller than her, with an athletic built body and a yes, no hair on her head, among other things.

"God almighty, in heaven, your creator, sent me," Cephia interpreted back.

"Well then, archangel, or whatever bullshit you call yourself, it's high time you get out of our way so we can go find out exactly what you did to my men!" Colonel Carkenbo snapped back menacingly, and with one flip of his hand, the silencer rigged assault submachinegun came up. Several bullets came out of its barrel, fast and hot, hitting Cephia in the chest and neck.

The archangel stiffened, her body stumbling backwards. Boof! Boof! Boof, boof, boof! The dull thuds of the deadly, heavy caliber bullets hitting her body at close range was clearly audible after Colonel Carkenbo fired off several more rounds at her. That was why he always chose this weapon, because this submachine gun was capable of inflicting lethal damage with just one shot at a target. But with several rounds fired, the deadly, heavy caliber bullets would create a total shattering impact capable of not only shredding up everything in their way, but also blasting material outwards. Cephia then lost her balance and hit the ground with a heavy thud. Even as her body appeared to be grasping at the last straws of life, exhibiting seizure activity from where it lay on the sandy ground, Colonel Carkenbo briskly walked over to where she had fallen and fired off more rounds into her upper body. He stopped when the jerking stopped.

"Whoever you are, or whatever you are, I don't have time to bullshit around! I said I need you out of my way, and I meant it!" the colonel said in a decisive manner, staring down at her motionless body as he shoved the gun back in its body side holster. "And unlike what you said you did to my men, what was it again… silenced them temporarily? Well, I am getting you out of my way permanently! Just to make sure you don't interfere with this mission ever again. Come on Jiang, let's go find the rest of the team."

"No, you're not!"

Cephia's strong, chilling menacing voice was unmistakable as she suddenly resounded herself, this time without the ghostly utter sounds involved. As the colonel turned around to leave, an iron clamp - like grip took hold of his booted leg, suddenly holding him in place. And then with one heave of Cephia's gripping hand, colonel Carkenbo's body was tossed into the air. His body flew past and above commando Jiang's head and smashed into the brick wall behind her. His body plummeted to the ground and remained motionless.

As she slowly rose to her feet, the archangel bent her upper body down, opened her mouth, and with a light gagging sound, she spit out all the bullets that had been shot into her body while she lay unresponsive on the ground, on to the ground. She then shook her head vigorously, left and right, twice, and commando Jiang Hong saw the bullets that were shot into her neck pop out of their puncture, entry holes and fall on the ground at her feet. Those puncture wounds ther. quickly and completely self-sealed.

"What the... hell!" Commando Jiang Hong exclaimed in utter disbelief, taking several steps back.

"Now do you believe? I am not human like you. I am an archangel from heaven, and you can't kill me," Cephia stated as she resumed her upright position. "Or do you need more convincing?"

"Yea, no kidding, I now see that!" Commando Jiang replied. "But I've got to do what I came to do, even if it means resisting the unbelievable and or challenging the impossible!"

Since every one of her teammates seemed to be out of the game, she now believed that it was up to her to accomplish the mission, with or without them. After all, she was the second in command of the mission, and her superiors back in China had strictly emphasized on the rule that they only wanted to hear success out of this mission and nothing else. What she didn't realize was that the Archangel could hear her mind and knew exactly what she was going to do. And thus, she tensed herself for the next moment.

And with those words, Commando Jiang leaped high off the ground and towards the wall. Her feet connected with the wall and then she bounced off, spun around in midair and quickly administered a neck twisting kick at Cephia's head before landing on the ground on her fours a few yards away, arms and legs spreads out. Cephia stumbled a step or two backwards but remained upright. But there was no time for commando Jiang to contemplate the effects of her attack, for this adversary needed to be taken out fast if she was to try and accomplish this mission on time. She came off the ground fast, leaping like a big, fierce wild feline pouncing on its prey. Even as she sprang into action, each of her hands took hold of a stiletto knife that had been harbored on each flank side of her body. She came in spinning and sunk each knife deep into Cephia's body. She felt the sharp blades enter deep to the hilt on each side of Cephia's rib cage and then jumped clear.

Commando Jiang heard the archangel exhale loudly and knew then that she had punctured those lungs. As Cephia grabbed at the knife handles to pull them out, Commando Jiang jumped back in and administered a series of rapid fist blows at the archangel's head and neck, blows that could have, together with the other deadly blows already inflicted, rendered a normal adversary useless and dead. Then she jumped away again, a little bit further away this time. She was ready to pounce back in again.

But not this one! To her unimaginable disbelief, Commando Jiang saw Cephia's head spin around in a total circle on her neck and come back into place again. At the same very time, Cephia jerked the two stiletto knives out of her sides and threw them at her. The knives fell on the ground in front of the commando's feet.

"Holy crap!" Commando Jiang exclaimed in utter disbelief of what she just saw, shaking her head to make sure she wasn't dreaming. She looked down at the blades. They had no single drop of blood on them!

"Desist your resistance now, or you will also end up like your friends!" the archangel snapped at her, now sounding impatient, and then without warning, she suddenly leapt off the ground herself, vaulting sideways into the air, and landed smack on her feet right next to the fierce commando.

"My friend, that's not going to happen!" Commando Jiang snapped back, and then lashed out again at the Archangel's face with her right- hand fist. But Cephia grabbed hold of the flying wrist with her left hand, yanked the commando Jiang in closer, and then viciously chopped at the commando's stretched out arm with her right hand. The sudden intense, jolting pain shot through the commando Jiang's arm and into her right shoulder, making her grimace. Grabbing hold of the same hand with both of hers, the archangel swung commando Jiang around quickly, spinning her into midair and tossing her at the brick wall like she was a small sack of potatoes!

But Commando Jiang stretched out her legs, her feet once again connected with the wall, and bounced off it in a tilted twist, and then her body landed back on the ground a few yards away in a straddled position using her left arm and two legs. But the aching, throbbing pain in her right arm was too much, and she struggled to hoist herself up. But in a flash second Cephia was back at the commando's side. Commando Jiang didn't even know how Cephia got there so superfast. Now Cephia steel – gripped commando Jiang's neck with her left hand. In the following few next seconds, Cephia lifted the vigorously writhing and resisting commando off the ground until both her feet were dangling in the air, and then clubbed her midsection with two rapid right-hand fist blows, brought her down lower, and then whip slapped the commando in the face three times with intense force, using her right hand. The midsection blows completely forced air out of Jiang's body, making her instantly puke out all the contents in her stomach. The heavy, slapping blows to her face hit her with such great force they jerked her head from one side to another and then back. Commando Jiang Hong was now definitely rendered almost unconscious, her vision completely blurred.

Cephia dropped her to the ground, stepped back and looked down at the now blood – oozing, vomit drenched commando. This time around, commando Jiang did not get up. Instead, she fully collapsed on her back, her eyes fixated to the sky above her. Cephia placed her right foot on the commando's ribs and pressed down. Commando Jiang cried out in pain, her upper body flexing upwards off the ground.

"You tried, human. But now you too get to be silenced!" Cephia said. "It is now time for me to attend to God's business."

But suddenly she removed her foot from commando Jiang's rib cage and her eyes moved to the wall. As commando Jiang fell back to the ground, Cephia retreated back several steps from where Commando Jiang laid, unable to move herself anymore. At this moment, too, Commando Jiang very slowly moved her head to look at the archangel. The archangel suddenly hastened forward, skipped over the commando's body, and commando Jiang faintly looked on, she leaped high in the air, her body floated over to and above the top of castle's brick wall fence, and then descended out of sight on the other side.

371

Commando Jiang breathed in relief and tried to sit up, but the effort was too painful for her body, and she immediately fell back to the ground. She felt tears roll down her eyes, and even that made her grimace with pain. The last time she cried was forty years ago, when she was an average teenager, and after receiving a spanking for doing something that angered her mother. She now blamed herself for putting herself in this helpless position. She should have known better not to challenge the archangel, especially after being a first-class witness to the fact that Colonel Carkenbo's bullets had not stopped her at all, and after seeing what she did to him afterwards, not to mention how the archangel had discharged the bullets out of her body. She should have believed then and backed off, or even ran away. For this, she now agreed, was not a normal human being at all! She had to be from another world, a supernatural being. Or, to sum it up, and as indeed she had revealed to them, she was an archangel from heaven above!

The Archangel's body floated down onto the dusty ground of the compound fronting the inside of the castle gates, separated by a moat from the castle's main entrance. The bridge that enabled the connection of this area over the moat to the castle's yard had been pulled back up, so there was no other way for anyone coming through the gates to cross over to the castle's main access entrance except, perhaps, by swimming their way through the dirty, stagnant, crocodile loaded moat water. But the moment her feet touched the ground beneath her, Cephia quickly observed her surroundings, her head swiveling around again in a full, complete, circle or turn around on her neck. With her arms slightly spread out from her body sides, she slightly bowed her head down, and instantly her body became clothed in an irregular, hooded, button – free, long dark brown leather coat all the way to her ankles. The color matched what she was already wearing. When she raised her head up again, her head was now completely covered by the hoody except for the mouth and nose, and her hands were concealed inside the arms of the long coat.

Cephia looked gothic as she then slowly made her way to the moat and simply walked over the water like it was a hard surface, crossing over to the other side. She had only walked a few steps on the flat, concrete surface that led to the castle's main door entrance after crossing the moat when suddenly the entire area was brightly illuminated by fluorescent lights. Cephia stopped moving, and although her eyes were completely obscured by the hood of her coat, she could perfectly see her surroundings, where several guardsmen were poised in waiting with their guns and dogs. But with the lights now on, the guards stepped out of their cover from all around the place and slowly converged on her, guns pointed at her. In seconds, Cephia summed them up to be a total of thirty-eight armed guards coming out into the open. The dogs, perhaps trained to harass unknown trespassers by growling menacingly, rendered the situation a bad sense of deadly hostility.

"Aldhlaab, silans! nunc!" Cephia suddenly shouted out.

None of the guards understood the words she said, or why she suddenly shouted them out, but to their surprise, the dogs instantly ceased their menacing growling and barking, sat down square on their haunches, and despite the guards forcefully pulling on their leashes, refused to move forward.

While other guards tried to work the dogs into advancing on her, other guards cautiously approached her, their guns trained on her, ready to shoot.

"Put your hands up and behind your head, and get down on your knees, or you will be shot immediately!" one of them said quickly. "You are trespassing on private grounds, and we are going to have to apprehend you. How did you get in anyway? The gates are locked, and the moat bridge is up. Unless you climbed over the wall, but that's a very difficult thing to do. And you are not dripping with the filthy moat water either!"

"I am inside, right? How I got in doesn't really matter anymore. Now, take me to your master!" Cephia said, getting down to her knees and putting her hands behind her head. She said this in a calm, laid back, soft voice.

"Yes, he's been eagerly waiting for you Americans to show up," the same guard said. He pulled out a radio set from one of his jacket pockets and pressed a button on it. "Sir, we've got the American!"

"American? Or Americans?" came the response from radio.

"American, sir. Only one, and it's a woman, sir." The guard answered.

"Hmmm… that's strange, but okay, bring her in, and then make sure you search the rest of the grounds, and even beyond the bridge, to make sure there are no more unwanted people hiding out there on the premises," captain Kakra's orders came through loud and clear. "The owner wants to see them himself."

"Yes, sir," the guard said. Then he switched channels on his walkie-talkie issued some orders. "All ground units, engage thorough search and check on castle grounds within the security perimeter, now! Report back immediately if you find any unknowns. I repeat, conduct secure check on the castle's entire internal grounds and report back anything unknown to me immediately."

Sticking the walkie talkie back into the pocket, he turned to Cephia. "Ok, let's go, now! Today is your lucky day, American woman. Normally, the rule is to shoot down any unknown person found on these premises on sight, immediately and with no exceptions! I would have done it myself. But the boss wants to see you first before I kill you. Now, get up and move!"

He then suddenly shoved Cephia forward, a move that was done so roughly she almost fell down. The archangel did not object, despite stumbling forward. After that, she calmly walked on, flanked by at least twenty armed guards, and entered the building. As soon as she was inside the building, the dogs suddenly got off their haunches and started moving again. But they remained mysteriously silent. It was like they were coming out of a deep trance and were not fully wake yet. The moat bridge was let down and the guards started searching the premises with the dogs.

When they got to the elevators inside the building, the same guard roughly shoved Cephia forward and into an elevator when it opened, making her stumble again. Once again, she ignored the rude behavior, reminding herself that she was their prisoner, and this was not the time to start a fight or commotion. Then everybody else got in. She was now sandwiched in between a group of gun toting humans, who were completely unaware of the fact that standing in their midst is the deadliest entity in their entire universe at present, an agent with the maximum capability of implementing extremely intense and maximized levels of destructive battle combat, using means and methods so lethal and or deadly in nature, and at a magnitude that is totally and completely beyond possible human comprehension.

This archangel, the epiphany of heaven's already declared Para bellum ultimatum, is the fire that burns fire out! The Sanctus ignis!

They exited the elevator when it came to the underground floor and then with Cephia still sandwiched between the men with their guns, they walked through a well illuminated hallway that finally led them to a closed double door entry. The rough guard opened the door and they ushered her into the center of the underground mess hall, where captain Kakra was patiently waiting. The rough guard suddenly kicked at the back of Cephia's legs, causing her knees to buckle and subsequently forcing her to kneel down on the floor. She bowed her head down, which made her whole head to be totally concealed by the hood of her coat.

"Hey man, take it easy on our captive, will ya?" captain Kakra snapped at the guard. "Being a prisoner of war does not necessarily mean that the individual in that predicament is to be subjected to unwarranted harassment or mistreatment. Do you understand?"

"Yes sir, I understand, sir!" the guard responded quickly. He then stepped away from Cephia as captain Kakra slowly approached the unknown archangel.

"So, you're one of those commandos sent to destroy our project, huh?" he said, standing a few yards away from, and looking down at Cephia. "Where are rest of them? Where are your buddies?"

"I have no buddies. I came alone." Cephia answered calmly.

"You mean to tell me that you are the only one they sent to carry out this mission of destruction?" Captain Kakra asked, sounding very amused. "Why? did they think this was going to be some kind of school, full of kindergarten children with toys? Look around for yourself, and then tell me what you see. We are a self-protected facility with a battalion of very carefully selected, well trained guard soldiers, hell bent to do what they were hired to do, and that is to protect this facility and its operations from any outside interference at any cost. And so, I hope you do understand when I say that I am totally baffled when you tell me that your almighty government sent a single commando to carry out the impossible task of destroying an operation of this nature, because it is well operated and guarded!"

"It depends on which government you are talking about," Cephia responded back.

"The United Nations, of course, which is itself governed by the American government and its allies," captain Kakra said. "The group that thinks they own this world. But no, they don't! God intended to have this world shared, and not controlled by a minority few."

"Yet your world is in total aberration from what God wants!" Cephia responded back. "Owe it to the devil. It's the devil's influence that's leading humanity to the brink of self-destruction and extinction due to its macabre presence. It is leading this world to total nihilism. To stop this from happening, humanity must be imbued again with God's mighty ways, glory, grace, and presence. Otherwise, all will be lost!"

"You're thinking and behaving like everybody else, playing the religion game!" Captain Kakra responded back, and now pacing around the room. "Playing the blame games. Now what has the devil got to do with what's going on, uh? Why does everybody try to blame their failures, mishaps, misdeeds and perhaps their faults on someone or something they have never physically met or seen in real time? Take for instance, you! Tell me something. Have you ever met with, or seen the devil?"

"No, not yet. But as for you, you have met the devil, and you are now, perhaps unknowingly, too busy playing his games for him," Cephia answered back.

The captain stopped pacing and frowned. "Hmmm, maybe I have," he said. "But so what? After all, most of the people in this world that are supposed to lead us into wellbeing and meaningful development look no further than to the devil. They act devious, they operate using evil ways, means, and tactics. They kill people, destroy people's livelihoods, and derail ancient traditions and generational formats, just to enrich themselves. Look at you and me. Is there any difference? We are coerced into doing bad things to people by our bosses, in the name of country and flag. No, I am not playing the devil's games. I am just simply following orders as per my job, just like you!"

"You're wrong on that. While my boss is the holiest of the holy, yours is a dastard!" Cephia responded back, and then continued "Your so-called boss is the epiphany of wickedness, evil, and treachery. It's your so-called boss's actions that have now provoked the ire of the one and only almighty God, in heaven. Do you want to know what God is saying now? He's saying that enough is enough! His anger has reached an apotheosis level."

"Wait a minute. Are you trying to tell me you were sent here by God? That you really are not part of the American - led team we've been expecting to come after us?" Captain Kakra asked the archangel, halting his pacing and turning around to look at Cephia closely. For some reason, he was beginning feel nervous about the individual before him. Something wasn't right, but in the sense that something was uniquely different with this person. He could feel it deep inside him!

"That's what I have been trying to tell you all along, that I am the only one God sent here," Cephia replied, her head still bowed down, her face still obscured by her overcoat's hoody as she patiently maintained her position on her knees on the floor. "I have nothing to do with the human force out there."

"Oooh, I see. Okay then. Since you define yourself as a divine entity, we're going to try to prove your claims," Captain Kakra said. "First, divine individuals look different from the rest of us earthlings. So, let's start by completely disrobing you. Hey, you, Kamuzu, help our self - confessed divine take her coat off first."

"Gladly, captain," the guard said, immediately stepping forward. "I have been really wanting to know how she really looks like without her gothic looking coat on. Maybe later I will also get to know how she feels in the inside too."

That made the other guards laugh, but the captain was still not having it. "I didn't say that was going to happen, Kamuzu, and for the last time, I am warning you. Mind your conduct around her, or I will be forced to deactivate you by making sure you don't see the dawn of tomorrow!"

Kamuzu was the guard who had apprehended the archangel earlier and had played the rough hand with her. Her head still bowed down, Cephia slowly turned her head sideways and stared at the guard.

"You! I seriously suggest that you don't put your filthy hands on me, or on my coat," she said, her voice still calm. "Your entire soul is bedeviled with unkindly deeds and acts of wickedness that need to be addressed before your divine maker decides your fate. You're almost as vile as the devil himself, and we cannot, at this time of your life, accept your presence before us. So, if you touch any part of me, you will immediately be shunned by my holy fire as it attempts to cleanse your filth off me. And believe me, you will regret what happens to you after it happens to you. You would rather have me take this coat off myself, and only when I am ready to do so."

"Sorry my friend. Captain's orders!" the guard said, reaching out and placing both his hands on her shoulders to yank her coat off her body. The lights in the room suddenly dimmed, and then a loud, big spark of static electricity suddenly occurred around his hands, vanishing in about two seconds, but leaving behind a puff of dark grey smoke and a sizzling sound effect. The guard screamed loudly and withdrew his hands immediately, but it was too late. Everyone else, including captain Kakra, flinched at the sight of his badly and completely charred hands and the foul stench of burned flesh that came off them. It was like he had been burned by a one hundred percent corrosive acid, to the bone! All his fingers now looked like shriveled, burned, bacon strips! Overly terrified and in excruciating pain, the guard ran out of the room still screaming at the top of his voice. The lights resumed their normal brightness.

"I warned him," Cephia said calmly and with a sigh, slowly turning her head back into the bowed down, lowered chin, position. "Anyone else care to try, hmmm? Maybe one of you has a clean soul and won't be affected by my burning fire."

Everyone remained where they were standing, including Captain Kakra who had immediately jumped back when the guard got burned. Not even one of them dared talk back.

"Now what's going on here?" Someone else growled loudly in a heavy and dramatically hoarse voice.

Everyone, except Cephia, now turned around to see the masked principal with the three escorts enter the mess hall from one of the connecting doors.

"Boss, we have a prisoner here, caught trespassing on the grounds beyond the main gate, and whose body can't be touched by anyone sinful!" Captain Kakra responded quickly. "Otherwise, the sinner gets scotched by a fire off her body! One of my guards tried to disrobe her and his hands got burned badly! We brought her in because we thought she was part of the American-led team."

"I say, don't waste my time with such pitiful, human sorcery!" the principal said, pointing at the archangel. "I am definitely the least impressed by the dismal standards of magical impressions in your world!"

"But boss, I don't think this was just simple magic," Captain Kakra said. "We are all first-class witnesses of the incident that happened to Kamuzu's hands. And this was after he was warned by the prisoner not to touch her or her coat, but he went ahead and laid his hands on her coat shoulders anyway. I can call the guard back so you can see for yourself, boss. It was a terrible thing to witness, and I can still smell that terrible stench of burnt flesh in the air. I am beginning to think that God might be involved in all this. And when that happens, nothing appears to be the same anymore!"

"Spare me your weak, fearful rant, Captain, lest you anger me to the point where I have to kill you instantly. And do not ever mention God in my presence again, ever!" Retorted the principal, waving a hand in dismissal. "I am declaring the fact that whatever you or anybody else here may have witnessed is simply feigned conjuring. End of story! Stand aside now, captain, I will take it over from here!"

"Yes, sir boss, as you wish," Captain Kakra acknowledged, and giving a brief salute. After that, he retreated back and away from the archangel, joining the rest of his armed guards who were now standing several yards away from her after witnessing what happened to their fellow guardsman.

"Now, let's see what we have here," the principal said, taking a few steps closer to the isolated kneeling figure of the archangel in the center of the big room and who now had both her arms folded up on her chest. "So, you can do some bad magic, huh? Maybe you can show us some more of your tricks before we finally get to make an example out of you to all those others who dare try to interfere or mess with me and my business."

Without using her arms, her hooded head still lowered, Cephia the archangel rose from the floor, slowly and with ease until she was fully upright. Her arms suddenly fell to her sides and her hands were again concealed inside the coat arms. Then she slowly raised her head and directly faced the devil incarnate.

"Let's cut the small talk out, shall we, devil incarnate?" She said in a calm but very audible, strong voice. It was no longer that soft voice she used with the humans. "Do you realize that what you are planning to do will amount to a horrific level of cataclysm? And as such, you are a bane to the heavens, a belligerent feral spirit from hell ably manipulating humanity to self-destruction. Your actions have provoked seething, restless anger from the heavens, and that's why I am here. To save what is left of God's seventh dimension and to restore God's order before all is lost to hell - like cries of total grief, agony and terror!"

"If that's the case, then why don't I feel heavenly capacity around here?" the devil's incarnate responded back, head shaking slowly. "Because all I just heard is plain speech from a dolt! What am I supposed to do, huh? Believe in all that bullshit? You think you can just walk in here and threaten me with some obnoxious magic and speech and then expect me to cower in fear? Well, that's not going to happen. This is my world and my world alone! Your very presence here offends me and is considered a total abomination by I and my followers!"

Cephia briefly turned her attention to Captain Kakra and his guards. "The God I serve is also a God of mercy, so I am going to give all of you the choice to determine your fate. Leave now, and your day of judgement will remain as originally scheduled. But if you choose to stay and serve this evil spirit, then your time is done, and I will judge you per my mandate. I will destroy your body and soul!"

Captain Kakra looked at the archangel and grimaced. He then said, "Thank you for allowing us to make that choice, even though this privilege afforded to us is riddled with threats. But here is the thing. We're here to do a job that our boss here is paying us well to do. We follow his orders, and as long as he has not terminated our function, we are not going anywhere, and we will do what he says!"

"Very well," Cephia acknowledged. She then turned back around to face the principal and the three aides. "And as for you, not only am I here to stop you from proceeding with your so-called business, I am also here to destroy you to the core. I am here to free the soul that you have taken over and then send you back to hell. It will all end here, today, now!"

The devil - incarnate raised both hands in exclamation, looking left and right at his escorts, who smiled back. Spreading both arms out, the principal responded back, "So you are going to destroy me, huh? How? Do you know how many people have already tried to do that and failed miserably, most of them ending up dead? Please, be my guest. But as far as me and my people are concerned, all we've just gotten from you is talk, talk, and talk! Gibberish! Please don't keep us waiting any longer. Why the hell don't you show us more of your marginalized sorcery?"

"Yes devil, it ends right now!" the archangel reiterated, her coat hood flipping itself off her head. Her eyes were now two intensely sparkling yellow sapphires with no pupils. She stretched her arms sideways, and her long coat automatically flew off her body, vanishing in a "puff" in the air and revealing all the stainless- steel weaponry attached to her body with no visible straps holding them in place, and the metallic bracelets on her arms. The rest of her light skinned body, including her head, was now all marked with glowing purple, tattoos. And now all the bracelets on her arms started vibrating, nonstop, and making the "cling clang" noise.

The devil looked once into the archangel's sparkling eyes and suddenly became very startled. Now hysterical with fear, the principal immediately shouted out. "Kill that woman! kill that bitch, now! She's a holy! All of you, now! Kill her! Go! Goooooo!!!"

Cephia shifted her arms upwards, stretching them out in front of her and pointing them at the devil, and then thrust both hands open.

The bracelets flew off her arm in rapid succession and hit the devil's incarnate in front part of the neck, chest, abdominal wall, pelvic area and both thighs. The moment those bracelets hit the devil incarnate' s body, they embedded themselves and started glowing like superheated, red-hot coils. The devil within howled out loud in instant, overwhelming

381

pain, and its incarnation fell down to the floor, going into direct seizure mode.

"Sah hamra im li ignis gris yahim zarib ignis!" Cephia cried out loudly.

"I give you the fire that burnt out fire!"

Then pandemonium broke out. The devil's three aides sprang into action, their bodies responding by going into instant, progressive transformation.

Meanwhile, Cephia left the floor, leaping high up into the space above, and her body spinning around in midair to face Captain Kakra and his guards below her. They were now responding to the devil's orders, scrambling to aim their guns at her. Her arms and legs spread out like a swooping eagle coming down on its prey, her action slowed down as she descended down on them, timely suspending her in the empty air space. Then she suddenly landed smack down on her feet, and in her left hand was the tool that looked like a heavy duty four-way lug wrench. Quickly touching the left hand with the right, an exact replica of the same tool suddenly appeared in her right hand, and then she started spinning both tools like they are rotor blades, extremely fast, in front of her. At the same time, the armed guards opened fire on her. But their bullets couldn't get past the super - spinning tools in her hands, for each bullet that hit the spinning cycles was instantly shredded into tiny particles! This went on for at least five minutes as Cephia manipulated the weapons left and right, up and down, responding to those guards who were trying to sneak in shots using the side, and not direct or frontal, assault tactics. The noise was deafening, and the room was filled with a lot of blue smoke from the gun shots.

And then she opened her mouth, wide, revealing her golden teeth for a couple of seconds. A swarm of hundreds of yellow jackets spewed out of her wide-open mouth by the hundreds and descended down on the captain and his guard group, spreading out everywhere and instantly going into aggressive sting mode. Some of the guards managed to fire a few shots from their guns, but it was too late. As the guards screamed loudly and tried to ward out the stinging insects,

Cephia closed her mouth, threw the spinning weapons up into the air, and when they came down, they embedded themselves into her body, disappearing into it. Instantly turning around, she then faced her next challenge. But what she was facing next was even more dynamic!

The short, stocky black man had completely transformed into this all hairy, very muscular, partially clothed, Cro -Magnon man with two big arms on each side of his body, and big feet. His head resembled that of an orangutan head with a full mane of facial hair. He was now a big, six feet plus tall, hairy monster of unknown ape – like origin, standing on its two feet, beating his chest with all its fists, bearing massive gray teeth and bellowing loudly as he got ready to attack. One of captain Kakra's guards, trying to run away from the stinging insects, ran into the Cro – magnon's direct path. His hands grabbed at guard's body from both sides, and instantly tore him into two parts, spilling body contents everywhere before tossing the dismembered body to the side like it was a rag doll! And when another guard got into his path again, the Cro -magnon lashed out with a clenched right fist, hitting the guard hard and sending his body flying high until it slammed into the ceiling above and then slammed down to the floor. The Cro – magnon man then bellowed loudly and turned around to face the archangel. Thumping his chest with his four hands, he advanced forward.

The two women, of course, completely transformed themselves into their big dog forms, their big mandibles open and showing their massive white teeth. They growled menacingly as they, too, advanced on Cephia.

Cephia quickly raised her hands up and the black gloves automatically flew off her hands and remained suspended in the air in front of her. As the gloves flew off her hands, a pair of double-edged knives that resembled World War two, ten inch, Garand Bayonets popped off her back and landed into the grasp of the gloves. It was like the gloves were being manipulated by invisible hands and body. The gloves and their knives flew away towards the loudly bellowing Cro -Magnon monster, instantly engaging him in a rapid, aggressive, antagonizing brawl of thrusts, swipes and jabs. The offensive gloves with their knives now prevented the monster from advancing towards Cephia. Each movement he made with his hands and feet was met with aggressive knife attacks that sliced or pieced away at his body, causing him to instantly bleed.

Cephia's right hand then flexed out up and towards her back. The Spear - like monument popped off her back and landed into her open hand like it was being pulled by a strong magnet. Bringing it down to the front of her body, she held it with both hands and stretched it out until it was a full, double headed spear.

"Damilla savhalsa, kum hamra diy!" she hissed the order to the spear. "Go, help take care of that one, now!"

And with those words, she threw the spear at the Cro-Magnon man with her right hand like she was throwing a javelin. It did not hit the beast, but instead it landed in the way and systematically blocked him from moving forward, just like the gloves with the knives. As he tried to forcefully move forward towards Cephia, the gloves with the knives swiped, slashed and pierced at the monster's face, neck and chest while the double headed spear went into rapid self-thrusting action, its double-edged blades aggressively slamming and piecing into the beast's abdomen, thighs, and legs. The beast howled loudly in pain as it started bleeding everywhere. There was a one-time louder than normal bellow from his mouth when the knives sliced at the front of his neck, pulled back, and then flew in with full force to thrust into his neck again, pulled out again and thrust, with full force again, into his face, piercing through his eye sockets, pulled out and repeated the aggressive attack again on the eyes. With this second at his eyes, they suddenly popped out of their sockets, oozing out like jelly and rolling down his face, while his nose and mouth got sliced several times until they looked minced. The knife wielding gloves changed course and repeatedly warded off the monster's six swinging arms by swiping and piecing, cutting off its hairy fingers and opening both wrists' blood vessels!

The double edge spear kept thrusting, in rapid random successions, piecing viciously into his abdomen, front pelvic area, thighs and knees until he could not sustain his weight any longer because of the deep puncture wounds inflicted on his body and which were now bleeding profusely. Still howling loudly, the Cro - Magnon man beast collapsed to his knees, but still trying to savagely slash with his four hairy, deadly claws at his mostly invisible adversaries. He finally pitched forward and hit the floor with a heavy thud, remaining still. His now naked body

384

slowly transformed itself back into the hefty, stocky black human male, now looking bloody and gutted all over his body. The four armed, Cro – magnon monster was dead without having his chance at directly challenging the archangel in combat.

On the other side of this in – house battle, it didn't look good either. With the hot coil rings burning up the devil incarnate's body insides, blood started oozing out of the mask's eyes, nose, and mouth structures and from edges around the face. The devil's incarnate was trying to get up from the floor, but then fell back down and started seizing again. Cephia took all this in with one sweeping glance and then turned her focus to the two big, growling, snarling dogs.

They were now circling around her, their eyes steel blue and blank, until she stood in between them. They were getting ready to pounce on her from both sides, like they did with major Haraabi before they ripped both of his arms off his body.

"Sau malum gadim enri, sartai malum enim mori. Mou gaduhm sohimra! morezei Sohimra gaduhmnai. Sau himra enri, sarta? Li dekri demua!" Cephia hissed at them.

"The evil that made you is no more. Now death is coming to you too. Prepare to die. Or are you already ready? then come on!"

They launched their attack, their mandibles wide open, ready to latch on to flesh and bone. But she wasn't there. Cephia leapt out of place, vaulting backwards so quick the vicious animals missed the move, and their heads butted with a thud! Both dogs fell back to the floor, whimpering loudly. Cephia landed back smack on her two feet and faced the animals again. They flipped right back up, snarled at her, and then attacked immediately. At that moment, two long knives popped off her body and fell into her open hands. The gleaming, double-edged knives had fire sparks coming off their blades. She whapped the blades together twice, very fast, and then braced herself for the assault.

Cephia lashed out with a low flying left foot kick at one of the monstrous dogs, her metal clad boot shoe connecting with its lower neck. The blow flipped the animal over, sending it rolling into the air and slamming it into a wall a few yards away. Then in the next flash moment, she lashed out with her right foot at the other dog, aiming at the front of its head. The dog's gaping mandibles latched on to the foot, tight, momentarily retaining Cephia on her left leg. But before the deadly jaws implemented their total bite and rip effect, the metallic edges of Cephia's flat soled boot shoe snapped open, releasing thin, double edged nail knives outwards on the top, right, left and bottom of the shoe. The sharp knives instantly wedged through the interior of the monster dog's mouth, piercing their way through. Cephia then flexed the leg back, pulling the animal inwards, and lashed out in a fast right-hand slash move at the animal's head with the dagger in her right hand. The dog's head was sliced wide open from below the eyes, completely separating the top from the bottom. The animal's mandible grip on her foot immediately loosened and it collapsed on the floor, dead. Cephia pulled her foot away, the knives retracted back into the edges of her shoe, and then was back on her two feet again. She now eyed the other big dog closely.

The other monster dog quickly rebounded from the hard kick and slam, but then stopped when its eyes locked on the dead body of its partner in crime. Snarling loudly, it looked up at Cephia, edged forward towards her, then stopped. The big animal was hesitating.

"Diz migri tempus est mori, etiam! muqadas, kyia aap hain, huh?" Cephia said, stepping forward.

"It's time for you to die, too! Now you're scared, huh?"

On the dog's left side, just a few yards away, the masked devil's incarnate was barely clinging on to life, the total internal body defilement by the holy fire almost complete. The devil's incarnate was also mumbling words, barely audible, and at the same time stretching its right arm out, trying to reach out to the monster dog, which also now changed its focus from the archangel to the masked individual. Suddenly, the big dog begun changing back to its human form, and the transition was happening fast. Realizing what was about to happen, Cephia quickly stretched out her right arm, and opened her right hand, letting go of the dagger which, in a flash second, reattached itself to her body.

"Inihri Mua!" Cephia said quickly. The moment she said these words, the double headed spear fast swished from its position where it had done its last self-thrust into the Cro-Magnon beast's body, and into her open right hand. At about the same exact time, Kimba's transformation back into human form became complete. She swung around and reached out for the devil incarnate's hand with her's.

"No mocri dihakma, Satan!" Cephia hissed loudly. "That's not decreed to happen, Satan!"

The two heads of the spear in her hand suddenly glowed red as Cephia instantly threw it with deadly accuracy at Kimba. The moment the tips of the glowing spear heads made contact with her body, Kimba's entire human structure completely exploded into tiny pieces of flesh that splashed all over the floor, ceiling and nearby walls, and just as the devil's fingers were about to touch the transformed dog woman's. The small, bloody chunks of Kimba's human remains then completely self-charred, leaving behind dried residual, some pieces exhibiting a dark vapor - rise. Kimba was completely incinerated.

Then the spear retracted itself back into the archangel's hand, just like a boomerang, in a snap moment. The archangel then threw it up in the air above her, and as it came back down, it shortened itself and then reattached itself to her back. Cephia then stretched out both her hands again. Her gloves, still holding the knives, floated back to her, released the knives which reattached themselves to her body like a fast magnet pull, and then they fitted themselves back on to her stretched out hands like a second skin fitting.

Cephia had just prevented the devil from transferring itself from its previous, degraded body to Kimba's. A simple touch to her fingers while she was still in her human form was all it would have taken for that taken. Once inside Kimba's body, the devil's powers could have tripled, making it possible for the devil to escape unharmed, and enabling the devil to get out of the room, take possession of the deadly viral strains and dispose them to the open world.

The Devil's incarnate fell back on the floor, lifeless!

Then the ugly mask slowly lifted itself off the incarnate's head and floated over in the air to where Cephia was still standing, confronting her at face level. The archangel did not budge an inch and stared right back at the ugly thing. Then the mask spoke.

"Demuz e zamiha krit yish, Ketrush denmish intam cribna!" it growled menacingly.

"This is my world too, and I will find me another home!"

Cephia's eyes suddenly opened wide, and a ray of visible green, vaporized air streamed out of each eye, straight on to, and then engulfing, the entire mask. The mask released a horrifying scream, a sorrowful sound like that of a tired, sick old man crying out in pain. Then it suddenly shriveled up, like a piece of soft plastic material affected by high heat. It fell to the floor, looking like a dirty, crumpled, rolled up piece of aluminum foil paper or totally crushed up soda can.

"La, el hellaz 'al infierno j'ai dit!" Cephia responded back. "No, return to hell I said!"

Cephia looked down at the crumpled remains of the thing, shook her head slowly, and then walked over it to where the principal's body lay, unresponsive and unmasked, and stared down at it.

The head was that of a very pretty woman, her beautiful, long, silky black hair spread out underneath her head, her eyes still wide open, her mouth agape and revealing beautiful, well aligned teeth. Even with her olive skin tone beginning to pale as a result of death, this woman still exhibited intense, unimaginable beauty. The devil surely knows how to choose his temples.

"Kumoshile!" Cephia said in a low tone voice. "Wasted!"

Her eyes returned to normal, and she quickly looked around her. The only human still standing upright was captain Kakra. He was standing against the wall, unable to move. A thick swarm of hundred or more, high–pitched buzzing, yellow jackets were floating up and down everywhere in the room, but there was this one shiny yellow jacket that stood out of the swarm and right at the tip of his nose, that remained steady in place, facing him. One move from him, and this insect would unleash its horrific sting on him. Cephia briskly walked over to where he was, her face grim, her body still tense from her previous encounters, and stared at the terrified man up-close.

"So, do you see, and now believe in, the power of God?" she asked. Captain Kakra, shaking all over and looking so terrified, nodded his head quickly in affirmation. "By the way, it only takes one sting from any one of these insects to fatally kill a human. The super venom from that sting will completely paralyze the function of the human system in exactly fourteen seconds, and then death will follow in the next seven. All your men in this room are dead now. But because you mentioned God to the devil, I instructed them not to kill you!"

After saying that, Cephia turned around, opened her mouth, and the entire volume of unstable, loudly buzzing yellow jackets plus the one in front of captain Kakra, suddenly changed direction flew towards her, entered and disappeared into her mouth. Not a single one remained behind. After they were all gone inside, she closed her mouth.

The building suddenly shook. Boom! An explosion had just gone off somewhere, though sounding distant. The captain stared at Cephia, looking more terrified.

"Please… please, don't destroy the building while I am still in it," he pleaded. "I don't want to die here. Let me get out first."

"Hmmm, that's not me. It's the American team that you have been waiting for. They are finally here to take you down!" the archangel replied. "As for me, I still have God's work to take care of. You've still got enough time to get out, and when you get out, go back to your home, to your people, to your nation, and for the rest of your life talk about the glory and power of God. Tell your people that God in heaven is real and is everywhere in this world that he created. That's all I want you to do in order to show your gratitude to me for sparing your life today."

And with those words, she turned around and walked away from him. She walked to the door that connected to the hallway that led to the laboratory and disappeared inside.

Inside the laboratory, Chief scientist Ning Pei Pei looked up from the microscope and nodded his head at his assistant.

"We're all good to go. I have super perfected the strain. This final enhancement is so strong it will bring even the so - called most developed, powerful nations to their knees," he said, smiling widely. "No need to check it anymore. And I am sure the boss man, even though he scares the hell out of me with that stupid, ugly mask on his face, will be very content. Do you have all the one hundred and ninety- five strain samples ready? I did promise to deliver them to him tonight."

"Yes, Doctor Pei. They are all parked in these three attaché cases, ready for dispatch into the environment," One of his three assistants in the office with him quickly replied. "We disguised them well, labelled as small tester perfumes and cologne."

"Good job, people, good job!" The chief scientist loudly applauded. "I do have the four master antidotes samples with me here in this padfolio, all wrapped up in plastic med bottles. Easy to pass through the airport. Now let me inoculate you with the antidote so that you remain safe from the strains when we release them into the general public. Hurry up now, people. Time is of the essence!"

All three assistants rolled up their sleeves for the shot.

Doctor Pei placed the padfolio on the table, opened it, and carefully removed a vial from it. One of the assistants handed over three small gage needles with syringes, which he unwrapped and then used each one to withdrawal exactly one milliliter of the light orange liquid from the vial. After that, he injected the liquid into the assistants' arms. "You're all now inoculated from the pandemic. You have nothing to worry about when it starts. Oh, by the way, with your blood, just a drop of it mixed in one gallon of water or any other light liquid, you will be able to heal at least ten people of your choice by having them drink it. Save your loved ones' lives. Ok people, our work is done, so let's get out of here. Captain Kakra is supposed to address the workers here in about one hour from now. Final address. Everyone is going home! He will pass the rest of the final checks. I already gave you yours. We leave immediately."

"Dr. Pei, can we take a picture with you?" another assistant asked. "We've all been locked up and working together tirelessly with you for some long time. I would like to remember everyone."

"Ah… yes. Sure!" Doctor Pei consented.

The four of them lined up together and the selfie was done, after which the doctor placed the antidote vial back into the padfolio and locked it. Each of his three assistants picked up a briefcase and they all matched out of the tiny office.

Boom! Boom! More distant explosions went off. Now everyone in the lab area stopped what they were doing and looked at each other. Nobody seemed to know what was going on. No one had ever experienced such big explosions around here.

"What the hell is going on?" one of Doctor Pei's assistants verbalized what was on everyone's mind.

"Well, that captain man better come in and explain what the hell is going on out there!" Doctor Pei responded angrily. "I am sick and tired of living and working in a place where everything is always more than often militaristic!"

Whether by coincidence or not, his quest was suddenly answered, perhaps indirectly. Captain Kakra's voice suddenly erupted through the castle's modern public address system.

"Attention all workers inside the building. You need to vacate the building immediately. This is not a drill. I repeat, vacate the building immediately!" the captain's voice came through loud and clear.

There was general silence in the laboratory as everyone tried to contemplate the abrupt message.

Boom, boom! Two more explosions were heard, breaking through the icy silence. Now everyone stopped what they were doing and immediately started running to the door. Their mini stampede was cut short when suddenly the double doors to the lab burst open in wards and the two guard soldiers fell through to the floor. It was like they had been hit by an extremely heavy wind blast with a big whooshing sound to it. Even the doors were left hanging loose on their hinges. The two guards crushed on the floor right in front of the shocked laboratory staff and remained down, unresponsive, with their guns still in their hands. A few seconds after that, a lone figure walked in through the shattered doorway and stood in front of them. A stunning, bold headed female strangely dressed in a sleeveless robe with a lot of metallic stuff attached to her body.

"You, put those boxes down and then get out of here!" Cephia said calmly, pointing a wide finger at Doctor Pei's three assistants and then at the scientist himself. "And you, scientist, hand over that storage box in your hand to me. Hand it over Now!"

"Excuse me... and who are you exactly?" Doctor Pei asked immediately, sounding somewhat concerned by the strange way this newcomer showed up in his laboratory. "I don't seem to know you… and neither do I recall having seen you around here before."

"I am Cephia. You don't know me, because we have never met before, and that's because I arrived here today," The archangel replied. "Now, hand over the box, and the people with you should put those other bigger boxes down. Then all of you must leave, immediately."

"Eeeh, eeeh, eeeh… Now, hold your horses, woman!" the chief scientist responded back, gathering his wits. "What makes you think that you can just suddenly walk in here and tell us what to do? You want me to simply hand over the results of my finest work, ever, to you, and then simply walk away from it? Anyway, I am also, actually on my way to deliver the same results to someone else, that someone being the one who's paid me to do the research and provide the clinical output. That someone else is very much not you. Does it make sense to you, what I am saying? So, sorry! I am not about to relinquish the clinical results of my fine work to you. At least that's not happening today, and certainly not in the nearest future!"

Cephia stared at the chief scientist, who was standing several yards away from her, and a look of contempt came over her face. She took one step forward and in a blink of an eye she was standing in front of him, face to face. Nobody knew how she had moved so fast. What everybody inside the laboratory at that time witnessed was a slight movement of Cephia's body and then there she was in front of him. Her right hand went to the back of his neck and squeezed.

"I can tell you what to do because I can!" She said to him. "You will hand over that box to me or I will take it from you myself, and that's because it is meant to be. I am looking into your eyes now, which lead me into your soul, and I see that you're the designer of the core of this pure evil. How can you feel so redeemed by creating something that is going to be the demise of so many? Your so – called finest work has simply made you the devil's covered, yet very filthy, dirty hand. But since the biggest determinant of your achievements has been through your eyes, we shall now make sure that your eyes will never be used again by you to facilitate the evil genius!"

With those words, Cephia opened her mouth slightly and exhaled a gentle whiff of air into Doctor Pei's face, specifically over his eyes. The

392

two little glass panels in his highly polished, horn-rimmed spectacles cracked and shattered when her breath air hit them, falling out of their frames on to the floor. And then doctor Pei's vision completely disappeared. He was totally engulfed in darkness. Cephia let go of his neck, took the padfolio from his hand, and then shoved him backwards.

"What have you done to me? I can't see!" Doctor Pei screamed out. "Someone, please, help me! She's made me blind! Help, someone, please I beg you, I can't see anymore…"

As the chief scientist's cry became a terrified, shock filled plea for help, he started running in circles, grabbing at everything in his way, running into the walls and bumping into things. The group of equally terrified and shocked witnesses of this phenomenal incident, who were generally his laboratory staff, quickly gave way to the now raving, hysterical scientist who had for some long time been their determined, unyielding, very efficient and able boss. They literally stepped away from him, dodging his every move. Cephia now turned around and faced Doctor Pei's now visibly horrified three assistants.

"Now let me tell you one more time, because there won't be another!" she said, glaring at them. "Put those boxes down, all together, and then leave. Now!"

Dr. Pei's three assistants, two men and one woman, looked at their agonizing boss, and then at the poised, glaring, archangel whose chest was rising up and down fast, indicating her growing impatience. They quickly and simultaneously put the suitcases down on the floor.

Boom! Another explosion went off. This one seemed to be closer, for the walls reverberated.

"Now, all of you, get out of here. Leave!" the archangel commanded, her voice stern and forceful.

There were about thirty people present in the laboratory, dressed in clinical protective gear of different colors, and now they dropped down whatever they had in their hands, and all ran for the exit, staying clear of the archangel as they rushed past her. In a matter of just seconds, the room was empty except for the agonizingly hysterical, crying Doctor Pei and the archangel herself.

Ignoring the loud screams for help from Doctor Pei, Cephia slowly approached the three suitcases that contained the world's deadliest virus strain. Never had the seventh dimension come so close to a self - destructive catastrophe of such epic proportion, for had the devil's plan been implemented, humanity would have crossed the lines beyond mass death and into self-induced near – extinction, taking the rest of this world's occupants with it! She placed the padfolio that contained the antidote master samples on top of one of the suitcases.

The three Doctor Pei's assistants, together with the rest of the laboratory staff, rushed through the hallway and entered the mess hall. They all stopped when they laid their eyes on the mess left behind by the archangel. They were immediately shocked, and horrified, by what they saw. A woman screamed loudly in fear, and a man wretched as he started gagging, and then started vomiting.

Captain Kakra was still in the mess room and when he saw them, he beckoned to them. "This way, follow me. I will get you out of here!"

Boom! Boom! Another wave of explosions was heard and felt. Everybody once again jumped and quickly followed Captain Kakra to the nearest exit out of the bloodied mess hall that was littered with dead bodies all over. All of them did except one, the woman, the only female assistant to the chief scientist. Her name was Imrana.

"We can't just leave him to die in there, alone and blind!" she verbally and loudly said to herself. "He may be paying the price for whatever his misdeeds are, but he still deserves better than that. I am going to go back into the laboratory to get him out of there! I don't care what that weird woman will say or do to me! Can someone please come with me to help get him out? I don't think I can do it by myself."

But every one of those thirty something people had already left the mess hall, following Captain Kakra.

Her heart beating fast, Imrana turned around and ran back into the same hallway she had just come out of. Never had she ran so fast in her life. But as she got close to the totally shattered laboratory she slowed down, and fearfully crouched down to peep into inside of the laboratory first before fully going in. What she saw next was completely astounding, shockingly mesmerizing, and spellbinding!

She saw Cephia, who was now standing close to the bundle of the stuff she had taken from the three of them and Doctor Pei, slowly raise her arms up above her head, and her face looking upwards in the same direction. Her lips were moving, but Imrana could not hear what the archangel was saying. Even then, a rising loud, grinding sound, much like that of moving thunder in the sky, was evolving inside the room and that, by itself, was enough to prevent her from hearing what was being said. As the ceiling lights dimmed out low, everything in the area began shaking, including the machines and other heavy items like the freezer units. The storage cabinets on the walls, where extra materials like chemicals and hand equipment are stored, all burst open, the contents falling to the floor and scattering everywhere. It was like a strong gust of air was tearing through the room with enormous force. Then the portable machines, the rolling trolleys, the fridges and other movable heavy stuff rose off the floor, remaining suspended up at least two feet off the floor! Imrana cowered down in fear as she clearly watched what was happening.

Then the room suddenly started feeling up with a spectacular array of small, brightly flashing little lights, much like hundreds of tiny fireflies, all in different colors, floating everywhere. These little lights then slowly converged on the archangel, completely covering her entire body. After a period of about sixty seconds, they floated off her body to reveal a translucent human form, with sparkling emerald green eyes with no pupils. The top of her head was surrounded by a bright, golden disk of light that illuminated the entire room around her. The human form itself was now also totally suspended in the air, off the floor, supported by two big golden wings that were flapping up and down in slow motion, much like a hoovering bird of prey. The archangel's arms started growing long, extending downwards like long fillers with hands until they touched small heap of Dr. Pei's deadly bundle.

The Archangel's face tilted downwards, and behold, straight beams of bright yellow light streamed out of her eyes, nostrils and open mouth, completely splashing on, and illuminating, the packages to the point where they were completely transparent and all their contents visible. Then a visible vapor started coming off and out of the entire bundle, like slow steam. As Imrana looked on, the bundle and the steamy vapor turned crimson red. The entire baggage started breaking up into tiny pieces, eventually turning into dusty, shredded materials until it all became powdery. The entire bundle of suitcases and the padfolio containing the deadly bacteria and the bottles of its antidote, now turned into a thick rotating ball of dusty red vapor as the streaming beams of concentrated yellow light continued to focus on it. Suddenly, a momentary flash of brighter, blinding light, happened! The spark of light was so bright that Imrana was inevitably forced to momentarily look away. It was also at this time that a rumbling heavy noise with heavy vibrations, which she felt through the floor under her feet, followed.

When she looked back again, the entire bundle was gone, and everything was back in place. Even the stuff that had fallen out of the wall cabinets and shelves was off the floor and back into the cabinets, doors closed. The heavier floor stuff like the small machines, fridges and freezers, trolleys, chairs or stools had all fallen back down in position. The grinding noised stopped, and so did the rumbling in the floor. The ceiling lights adjusted back to full, illuminating the room brightly again.

But the sparkling, translucent full human figure of the archangel remained, the giant wings still flapping as it floated around in the room and the hundreds of tiny flashing lights followed her every move. The beams of light coming out of the archangel's head were also gone.

The golden disc of light, or halo, on top of her head still remained, its illumination surpassing that of the room lights. The archangel then slowly, and gracefully, descended back down to the floor. Her wings folded like those of a nestling butterfly. Once her feet touched the floor, the spectacular, stunning figure with wings walked over to where Dr. Pei was crouched up in one corner of the room and stared down at him. He was drenched in sweat, his hair shiny with beads of perspiration. His lips were trembling uncontrollably, just like the rest of his body.

Finally gathering up courage, Imrana jumped out of her own corner from the side of the shattered entrance and rushed into the laboratory, confronting the golden winged archangel. "Stop! Please don't kill him... spare his life. Please. I know that he has messed up, that he was knowingly betraying humanity with his genius, yet evil doings! But he has already endured enough punishment, holy angel. I pray that's enough. I plead with you on his behalf. Please give him a second chance at life again," she said, going down to her knees before the archangel as she stared up at the touring figure, tears rolling down her eyes.

The fully evolved archangel slowly turned around, with a lot of ease, looked down at her briefly, and then her attention went back to the downed scientist. Imrana could feel the heat waves coming off the divine entity.

"Please, God… wherever you are… I pray, spare his life," she insisted, and reaching up, she placed her hands on the archangel's arm. But Imrana didn't know what she had really touched, because despite the fact that there was this bright yellow, gently flowing, silky clothing over and or around that part of the archangel's body, it felt like she was touching revolving air, and it felt so warm and good. Imrana let go and stared at her own hands in wonder. The tiny, bright colored, glowing particles were all over her hand. It was as if she had smeared herself with them. Then she did it again, this time her hands touched the archangel's leg, starting with her knee and sliding down to her foot.

And unlike the previous occurrence with the rough -acting guard, her hands did not burn after she touched the holy one!

The shiny, translucent archangel once again slowly turned her gaze away from the distressed scientist to look down at the human female who was on her knees before her, tears still rolling down her eyes. At the same time, Imrana looked up again and their eyes locked. It was a moment of immense and intense, everlasting impact on the human subject, for what Imrana saw in the archangel's face was beyond describing, beyond comprehension, so overwhelming, and forever mesmerizing deep down her to soul. It was the most magnificent apparition, a revelation that mirrored the beauty of humanity in its purest form, a face so undeniably saintly, and she felt this unworldly, pure of the purest innocence of a newly born off spring flowing down into her with this total sense or feeling of gladness, of overwhelming relief and joy. It was a gift of breathless, timeless wonder! She felt light, like she was floating in space or something, in an abyss full of warm sunshine. And even though she didn't know it, the ultimate weight of seven hundred and seventy-seven burdens of life, born and bred to the human soul at birth, had been lifted off, and out of, her humanity! And because of this, Imrana completely passed out, her body flopping down to the floor and remaining still. Yet she could hear the archangel talking. It was like an ongoing dream.

"Hmmm... you selflessly plead for another's life," the archangel whispered, a graceful smile coming over her face. "I can well see that you carry the unique emblem of near - perfect goodness, a selflessness and good will towards others that goes beyond your own fears of the unknown, the real reason why you so much remain unscorched when you touched me. I shall spare your friend's life, but I cannot restore his sight, for taking it away was a directive from God, the purest of the purest light itself. And that which is said or done by the most divine of the divine, the holy spirit in heaven, I myself cannot undo, until the light shines this man's way again."

Doctor Pei suddenly arose from his fetal position in one corner of the room, getting up to his knees. Even in his total blindness, he had clearly witnessed everything, including the archangel's transformations. At the same time, the archangel's big golden wings completely folded down behind her, and the hundreds of tiny, sparkling and glowing, multicolored lights engulfed themselves into one whole and then diminished into nothingness. The archangel's translucent body redeemed itself into its human form of the stunning female warrior, Cephia, in her unique garbs.

For the first time, and without really knowing how it came to him, Doctor Pei now fully realized what had really happened to him. He had just fully experienced an altercation with an almighty, divine agent. The fact that he was still alive meant that he had just been spared from heaven's wrath. Going on all fours, he bowed down before God's mighty right hand, Cephia the archangel.

But Cephia's attention was now focused on Imrana.

"Arise, good maiden of the Seventh dimension," Cephia said to the unresponsive woman on the floor before her. "From now on, peace will be with you, forever and ever. You will never be afraid of anything again, and all that you wish for will be granted."

Imrana opened her eyes. She looked up at Cephia and smiled. The archangel smiled back and offered her hand. Imrana took hold of the warm hand, which was now all human flesh, and she felt herself being effortlessly hoisted up like she was weightless.

"Thank you," she mumbled.

"Imrana, I am archangel Cephia, sent directly from heaven to deal with one of the deadliest evil undertakings in your world," the archangel said. "It is now over, erased forever using the maximum divine fire of all fires, to nothingness by me. And as for your request, I have spared your friend's life. Now arise, go take hold of his hand and help him up. And then I shall get both of you out of here."

Imrana did as she was told. She walked over to where Doctor Pei was still kneeling on his fours and lightly tapped his shoulder. "Dr. Pei, get up. I came back to get you. We are getting out of here," she said to him. She gently touched his right hand with her's.

Still looking fearful, and tearful, the blinded scientist linked his right hand to her's and hoisted himself up off the floor. Imrana looked at the archangel and nodded to her, signaling that she was ready.

Cephia raised her right hand up. The double headed short spear moved itself from her back and into her open hand again. Once it was in her grasp, Cephia mumbled some words and pointed it at the ceiling above. A lot of rambling followed and once again the entire structure shook. And then once again the unimaginable started happening quickly. As Imrana looked on, the ceiling above started separating, parting into separate sides, the heavy tiles that made up the castle roof sliding over each other until the entire ceiling split up like two separate walls to the left and to the right to reveal the dark - clouded sky outside. Even the greyish vapor of the heavy mist was visible as it flowed in from the outside through the big open gap in the ceiling. "Hold on tight to his hand and do not let go. I will keep hold of your other hand. We are taking a shortcut," she said to Imrana.

Imrana nodded in affirmation.

The archangel's golden wings suddenly unfolded and started flapping heavily. Their powerful "zoop, zoop, zoop" motion created a firm heavy air current in the surrounding environment around them and then with her hand still pointing the spear at the parted ceiling above, she rose, her feet leaving the floor, going upwards higher and higher, pulling the two humans with her. For Imrana, all she felt was the warm hand holding hers and her other hand locked around Doctor Pei's. Also, to her surprise, the scientist completely felt weightless in her grasp as they rose with the Archangel. For some reason, she didn't feel afraid at all and was even able to look down at her load, who appeared to be seemingly looking upwards. They continued rising, through the newly created gap in the ceiling, until they were completely out and above the castle.

And oh, what a view! Imrana was seeing fire, burning all around the big building, but which itself still looked intact. At a certain level up there, they appeared to go sideways, slightly away from the structure, and then they suddenly started descending, slowly and steadily. She could still hear the flapping of the heavy wings as the ground below became visible and then her feet finally touched it. Firmly on the ground, she released the scientist from her grasp but still held on to the archangel's.

But Cephia gently freed herself from Imrana's hold. All that Imrana felt was the warm hand fading out of her grasp, like warm air flowing through and over her hand. She looked around her. They were outside the walls of the castle, beyond the gates. But part of these walls had already crumbled to the ground, leaving the castle completely exposed to the outside. Even the big gates were, as Imrana could see from where she was several yards away, down. Their hinges had been blown off the walls poles they had been attached to.

"Did you do all this too? I mean, the destruction of the castle's protective wall?" she asked the archangel.

"No, that wasn't me. I have nothing to do with the walls, for they don't bother me," Cephia replied, her golden wings flapping up and down slowly. "The invading human force from a place in your world, called America, caused the destruction."

Colonel Carkenbo's bombs had done a lot of damage to the outside, while Cephia cleared up stuff in the inside, of the old castle.

"Wow! But where are they? Did they go inside?" Imrana asked.

"No. They too are out here with you, and when they come around, they will help you and your friend here," Cephia said to her. "I must leave you now, my dear. I am still finishing up with God's business. Now that you have directly touched my hand and remain intact, you have become part of me and can call upon me at any time in your life if you need help with anything, anywhere, at any time, Imrana. We're with you now forever."

"What about me? What's next for me? I am devasted because I can't see anymore," Dr. Pei said loudly. "At least give me back my sight, and I promise you I will never do that evil job again! I will only do good."

Cephia briefly stared at Dr. Pei but said nothing back to him.

Instead, she turned her attention back to Imrana.

"You mean you are now my guardian angel?" Imrana asked, now facing Cephia.

"Yes. I have taken over from your personal angel," Cephia said, "You are a very special person, Imrana. I am glad to have you under my coverage. So now goodbye, my friend. Make sure your friend gets back to his homeland. He will remain blind for the rest of his life as a punishment for knowingly doing the devil's work, for being the devil's right-hand tool. And like I said earlier, this punishment cannot be altered by anyone except God, through his most senior archangels."

And with that, the archangel Cephia turned around and walked a few yards away from them before flapping her wings faster and lifting off the ground, flying higher up until she was directly over the entire castle and its grounds. Visibility had gotten better as the heavy mist was now strangely fading away, and the afternoon sunrays were beginning to filter through. She remained suspended in the air, her great wings flapping gently, as she surveyed the situation below. A bright ray of sunshine came through the fast-dissipating dark clouds, illuminating her hovering figure brightly.

From a distance on the ground below, several yards away from where Imrana and Dr. Pei were, Colonel Carkenbo suddenly woke up from his unconsciousness. His entire body felt very sore, every major joint in his body hurting like hell. When he spotted commando Jiang on the ground a few yards away from him, he painfully got up from the ground and made his way to where she was. She, too, had finally managed to sit up, and just like the colonel, she was still grimacing with pain and felt very sore everywhere on her body. He slowly squatted down next to her. Together they were now trying to figure out what had happened when Commando Jiang saw Cephia in the air with her big golden wings flapping, hovering above the castle.

"See that up there?" commando Jiang quickly said to him, pointing at Cephia. "That's what hit all of us!"

Colonel Carkenbo looked up at the sky, his eyes squinting. "What the hell is that?" He asked.

"A winged, sort of… human, but one that is likely one hundred times superior to us in combat, and most likely everything else," commando Jiang replied. "She is the one who single handedly stopped us from going ahead with our mission at this point".

"Then I am going to shoot that bitch down!" The Colonel said, sounding furious. He spotted his submachinegun on the ground a few yards away and started getting up to get it. But commando Jiang grabbed at his arm and pulled him back down.

"Don't try to stop her again, boss, because you won't win. Just let it be!" Commando Jiang said to him. "She's an archangel from heaven above. She's been sent to deal with the same problem our mission was supposed to deal with. And I am sure she's already done with it."

"I don't give a damn what she is, Jiang. This was our mission to accomplish, and I will kill anyone, anything, that tries to interfere with it!" the colonel said "And I don't care what, at this moment, you believe in either. I am going after it, with or without you!"

"Godamned it, Colonel! look at me! Take a good look at me! Do you think I would be seating here on my ass like some stupid dummy, instead of doing the job?" Commando Jiang shouted back at him. "While you were all down, I envisioned myself doing it on my own, carrying forward with the mission, but she stopped me! She whooped my ass so bad I thought I was going to die! She actually spared our lives, colonel, but I have this feeling that she won't do so again if we go after her again. So, I am asking you, do you really want to die this time around, huh? Is that what you want? Because from what I witnessed, it's impossible to kill her, and fighting her is pure suicide! Don't you get it? She is the impossible itself! She knocked out the rest of our team, skilled combatants like me and you. You yourself shot her several times with that very gun you're trying to retrieve, and there she is, still alive!"

Commando Jiang shook her head, looked down at the ground between her legs, sighing heavily. When she looked up, Colonel Carkenbo was staring at her like she was crazy. She could tell he was still not totally convinced. Godamned you, colonel! We came here with the intention to hit and survive, not hit and get killed! So, she resumed with her rattling about the mighty archangel above them.

"Let me tell you exactly what happened to those bullets you pumped into her body," commando Jiang said. "She puked all of them out. I saw it happen myself. Other bullets simply popped out of her body and the entry wounds immediately closed! Those bullets are on the ground somewhere a few yards away from here, if you want to check me out. Then I sunk two stiletto knives into her sides, fuckin' organ piercers, using killer slicer blows, and I knew exactly what I was doing. Those blows could have and precisely killed any human being or other animal for that matter. But she simply pulled them out and then went on to attack me like nothing had happened. I can tell you this now colonel, I have never been beat up like that before! It was so bad I broke out in tears! She could have killed me, but she didn't. She simply told me to stand down! That tells me that it wasn't us she was after. She simply wanted us out of the way!"

"She still interfered with my mission and shall pay the price for it!" the Colonel insisted, adamantly. "We are not even sure that she's on the good side with us or what exactly her intentions are. As far as I am concerned that bacteria could still be in there being languished around by some crazy son of a bitch trying to mess up the world!"

"Am afraid she's right. The archangel is real, and you can't win with her. She's too mighty!" another voice close by said. "And as for the deadly bacteria strains, it's all gone, destroyed. I myself witnessed the destruction. She did it herself, the archangel!"

The two soldiers both quickly responded by turning around to see a woman in a soiled white laboratory over coat, supporting what looked like a worn out, dilapidated old man with one of her arms. She was pointing up with her other hand at the archangel who was still hovering above the castle grounds.

403

"And who the hell are you people?" Colonel Carkenbo asked immediately.

"This man here with me is Dr. Pei, the chief scientist who was in charge of the entire process of developing the deadly bacterial strain," the woman said. "And I am Imrana, one of his assistants. The archangel flew us out of the building using her mighty wings. You must be the Americans she was talking about. She said you are the cause of the explosions that inflicted the damage to the castle walls."

"Hmmm… so she already knew what we were planning to do, let us come over this far, and then stopped us from going any further!" Commando Jiang said.

"She stopped you because there was an evil being in the building so powerful that you were no match against it," Doctor Pei spoke out in a harsh, hoarse voice to emphasize his point. "The personality behind this whole thing was a very terrifying individual wearing an ugly, equally terrifying mask, and wielding such immense supernatural powers as never seen before. Just like with the archangel, you were no match for this individual, who already knew that you were coming and was looking forward to kill all of you! I repeat, no human being was a match for this possessed, evil entity. Only an individual of such powerful divine nature, like this Angel, could face and destroy this evil, which I now believe she did."

"Ok, but I still believe that your archangel should have sat back and let us take care of business for her," The colonel said. "Now I don't know what to say in my report. That this strange, winged human suddenly showed up and did the job for us? What proof do I have now to show that I have effectively accomplished the task I was assigned to do?"

"And you son of a bitch was part of this, huh? You were working for this so - called evil entity while you knew all along that it was the wrong thing, but did it anyway? You were planning to destroy our world, murder millions of people! I think I should end your life too, right now! I should send you to the same fate as your evil master!" commando Jiang said fiercely. She suddenly pulled a double-edged knife out of one of her side pockets and pointed it at Doctor Pei.

"No, no, please don't kill me. I can be your proof that this was indeed real, and that it's now over with!" Doctor Pei said. "I can testify to everything that was going on here. I recorded everything on a cloud file via a hidden camera in the laboratory, just as I always do with all my research and works. Everything that went on in that laboratory was being secretly recorded. I promise you that I will avail everything to you, whenever you need it, as testimony for the success of your mission. Just get me to a medical doctor. Please."

"And I stand in on his behalf, for he's already been punished for his wrong doing," Imrana said. "The archangel didn't end his life but blinded him for life. He no longer can see. It's all good now. No need for you to kill him."

"We are going to need him to testify, Jiang," Colonel Carkenbo agreed. "Let's go look for the others, and I hope they are ok. Maybe we can all get to go inside the castle and look around, get to see what damage this archangel individual has done!"

"Ok, I agree with you, boss. But you must also agree with me that we should let the archangel be," Commando Jiang said, slowly putting the big knife back into its original place. "I am sorry I got carried away by the moment. The others shouldn't be far away from here. Let's go look for them now."

But they didn't have to go look for the others. One by one the other team members started showing up, and they all had one thing in common to say. That someone, or something, so strong and powerful had attacked them from nowhere and knocked them out. They had no clue of who or what it was.

"That's who attacked and knocked you out," Commando Jiang said, pointing with her hand again at the archangel, who was still hovering in the air space above the castle, her big golden wings magnificently shiny amidst the misty grey environment and the single beam of sunlight that streamed upon her from above. "Did the same thing to me and colonel. She prevented all of us from going in and doing our job. She also said her actions would save us from getting killed."

Every one of the commandos stood transfixed as they stared up at the striking, humanlike figure, with her big golden wings flapping up and down gently, several yards away and above their heads in the air. It was hard to believe at first, for no one had ever seen anything this, nor dreamt of seeing such stuff. They were all speechless.

405

The archangel suddenly started descending. They saw her gently land in front of the mixed, visibly mesmerized crowd of workers who had just fled out of the castle. Her big wings still rose up and down gently as she faced them. A few tried to run back into the castle. One of those who tried to get away was the guard with the scotched hands. Some guards started raising their guns, but captain Kakra waved them down.

"Come on guys. Let's all go into the castle and find out what this is all about," Colonel Carkenbo said, breaking the silence, and then turning around to look at Imrana and Doctor Pei. "You two remain here and wait for us, since you have already had close encounters with the Angel. You will travel with us so that you can testify about this event. We will help you get off the Island too."

"Yes sir, as you wish," Imrana answered, sounding relieved. She let go of Doctor Pei and slowly sat down on the ground. "We shall be right here when you come back." Doctor Pei followed her response by flopping down to the ground right next to her.

The short, automated bridge over the deep moat had been lowered down and they were able to cross over the water and on to the castle's big front yard in front of its entrance, where the transfixed crowd was.

As Colonel Carkenbo and his team entered the castle grounds and approached Cephia, her head slowly turned to look at them. Once again it went all the way round in a complete circle, coming back to face the crowd, and everyone clearly saw that. Upon seeing that, some of the men on the Colonel's team stopped walking. But the colonel and commando Jiang continued walking towards her. A few yards away from her, they stopped.

Captain Kakra suddenly went down to one knee before the archangel, bowing his head down. Without hesitating, the rest of the individuals in the crowd did the same. Colonel Carkenbo and commando Jiang looked at each other briefly, and then they both went down on their knee, bowing their heads down like everyone else. The rest of the team also did the same thing.

Cephia's wings stopped flapping and slowly folded back behind her as she finally spoke.

406

"Your job is done here. It's time for you to go back to your homes and rejoice in the glory of God above," she said, her voice coming out in multiple echoes. To her audience, it sounded like her voice was coming to them from all around. It was like a very clear, well balanced multiple speaker system. "Arise now, children of man. There is nothing left to fear anymore."

"What, or who, exactly are you?" someone from the crowd asked loudly, but fearfully, as everyone stood up again. It was the guard with the scotched hands. Someone had helped wrap up both hands in clean bandages from an emergency kit.

"I am archangel Cephia, created out of Archangel Gabriel by the almighty God, the holy of the holiest, and the forever shining light. The ones in heaven call me Gabriel's little sister," The archangel replied. "I was dispatched directly from heaven to stop, and completely destroy, the evil that was about to bring and cause unimaginable suffering and death to your world as you know it. I have also been tasked to deliver a message from God above to mankind, starting with you here today, and it is simple message. That God still loves you and will not let humanity perish this way. But mankind must first turn back to God and redeem your trust from heaven. It doesn't matter where you hail from, or what you look like, who you're, or what you believe in or do. You are all one and the same in the eyes of God. You're all God's creations, God's children, subject to God's ways, God's rules. No exceptions. Because everyone of you here, and anywhere else in this world, I can only confirm this to you, that just as you're born, so will you die. Some sooner than others, but you will face the same fate, no exceptions. So, it's now time for you to go back to your homes with this message deep down in your hearts, in your souls, for today you have been saved to receive it. Go start a new life in which you give thanks to God every day. But most important of all, repeat the message to your people, to everyone you see, everyone who can hear you."

"You're sending us home, but we have not even been paid our last wages," someone else said. "How are supposed to start this life you are talking about?"

"You have all already been well remunerated," The archangel responded back. "It's all in your bags, pockets or satchels. So, I say to you again, go back to your homes and remember the goodness of God every day of your life, and repeat the message given to you today."

As most of the crowd quickly searched deep into their pockets and bags, and to their total surprise, and delight, they found bundles of international currency money in their grasp. The excitement grew louder as their delight was verbalized.

Everyone in the crowd appeared to be delighted, except, of course, Colonel Carkenbo and his team. Making his way around the crowd and to the front where he could face the archangel directly, with his team following behind him, the colonel got ready to voice his discontent.

He paused for a moment to take in the full view, up-close, of the entity before him. She was stunningly beautiful, well built, and had that aura of purity around her, like someone who instantly commands a following. But she was obviously not of this world. The stuff on her body, the emerald-green eyes with the bright yellow twinkles, and of course the big golden wings clearly denoted that. There was also that faintly glowing ring of yellow light around the top of her head. Every time she said something, the ring glowed brighter. When she stopped talking, the ring faded into a faint glow again.

"So why did you stop us from going into the castle to destroy this evil?" Colonel Carkenbo asked, raising his voice. "We had it all planned out, we were well armed, capable, and ready."

"First of all, your human response was not fully united, as those elsewhere amongst you had already collaborated with the devil, making him aware of your mission and the intention to destroy his interests," the archangel replied. This time, her entire self-turned around to face the human fighter team. "And so, the devil already knew that you were coming. The devil, due to his supernatural powers, had already sensed your presence on the island by the time you made your way to the castle, knew when you and was simply waiting for you to come into his claimed house and then kill you. Although the devil's incarnate had enhanced powers to know all this, you also been betrayed by your kind. You cannot win the battle with the devil if any amongst you is in line with him. You must all unite as one to fight the common enemy. But even given all the human faults, it is a fact that this enemy was too strong for you and your friends to destroy, and you were all bound to perish. I had to come in and stop you from being completely destroyed by the devil, not the other way around."

"But we were to do what it takes to do the job, even if it meant dying while trying," Commando Jiang added. "Instead of stopping us, why didn't you just simply join our team to help destroy this enemy? You just told us that only if we are united as one shall we be able to overpower the evil. You instead chose to stop us and go in solo, which underscores your point."

The archangel smiled as she stared straight at commando Jiang, and then replied. "I am not one of you, earthly warrior, so my ways are different from yours. God's ways are different from the human ways, so they cannot interact. And so, because I am of God in heaven, I can't unite with you in a joint effort. At least not directly. I can only help you in ways unknown to you, and that's also with by order from heaven. And with this particular case in point, there was no way that could happen. This was a timed war for heaven to fulfil."

"But still you should have let us try," another member of the team said. "Like she just told you, we were ready to die trying."

Now the smile disappeared from Cephia's face and was replaced by a grim look. "Let me put this way, earthly warriors. It simply wasn't your time to die. Not at this time, per God's orders. Each life here has a beginning, a destiny and or perhaps a purpose, and then an end. We in heaven determine that. And so, I say to you now, even though it could have happened, we decided this wasn't the day or time. Because the devil was involved, we decided to fight your battle for you, instead of you becoming collateral damage, because, indeed, this was a matter between heaven and Satan. So, I took over your guardian angels' jobs so guarantee your calendars don't end on this day. Without my intervention, the devil would have easily claimed your souls today using the evil inside the castle, the one that I have just destroyed. So, it all ends here. After all, isn't it better for you to be able to go back home and claim victory over the devil while you are alive?"

Before the team could respond again, a man hastily made his way through the excited crowd until he reached where captain Kakra stood, who himself looked amazed at the apparent good fortunes of his workers. He himself had no clue how all that money had gotten into these people's pockets. The man, in a guard's uniform, handed him a set of keys, saluted, and then stepped back into the crowd. The captain stared at the bunch of keys in his hands, all attached to on metal ring. He knew what they were but had not seen them in a long time. When Major Haraabi left, the main keys to the castle seemed to have vanished with him. Now how in the world did they suddenly show up? He looked up to again to see the person who had delivered the, but the individual had already immersed himself into the crowd. It was then that he heard the voice in his head, gentle and very clear.

"Bring those keys to me, captain, so that I can return deliver them to the rightful owners of this castle," The voice said. "The castle must be returned back to its rightful owners, and that will happen tonight."

Captain Kakra slowly turned around and stared at the archangel, who stood several yards away from where he was. Cephia smiled, slowly nodded her head at him and then stretched out her open right in his direction.

"Of course," the captain acknowledged rather loudly. He slowly made his way through the crowd to where Cephia stood and as he placed the bundle of keys in her open hand, he reached over and kissed it. He again went down on one knee. "Thank you for sparing my life today, for giving me a second chance." After saying that, he got up and rejoined himself to the crowd of workers.

Cephia nodded briefly at him, taking possession of the keys without saying a word. She now stood between the crowd and the world's joint, elite, military force.

"I must leave you all now," Cephia said to the crowd in a loud and clear voice, raising her face again to face them. "Remember the almighty God in heaven all the time. He's alive. You're never, ever, alone. We will always be there to protect you whenever necessary."

Before anyone else could respond to her imminently declared departure, Cephia's big, glowing golden wings suddenly spread out, like a startup umbrella canopy. Once again, the crowd stood back in awe as the magnificent figure rose before them, flapping her wings majestically. The archangel hovered above the crowd for at least two full minutes, looking down at them with a smile on her face, her golden teeth gleaming in the sun. It was like she was checking on them for the very last time to make sure they were okay, and then her wings flapped faster, and she flew backwards and further up in the air. When she could only see them in minute form, Cephia turned around and flew away, disappearing into the clouds. As for the crowd below, every individual remained looking up at the sky until her figure was no longer visible. Then the crowd started breaking apart, everyone headed for the gates, everybody talking loudly.

Captain Kakra walked over to where Colonel Carkenbo and his team stood as they started planning their next movement.

"You must be the American team," he said, offering his hand. He quickly withdrew it when the colonel didn't offer his back but instead stared at him with an angry mean look. "I am Captain Kakra, and until now I was in charge of the castle's entire security. She told you the truth, the archangel. The horrifying masked devil was ready for you and was going to kill all of you. You were no match for this thing, guys, for I saw what happened in there, firsthand, and boy, it was unbelievable, unprecedented, never seen anything like that in my entire life. The warrying factions were not of this world, their actions absolutely intense, powerful and very deadly!"

"And you were part of this whole thing, an operation that was about to destroy this world? You were protecting it, letting it happen! And now you have the audacity to talk to me?" Colonel Carkenbo responded back to him menacingly. "Do me a favor, captain whatever. Stay out of my way and my sight! That way I won't be forced to shoot you!"

"Hey, man, no need for all that hostility. You heard the archangel, she said this war was over," Captain Kakra said standing back. "You must understand that I only worked here, just like everybody else. Just like you, we were here to simply make some money and then go home. We absolutely had nothing to do with the devil's plans or intentions. And now we are glad we came out alive. Some did not make it!"

"Hey, you heard the man, he doesn't want to see you or talk to you. So, get lost, will ya?" one of the team members, commando Phillip Bhekumbuso from South Africa stepped in, giving the captain a grim look. "Like Michael Jackson said in his song, just beat it! Now! End of story!"

411

"Okay, okay, guys. Was just being friendly, maybe give you a fill of the events that transpired in there," Captain Kakra said quickly as he backed away from the commando group. The commando had his hand on a revolver on his hip, like he was about to pull it out and shoot him. "But ok, you guys have a good life, then!"

And with that, Captain Kakra walked away, shaking his bruised head repeatedly, surprised by the unwelcoming response from "the Americans". Time to go home, he told himself. He had a backpack on his back full of money from only God knows where, so no worries.

He joined a group of men and women on the far right and together they made their way off the castle grounds, joining with the rest of the crowd. Everyone was moving in the same direction. Towards the coastal front.

Colonel Carkenbo and his team pulled out their satellite enabled phones and started arranging for evacuation.

The old man in the village had just finished taking his evening bath inside his small, walled – off, private outside bathing area, and was back into his small, one - room brick house, lighting up a kerosene lantern. He was in the action of rolling out his mat for evening prayers which he did every day, morning and before going to bed, when there was a knock at his door. As the village's paramount elder, his house was always open for everyone, at any time, young or old, and he never locked the door.

"Do come in," he announced, as he sat down in his high - backed rocking chair behind a wooden table with three chairs in front of it.

The door opened, slowly, and then Cephia walked in. A gush of fresh air with a rose petal scent followed her, rolling through the one room house in a whirring fashion. The joint lighting from the old man's kerosene lantern extinguished itself completely. But there was no darkness in the room at all, for the archangel had a very bright light coming off her body and it completely illuminated the entire room brightly. From the outside, one would think an electric fluorescent light was on inside the old man's room. Just like the other village members, the old man never ever used electricity. And he didn't want it either. He was stuck in his old world.

412

The old man's eyes widened in shock, and he quickly scrambled to get to his knees, knocking over the small table in the middle of the room that had some personal items on top of it that included a couple of metallic tea mugs and food plates, and a small handheld shortwave radio. He himself almost fell forward face down.

But Cephia quickly reached over and gently took hold of his arm, settling him back in his chair. "Arise, old man. You don't have to kneel down before me, for your soul is already sacred enough to be exempt from that. You're already a saint attached to the spirit of a people, your people, a nation. And besides, you are too tired to do so."

After she had settled him back into his chair, Cephia then raised her right hand, palm down, and as she did so, the small table reset itself upwards, and so did everything that had fallen off it, the items neatly rearranging themselves back on top of it. Cephia glanced at one of the three wooden chairs, and it moved towards her by itself until she sat down in it. The old man still didn't say anything. The archangel's sudden reappearance right into his house had completely terrified him into silence.

"I have brought you back the keys to the castle. It's back in your hands now and we will make sure nobody takes it away from you and your people again," Cephia told him, her face glowing in the light. The keys were latched to her left wrist. She took them off with her right hand and placed them on the table in front of him. "I shall also make sure that by the time you get to it, any traces or residue of the evil that had been occupying it will have been erased completely. Just stay away from the castle area for the next two nights. No one must even go near it. The full regal rights of your traditional heritage will also be fully restored. My job is done here. But before I leave, is there anything you want to ask of me? Perhaps something I can do to help relieve the burden of maintaining your people?"

The old man blinked, his thick gray eyebrows rising up and down slowly above his eyes. He breathed in and out heavily, and when he spoke, his voice was hoarse and grave, like someone who is very tired.

"Take me home with you. One hundred and fifty-one years is enough for me. I can't do it anymore. I am tired and burned out. I want to rest," he said. "After all, I have lived to witness what I have been praying for,

413

and that is the promise by heaven to return our freedom and heritage to us, the Turikai. But I didn't expect to be faced to face with an archangel from heaven! It's like seeing God himself, which is terrifying. I don't need anything more from this world. So that's why I am asking you to take me with you back to heaven or wherever it's peaceful."

"Ok, old man. It's a fair request, one that I will present to heaven when I report back before God, for consideration," Cephia replied. "But I cannot take you with me right now because I am not quite done yet with my mission here. Also, I am not a soul carrier. That is the job for another Archangel, together with your guardian angel who, by the way, will need to be reassigned first to another saint before you're released. But I promise you, I will deliver a first-class report on your request and heaven will respond to it soon and accordingly. It won't be long, I promise."

"Thank you. I will remain patient, I will wait," the old man said, bowing his head down slowly and inevitably closing his eyes. "And thank you for coming down to save us."

The old man slowly raised his head up and opened his eyes.

There was no bright light in the room anymore, and the archangel was gone. The lantern in the room had lit itself up again, giving him the usual normal light. The fresh smell of roses was still there, further proving that this wasn't just a dream. Even the chair in which she had sat was still in the same position that she had placed it and sat in it. Everything else still looked the same. The door didn't even open or close. But still, the old man slowly blinked several times and then shook his head. He was beginning to seriously doubt himself. He was thinking that his super old age was beginning to play mind games on him. But as he was about to get to his knees to proceed with his final prayer of the day, he saw something else on top of the table and blinked again. He looked closely again at the small table in front of him. That something else was the set of keys to the castle that the Archangel had brought to him. They were still in the exact spot where she had placed them. He put his hand on them. They were real, metal keys and they felt strangely warm. So, it is true. The mighty looking, beautiful archangel was really here. It wasn't just an effigy of his imagination!

Trembling uncontrollably, the old man slowly went down to his knees to pray.

Elsewhere in the island country, an anxious president Piajohnney Moongoo stayed back in his office much later that evening, seated in the comfortable, all leather, presidential, executive chair behind the big, glass topped, executive presidential desk with everything neatly arranged. Usually, he would be surrounded by his advisors who would be helping him grapple with the day's issues concerning governing the country or dealing with social – economic and local political instabilities or meeting foreign dignitaries who preferred to meet with him after his local affairs had been settled. But today he specifically preferred to be left alone and had instructed his personal executive secretary to cancel or suspend all activities on his official calendar. And this was because the concern at hand was rather a personal one.

He was specifically concerned about his dealings with the personality everyone referred to as The Principal, the somewhat terrifying masked figure behind his newest business endeavor, or adventure, as he liked calling it. For the first time in his life, though, he felt that he had no control whatsoever in what he was involved in, and he didn't like that feeling at all. He liked being in control, to have a say in the direction of things, that way he's able to monitor the progress of his business dealings. But for some unknown reason, this was different. He had no clue of what was happening or what was going to happen next. He was completely shut out of the entire process. He also didn't like the feeling that he felt somewhat scared of the masked figure. He had only met the individual three times, the last one being just a few hours ago, but he had to admit to himself that these meetings weren't easy time, for there was something eerie about this individual with that terrifying mask that he deemed devilish. And ever since he had started dealing with the masked Principal, a strange feeling of unease had taken over, prevailing and causing him to become restless and insomniac at night. He even had nightmares over the cryptic personality.

At the urging of his wife, who duly witnessed his new onset of frantic nightmare episodes which disturbed her own rest time and therefore caused alarm and concern, he had sought out advise from his personal physician, something he rarely did. The physician had run a battery of tests on him, found nothing negatively profound with his health, and recommended that the President take a break from the daily demands of his Presidential duties for at least a couple of weeks. Go on vacation somewhere outside the country, perhaps. Put his mind to rest for a moment. He was now pondering that advise, although he knew very well that the real problem behind these nightmares wasn't exhaustion.

But his real concern now was why he had not heard from the masked Principal yet. He was supposed to have gotten feedback by now from the devilish Principal. President Moongoo also really wanted this whole thing wrapped up and over with. He wanted the mysterious figure out of his head, out of his country. But he was also still very interested, though, in knowing the outcome of the deal, as the concept behind the project predicted huge profit margins for himself and others who had invested in it. But now, and again for some unknown reason, he couldn't help feeling that something wasn't right now about the mysterious figure and the business deal.

There were three special telephone sets on his desk, each one with a specific purpose. A red set for dangerous situations in the country and which required his immediate attention, a blue set for his security detail, and a green set for interoffice communication, manned by his executive personal secretary. He also had two cellphones, one for his personal business and the other for communication with his wife and family, and both were also on the table in front of him.

There was a gentle knock at the door, which woke him up from his deep thoughts. During these late hours, the only person who came to his office, mostly for what he termed personal visits, was his executive personal secretary, Mamilla, and she always announced herself at the door with a gentle knock. She was also the only person, apart from his immediate family, that was allowed in without due notice by his tight security team. Even his security chief always called him on the blue phone first before coming in, and mostly to check on him.

"Come in, my dear," he responded to the knock, sitting up and straightening himself.

The door opened and the gentle knocker walked in.

But it wasn't personal secretary Mamilla. Instead, it was a young oriental man, likely in his twenties, tall and muscular, with no facial hair except for neatly trimmed eyebrows, and completely bold headed. But the most striking or notable feature about the new entry was that he was completely clad in an orange, Theravada monk costume, and wore open sandals instead of shoes, something that was rarely seen inside this office, or even outside the official presidential building.

Despite his unique, yet simple appeal, the man immediately presented an aura of elegance around him.

The monk man quietly closed the door behind him and then looked around him. His eyes focused on a straight-backed chair, about two meters away, that was centered right in front of the Presidential table. It was the chair used by personal secretary Mamilla when taking dictation from the President. The Monk sat down in it, directly facing the President. Despite the smile on the monk's face, President Piajohnney Mocngo's first reaction was to reach for the blue phone.

"I am afraid that won't be necessary, Mr. President," the monk said in clear, crisp English. The President himself was a Cambridge graduate.

"You don't walk in here and tell me what to do, aah!" the President stated in a menacing voice. He picked up the receiver and listened. There was no dialing tone from it. There was an extra red button on the set that allowed him to initiate an automatic emergency call without using the receiver. He only had to push it once to jumpstart the security detail's immediate, tactical convergence to his office. He jabbed it several times with one of his fingers, and then sat back and stared at the monk man before him.

"That won't work either, Mr. President. And besides, even if it was to work, by the time your security detail arrived I would be done and gone," the monk man said calmly.

"Who the hell are you and how did you get in here?" the President asked, staring angrily at the monk. "No one comes into this office to see me without prior notification or authorization by me or my team. It's called protocol! My security should have alerted me about it in the first place, then my secretary. Basing on all that, and as far as I am concerned, there was no inclusion of a monk visit on my program today. Besides, it's too late in the evening and I had personally ordered that all official programs for this evening be put on hold. I needed some private, personal time and you're now encroaching on it!"

417

"I already know all about your protocol and how your security works," the monk man said. "I also know that you ordered cancellation of all official and non-official activity off your Presidential agenda, this evening, which is why I chose this time to come and meet with you. Neither your security detail nor your secretary knows about this meeting, and did not even see me coming in. My visit is meant to be a private event with only you in attendance, President Moongoo."

"So, in this case you chose the wrong time, monk man," the President retorted. "If you truly know about me and my presidential protocol, and I don't understand how, then you should have known, too, that my private time means exactly that - my private time! It excludes everybody, and so you're not supposed to be here now!"

"Everybody except your dear personal secretary, huh? Noted!" the monk man said. "But no worries, she will be here as planned. I am the one who deliberately delayed her attendance this evening. I wanted talk to you first, get it out of the way. Just like you, I am a very busy individual, but my commencement here is deemed a high priority and had to happen today, at this time."

"Frankly speaking, I am not understanding what this is all about or what's really going on, but ok. Now, what can I do for you, monk? Or should I simply ask, what do you want?" the President asked, sitting forward in his chair, arms resting on the desk, and staring straight into the smiling, bespectacled monk's eyes.

"My name is Zeal, and I want to talk to you about your deal with the devil, Mr. President," the Monk man said.

"I am sorry, but I am not sure if I am understanding or hearing you right. Did you just say "my" deal with the devil?" the President asked, looking clearly confused. "What deal? And what devil?"

"The deal you finalized late this morning with the masked devil, to be specific," the monk replied. "You intended to, and almost made it possible, for the devil's plan to happen by authorizing the use of this land to facilitate and or accommodate the devil's incredibly evil intentions. And for what reason, President Piajohnney Moongoo? Greed! You still want more, right? But we know that God has blessed you with everything that any human being could possibly dream of. You name it, you have it. The problem here is that you did not stop to

418

think about the consequences resulting from your actions, that millions of lives will be destroyed, lost forever. The least you would have done, perhaps in gratitude for what God has blessed you with, is to totally abstain from participating in the devil's plan, and from doing what is clearly wrong."

"Why is everyone all of a sudden so concerned about my interests in this?" the President responded in differently. "I saw a good deal and responded to it like any other seasoned businessman. It's just business as usual for me. Where do you hail from anyway, and how come you know so much about my deal and conversation with the masked fella, hmmm? Are you part of it too? did he send you to come talk to me about it? I have been waiting to hear from him all this time personally and instead he sends me an emissary of some sorts, who's disguised as a monk. Listen, go back and tell him it doesn't work like that with me. I need to hear from him first-hand, and fast. I need to know about our deal."

Zeal the monk now slightly leaned forward. He was still smiling. "Yes, I am part of it too, but in a different way," he replied to the president. "First, I am not the devil's emissary, but I am a real monk. Second, I am not part of your so-called business deal. I am very much on the opposite side of that. Unlike you, I am part of a team that is here to save life, not destroy it. Third, unlike you, I am not in it for gain, but to restore God's righteousness. Forth, and most important of all, I am both heaven sent, and heaven bound. Hence, I am here to deliver a verdict from heaven, to tell you that you were wrong and will be punished for not using God's blessings to you to help others. You have betrayed God's trust.

"And you think I will buy into all that heaven telltale, huh?" retorted President Piajohnney Moongoo, shrugging his shoulders impatiently. "I don't even believe there is God anymore. It's all about money these days, my friend. Show me the money, and I will worship you! But now you Listen to me carefully. I am still the President of this sovereign country, and you don't just get to walk into my office, unauthorized, and threaten me. First, you're not even a citizen of this country, so I don't have to sit here and listen to you. Instead, I can have you arrested and imprisoned, if not shot, immediately! Secondly, stop meddling in my personal business or I will have you extradited to your country so fast your embassy won't even have a sniff of your orange attire! Thirdly, so what if I did wrong? In that case it's between me and my maker, not some mysterious earthly monk. So, get out of my office right now, don't look back, and don't ever come back. Tomorrow I will launch an investigation to find out who let you in here. Now go! I have bigger things to stress about, like that mysterious thing violating my country's airspace."

"I wish it was that simple, Mr. President," Monk Zeal said, his face now turning grim. "Remember, every business comes with a risk, and you have risked it all, president Piajohnney Moongoo. The verdict has already been rendered and will be immediately effective when I get up from this chair."

The monk then closed his eyes and bowed down his head until his chin touched his chest. His legs joined together, and his arms folded in front of his abdomen.

Even as he said those last words, Zeal the monk was already rising up from the chair. But for President Piajohnney Moongoo, the monk's movement was rather confusing. From his point of view, it seemed like he was experiencing double vision, because he could see the monk getting up from the chair, yet the same monk was still seated down in that same chair. The seated monk seemed to be projecting himself forward like an image bursting out of a straight beam of light and coming towards him. President Piajohnney Moongoo tried to move out of the way, only to realize that he can't move, that he was transfixed. Then he suddenly felt, and then saw, himself coming out of his own body, which remained in the Presidential chair. It was all very terrifying, and as he looked on, the projected monk reached out with his now stretched out right hand and his open palm touched his Projected self's head. There was a flash of light, and then President Piajohnney Moongoo's projected body was thrust back into his physical body in the Presidential chair and with such force that the heavy leather chair tilted backwards but then slammed back into position with him in it.

His body suddenly experienced a massive shiver, and then went cold. Yet he could still see what was happening in front of him. He just couldn't talk or move. He was able to see the projected monk return to

420

his own physical body in the chair behind him. He then saw the monk slowly stand up and look down at him.

"It is done. Piajohnney Moongoo, you have now lost it all," He heard the monk say.

"What did you do to me, you son of a bitch?" the president shouted out. But it was all in his mind. He couldn't open his mouth or move any part of him anymore.

The monk simply smiled back at him, because he could hear every thought inside the President's mind. He then walked out of the room, closing the door quietly behind him.

On his way out, through the fully illuminated, wall to wall carpeted hallway that led to and from the President's office, Zeal bypassed the President's elegant, immaculately dressed, heavily perfumed, long legged, hip–swinging executive personal secretary, the very pretty and or beautiful Mamilla. She was on her way to the personal visit. At this time, Zeal the monk had closed himself off again from other eyes as he didn't want to arouse unnecessary commotion that would be sorely based on just his outlook. An elevator opened and two men in suits and holding folders came out. He walked into it, and once the elevator doors closed again, he immediately transformed back into physical form, now visible to human eyes. And oh yes, he could hear the high-pitched scream that came out of the President's executive office after Mamilla entered it. On the ground floor, the monk walked out of the elevator, bowing to everyone around in greeting, and then to the outside where a gleaming, chauffeured red Jaguar sedan was waiting for him. He got in, closed the door, and the vehicle drove away.

It was all over the news platforms the next day, nationwide and internationally. Breaking news: President Piajohnney Moongoo of the Turikai Republic had suffered a massive stroke while working late in his office. He was rushed to the hospital where it was determined, after a thorough evaluation, that not only would he never be able to function on his own, but that he will also never be able to talk again. In a much tearful, brief speech, and flanked by all her children and grandchildren, the first lady Lala Moongoo mentioned that the President had lately been working so hard for the country and appeared very stressed. She mentioned that her husband's personal physician had even recommended that the President take a break from his job, perhaps take a small vacation, but the President refused to heed to the advice, saying his nation came first before any vacation. She conferred that the President was extremely concerned about the recent incident in the sky.

His Vice President, who's also the current king of the indigenous Turikai people, had already been sworn in as the new president, per the constitution, after it was determined that president Moongoo was no longer able to lead the nation, and to stay in office for the next five years to finish up his predecessor's reelection years. New elections were to be held then. The new president made a few sweeping changes in his first days in office, and one of them was to restore the full rights of the indigenous Turikai people, and to start development in those areas outside the capital city where his people mainly held root, something that his predecessors had greatly ignored.

And so came true the promise made to the old man by an archangel from heaven. All that had been taken from the indigenous people of the Turikai nation was now returned to them.

# Chapter Eleven

*T*he Vonsberg family could hardly go back to sleep after their overnight encounter with the angels and the bad people, and when they did finally go to sleep, they woke up much later in the afternoon the next day. The nonstop ringing of the doorbell was what woke up Bernhardt Vonsberg, who was asleep in a nearby, ground floor guest room with his wife Myra. It was also when he realized that it was three o'clock in the afternoon.

It was the county sheriff and his deputy.

"Howdy neighbor, I am sheriff John Mccrally and this is my deputy Vickie O'Callaghan," the sheriff introduced himself. "Your gates are wide open, so we let ourselves onto your property. Sorry about that."

"Sheriff, deputy O'Callaghan," Bernhardt Vonsberg finally acknowledged after a brief hesitation. He barely knew these people because the Vonsbergs only occasionally stayed at this house for a few days mostly during the fall season. "I don't think that matters anymore. We feel safe here. And also… you're the police. What can I do for you?"

"Say, folks out there in the neighborhood reported to us early this morning that there were some pretty heavy, loud, and fiery explosions around here that lasted for at least over thirty minutes," The Sheriff said. "Them folks seem to think it all came off this property. So, we're here to investigate. Initially we see nothing out here, not even a tale -tell sign anywhere, of what could have been a gun or explosives site.

But if you don't mind, I and my deputy here are going to look around more on your property, just to make sure everything is alright."

"I am not aware of anything like that happening on my property, but, sure, go ahead, Sheriff . Just let me know if you find anything," Bernhardt Vonsberg found himself saying, this time without any hesitation.

"Thank you, partner. We won't take long", the sheriff said, and then they both walked away. Bernhardt Vonsberg's heart started beating faster as he stepped out of the house and onto the front balcony. What he saw was rather very astonishing to him.

The entire front compound was completely clean and back to it's normal. All outdoor structures were completely up and restored, all plants, like the short trees lining the driveway were upright, the flower beds looking undisturbed and normal, all light poles that had been otherwise damaged were all straight up. Lastly, there was no evidence of any human remains or other debris that had been the result of terrifying scuffle between the angels and the bad people. The big suburban vehicle, just like the rest of the remains of the bad people's destroyed vehicles, and the only object that seemed to have survived the angels' destruction, was also gone. In fact, compared to when they had arrived the previous day at the property, the compound even looked cleaner.

Bernhardt Vonsberg shook his head in wonder and stepped back into the house, leaving the door open. Maybe it was in his head, all this that happened. He clearly needed to wake up then, if that was the case. He walked over to the coffee maker in the kitchen, made himself a cup of black coffee, and then sat down in one of the chairs and waited for period of about fifteen minutes as he sipped on it. There was a knock at the door. The Sheriff and his deputy were back. He got up and went to the door.

"Absolutely nothin' out there, partner," the sheriff said, sounding disappointed. "Everything looks good and in place. By the way, that coffee does sure smell good. What is it, Colombian? Oh dammit! We sure do apologize for disturbing your peace this afternoon, aah, Mr."

"Ethiopian mountain coffee. Would you like me to make you a cup? It won't take but a few minutes to brew," Bernhardt Vonsberg offered.

"One more thing, if you don't mind me asking. You're here alone or you have other people on board?" deputy sheriff O'Callaghan asked.

"I am here with my family. They're all in there, sleeping. We had a long night up, watching movies," Bernhardt Vonsberg replied.

"Can I take a quick look around inside your house, make sure everyone is alright?" the deputy sheriff asked. "Or do you want us to come back with a warrant to do that? Sorry, but we here at county do things a little bit differently, and we conduct thorough investigations, meaning we leave no stone unturned. It's all in the name of safety for our community."

"No, you don't have to go get a warrant. I don't have anything to hide," Bernhardt Vonsberg said with a faint smile on his face. He stepped aside to let the deputy in. "Please come right in and do whatever you have to do."

"Thank you, sir," Deputy O'Callaghan said, and then with her hand close to her holstered gun, she walked in and started her look around. It took her about ten minutes to check out the big house's interior, including upstairs, careful not to wake up anybody, and of course she found nothing suspicious. Bernhardt understood, though. It was just that real, good old fashioned, Texas law enforcement. They always conduct their business professionally and seriously. "Don't mess with Texas", as it's all well-known all over the lone - star state!

"All clear," the deputy sheriff reported back after her checkup. "Thank you so much for your cooperation, sir."

Bernhardt nodded in affirmation. "Coffee, guys?"

"Nah, we galla get going, but thanks. And if you hear anything about these disturbances, say when you or any member of your family is out and about, don't hesitate to let us know," the deputy sheriff, who looked much younger than her old boss, said. "A long serving state trooper was also brutally murdered last night while on duty not so far away from here. A man hunt for his killers is currently on going in all areas within three hundred miles radius of the highway. We're advising that you stay cautious of your environment and stay safe, sir."

"That's damn right. Now you have yourself a great day, will ya, Mr.," the sheriff said, and together they made their way back to their police cruiser, got into it, and drove away. Bernhardt Vonsberg sighed in relief, shook his head probably in wonder at how things were all working out, and then slowly closed the front door, making sure it's locked behind him. After that, he made his way back to the guest room where his wife was still sleeping and closed the door behind him.

Rashid Rahman and Misty Munro stayed at his place in Corpus Christi, Texas, for at least three months after surgery was done on her injured hand to allow it to heal, and then he flew her to Israel where she got to meet his brother. It was a very rejuvenating, heartwarming visit for Misty Munro, who had never left her home state of Texas or her country, and it was while they were in Israel that Rashid Rahman fully proposed to her and placed the engagement ring on her finger. Shortly afterwards, the newly engaged couple flew back to the United States. About three months later, his brother and family flew over from Israel to the United States and attended their wedding. It was held in a park on a Saturday evening where a Pastor and an Imam were both present to oversee and bless their union.

Misty's mother, stepfather, a bunch of relatives from her father's side, and of course a group of Misty's friends from her hospital workplace also attended the wedding. It was a beautiful, exciting, but low – key ceremony, nothing fancy. About two months after the wedding, and with his brother and family having returned to Israel, Rashid and Misty sold their Corpus Christi house and moved to a much bigger house in Rockport, Texas, which they decided to make their permanent homeplace until further notice. And in one corner of their living room, on a small table covered with a clean piece of red cloth, was Misty's bible and Rashid's Koran. And at this time, too, they were expecting their first child.

United states Senator Mitchell Binion was confronted by U.S government cybersecurity agents the next day after his ordeal with the two men. They wanted to know why he made a download of a sensitive, classified file, even though he was deputy chairman of the foreign affairs intelligence committee. He told them that he just wanted to see if all that stuff can fit on a single drive, which, to his surprise, it did, but that was all. He even offered the drive back. With the backing of his influential friends on the committee and other related areas, he was quietly placed on administrative live while an investigation was conducted into all his activities. He had to hand over his passport and all the special items attached to his position that allowed him privileged and official access to his offices and government entities all over the country. In fact, he was placed under house arrest with no visitors to his house except his family and these had to be verified by government security agents placed at his home. All his telephone activities, incoming and outgoing mail, were now being screened and his computer was confiscated. Special catering was set up to provide him with all the food and other basic stuff that he needed until the investigation was over.

During this time at home, Senator Binion used his photocopier machine to make clear copies of the photos of his wife and that other man, put them in a certified mailing envelope addressed to his wife plus a note asking for an immediate, uncontested divorce, and then had the agents mail it out for him.

The investigation lasted for three weeks, and during this time, just to protect her, he did not, in any way or form, contact Marija directly, but had a friend keep tabs on her with special instructions to only get back to him if there was a problem.

Also, during the last week of the investigation, he got a certified letter from his wife Greta. It was a response to the one he had sent her, and in it she simply agreed to the divorce, asked him to mail her all the paperwork for her to sign, said she was sorry that it all ended this way and signed it off with a simple goodbye. At the bottom of the one paragraph letter, she added a foot note that he may mail her some or all her personal stuff if he wanted to, otherwise she didn't need anything else from him, was done and never coming back. Senator Binion then contacted his lawyer and instructed him to draw up the divorce and send it to her. As for her personal stuff, he bagged everything up and put it in the trash container outside.

The investigation finally ended, and it was determined that there was nothing concerning the government that was seriously compromised, but restrictions on some of his key government access privileges were put in place for one year. And so apart from a strict warning never to do this kind of thing again and the restrictions, he was released back to his normal life and functions. A week later his lawyer called him to tell him that Ms. Greta Binion had signed the divorce papers and sent them back to him. The lawyer had already ratified them and put them in the court docket for a judge to review and sign off. And since the divorce was uncontested, it was pretty much a done deal, and the senator was suddenly an unmarried man. A couple of months later Marija moved in with him and was able to have full access to maternity healthcare using his medical privileges. A full DNA testing panel was conducted to prove that the baby she is carrying was indeed his, much to his surprise because she Marija herself asked for it. A private engagement ceremony followed. They planned to marry after the baby was born, which was expected to happen in about seven months. And it was a little bit shortly after this time frame that a very healthy Mitchel Binion the third was born.

The couple got married a year later. It was also at this time that Senator Binion announced his bid to run for president of the United States.

Ruma Crane, Woodrow Crane's daughter, had never experienced so much peace and love in her life like she was receiving at the small Coventry known as "The sisters of The Holy Ghost". From the moment she had made her debut into the place, she had been treated special, and as one of them. She now had her own very clean room and bed, her own bathroom, and everything was so neatly arranged for her. She quickly got involved in the convent's daily routines of prayers and service. These people even went out of their way to do a lot of good for other people who couldn't help themselves, she found out, and she loved it! She loved her new life so much that she soon became the leader of the convent's community outreach service, where she met with, and directed all kinds of services to the needy. The mother superior was so nice, and treated her with utmost respect and kindness, giving her all the support, she needed. It was through these services that she met with her biological mother again, embracing her and thanking her for taking care of her when she was a little girl.

But Ruma's mother was the most surprised to see her daughter as a nun. The transformation was phenomenal. Surprisingly, her mother did not ask about her father at all during their joyful reunion.

It was if she had been completely born again, into a new, totally different life all together. Her past life virtually ceased to exist in her conscious mind. For some reason, whatever went on during her stay with her father became vague memory, however much she questioned herself on what went on during that time of her life or why she had embraced such a violent world. It was as if there was a block on her memory. But one thing she did not ever forget. And that was the sight of those angels when they surrounded her, their leader with the sweet-smelling breath speaking to her and then touching her head, and her sudden appearance outside the Coventry. It was a vision that was to forever haunt her, one that she would eventually take to her grave with her.

The Texas highway patrol association, together with other law enforcement agencies, finally found out who they think killed veteran patrol officer Gregory Walker and the other officers involved. What they found several hours later into the next day was a crushed up, or mangled, black Chevy suburban sports utility vehicle with dead bodies of four men, and a lot of sophisticated assault weaponry inside it. It was found miles away from the scene of the hideous crime that took the officers' lives, in a deep ravine off a ragged road in a remote, deserted area near Austin, Texas. It looked like the driver of the big car had lost control of the vehicle, veered of the road, plunging the vehicle and its occupants into the deep, rock filled ravine. The speedometer reading was stuck at a 120 miles per hour reading. A hiker found the wreck and called the police. The bullets from the guns in the car were matched to the bullets extracted from Gregory Walker's body and the bodies of the responding units that were tragically killed on that day. Fingerprints of the dead men in that car were also found on the weapons.

One of the dead men in that vehicle was identified as Woodrow Crane, a veteran Marine Officer and private businessman. The coroner's office reported that Crane's cause of death was, mysteriously, asphyxiation. Even then, his body had no signs of strangulation or restraint. But it was completely drained of its natural color. It was as if his skin had been bleached. They tracked down his estranged ex – wife, through court records, but she told them she had nothing to do with him at all for a long time. Asked about her daughter with him, she said that she didn't know her whereabouts after he took the girl away from her and threatened to kill her if she tried to interfere with his personalized custody of her. The investigating agency then tried to look for the couple's daughter, Ruma Crane, but there was no trace of her. She wasn't even on any active registry list. Ruma Crane had mysteriously vanished. Woodrow Crane's other children, although named in his will as beneficiaries of his million-dollar fortune, declined to comment on their father's life functions and or activities, mostly because they didn't really know that much about him except that he was their father.

And there was nothing else available to link Woodrow Crane to anything else. All they had was his body and the guns. The car's interior had his fingerprints and those of the other dead men everywhere in it, nobody else's. It was then concluded that Woodrow Crane and his crew had died in an accident as they tried to flee from the police.

Gregory Walker's wife, Lori Walker stated in the reading of his obituary, read for her by her brother, that her husband seemed to be disturbed lately and she had to remind him about their committed love to each other. She was sad because he died without acknowledging what the problem was and urged other law enforcement personnel couples to love each other every day by talking about issues affecting their lives. She later received a two and a half million dollars package which was her late husband's life insurance and other job benefits. The Texas law enforcement association planned to erect a statue of the fallen veteran officer in his memory.

So, what happened to Anna – Maria, a.k.a Pony, and her family? After the family of three came to a mutual consensus to let Ms. Zeal take them to wherever she wanted them to be, the angel drove them back to Incheon airport, where a big, sky – blue, jet airplane was stored in a private hanger. When they arrived at the airport, the big jet plane, which had a big, clear label on it that said "Sky Angel One" on it, was being pulled out of its hanger by an airplane hauler and on to what a private airplane runway. But first, before that, she drove them to another area or section of the city of Seoul, to a relatively secluded neighborhood of a gated community with spaced out, well built, houses in it. There she pulled up in the driveway of one of the big houses, got out of the car, and after the car's back passenger doors automatically opened, she asked the three females to follow her to the inside. Inside the house was warm and cozy, brightly illuminated, and smelled like freshly baked cookies. There was no one in the house, but everything looked very clean and very neatly arranged.

"So, what is this place? Is this your house?" Pony asked naturally, a part of her basic survival instinct.

"This is one of our designated safe neighborhoods. Each nation in the seventh dimension has areas, called Angel spots, where Angels arrive first to outfit themselves for their earthly experience," Ms. Zeal said. "We also use the spots to carry out basic operational needs to suite our agendas as needed. Like now, I brought you here so you can freshen up and look presentable to the outside world, your world."

"There are four bedrooms in this house. One is for you, another for your mom, and the other for my beloved friend, little Sue – Ann.

The fourth bedroom is for Angel use only," she told them. "Everything in each of these rooms has been set up to specifically suite your personal preferences, in your exact sizes and comfort, per my request. That's why each room is specifically allocated to each one of you. You go to the first room on your left, Sue - Ann in the middle room, and your mom to the next one. Each room has a bath attached to it. Last, there is some food in the kitchen area. Find you something to eat before we leave. We leave in exactly one hour."

And with that, Ms. Zeal gently patted Sue – Ann on her back, smiled at the other two females broadly, and then left the living room, entering the fourth room, which was next to their mother's and closing the door behind her.

"Ok, girls, you heard what she said. I am going to my room now. See you again in a few minutes," Mom said, and turning around, she slowly made her way to her designated room and closed the door behind her. She still exhibits weakness, Pony noted quickly. Despite the angelic intervention on her mother, Pony was still worried about her overall functional ability. Pony also insisted on going in with her sister first, and then they would both go to her room after. Sue Ann was all happy with that arrangement.

The three human females took at least over thirty minutes to freshen up, and even then, all three felt they were being extremely rushed. And as stated by Ms. Zeal, each one had the exact much up of their personal preferences, and with a variety of choices, including perfumes, earrings and necklaces. It was forty-five minutes later when they heard Ms. Zeal loudly calling from the living room, reminding them it that it is almost time up. When they finally came out of the room, each was neatly dressed in a floral dress with a matching purse and shoes, except for Pony who had on jeans and white polar neck top and for the first time in a long, long time, simple slip-on shoes. No more boots.

They had a few minutes of grabbing a slice of cake and milk for Pony and Mom, cake and juice for Sue – Ann, and then left the house.

Ms. Zeal drove them to Incheon international airport, where "Sky Angel - one" was waiting for them. The group was led to the plane through a private access channel by a group of smiling airport staff and then led up the stairway into it. After that, the plane's crew took over. Inside of the plane was like the inside of a well-furnished house, with beds, a playroom with a lot of children play stuff, including a small piano. The plane also had a small home theater area. The airplanes' crew were extremely cordial and made sure the travelers were all comfortable. Surprisingly, two of the flight crew were little girls of the same age as Sue – Ann, and soon they whisked her away to the playroom. Mom wanted to go to sleep, and Ms. Zeal personally made sure she was well tucked into a nice bed in one of the sleeping rooms in the plane. Mom was still recovering from her death recall and still needed the attention of the senior angel.

Pony found a comfortable corner in the home theater area and sat down, asking the flight attendant to bring her a glass of warm apple cider, if they had any. Ms. Zeal soon joined her, seating herself next to her. She took her eyes glasses off , once again revealing the deep blue, pupilless eyes.

"So where are we now headed to, Angel?" Pony asked, as she took her glass of warm apple cider from the flight attendant and nodded a thanks to her.

"To your new home. For now, you will live in a country in the south Pacific Ocean called Vanuatu," Ms. Zeal replied. "It's a paradise out there and you will be safe there until we see it fit for you to return to the rest of the world. Our angel designees will be working with all three of you to help you adopt to your new environment. Guard angels will also be around to make sure that the no evil intentions interfere with your stay. Would you like to look at it, via this theater screen, to see how it looks like? I can always change the destination if you don't like Vanuatu."

"Yeah sure, let's take a sneak preview of it," Pony replied without hesitation.

The show lasted thirty minutes, vividly describing the southern pacific nation of Vanuatu in real time. When it was over, Pony, who had been to a few similar places worldwide but none like it, agreed that she really liked it.

"Good. I will also show it to the rest of your family when they are ready," Ms. Zeal said. "You have a bed on the plane if you feel like taking a nap, you know. The flight is a little over twenty hours. I hear sitting up that long can be tiring for you humans, especially if you've had a long, engaging day like yours."

"Thanks for the offer, but no. I will stay up in this chair until we reach our destination," Pony replied. "I am very comfortable where I am right now."

"I can see you are still very apprehensive, Anna Maria" Ms. Zeal said. "But now you can relax. You're safe with us, all of you."

"Yes, I am always apprehensive," Pony acknowledged without looking at her. "Besides, angel, I always want to see where I am going, but I also have a lot to think about. Can't do that while asleep. But I bet you angels can."

"No, not really true, that," Ms. Zeal said. "Because when we go to sleep, or rest, we completely shut down. We angels don't sleep the same way you humans do. When we go to sleep, we sleep for a long time, perhaps for up to ten human years maximum. During this time, we are retuned or reset back to heaven's standard. When we wake up, we can stay up for as long as one full heaven standard year, what you humans call a century, doing God's work, until another round of angels wakes up and replaces us. Only the archangels have the choice to sleep and wake up at will. Senior angels, a step down from the archangel level, sleep fewer years. Fascinating, isn't it?"

"Yes, quite fascinating, but also mysterious stuff!" Pony replied, shaking her head slowly.

"Alright Anna – Maria," Ms. Zeal said, smiling at her. "I will let you be for now; let you catch up with your thinking. I will be in the cockpit if you need me."

With that, Ms. Zeal got up from her seat and left.

Later, Pony decided to stretcher her legs out. She got up and left the theater room. She met one of the flight attendants in the corridor.

"Excuse me, where is my little sister?" she asked.

"This way, I will show you. She's taking a nap with her new friends," the attendants replied politely. She led Pony to one of the side doors in the well-lit, plane hallway and opened it. There were three beds in it, all occupied. Sue - Ann was in one of them, in the middle, flanked by the two other little girls, all sound asleep. She closed the door quietly, then asked for her mother. To her surprise, she found her mother up, playing a game of cards with Ms. Zeal. The two women looked up at her and smiled as she stood in the doorway.

"I thought you were in the cockpit with the pilots?" Pony asked Ms. Zeal, after giving her mother a brief hug.

"Well, I changed my mind and instead came to check on your mother. She's still healing, you know. And now I find her to be a very fascinating and quite wonderful individual," the angel said. "But you can peek into the cockpit, Anna - Maria. It's quite different from the human flying machine. One of the attendants can take you there."

Plane cockpits always fascinated her, and so she decided to go look at this one. But that's something that she was already wanting to do on this flight but had not mentioned her intentions to anyone. So how did Ms. Zeal know that she wanted to go to the cockpit? This was all mind boggling, she told herself. And now one of the flight attendants was already patiently standing in the hallway read to take her to the cockpit.

To her total surprise, they were no pilots in it. The plane was flying completely unattended. She also noted that the instrument panel, the equivalent of a car's dashboard, had nothing on it at all except one control wheel in front of one of the two chairs, as compared to the usual planes. The control wheel kept moving slowly by itself. The cockpit contained two seats and was all glass around it, so the occupants can look at the outside from all around them.

"Where are the pilots?" She asked the attendant, sounding a little bit anxious.

"This plane doesn't need a pilot, Anna - Maria," the attendant replied, smiling broadly. "The seats are there to make it look like a normal human - made plane to the humans in this world. But unlike the human - made plane, this plane is its own pilot, with everything controlled by a team of Angels invisible to the human eye, inside and outside the plane. The senior angel gives it instructions as to where to go and how fast it should go to that destination, and then it flies itself. It can fly at regular, normal speed, or at supersonic, speed of sound levels. Right now, we are flying normal. The senior angel on board does not see the need to rush."

"Wow! Can pilots in other... well human or even non – human controlled aircrafts see or detect your plane, from out there?" Pony asked.

"Not exactly," the attendant replied. "Only if we want them to see us. We can't even be detected by human radar once we leave the airport. We are only detected by human radar systems on only a few selected airports or detecting units, carefully chosen by the Holy Angel network. This airplane, lady, can land anywhere, on any terrain, on any water body, that being sea, ocean, lake or river, on ice or soft sand, mountain top, even cling to the side of a big building like an insect. It can be still in air space without tilting or shaking. It can fly vertical like a rocket, roll like a big fish in the sea, or fly sideways like a sparrow. It can submerge into a water body like submarine, if necessary. It's simply amazing."

"So, what level in the angel hierarchy are you?" Pony asked the flight attendant, who had sat down in one of the cockpit seats and was now facing her as she talked to her. "You pretty much look human to me. I mean... you don't have blue pupilless eyes or visible wings or some other visible, non – human attribute, but I assume that to be a flight attendant on a divine machine like this you must be one of them."

435

"Junior Angel, way down the ladder," the attendant replied excitedly. "I am still human like you, but an enhanced human. Because of certain things that I did when I was still fully human, a senior Angel adopted me and anointed me to be part of their system, a representative of the divine network called an "Angel designee", but also ranked junior angel. In other words, I am still human, but I have been given certain special attributes that completely elevate me beyond certain human levels and capabilities. For example, as per my current job, I can speak any language in the world at once, depending on where I am on the planet. I can also talk to any of God's creatures, can hear trees whispering to each other, can evaluate and or analyze wind sound, which gives me the ability to tell what weather is coming, how severe it will be, and may be able to alter its inclination. I also prepare souls of those who are about to die, get them ready for the transition. In other words, I have been assigned to the transition business. Only when my human life ends shall I then be reevaluated and turn into a full angel."

"Wow! Are they hiring?" Pony asked. And both women burst out laughing heartily. "I mean, it seems to be exciting."

"They're 'hiring' all the time, but a senior angel must sponsor you. My name is Tamaleya, by the way. Now let me let you in on one secret," the attendant said, coming closer to Pony by touching a spot on the cockpit chair that made it automatically shift forward in Pony's direction. "You see those two little children who are playing with your little sister, they are both full angels already. They are both of a higher rank than I am, higher than any of us adult flight attendants on this plane."

"So, they already passed on, first, and then came back as full angels?" Pony asked.

"Yes." Tamaleya replied.

"So, what is their purpose on the flight?" Pony asked.

"They're here to nurture your little sister, to make her feel comfortable and at home," The flight attendant replied. "On special request from your senior angel, Zeal. She made the request, and they magically appeared on board."

But now, Tamaleya had Pony instantly thinking. Oh my god, the senior angel is planning to turn my sister into one of them. It's the plan all along. Take her away from me. But I am not ready to lose my little sister yet, because she's the only sister I have in this world, my only true friend, and I love her beyond love itself. I better go talk to Ms. Zeal and stop her from doing that. I must warn her that if she tampers with my baby sister, she's going to have to deal with me first.

"You don't have to worry about that, Anna – Maria," a calm voice from behind her said. "You have my word on that. Besides, I would like Sue - Ann to enjoy her full life as God intended it to be, with her family, and I am willing to wait for her to go through that phase before I even designate her."

Pony sharply turned around to see Ms. Zeal standing in the doorway of the cockpit, hands folded in front of her.

"You're eavesdropping on our conversation and on my thoughts, Ms. Zeal, and without my permission. In my world, that's not right!" Pony said immediately, sounding annoyed.

"I don't have to ask for your permission on that, Anna – Maria," the Angel replied, not bothered by the human's verbal scolding. "It's part of my job to do that, it's part of who I am, whether you agree to it or not. I am here to protect you, body, mind and soul. It means that I have full access to the whole you. Right now, I can sense all your body functions, including your emotions and thoughts about the future as per every second that goes by in your human life. But relax, come with me, I want to show you and your family something interesting. Your sister is now wide awake, and I got your mother ready to see it too."

Pony winked at the flight attendant, who winked back, and then followed Ms. Zeal out of the cockpit. When they entered the main lounge of the plane, which could stand for super first class on a regular human passenger airplane, Sue – Ann broke free from her mother and rushed into her sister's arms.

"I missed you while I was sleeping, Anna – Maria," she said, holding on to her big sister tightly.

"The last time I saw you, you and your new friends here were all fast asleep, Sue – Ann." Pony said.

The two other little girls looked up at Pony and smiled but said nothing.

"Ok my friends. Are you all ready for the special treat?" Ms. Zeal asked. "It's part of the entertainment given to our first-time guests on the plane."

"Ready when you're," Sue – Ann said, already sounding excited.

Ms. Zeal raised her arms and waved them up and down twice, like a choir conductor. Suddenly, the entire plane's metallic frame structure disappeared and was replaced by clear glass to reveal the outside environment of the sky, with all the stars and clouds around them, some floating by, some stationary. It was night time in this time zone, and a big, full yellow moon was visible to them. Some stars were huge, some were quite small, some extremely bright, others dim. It felt like they were travelling through a space galaxy and were right in the middle of everything. It was an extremely amazing, breathing taking sight for the new riders.

"Behold, one of the many of the almighty God's wonders, folks," Ms. Zeal said. "And there is more to see beyond this spectrum, like an occasional group of angels being streamed to your world below. We won't be seeing them on this route, though. That part is exclusive in a different way and happens every ten or so human years. It also happens when the almighty God, the light, the Holiest of the holy spirits, is responding to something out of the normal, like this time around. We were quickly streamed to earth to stop the devil from causing mankind to self -destruct. It is the reason why this summer is so hot, that the tropics are experiencing more than usual humidity with increased torrential rains, that sea levels are randomly and dangerously rising and in some places are causing tsunamis, why certain dormant volcanos are suddenly erupting. It is why this year's winter is going to be unusually more severe in the cold seasoned places, even those places that usually have mild winter seasons. We are simply arriving."

For the next fifteen minutes or so, Ms. Zeal allowed her new passengers to soak in the glory of the galaxy, uninterrupted, and then closed the plane again. And soon everybody went sleep, even Pony. Only Ms. Zeal and the flight attendants remained alert and awake.

Eighteen hours later after the show, the plane quietly landed on one of the islands of Vanuatu, the south Pacific Ocean nation. Ms. Zeal woke Pony up, who appeared to be surprised, or rather embarrassed, that she had fallen asleep.

"We have arrived, Anna – Maria," Ms. Zeal said to her. "Now remember, this is going to be your home for some time now. There are others like you here too, from all over the world, all brought here to safety and wellbeing by angels like me, so you won't be lonely. I will be leaving you soon, but not right away. I am going to make sure that before I leave, you're all well acclimated."

"Have you talked to my mother about this?" Pony asked.

"Yes, I have, and she's ok with everything, because she now fully believes in the power of God and the angels," Ms. Zeal replied, smiling. "I will leave it to you to explain the changes to your little sister, but I know for sure she will be fine with all of it."

Much later, about three months after their debut on the island, Ms. Zeal left Vanuatu for an unknown destination, on a similar airplane, and Pony and her family would never get to see her again until seven years later.

# EPILOGUE

**His names were Luis Perez St. Perez.**

And once again, folks, this is Reverend Robert Moolimer, the pastor of a small, non – denominational Christian faith church out here in Dallas, Texas, in the United States of America. If you may recall, I spoke to you about the issues concerning our lives as humans versus the existence of immortals on the other side of the spectrum. That same prologue laid the foundation for the understanding of the rather complex series of events that took place as narrated in this book.

Well, what I am about to finally talk about in this conclusion all began when one Sunday morning, right before church service began, a member of my congregation introduced to me, and my wife Sylvia, a young man from Guatemala. The introducing member, herself a student at the university of Texas in Arlington, told us that the young man was new to the area and was looking for a place of worship to go to every Sunday and as needed during the week. He was neatly dressed in a plain white, long-sleeved shirt, black dress pants and shoes, and carried a small notepad with him.

Of course, we warmly welcomed him to our church, and I told him that at any given time he wanted to come in and pray on a non – Sunday day he was more than welcome to give me a call so I can come open the church doors for him. He did indeed, after this first meeting, call me later in the middle of the week to come open the church doors for him so he can do his worship, but he also asked to speak to me in private after he was done. Without even asking him what this was going to be about I looked at my schedule that was rather hectic, found a light day on it and agreed to meet with him on the next Friday, in the same week.

I remember that day when we first met in private. Luis Perez St Perez turned out to be a very nice, charming, and soft-spoken young man. He thanked me for granting him this meeting and then proceeded to tell me that God had sent him to talk to me about issues concerning this world. Surprised, I asked him why I was the choice for this kind of thing. He said he didn't know why either, but that God communicates to him through a network of Angels and had done so since he was ten years old. Initially, he said, he thought that maybe he was going crazy, but after certain things subsequently happened to him, he learned to listen to these voices that came to him at any given time, sometimes through dreams and sometimes directly. It was like his life had been taken over by some unknown entity. He said the same voices led him to the United States of America, which by the way, after following all the instructions from the voices, entrance to the country was a breeze through. The same voices that had instructed him to seek out the university of North Texas for his studies ultimately led him to meet the right person to link him to me. He mentioned that what he was telling me right now was simply a summary of what he had gone through, and that was because he didn't want to waste time going through all the details of personal events that happened to him in those past years that eventually culminated into this meeting. He said that he had very important things from heaven to tell me so that I can in turn tell the world.

At first, I didn't know what to say or believe, but I was willing to listen to what he had to tell me, and as I came to find out later, what he was communicating to me turned out to be real and very correct. The deeper I got into it, the more my eyes and mind got opened to his truth. How did it get to this level? Because I, in fact, checked out almost everything he was telling me. But this was not because I wanted to prove him wrong at some point. It was because he himself wanted me to go find out for and by myself, that indeed it was heaven talking to me through him. Not only did he encourage me to go out there into the world and investigate the truth of what he was telling me, he also sponsored all my travel expenses.

My travels took me to the township of Namugongo in Uganda, East Africa, where I was able to meet and confirm everything of that segment of his revelations. I spoke to Mother Edina herself who even told me that her angel, Orayah, had told her that I would be sent to her by a young man from far away. I met with all her folks and their friends, including Mufti Musa and his wife, Halima. It was during this visit that the family fully explained, and gave me copies of their records, of the incidents that totally changed their lives ever since Mother Edina first started having her visions. The main four people mostly involved in these events took turns, each in their own way, to narrate and describe that night the angel appeared to them in Mother Edina's room. It was so astonishing to hear this part, for it was so compelling and so fascinating. The other thing that we noticed too was that it was mostly the men, meaning the bishop, the reverend, and the mufti, that conducted the narration, with very brief interventions now and then from Rebecca. Otherwise, their three women, who came to meet with us and share an evening dinner prepared for us by the reverend, sat together in one corner of the living room and simply smiled at us without saying anything.

By the way, I and my wife Sylvia had to go back to Uganda a few months later after this meeting to be at Mother Edina's funeral. Her family told me that she had told them that at her persistent request, Angel Orayah had promised to take her to, and show her, the ultimate light, which is God in heaven, and introduce her to all his angels and prophets. The real gist of this final revelation of going to see God was that she told them the date Orayah had told her this could happen. And sure enough, on that day, and after going to bed with a big smile on her face and seemingly excited, and after requesting that her family dress her up in her favorite dress, necklace and shoes the night before, and then she was found dead in her bed, the strange smile still on her face. Even during her wake, she still retained the smile! She also died twenty- four hours shy of her one hundredth birthday!

I followed up with meetings with folks like Misty Munro and her husband, Rashid Rahman, and with miss Ruma, who had changed her name to sister Hannah James. They all confirmed and talked about their events and how terrifying it was. It was difficult, though, to get Ruma to confront her past, because she appeared to have almost no recall. but at the urging of her mother superior, she opened. Going back to her room, she came back with a small diary in which she had written everything concerning her past life including what she remembered of her parents. She said she wrote all that stuff in the fi rst week of her arrival and acceptance to the convent. With tears in her face, Ruma said that we can keep the journal, but adding that once we take it, her past wil be completely gone from her, and she didn't want to see us again. We agreed to that. The journal vividly described everything that went on, even the part where state patrol man Greg walker was shot down. There was evidence on record of the death of officer Greg walker and other patrol officers on that fateful day, with the conclusion that they found his killers who apparently had died in a mysterious car accident. At the request of the mother superior, we abstained from revealing the information to Texas law enforcement, since the investigation appeared to be concluded and the case closed. I was even able to meet with, and talk to, the female rookie officer who survived the fatal onslaught. She had fully recovered and was now back on the beat. She described, with tears in her face, that fatal night, and how thankful she was to God that she was alive and moving on.

I finally managed to secure an appointment with billionaire Bernhardt Vonsberg and his family on a late Sunday evening at their home in Southlake, Texas, but after providing all my credentials and carefully explaining to him as to why I wanted to interview them. During this special evening, they candidly opened and told me their story of that night. Benita Vonsberg said she was still waiting to see the male Angel Zeal again. Bernhardt Vonsberg was able to confirm the initial meeting with Major Haraabi at which where he introduced, and then talked about the devil's prospects, the beginning of everything, and was able to confi rm with flight documents of that day, and how he missed the doomed flight on which other fellow investors had died.

Sylvia and I visited the site of what used to be major Haraabi's apartment in England, which had been scourged by a mysterious fire. The remains were still intact, but the area was closed off with police yellow tape. Indeed, the apartment owners confirmed that he used to live there by showing us the leasing records. But the part where the devil's incarnate and her group killed Major Haraabi and then departed for France to meet with the queen crow was filled in by Luis Perez St Perez. But he provided us with the address of the devil's mansion, and we were able to view the structure, which was now looking bushy and dark with no one there anymore to take care of the place.

Then Luis Perez St Perez asked me to go to Italy and confirm stuff with ex- Italian carabinieri captain Jacques Kakra. After searching

443

through certain records, courtesy of Italian authorities, I was able to track down, and meet with the captain. He too gave us his version of the story, describing Cephia vividly and passionately, and narrating about the events of that day that the final confrontation happened. Captain Kakra cried tears in front of me as he did this, saying that in his entire life nothing could have prepared him for that day, and that his life has never been the same ever since. He strongly dwelt on the fact that Angels are very real and that we should pray to God and give thanks every day!

I didn't get to interview every member of colonel Carkenbo's team, including the colonel himself, who had been promoted to brigadier general. But Brigadier General Carkenbo simply declined to meet with me. He didn't want to talk about anything concerning that mission, stating that he was also under a gag order by the department of defense not to do so. I got to interview commando Philip Bakambuso from South Africa, and then the big German commando. Man, that guy was big and muscular! They both confirmed the attack on them outside the castle's perimeters and seeing the winged Archangel with their own eyes.

Surprisingly though, and after going through some solid red tape, the Chinese government granted me access to commando Jiang Hong, who herself, like major general Carkenbo, had also been promoted a high ranking, decorated officer in the people's liberation army. Jiang Hong provided me with a vivid narration of her encounters with Archangel Cephia which exactly matched Captain Kakra's descriptions during his narration. She too stated that this mission was unlike any other she had been on, and will remember it to her dying day, saying that it was too incredible even to just talk about it.

I attended the investigative trial of the still very blind scientist Dr. Ning Pei Pei, who testified that as an employee of a wealthy individual known only as the principal, he had helped develop, test, and make ready the deadly mass destruction, virus – bacteria hybrid, but denied knowing what the real motive behind its production was. The scientist still remains incarcerated at an unknown location.

After that, I and Luis Perez St. Perez finally travelled to the island nation of the Turikai republic, using the Libyan coast route, and there,

444

too, the flight control tower crew confirmed the terrifying noise in the sky, stating that up to this time they have not figured out yet exactly what was in the cloud - covered sky that heavily misty day, which had even caused a temporary regionwide power blackout. The flight tower had been repaired and or rebuilt already, so I wasn't able to see what damage was caused. The flight control crew on that day had since returned to their duties after hospital treatment and described to us what that massive noise had done to their health.

From that area we hired a motorized boat to cross us over to the Turikai republic. We could have flown in by helicopter, but I wanted to feel the route taken by the commandos on their way to the doomed castle.

Now by "we" I now also include a group of several other people which included a senior representative from the Vatican, a senior representative from Canterbury, a deputy minister of India's ministry of religious affairs, a senior Mossad official from Israel, a senior official from the South African state security agency, a high ranking member of the General intelligence Directorate of the Kingdom of Saudi Arabia, a senior official from Britain's MI6, a senior agent of the united states' CIA, the United nations director of world affairs, and China's intelligence service, or Guoanbu, sent commando Jiang Hong back, plus two professional camera men to shoot pictures and record the this remarkable, unprecedented history making trip and event. Also, this was the first trip that Luis Perez St Perez accompanied me on my investigation. My wife, Sylvia, did not come with me on this one. All of us were on one big, motorized boat, escorted by a series of other security power boats.

The trip was geared towards taking a physical, up-close look at the epic center of evil which could have paralyzed the world into near extinction. There was also the eagerness by some of us to set foot in a place disrupted by out of this world, perhaps paranormal or supernatural activity, the actions of an Archangel against the devil. But most of the participants didn't know this. Only myself, Luis Perez St Perez, the Vatican, Canterbury, India Ministry official, the Saudi official and of course commando Jiang Hong knew the divinely - bound significance of being here.

445

We met with the old man, who was now frail and weak but able to talk. After introducing ourselves through a local guide and interpreter who was kindly provided by the new President's office, we were able to talk to him in form of a brief interview. He confirmed the appearance of the American – led commando group, how he had pointed them in the right direction, and then confirmed the appearance of the Archangel. He then gave me the keys to the castle, given to him by Cephia, and asked us to deliver them to the President of the republic, who was also his king, after we were done visiting the castle. One week after our visit to the island republic, I received a telephone call from the President himself to inform me that the old man finally died in his sleep.

Everything was still as is, including the laboratory with its destructed archangel's path through its ceiling, while airlifting Imrana and her scientist boss out of the building. The machinery, the staff or workers' quarters, and evidence of the damaged meeting room where the confrontation between the Archangel and the devil incarnate had occurred was still vividly intact. But all human remains, the inevitable collateral damage of the deadly confrontation, had been removed and buried by the indigenous people and government workers.

Pictures of the place, inside and outside, were taken, lab samples collected, some items picked up, and then we all left the place. Even in its emptiness, the eeriness in the place was signifi cantly present and strongly felt.

Our delegation was finally met by the king of the Turikai people, who was also the current President of the nation. Never had his country received so much "silent" attention from the outside world, he said. The President then handed to me a small package which he said I might find useful to my divine - bound investigation. I opened the package immediately I got back to my hotel and in it were transcripts of his predecessor's true testimony of what had happened to him. Although he couldn't talk, technology had made it possible for the now fully paralyzed, wheelchair bound, ex – president Moongoo to narrate his events, starting from when he had met the devil incarnate and up to when the monk individual left his office, living him paralyzed, speechless, but with his brain still fully functional. At the end of his transcript, he issued a full apology to his country and family. Although

446

the transcript had been sealed as a classified, top-secret document by the Turikai government, the President felt that it was necessary for me to have and include in my record of events pertinent my investigation. It was a stunning revelation, but then, also, Luis Perez St Perez had told me that angels are "invisibly" involved in my investigation and would open means and ways for me that would have otherwise been impossible to access. This was one of them.

But perhaps the best and most intriguing part of my investigative journeys was the trip to Vanuatu, the island nation in south Oceania, for me to verify and or confirm the events and or circumstances surrounding the one enigmatic figure in this epic saga, the dynamic personality called Pony, and also known as Anna – Maria. She was the person who had warned the world about the impending doom project. And this time, again, Luis Perez St Perez travelled with me.

Now a mother of one son, she wasn't afraid to proclaim that this was a product of her union with Major Haraabi. At the time of her separation from the late Haraabi, who up to this time she did not believe he was dead until Luis Perez St Perez told her about it, confirming what Ms. Zeal had told her about the same subject in ethe same way as he did, she had not figured out that she was pregnant with his child. She appeared shocked when Luis Perez St Perez mentioned that the reason why she suddenly felt nauseated on her flight to South Korea to find her family was because Major Haraabi, at that exact time, was dying, and that his last thoughts were of him seeking forgiveness from her. Yet Pony had not mentioned that part of feeling sick on the plane to us at all.

And so, it was indeed a miracle that the baby boy had endured all the beating she had suffered as she tried to make her way out of the evil hotel building. She was told by Luis Perez St Perez that the baby, who she named Ji - Hoon Haraabi, was simply meant to be.

We had a candid conversation with Pony, in which she described her entire time with the devil's organization, how she and Haraabi met, the Katarina problems, and the terrifying ordeal of trying to rescue her family, including the time when her mother purportedly died, only to be resuscitated back to life by Angel Zeal. She described the journey to Vanuatu and meeting with the Angel designees. We met with her

447

mother and her now teenage sister, who both testified to the events of that time.

Pony said that she hopes that her past was over with. Both her and her family very much loved it here in Vanuatu, but that although they have not yet considered living elsewhere yet, they still missed their home country, South Korea. Pony added that Angel Zeal's warning that she should stay away from her home country for now until she was advised to do so by the Ms Zeal herself or through the Heavenly Angel network. She then took us around the capital city, Port Vila, and took us on boat rides all over the different islands that make up the beautiful country. We stayed in Vanuatu for one week, and then returned to the United States.

After a week of rest, sylvia and I flew to France and were able to see the darkened, still completely sealed off, mansion of the crows in the old French town. We took pictures of it from the outside of the fenced off perimeter. We then returned to home to the United States where I started working on the compilations, to make them into the whole story you just read.

It took me a little over fifteen months, after concluding my investigations, to put all this together for the world's record, including the main message passed over by Archangel Cephia, that humanity was one whole worldwide, regardless of race, color, religious affiliations, language, flag or creed, and that there was only one God, seated in heaven, the undying light, presiding over all on this planet and beyond. Only through realizing this shall there be peace on earth, which is God's Seventh Dimension. And so, at the eve of concluding the archiving of the events of this epic story of divine intervention, and particularly for the record, I posed these questions to Luis Perez St Perez, the mysterious young man from Guatemala as we sat face to face in my small church office.

"So, for the record, you, Luis Perez St Perez, claim that you're an angel designee who's been placed in charge of keeping up with, keeping track of, and finally revealing these important events to me after they evolved. You also claim that one of your strongest attributes as an angel designee is that senior angels based in heaven can communicate to you through dreams, and sometimes directly, right?

"That's correct, reverend Moolimer," he replied calmly. "And I have proven it to you, haven't I? Everything I have told you has turned out to be correct, and at no cost to you."

"And if you don't mind me asking, where did you get all that money from? I am asking about the money that has funded my entire investigative research all this time?" I asked.

"I don't know where it comes from," he replied. "All I know is that when I came to the United States of America, I had a daydream while I took a nap in a hotel. In it, a person, whose face I couldn't see, told me to open an account with the first bank I got to. So, when I came to the university, and after my first day of orientation, there was a notice board on which a flyer advertising a bank was pinned. I picked it up, found the directions, got to the bank and opened an account in my names. The bank official, whose name tag read "Ajiona Zeal" told me not to worry about an initial deposit. The next thing I knew I was receiving bank statements showing me money on my account. And so as long as I continued working with you, and continuing my research on divinity related studies, my account remained loaded with money. That's how I funded all your travels. As I told you in the beginning, it's the full Angels at work here, reverend."

"Full Angels?" I queried back, confused by his statement.

"You asked me if I am an Angel designee, which I said I am," he replied. "But Angel designees don't work like full angels, the real winged, but mostly invisible, individuals in our world. While they work

God's beat, full angels are allowed to choose any human being they feel meets the standards of God's call and delegate some of their work programs to or through them. I wouldn't be able to do and or set up everything we have done if I wasn't under the directorate of a full, or even senior angel."

"Now tell me something, Luis, and if you don't have the answer, that's ok. So where is Archangel Cephia now?" I asked. "Did she go back to heaven, now that her triumph over evil has been achieved, her mission accomplished?"

"I actually saved that for the last part of my revelations to you and the world," Luis Perez St Perez replied. "On the contrary, she did not go back to Heaven as promised by her big brother Gabriel, one of the most senior of the Archangels. She was, instead, temporarily barred from going back."

"Barred from going back?" I asked, keen to hear why. "Do we know why? Did Gabriel come down to our world to tell her that she was barred from returning?"

"Yes, Gabriel chose to personally deliver God's new orders to her, since he was the one who had recommended that she should descend to the seventh dimension to lead the campaign to defeat the devil," Luis Perez St Perez replied. "You see, Gabriel had considered this as one of the many hands on, training sessions in the art of heavenly warfare for the young Archangel, since she had never been exposed to such before. But even when in training mode, Cephia had performed excellently. And so, since the devil, by heavenly standards, has not been totally or definitely vanquished from God's precious Seventh dimension, more trouble is expected amongst humans. The council of heaven's archangels, headed by Archangel Michael who is also armed with God's mandate, voted to extend her stay, which was totally the opposite of her expectations, for she wanted to go back home. Cephia was clearly angered and called out to God directly for breaking the promise to get her back home after the job was done."

"What exactly do you mean by "called out to God"?" I asked, for clarification purposes.

"She verbally chastised God for not delivering on his promise, which was definitely her need to return home," Luis Pere St Perez replied.

"Wow!" I exclaimed. "And man, don't we all. We all sometimes get riled up if God doesn't respond to our prayers promptly basing on our selfish wants or needs, forgetting that he has his own ways and time for doing things. So, what happened next?"

"That's very true about us humans. But anyway, for calling out to God like that, she was punished," Luis Perez St Perez responded back and then continued. "In heaven, I am told, the single major rule is to obey the will of the holy spirit without question. No one in heaven, not even his most precious Archangels Michael and Gabriel, are allowed to object to God's commandments or call out to the will of the holy spirit, even if they have grievances. No one challenges God's decisions. The almighty God denies, alters or changes, forgives, punishes, resolves or judges all before him, but most important of all, at will."

"What was, or let's say, what is, the punishment given to Cephia?" I asked, becoming very attentively eager know how God punishes his angels. I was envisioning it to be a spanking, or some kind of time out for an offense like Cephia's call out to the almighty.

"According to what was revealed to me for your earthly records or archives, Archangel Cephia was clipped," Luis Perez St Perez said. "This, perhaps, is the worst punishment to be inflicted on a heavenly angel, and is secondary to being completely banished from heaven, which is the worst punishment that can be inflicted on an angel or archangel." "Clipped?" I asked, intrigued by the word.

"Yes. As explained to me, it means that her wings were removed from her, and the powers of heaven's mandate withdrawn," he explained to me. "To remove an angel's wings demobilizes the angel and the angel's free will to roam heaven and heaven's entities. It also reduces the angel to non -divine creature level. That angel can no longer fit in with his or her peers. Withdrawing heaven's mandate means the angel is no longer protected by heaven. Heaven will monitor, but not protect, the clipped angel until heaven's most senior archangels' rule that the clipped angel is still worthy of heaven's appeal. A final judgement will then be rendered which determines whether that angel's heavenly status should be reinstated or not. But because Cephia is an archangel herself, and Gabriel's little sister, her punishment is of a temporary status. Which brings me to her punishment part. Cephia has been temporarily banished to the seventh dimension, the very place she had been sent to cleanse. She will roam the earth for forty days and nights with no protection and no wings, only relying on the battle skills provided to her during her training as one of heaven's war archangels. For a junior archangel like her, it's likely going to be a terrible thing. It's like being an involuntary immigrant in a new, possibly very hostile, territory. What will happen to her next remains to be seen."

"So, then she's still down here with us, right?" I asked.

"Yes, she is," he confirmed. "Her punishment, I was told, will begin in seven months and seven days. Actually, today is the last day of those last seven days. She will be ushered out of an area on earth called the Ring of Fire which is one of heaven's gates to the seventh dimension. It was inside this ring of fire that she met with Gabriel for her sentence. When she's finally released into her punishment, the volcanos in the ring of fire will erupt as heaven's gates get closed to her. Even the ocean's levels will rise as this happens, the moon will hide behind dark clouds, and trees around that area or within a radius of seven hundred miles from the ring of fire will completely shade all their leaves. And for twenty-four hours straight, the temperatures in all deserts around the world will change to harsher levels during the day and at night, this meaning that the cold deserts will super freeze, and the hot deserts will heat up beyond their usual, predicted normal levels. In the regular human world, it will see twenty-four hours of abnormal wind speeds and strength, rain, and dark skies. I was also told that all newborn human babies of this day in this world will have a strange birth mark or defect on them, a mark of God's anger towards his archangel. These newborn babies will be different to the world in many ways when and as they grow up. Some will exhibit unusual excellence while others will be notoriously exhibit terrible and disastrous failures."

"And that will be starting tomorrow?" I asked, staring out of my office window. It was already getting cloudy out there.

"Yes," Came the answer immediately.

"So now what's next for us, for this world of ours?" I finally asked.

"It means that for now, the world will have to battle its own evils until the Archangel Cephia is reinstated. Starting with tomorrow, all holy battles will stand down, including brand Zeal. Only heavenly acts of Mercy and special assistance will remain active. The angels who conduct these acts are not programmed for battle or war. They only deal with special needs from special prayers. They are called the On Call Angels," Luis Perez St Perez replied.

This was the last day of my several interactive meetings with the young Angel Designee known to me as Luis Perez St Perez, whose mission was to deliver a record of otherwise mostly unknown events that took place in our world that could have altered humanity forever.

My job was then to arrange these events into a chronologic order for humanity, hence this epic story we have today.

We had an early, evening dinner with him, that is me and my wife Sylvia, and then we drove him to the airport. He was going back to Guatemala to visit with his fiancée, he had told me, whom he hadn't seen for a while as he was busy conducting God's affairs. He said he would be coming back to the United States finish his final studies. But Luis Perez St Perez never did come back, and when I went to the university to see if he was back for his final classes, I was told there was no student by those names! Another mystery from God that I don't intend to solve now, or even ever. I even contacted the embassy of Guatemala in Washington D.C and after a few days they called me back and told me they have no such names registered in their citizenry data!

As to why I was chosen to be the one to work on and or simplify the divine record to human understanding, I have no answer yet. All I know is that this was just one of those defi ning periods in this world, and I am sure there are other events, similar to this one, that have happened here before, in our world, or as revealed by the heavens, in God's backyard, The Seventh Dimension. But what will happen tomorrow remains to be seen, because even for what's going to happen in the next breathing minute still remains Heaven's little secret until it is past.

I am Reverend, or Pastor, Robert Moolimer in Dallas, Texas, United States of America. Thank you for reading my archive.

## The End

*Coming up soon:*

I am Cephia: Rise of The Ungodly. It's the ultimate sequel to I AM CEPHIA: CEPHIA AND THE DEVIL'S PANDEMIC. The clipped

Archangel must now fight her own battles after she is banished from heaven and is left in our world without heavenly mandate or coverage. It's a war against ultimate evils as revenge is sought by the evil side in response to her annihilation of the devil incarnate.

"But is this heaven's final plan to get rid of the devil in the seventh dimension?"

# About the Author

Samuel Kironde Ndawula is a freelance writer. He lives in Texas, United States of America, with his family.

www.ingramcontent.com/pod-product-compliance
Lightning Source LLC
Chambersburg PA
CBHW020428130626
46549CB00001B/31